Structural Hearing

TONAL COHERENCE IN MUSIC

Structural Hearing

TONAL COHERENCE IN MUSIC

BY FELIX SALZER

WITH A FOREWORD BY LEOPOLD MANNES

TWO VOLUMES BOUND AS ONE

DOVER PUBLICATIONS, INC. • NEW YORK

This Dover edition, first published in 1982, is an
unabridged and corrected republication in one
paperback volume of the work originally published
by Charles Boni in 1952. The work was previously
published by Dover in 1962 in two clothbound
volumes. At that time the Preface to Dover Edition
was first added to the work.

International Standard Book Number: 0-486-22275-6

Manufactured in the United States of America
Dover Publications, Inc.
31 East 2nd Street, Mineola, N.Y. 11501

To the Memory of

Heinrich Schenker

1868—1935

Preface to Dover Edition

Since the publication of the first edition of *Structural Hearing*, it has been gratifying to receive the comments and suggestions of students, teachers, musicologists and others.

Many who have found the book useful have brought to my attention certain necessary changes and emendations in both the text and the musical examples. This new edition benefits from their helpful criticism.

To Charles Boni, the original publisher of *Structural Hearing*, I wish again to pay tribute. It was his foresight which helped the book to make its mark.

For more than four years the distribution of the book has been in the very capable hands of Mr. Hayward Cirker of Dover Publications, Inc. During that time I have come to admire the breadth of his interests and the sureness of his judgment.

It is a source of great satisfaction to me that this new edition appears under the Dover imprint.

F. S.

New York City

June 1961

VOLUME ONE

Foreword

To the gifted and experienced musician, music is a language—to be understood in sentences, paragraphs and chapters. The student who is still struggling with letters and words, so to speak, needs the guidance that will reveal to him the larger meanings of the musical language. Theory, as it is called, has always been upheld as the promised gateway to this broad understanding, but there are thousands upon thousands of eager young musicians as well as disappointed older ones who will testify to the seemingly unbridgeable gap between their theoretical studies and the living experience of music itself.

To tell the truth, musical theory as it is generally taught, consists of a more or less elaborate system by which small musical units may be identified (or written) according to their position and function with respect to the temporary tonal context. The larger units are merely labeled according to the recognizable thematic characteristics. The student who masters such a system has indeed learned something about music; but what he has learned is a nomenclature by which he can conduct a well-described "tour" through a composition, pointing out each landmark and its more obvious characteristics.

If music were only such a "conducted tour" it would never have the profound and moving effect upon us which has made it perhaps the greatest of all the arts. Obviously something far more fundamental and compelling is at work in this great language, something which conventional theory touches but has largely failed to reveal in its full extent. This "something" quite evidently consists of more than one element; but there is hardly a doubt that the greatest of these organic elements is that of tonality with the inevitable relationship of tonal direction to the element of rhythm—for this is the space-time continuum in which music lives. It appears that Heinrich Schenker was the first musical theorist who took the decisive step in defining these organic forces of the musical language; in particular, the tonal functions and relationships which form both the generative and cohesive forces in great music.

Schenker, however, never fully organized his writings from a pedagogical standpoint; nor are they by any means complete. Some of his explanations, moreover, are challenging and call for reexamination. In this extraordinary book Felix Salzer has, I believe, attempted and succeeded in a task of tremendous difficulty. Schenker's pioneer work has been modified, expanded and completed, in a sense, for the first time, so that its application to tonal music of all styles and periods can be understood. In order to achieve such a result, it has been necessary to write a book of considerable length and, in places, of some complexity. This is inevitably due to the fact that Dr. Salzer has faced fully the problems of his task and has tried to be as complete and exhaustive as possible.

In my many years as Associate Director and Director of The Mannes Music School (following a good many years devoted to the teaching of theory and composition), I have been in a position to observe the results of this approach to music upon the students themselves. Much of the material in this book has been used for several years in the regular theory classes of the School; it will undoubtedly become the official textbook for the course. I can say without hesitation that I have never seen such musical awareness on the part of theory students, nor such genuine enthusiasm for a theory course. What seems at first to be an almost unnecessarily diversified terminology, becomes later on an obviously necessary and logical approach, and furnishes a student with a means of analysis which can guide him through a work of any length and complexity. And what is still more important, it can guide him to that sort of listening which embraces the "paragraphs" and "chapters" of music—that instinctive understanding which marks the true musician.

I feel that the appearance of this book is a major event in the history of musical theory and understanding, and merits attention from musicians of all kinds.

LEOPOLD MANNES

ix

Contents

Part III

Introduction

This book is based on Heinrich Schenker's revolutionary conceptions of tonality and musical coherence. It has been motivated and guided by my great admiration for Schenker himself, as well as by my gratitude for those ideas and teachings which have given my musical life its purpose and direction.

It is not the aim of this book to apply Schenker's ideas to specific problems; this has already been done in books in both English and German. My purpose is to mold his concepts into a workable, systematic approach for use by teachers, students and performers, as well as by anyone seriously interested in the problems of musical continuity, coherence and structure.

Whoever undertakes the task of presenting Schenker's ideas outside the German-speaking world is confronted with the formidable question: "Why not translate Schenker's writings and let them speak for themselves?" There were many reasons for my decision to drop the idea of translation, with or without commentary. One important reason seemed to me to be the very gradual, yet at the same time very complex, manner in which Schenker's final conceptions took shape. Between the harmony book,[1] published in 1906, and the final work, *Der freie Satz*,[2] published after his death in 1935, his books and articles reveal the extraordinary growth of his ideas. However, to the musician still unfamiliar with his work, these publications do not present a systematic development from rudimentary ideas to their final form and definition. For instance, there seems to be a veritable break between the period in which he wrote his study of Beethoven's Ninth Symphony (1912)[3] and that in which the first issue of *Der Tonwille* (1921)[4] was

[1] *Neue Musikalische Theorien und Phantasien* (Vol. I, *Harmonielehre*). Universal-Edition, Vienna.
[2] *Neue Musikalische Theorien und Phantasien* (Vol. III). Universal-Edition, Vienna.
[3] *Beethovens Neunte Sinfonie*. Universal-Edition, Vienna.
[4] Universal-Edition, Vienna, 1921-1924.

published. New ideas suddenly appear, seemingly for the first time, and the gap between these two periods has never been explained. From then on, the development of the new ideas is more consistent; but although the bridge from old to new is understandable to one familiar with Schenker's approach, it presents a definite obstacle for the beginner. Even in the years between 1920 and 1935 various major changes both in the conception and in the working-out of ideas are evident in the various issues of *Der Tonwille* as well as in the three volumes of *Das Meisterwerk in der Musik;* [5] the reasons for these were never fully revealed. Although Schenker's students and others sufficiently interested in his work were able to follow his provocative and compelling way of thinking and reasoning (and were able in turn to give their students the necessary explanations), the fact remains that Schenker's last work, *Der freie Satz,* is a highly advanced and rather complex book for which adequate preparation simply does not exist.

These factors made translation, without at least a thorough and lengthy commentary, highly inadvisable. But there were two other decisive reasons that finally caused me to give up any idea of translation and to write a new book presenting his conceptions systematically. During the years following Schenker's death (January, 1935), partly as a result of discussions with other musicians and teachers but mainly through my own teaching experience, one thought became increasingly clear. To teach music theory, analysis and composition according to his ideas, it was necessary to formulate a new pedagogic approach to these ideas. Many points required clarification, and many terms needed more concise definitions; it became apparent, furthermore, that explanations ought to begin on a more elementary level. Understanding of tonal organisms is a problem of hearing; the ear has to be systematically trained to hear not only the succession of tones, melodic lines and chord progressions but also their structural significance and coherence. Thus a systematic approach evolved, starting from simple and short examples and leading, in gradual stages, to large and complex organisms. This approach I call "Structural Hearing."

The second reason for not translating is that Schenker, with very few exceptions, used as illustrations music of the eighteenth and nineteenth centuries only, the music which lay so close to his heart and mind. Within the last fifteen years I have become completely convinced, however, that his ideas apply to widely diverse styles of music and that the broad conception underlying his approach is not confined to any limited period of music history. This fact has not been recog-

[5] Drei Masken Verlag, Munich, 1925-1930.

nized sufficiently and has led to the belief that Schenker's writings are valuable only for eighteenth- and nineteenth-century music. Nothing could be more erroneous; it is hoped that the following pages will prove the fallacy of this contention.

Hence Schenker's basic premises are left untouched in this book, but within the new pedagogic approach, several definitions have been revised and the range of literature has been considerably widened. I am aware of the fact that these changes will be criticized by those who still cling with the spirit of orthodoxy to every word Schenker has pronounced and who oppose any deviation from or any development of his writings. I consider this attitude narrow-minded and short-sighted. It has proven to be detrimental to the dissemination of the approach as a whole, because, by its very dogmatism, it has tended to make hard and fast some misunderstandings to which Schenker's writings have been subjected. I am convinced that a free and unbiased investigation of his work, while making certain definite modifications necessary, shows its value as even greater and farther reaching than heretofore held possible. It seems to me that Schenker's concepts provide not only for an intimate understanding of musical architecture of the past centuries, but, once thoroughly understood, may contribute towards establishing a truly modern style of composition.

In planning the contents of this book it seemed necessary first to explain in outline the essence of his ideas and their vital significance for our times. I have therefore divided the book into three parts which differ somewhat in approach. The first part presents Schenker's conceptions, their purpose and the possibilities which they suggest. It is in no sense intended as a comprehensive survey but simply as an introduction to the fundamental ideas upon which the approach is based. The questions raised by the first part and many which it leaves untouched, will be answered in the second part—*The pedagogic and systematic approach to structural hearing.* Each of these parts, however, will be treated as a unit, each understandable and complete in itself, without reference to the other. This procedure necessarily entails a certain amount of repetition, especially between Chapter II of Part I and the early chapters of Part II. Such repetition is unavoidable if the second part is to be presented as a complete and detailed exposition of the approach. In addition, it can serve only to enhance the reader's understanding to find each idea, which served in the general outline, repeated and developed in its exact perspective within the detailed whole. The third part, finally, deals with the implications and consequences of structural hearing as they concern problems of musical understanding, interpretation and musicology.

The second volume contains analyses of compositions constituting a large cross-section of musical literature from the Middle Ages to the present day. Within the processes of structural hearing, keyboard exercises have proven to be very helpful. They too will be found in the second volume.

New York, January 1952   FELIX SALZER

Acknowledgments

It is with deep pleasure that I acknowledge my indebtedness to several musicians, students and friends.

Above all, my thanks go to Miss Adele T. Katz and Mr. Leopold Mannes. Miss Katz's intimate acquaintance with the problems discussed in this book has been of great assistance. Her constant encouragement has been most inspiring, and in all these years of preparation and research she has generously given from the rich fund of her knowledge and experience. The musical affinity which connects me with Leopold Mannes is a source of deep satisfaction to me. I am most grateful to him for constructive criticism and very valuable suggestions. It was upon his initiative that, several years ago, the theory department of The Mannes Music School was reorganized on the basis of the conceptions outlined in this book. This step, combined with the zeal and interest of a most cooperative student body, has been of immeasurable help to me.

I am indebted to Miss Gertrude Bamberger, Miss Eugenia Earle, Mrs. Katharine Foy and Miss Elizabeth Lansing for valuable suggestions. At various stages they have given their time freely to the careful scrutiny of parts of the manuscript. My thanks go, furthermore, to two young composers, Mr. Noel Sokoloff and Mr. Roy Travis, with whom I conducted extensive studies in contemporary music and music of the fifteenth and sixteenth centuries. Their enthusiasm has been inspiring, and very valuable advice on their part is here gratefully acknowledged.

In the final stages of writing, Mr. Saul Novack and Mr. Joel Newman have proven to be of greatest assistance. Mr. Novack has made significant contributions, especially to Chapters Seven and Eight and to Part III.

Mr. Newman has made most valuable suggestions, and both have edited the manuscript with great care. The expert work of autographing the musical illustrations has been done by Mr. Carl A. Rosenthal, a rare craftsman and musician. I am most grateful to my publisher, Mr. Charles Boni, for his enterprising spirit and his splendid cooperation. Thanks are also extended to Miss Ethel Matier for her help in various matters.

My acknowledgment to several publishers for permission to include copyrighted musical examples will be found in Volume II.

I cannot conclude without mentioning my wife's contribution. Without her unwavering interest, her understanding and confidence, this book would never have been completed.

F.S.

PART

I

Part I   Chapter One

New ideas, whether they support or oppose the customary trend of thinking, represent the spiritual and mental characteristics of the period into which they are born; they will always be symptomatic of that particular period in human history. Thus, before discussing ideas of a revolutionary nature on the structure and coherence of music, it seems of utmost importance to understand the characteristics of the musical period in which they have evolved. In more specific terms, we must understand the conditions under which music is at present developing, the role it plays in our stage of civilization and its relation to the cultural and spiritual trends of our time.

Whether ideas meet receptive or deaf ears, whether they are born to live and bear fruit or to die and be forgotten does not depend on their intrinsic value alone; it also depends on the condition of the soil, so to speak, on which they fall. History knows some instances in which new ideas have been readily absorbed and applied, but many more in which ideas have been allowed to lie fallow and to disseminate very slowly. The reasons for the fate of an idea are as manifold as are the reasons for its birth.

In attempting to characterize our times in relation to the development of music, we find that very diversified trends at first give a confusing, rather kaleidoscopic impression. In spite of this apparent confusion and our necessary lack of historical perspective, a picture may be drawn presenting two aspects which at first appear extremely contradictory, but which prove to be interdependent by balancing each other to a remarkable degree.

One of the more obvious characteristics of our cultural period is the intensity and extension of its musical activity. This intensity pervades all fields of music, be it composition, performance or teaching. The last decades have been marked by a tremendous increase in music-making in general. In terms of quantity alone, we can say that probably more people than ever before have been brought into contact with good music. The vast number of concerts given, in addition to radio programs and recordings, have done much to bring music to the people (in the literal sense of the word). Consequently more and more people are studying music seriously or taking music courses as part of their general education. This new interest, in turn, has encouraged and made possible the establishment of more music departments in colleges, universities and other institutions of higher education, which provide serious students and music lovers with heretofore unheard-of opportunities for music education.

Great progress has been made in the field of pedagogy. The technical standard of instrumental playing has been raised to a very remarkable degree; performances by children and young students give convincing proof of the high average of technical quality. This positive trend can also be observed in the unusually high standard of orchestral performance.

The bright side of this picture is also intensified by a growing interest in the theory of music and composition and the strong development of musicological research in universities. This has produced an increasing sense of responsibility concerning performance. The number of good or at least technically clean performances has grown appreciably in the last decades; the technique of rehearsal has become more precise. Problems of style are no longer the concern of a few musicians only; we have become style-conscious. Although stylistically incorrect performances certainly occur, they provoke healthy criticism and opposition due to the improved and deepened historical outlook of many musicians.

We also must acknowledge that now, in contrast to the situation prevailing at the beginning of this century, more is being done to help the young composer. Certainly there is still much room for improvement, but, on the whole, the lot of the contemporary composer has brightened somewhat. Performing artists are gradually including more contemporary works on their programs, and there is a happy trend on the part of some publishers to accept new works more readily. I believe that this is due to a more enlightened attitude on the part of the public.

All this, however, describes only one side of the picture; the other side offers a remarkable and rather ominous contrast. Under the pleasant veil of musical prosperity lie deep unrest and uncertainty; in spite of all this hustling musical life, we are living through a time of crisis. No wishful thinking can deny its existence; its symptoms are too obvious and too abundant to be denied. Every thinking and conscientious musician, whether he fights for a new musical idiom or a new theoretical approach or clings to tradition, must strive to understand the nature of this great unrest.

This is a crisis in fundamental musical concepts which naturally affects the composer. It in no way reflects upon the quantity of his production or upon the undoubted quality of many contemporary works. But to whatever degree the individual composer may be affected, we are undoubtedly passing through a period of strained and self-conscious composition. We are constantly groping and experimenting, searching for a new language, a new idiom, a new direction of musical thought. In this search for the new, however, we somehow do not act as free agents; for instead of letting all creative forces come into play, our generation has entered upon a frantic struggle for originality. From the necessity of finding new means of expression arises a misconception of the new as an end in itself. The elements of composition can be taught, but originality can never be taught or demanded from a student because it is entirely dependent upon inspiration. Since he will or will not attain originality according to his own talent, this demand is a tremendous handicap to him for it tends to force him to be new for the sake of the new. This artificial incentive too often kills the last vestiges of spontaneous impulse and creative naïveté and has led to creative self-consciousness. It is also significant that more than ever before the composer is taking an active part in discussion; leading composers hold important teaching positions; they write books and articles on a far greater scale than did composers of former times. All this points up more strongly how conscious the problems of composition have become.

Today's musical crisis centers on the problem of tonality. Tonality, new tonality, atonality, polytonality, twelve-tone music, neo-classicism, impressionism—all these terms may symbolize various and often conflicting currents, but they all vitally concern the substance of musical language.

There is a tendency to explain away the importance of the crisis by comparing it with former conflicts, for instance those of the sixteenth and seventeenth centuries. We are told to beware of exaggeration, that every period tends to overstate its own significance and that a crisis which seems far-reaching in our times may in the light of history prove to be far less important and significant than we judge it to be. In short, we are told that while we may consider the crisis in our time as involving the most fundamental conceptions, this crisis actually represents, historically speaking, just another change of style.

Although it is true that history shifts the emphasis of events, I believe that those who see in recent developments only another fight for a new style are overlooking a decisive point: the musical revolutions of the sixteenth and seventeenth centuries were revolutions within a generally accepted basic idiom of musical expression; they represented changes of style during the course of the development of a musical language, or changes within a language already developed. But none of them—neither the struggle over the opera at the end of the sixteenth and the beginning of the seventeenth century, nor the conflict between vocal and instrumental expression in the sixteenth century—affected the basic conception of tonality. These struggles ultimately reduce themselves to changes in styles and settings; this is true not only of the conflicts already mentioned, but of the development of the classical sonata form and of the strife over Gluck and the neo-German school led by Liszt and Wagner. While these conflicts essentially represent changes of style, they nonetheless gave great impetus to the development of tonality's expressive possibilities.

We must distinguish between changes of style on the basis of a developing or existing language and a crisis of the musical language itself. These earlier conflicts may have created much discussion at the time of their occurrence, but, what is of foremost importance, they left the language (i.e. the fundamental conception of musical utterance and continuity) basically untouched. They affected, so to speak, the appearance and dress, but not the body. They served to enrich, elaborate and even to change the dress in spectacular fashion, but they presented no attack on the body, i.e. the conceptions of musical continuity, coherence and structure.

Our period, however, is completely at odds about basic conceptions of musical utterance and coherence. This is therefore a conflict of language and not of style. Not one idiom has as yet divulged its possibilities convincingly to a majority of composers as a musical language, and what is even more important, none of them has reached that unconscious stage of musical expression so vital to the development of an artistic language or conception.

Whatever the future of art music may be, whether it lies in the twelve-tone system or any other of our present much-discussed idioms, there is hardly any doubt or disagreement about the fact that, for the present at least, the language of tonality has lost its universal power of musical expression. Some believe that it is disintegrating, having exhausted its possibilities. Others, however, believe that this language, after having gone through a period of crisis, is now emerging with major changes and new structural possibilities constituting an enrichment of its architectonic potentialities. This is also the view of this

author who firmly believes in the development of a "new" tonality made possible through the powerful influences of Hindemith, Bartók and Stravinsky. Time will provide the answer to this question. We shall probably go on groping and experimenting for some time to come; we must go on because only the constant efforts, conscious or unconscious, of this and the following generation will provide the much-needed answer and will give direction to future generations.

A crisis of a musical language or of a basic musical conception (tonality may be classified as both) can neither be condemned nor praised. It cannot be fought, but neither can its existence be denied; it is beyond all methodological interference. The course of cultural developments of such strength as the crisis of tonality can be influenced to a limited degree at best.

It is the way in which we deal with this crisis, our attitude towards it, which is of vital importance and which may have some direct bearing on future developments. It is certainly not beyond our power to influence this attitude.

We are searching; we are trying to understand; we are endeavoring to make conscious the unconscious. This is a general characteristic of our times, and it is true of our relation not only to music, but to the other arts and to science as well. It is our destiny and we must live up to it. We cannot afford to indulge in ostrich policies or to be complacent about our accomplishments. More self-criticism, a more honest appraisal of our situation, is imperative if we are at last to gain creative expression, free from the specter of originality *à tout prix*.

It is equally imperative that we be at all times receptive and responsive to the new, and I think we are now on the whole more open-minded than other periods have been. However, the tendency which we often observe to discuss modern compositions in vague generalities is not only unjust to contemporary composers, but is very detrimental to our attempts to meet the crisis. In the appraisal of new works, just as in the analysis of older compositions, there is an unfortunate tendency to be satisfied with vague categorizations according to such superficial stylistic criteria as "neo-classic," "neo-romantic," "linear," etc., or to describe their outer, visible appearance, so to speak, in terms of external aesthetic values. These terms, while having a definite place in the field of music criticism, hardly ever touch upon the actual musical utterance. Often terms such as "original," "bold" or "interesting" are profusely used but do not succeed in covering up what is lacking either in the music itself or in the listener's understanding.

Furthermore, it seems as though some musicians are so deadly afraid of "missing" a talent that they think it safer to praise most new compositions, thus demonstrating an appalling lack of judgment and discrimination. This curious attitude has indeed become a veritable obsession with all too many musicians, critics and teachers. Whether we are prejudiced and condemn or neglect works simply because they are new and sound unusual or for other narrow-minded reasons, or whether we go to the other extreme and lose our sense of judgment merely because the work is new and we are afraid to be blamed for not having recognized a talent—both attitudes seem to me equally detrimental to the development of music. Either will delay more than promote the process of finding a definite language of musical expression.

The roots of the tendency to be vague and to generalize lie in a widespread and marked uncertainty in regard to basic musical conceptions. This uncertainty leads naturally to vagueness in our musical terminology and only too often to outright superficiality of musical analysis and criticism. A great gap exists between the demands made upon the critic and teacher for understanding and guidance, on the one hand, and our ability to cope with these demands, on the other.

An ever-increasing number of musicians feel that they have been subjected to methods of musical theory and analysis which they now consider to be inadequate. As a result, some of them tend to reject every possible type of analysis and, as a consequence, resort to purely descriptive methods in which musical generalities play an unduly prominent part. They have given up hope of expecting any light from intrinsically musical explanations of musical contents. It is this situation which produces our ambiguous terminology. There are far too many who are spellbound by terms and who juggle slogans which do not gain significance from constant repetition, but only add to the confusion. In spite of all attempts to categorize, and in spite of the great increase in style-criticism, we can hardly think of a time when there were so many terms in use, while at the same time there was so much real confusion over basic musical conceptions.

One basic musical concept already mentioned, tonality, is to many a vague and only partly understood phenomenon whose potentialities are as yet unknown. Tonality, along with other fundamentals such as harmony, counterpoint and modulation, are defined in a great number of varied and often contradictory ways. Even the function and origin of form in music seems today to be a bewildering subject.

We can hardly decide now whether the crisis in musical language is the consequence of the confusion in basic musical conceptions or whether these ideas are bound to become confused when the instinct for the use of the language declines. Developments in the history of art move gradually, and it is certain that there is neither one cause nor one solution to all the conflicts which confront us. It is in our hands, however, to change the mental attitudes and the methods which tend to a vague, purely descriptive terminology of analysis and criticism, and to revise the whole field of theory and appreciation. I am convinced that nothing short of such a fundamental revision can give our musical thinking a new direction.

It is my belief that it was Heinrich Schenker who gave the powerful initiative to this much-needed revision. He has provided us with new ideas which clarify and revise conventional conceptions and which give new impulse and stimulus to our musical thinking. Above all he has brought the wide field of musical theory again into contact with the living motion of musical composition from which it had separated itself so very thoroughly. No one can predict in what way his ideas will influence the development of a new musical language, or to what extent they will affect problems of analysis, interpretation and composition. It seems certain, however, that understanding and assimilating them represents a necessary condition to sound musical development, out of which a solution of the crisis may later evolve.

Part I   Chapter Two

A.   Chord grammar—Chord significance

Schenker's conceptions are based on a fundamental observation, the recognition of which formed the starting point of his entire work—the distinction between what will be called *chord grammar* and *chord significance*. While this distinction may have been instinctively felt by other musicians, they do not seem to have recognized its vast implications nor to have drawn from it any tangible conclusions for the theory of music and composition. Schenker examined this distinction, and, following up its implications, arrived at new and far-reaching conclusions.

Chord grammar denotes the usual type of analysis in which separate designations and labels are assigned to triads, seventh chords, etc. It is a purely descriptive means of registering and labeling each chord and relating it to different key centers. Chord grammar is the backbone of our present-day harmonic analysis, which is primarily concerned with recognition of the grammatical status of each chord in a musical work. It breaks up a phrase into a group of isolated chord entities. The study of chord significance, on the other hand, reveals the meaning of a chord and the specific role it plays in a phrase or section of a work, or in the work in its entirety. Chord significance, since it discloses the function of a chord, goes far beyond grammatical description by pointing out the special, architectonic purpose of a chord within a phrase. As a first result of this distinction, Schenker found that the roles which chords play in a musical phrase or section are very diverse; even two grammatically identical chords appearing in the same phrase can fulfill totally different functions. Thus it follows that labeling chords according to their grammatical status never explains their functions or how they combine to create a unified whole.

As an illustration of the difference between chord grammar and chord significance, let us consider the opening measures of Bach's Prelude in Bb Major from Book I of the *Well-Tempered Clavier*. In addition to illustrating this distinction, this brief example also provides the opportunity to demonstrate some of its broader consequences. ►[Ex. I]◄

The Roman numerals appearing directly below the music represent the usual type of harmonic analysis, indicating the status of the chord in the key and its position (root position or inversion). The customary melodic analysis would point to a sequence embracing four tones (D-C-D-F) as a motive. The last group of four chords together with the tonic chord in the final measure would be indicated as a cadence. Because of this cadence as well as for the sake of variety, the melodic sequence would be considered changed in the third and fourth quarters of measure 2. Or, the presence of the sequence might lead to an alternative reading of the chords on the last eighth-note of meas. 1 and the fourth eighth-note of meas. 2 as secondary dominants of the preceding chords, despite the fact that the D chord is minor. This reading would result in the following harmonic analysis: I-V⁶-I-V-VI-III⁶-VI-V*of* VI-IV-I⁶-IV-V*of*IV-II, etc. Although this reading of the chords appears to be somewhat more discriminating than the first, the approach is essentially the same; it is purely descriptive and vertical. It completely dissects the phrase, turning an organic musical idea into a group of isolated chords and motives, each of which is represented as an independent entity through the application of grammatical symbols.

Many musicians feel that this type of analysis, though indispensable as groundwork, is incomplete, and that the most vital problems of the music have not been explained or even touched upon. What has this analysis revealed of the phrase's motion, and of the function of the chords and sequences within that motion? Has it been explained whether or not these tones, chords and motives are integral parts of an organic whole?

B. Music as directed motion—Structure and prolongation

We often hear and read about the motion of music and about a piece of music as an organic whole. But these facts are seldom subjected to analytical investigation. If, however, a musical phrase is an expression of motion, questions as to the musical meaning of this motion are in order and will have to be answered. To put these questions in more specific form: Where does the motion begin? What is its goal? And how does the composer reach that goal?

Like a logical argument or a literary composition, a musical work is directed; its direction is determined by the very goal towards which it moves. Thus the significance of tones and chords and the functions they fulfill depend upon this goal and the direction the motion takes to attain it. It was this observation which led Schenker to the conclusion that grammatically identical chords may play diverse roles. Obviously a bare description of grammatical facts fails to take into account the problems of musical direction.

To return to the fragment of the Bach Prelude, let us first discuss melodic direction in terms of the sequence. We hear the sequence begin on the Bb-Major tonic and come to an end upon the incomplete C-minor chord (meas. 2), at which point the motive changes. The sequential motion and the point of change have a twofold meaning: First, they unify the motion up to the point of change; second, this very unification serves in turn to stress the C-minor chord as a temporary goal, thus giving it more weight than the preceding submediant and subdominant chords. In the following chords, the emphasis falls upon the dominant seventh chord on F, the top voice circling around Eb, and this leads to the conclusion of the whole phrase on the Bb tonic. Thus the motion outlined in the whole phrase progresses from the initial Bb chord to the Bb chord in the third measure. The supertonic triad and the dominant seventh chord, as temporary goals, give specific shape to the outline; together with the two Bb-Major tonics, they form the progression I-II-V-I. This progression, supporting a motion in the top voice of D-Eb-Eb-D, governs the entire phrase and constitutes its *structural framework* or *fundamental structure*. Its members will be called *structural chords* (Graph a).

We come now to those chords in the phrase which do not serve as members of the I-II-V-I progression. What is their function in the motion and what purpose do they serve in maintaining the organic unity of the phrase? [1] Graph a has shown that instead of moving a tone upward from the Bb-Major to the C-minor chord, the possibility represented in Graph c, Bach inverted this obvious movement and descended a seventh in the outer voices. The filling in of this descending seventh engenders those intervening chords between the I and the II that contribute individuality and richness to the progression. These chords that fill the space of a seventh have a different origin and function from the chords that outline that space, the I and II. They constitute the means of passing from I to II, a motion emphasized and held together by the melodic character of the sequence (Graph b).

In this instance, the motion from I to II is achieved by means of the VI

---

[1] The use of half-notes for chords of the structural progression in the graphs is not intended to indicate time-values, but to differentiate structural points from chords having a different function. Roman numerals are applied only to chords defining the structural framework.

and the IV. Had Bach descended from the B♭-Major to the C-minor chord in a stepwise progression, the intermediate chords would be clearly defined as passing chords. Instead, however, he devised a musical pattern which moves in thirds through the G-minor and E♭-Major chords. Although the progression is not stepwise, these chords do in fact serve as passing chords. They are the connecting links between the I and the II, since they provide the motion between these structural chords. Both the structural and the passing chords are further strengthened through neighbor-note chords on the second and sixth eighth-notes, meas. 1, and the second eighth-note, meas. 2. The incomplete F-Major, D-minor and B♭-Major chords that follow the B♭-Major, G-minor and E♭-Major passing chords may be termed embellishing chords since they support embellishing tones of the melody. The primary function of these chords, as well as of the passing G-minor and E♭-Major chords, is to *prolong* the motion from the B♭-Major to the C-minor chord. Hence in distinction to the structural I and II, these passing, neighbor-note and embellishing chords are called *prolonging chords*. The G-minor and F-Major chords in first inversion appearing between the structural II and V have a similar origin; since they support G and F in the top voice, tones embellishing the structural tone E♭, they are embellishing and passing chords that prolong the motion from II to V.

It is now clear how the questions posed on page 11 regarding musical motion are to be answered with reference to the opening of the Bach Prelude. The reader, for final confirmation, should play or listen carefully first to Graphs a and b, and then to the quotation itself.

Schenker developed the distinction between chords of structure and chords of prolongation directly out of his differentiation between chord grammar and chord significance, and from his insistence upon taking the music's direction into consideration. This distinction between structure and prolongation became the backbone of his whole approach.[2] By means of this distinction we hear a work, not as a series of fragmentary and isolated phrases and sections, but as a single organic structure through whose prolongation the principle of artistic unity and variety is maintained. This way of understanding musical motion represents, I believe, the instinctive perception of the truly musical ear and can be termed "structural hearing."

[2] The analogous and equally important distinction between melody tones of structure and melody tones of prolongation will be discussed in more detail in Part II. The graphs in the present chapter necessarily show the melody's significance, and for the present the reader must be content to follow their indications as well as he can, and to concentrate more on the bass if necessary.

It is wrong to assume, however, that finding the structural framework constitutes the sole purpose of this approach. On the contrary, structural hearing implies much more. It enables us to listen to a work musically, because by grasping the structural outline of a piece we feel the full impact of its prolongations which are the flesh and blood of a composition. Thus the structural outline or framework represents the fundamental motion to the goal; it shows the direct, the shortest way to this goal. The whole interest and tension of a piece consists in the expansions, modifications, detours and elaborations of this basic direction, and these we call the prolongations. Their broad, complex and bold unfoldings and their artistic coherence can only be grasped and fully appreciated, however, if their basic direction (comprising the structural framework) has been understood. In the reciprocity between structure and prolongation lies the organic coherence of a musical work.

C. Harmony and Counterpoint

The distinction between structure and prolongation led Schenker to a new conception of the functions of harmony and counterpoint in creating organic unity. He came to the realization that, as has been suggested, not every chord is of harmonic origin. Although he surely was not the first to arrive at this conclusion, he was the first to prove that this concept has a revolutionary effect upon our understanding of music. To regard every chord as a harmonic individuality leads us back to chord grammar and all of its limitations. Similarly, to believe that counterpoint is confined only to so-called independent voice leading and to such techniques as imitation, stretto, canon and fugue, etc., overlooks the vital role it plays in every composition irrespective of its style, be it a fugue by Bach, a sonata by Haydn, a passage from a Wagner music-drama or a waltz by Johann Strauss.

Once we have realized the different functions chords can exercise we find that in addition to their structural or prolonging roles, they may have harmonic and contrapuntal functions as well. A detailed explanation of the harmonic concept will be given in Part II, Chapter IV. For the moment it will suffice to point out that this concept is based on the relationship of the fifth as expressed in the overtone series. Out of this relationship evolves the fundamental harmonic progression I-V-I. In addition to the fifth there is the weaker relation of the major third—weaker because it is farther removed from the fundamental. A chord thus demonstrates a harmonic function if it is a member either of the fundamental progression I-V-I or of one of the following progressions: I-II-V-I, I-III-V-I, I-IV-V-I. In these elaborated progressions, as we shall call them, the II, III and IV, respectively, bear a harmonic association either to the tonic or the dominant. The II demonstrates a fifth association with V, the III a third association with I, the IV a fifth (below) association with I. However, and this is most important, a II, III or IV exercises its harmonic function only if it appears in connection with I and V, elaborating the fundamental harmonic progression. In other words II, III and IV are not automatically harmonic chords; only if one of them is a member of a progression coming from I and proceeding to V, serving as an intermediary station in the fundamental harmonic movement from tonic to dominant, has it a harmonic function. Members of a harmonic progression need not appear in direct succession, as can be seen in the example from the Bach Prelude (Graph b of Ex. I), where the members of the progression I-II-V are separated by several intervening chords. In spite of their separation, the ear grasps their structural connection because they are equal in structural function and none of the other chords are on a par with them.

The term "harmony," therefore, should only be used for members of a harmonic progression; they are the "harmonies" in the truest sense of the word because they are connected on the basis of a harmonic association. On the other hand, all chords not based on harmonic association are products of motion, direction and embellishment and, paradoxical as it may sound, have a horizontal tendency. They result from the motion of voices since they are generated by voice leading and voice direction and will be called *contrapuntal chords*, in contrast to chords of harmonic origin. Thus in the phrase from the Prelude, all chords other than the I-II-V-I, the harmonic chords, are contrapuntal chords of various types.[3]

To conclude, in our example the harmonic chords are also structural chords, constituting the structural framework; the contrapuntal chords, on the other hand, are simultaneously chords of prolongation, because they prolong and elaborate the space between members of the harmonic progression.[4]

[3] These will be dealt with at length in Part II.
[4] The reader should not be led to believe that these chord functions are the only ones to be found. This is by no means the case; we shall have the opportunity later on to demonstrate the prolonging function of harmonic progressions within a larger framework, as well as the possible structural significance of contrapuntal chords.

D. Chord prolongation

Contrapuntal chords do not only appear *between* two members of a harmonic progression; very often they move *within* a single harmony or chord. In such cases the function of these contrapuntal chords is to prolong and elaborate that single harmony or chord. An example from a Chorale by Bach [5] will illustrate this type of prolongation. ►[Ex. II]◄

Graph a shows a motion in the outer voices, in which the top voice ascends a third and the bass descends an octave, filling in intervals of the B-minor chord. This process may be called the horizontalization of a chord. It imparts expression to a single chord, in this case a structural harmony (see Graphs a and b). It is the outer-voice motion which is essential; the chords resulting from this outer-voice motion only intensify it, and it is a striking fact that they have no value or *raison d'être* other than to unfold the governing B-minor tonic, to which they are subordinated. What has been achieved is the prolongation of a chord; we shall call this function *chord prolongation*.

The role of the chords *within* the horizontalized and thus prolonged B-minor chord is that of passing chords, not between two different harmonies but within the horizontalized intervals of a single harmony. This harmony, a prolonged structural tonic, moves to the dominant which in turn proceeds to the tonic, concluding the phrase outlined by a structural harmonic I-V-I progression. The difference in function between the prolonging dominant in meas. 1 and the structural dominant in meas. 2 furnishes an illustration of grammatically identical chords playing diverse roles.

It is now clear that the term, prolongation, may be applied to the expansion of a progression from one chord to another (see the Prelude) or to the expansion of a single chord; thus far we have been confronted with the prolongation of a progression from I to II (Prelude) and with the prolongation of a I (Chorale). The fact that the space between two chords may be prolonged and that various chords may serve to prolong one single chord, was a most important discovery which had its origin in the music of the Middle Ages.

These two types of prolongation influence the motion of a phrase in very different ways. The prolongation of a progression, as illustrated in the Bach Prelude, shows a strong impulse of direction since there is

[5] No. 294 in Riemenschneider's ed., *371 Harmonized Chorales and 69 Chorale Melodies with Figured Bass*. G. Schirmer, Inc., N.Y., 1941. All references to Bach Chorales follow the numbering in this edition, unless otherwise indicated.

a drive from one harmony to another (I to II). The passing chords intensify the feeling of drive and direction; the structural progression from I to II itself, if unprolonged, would scarcely have conveyed this impression of a drive to a goal. The stress here is more on direction than on expansion. In the Chorale phrase, however, the impulse of direction is weaker, because, for the greatest part of the phrase, the motion lies within a single prolonged harmony. The emphasis here is on expansion rather than direction, since the prolongation of a single chord checks the impulse to attain a new structural goal (in this case, the V). Thus in the Prelude, motion develops from the beginning and proceeds straight forward until the next structural goal, the II, is reached; in the Chorale, on the contrary, the chord prolongation causes a lingering, retarding effect, after which the progression to the new structural goal immediately takes place.

These two different types of motion are not without influence on interpretation.[6] Even in such simple examples it will seem natural that the gradual but well-directed drive to a goal will need different interpretative shadings from the "circling around" or "moving within" type of motion: These differences are inconspicuous, but nonetheless important; in many cases they are achieved quite unconsciously in performance on the basis of musical instinct. Certainly interpretation is also influenced by stylistic and historical considerations. We must never overlook the fact, however, that the problem of good interpretation lies to a great extent in the music itself and in its musical meaning.

E. Tonality

Through its power to subordinate tones and chords in order to extend a single chord in time, chord prolongation creates tonal entities; it is thus an organizing force. As such it became the essential factor in that great concept of musical organization which the music of western civilization has created and which we call tonality.

In the following phrase from a Bach Chorale ▶[Ex. III]◀ we encounter a chord prolongation which touches on the question of tonality, even if on a small scale.

Using the conventional method of harmonic analysis to explain this passage, a difficulty arises in connection with the use of a G-Major chord (meas. 2) in a phrase in A minor. What is its status, since it

---

[6] The application of structural hearing to problems of interpretation will become clearer as the book progresses.

evidences no harmonic relationship to the A-minor chord? [7] Does it represent a modulation to a new tonal center, even a "false" or "temporary" modulation to a new key? Since we hear this entire passage as an organic whole, despite the fermata, is there not a logical and musical explanation for the G-Major chord indicating that it is an integral part of a single structural framework expressing the tonality of A minor?

If we hear structurally, we find that the D-Major chord is not a modulatory agent to the key of G Major, but what is called an applied or secondary dominant. Any type of chord, whether it be harmonic, contrapuntal, structural or prolonging, can be preceded by an applied dominant chord. The function of the applied dominant is to provide additional color and to give emphasis to the following chord; it does not in any way affect the continued existence of a single key. From this point of view, the G-Major chord does not indicate a new tonal center. But what is its actual significance? If we listen to the melody carefully (Graph a), we realize that the downbeats of meas. 1 and 2 each give rise to ascents of a third (melodic parallelism) and to an added motive showing the skip of a third downwards; the downbeats are in stepwise progression; together with the downbeat of meas. 3 (which repeats the motive skipping down a third) they form an ascending third A-B-C of which the other melodic thirds are prolongations. The counterpoint to this ascending third A-B-C is A-G-A, Bach having chosen G of the natural minor scale instead of G♯. Since the top voice tone B is a passing note, and the bass tone G a neighboring note, the function of the resulting G-Major chord is that of a neighbor-passing chord [8] (Graph b). Because a neighbor note adds emphasis to the main note, in this case the tone A, and since the melodic ascending third horizontalizes an interval of the A-minor chord (Graphs b and c), we must interpret the G-Major chord as a chord moving within and circling around the A-minor chord, which it thus helps to prolong. The G chord has a contrapuntal, not a harmonic, association with the preceding and following A-minor chords and represents an integral part of one single prolonged A-minor tonic. This tonic then moves via an F-Major passing chord to the II , V and to the final I, which concludes the phrase. For final confirmation it would be advisable to play the tonal contents of meas. 1 to 3 (downbeat) in logical reverse, that is,

---

[7] To interpret the G-Major chord as a VII of the natural A-minor key is at best an explanation of that chord's grammatical status, and does not explain its function in an A-minor phrase.

[8] See p. 105 for an explanation of neighbor-passing chords.

from their structure to the phrase's completed form, as indicated by
►[Ex. IV]◄. I believe that this procedure completely illustrates the
basic unity of these measures.[9]

This example offers an excellent illustration of the different results
attained through chord grammar and harmonic analysis on the one
hand, and structural hearing on the other. To hear the G-Major chord
as a modulation to the key of G Major, even as a temporary de-
parture from the key of A minor, destroys the underlying significance
of this tonal unit expressing a single prolonged chord. Yet how
else than as a "temporary" modulation can harmonic analysis explain
the G-Major chord? Chord grammar, the basis of harmonic analysis,
provides for no other reading of the phrase. Based, however, on the
fundamental conception of structure and prolongation in general and
chord prolongation in particular there evolves an entirely new and far
broader concept of tonality, by which the G-Major chord is explicable
as an organic part of the whole passage. This concept of tonality actually demonstrates what the structural coherence of music means.

It is essential to realize that a chord, such as the G-Major one discussed above, may serve either in a harmonic or contrapuntal capacity
which in no way conflicts with the key in which it appears. If we hear
this G-Major chord as a neighbor-passing chord of the tonic A minor,
we can account for its presence in the A-minor key and only then do
we hear the whole quotation as an expression of structural coherence
and organic unity. To regard the G-Major chord as a modulation, even
if temporary, robs the motion of its unity by splitting it into two different keys.

This brings us to the usual conception of tonality as permitting a
series of shifting modulations to other keys, sometimes related, sometimes unrelated to the main key, with a return modulation to the initial
key at the end of the composition. According to this, the beginning
and the end of the composition guarantee the main tonality. But is this
what tonality actually means? Is it this conception which Bach, Mozart,
Beethoven, Chopin and countless other composers revealed in their
works? When Beethoven indicates that a movement of a sonata or of
a symphony is in a given key, are we to understand that only the
beginning and the end define that key, while the remaining sections
embrace many different keys?

The accepted definition of modulation is that it is the means of pass-

[9] This is one of the many instances where Bach carries the musical motion over
the fermata into the next phrase, thus creating a synthesis far stronger than revealed in the original melody.

ing out of one key into another in order to create richness and variety. Modulations are divided into two classes, those that are "temporary" or "false," in which the new key is of transient occurrence, and those that are "complete" and so of a more permanent nature. Yet what is meant by the term "temporary"? Does it imply that the main key actually has not been relinquished but only temporarily obscured? If so, and the main key is retained, can there simultaneously be even a temporary or passing modulation to a new tonal center? Or perhaps "temporary" means that the main key has been replaced by a new one but only for a short period. In this case, what is the function of the new key and how can we account for it within the main tonality? The new keys are usually explained on the basis of their harmonic relationship with the fundamental key, such as the key of the relative major, the dominant, the dominant of the dominant and so on. Often, however, the new keys cannot be explained on this basis. In fact, according to harmonic analysis, there are often so many modulations to temporary keys having no harmonic relation at all to the main key, that the key-signature indicated by the composer appears to be both contradictory and misleading. Furthermore, by pointing out a series of temporary keys without showing their function in the work (i.e. how they combine to create a unified whole), the analyst evades the question of the significance of these passages within the tonality indicated by the composer. The theory of constantly shifting modulations is thus a real descendant of chord grammar.

Let us now discuss problems of tonality and tonal coherence in a complete composition and then in a section of a large form. The two works to be cited differ widely in treatment, style and proportion but have the same harmonic framework outlining their respective tonalities. (In both the reader may experience difficulties with the structural explanation of the top voice. This topic will be taken up later; at this point he is advised to concentrate on the problem of tonality.)

The first of the examples is the Schubert Waltz in B minor, op. 18. ►[Ex. V]◄ The essential point of our discussion centers on the passage from the D-Major chord in meas. 8 to the D seventh chord in meas. 12. According to harmonic analysis, the D-Major chord (meas. 8) introduced by its own dominant, represents the tonic of a new key, the key of the relative major. Many persons will feel the continued presence of the D-Major key in the following measures because of the D pedal point and the outline of the D-Major chord in the top voice created by the sequential motive. They will then regard the chromatic chords in meas. 13 and 14 as a modulation back to B minor. On the basis of this

reading the Waltz modulates from B minor to D Major and back to
B minor. According to structural hearing, however, the D-Major section does not go *back* to the fundamental key but goes *on* to its ultimate goal, the dominant F♯-Major chord (meas. 15) and the tonic
(meas. 16). Therefore, a motion onward in one single direction, not
backwards, is indicated. This element of direction is of vital significance; we touch here upon a real difference of conception between our
approach and the customary method.

Thus the section usually regarded as in the key of D occurs within
the motion from the B-minor to the F♯-Major chord, that is, from the
tonic to the dominant of the fundamental tonality. What then is the
status and function of the measures commonly understood to be in D
Major? These measures exhibit a motion within the prolonged D-Major
chord, the mediant of B minor,[10] which serves as an intermediary goal
to which the motion from the tonic is directed and which in turn im-
pels the motion to the dominant. Thus the function of this D-Major
chord is that of a mediant in the structural I-III-V-I progression that
outlines the harmonic framework of a single B-minor tonality.

The reader may argue that the explanation of the D-Major section
as a prolonged III is merely another name for modulation without any
real distinction in their fundamental implications, and that the difference lies solely in terminology. This objection, however, is unfounded
because chord prolongation does not indicate a motion out of the key
to a new tonal center, not even a temporary one. On the contrary, it
implies the existence of one key only; by showing the function of the
D-Major chord as a member of the structural I-III-V-I progression,
the entire motion is kept within the outline of a single key.

Whereas the theory of modulation is based on the self-contradictory
conception of departing from a key while remaining within the key,
structural hearing proves that a piece with the key signature of B minor
is really in B minor only, because that key accounts for every chord,
with or without its prolongation, as an integral part of a musical organism defining *one* key. The old conception, on the other hand, makes
of the so-called main key a mere empty shell or a stylistic peculiarity
of a certain period.

The Schubert Waltz furnishes an illustration of another point of
major importance. Harmonic progressions which constitute the structural framework of short passages may at the same time serve as pro-

---

[10] In most textbooks the mediant of a minor key is indicated as an augmented
chord. But whenever the mediant is used as a member of a harmonic progression,
it *always* appears as a major chord, according to the natural or pure minor scale.

longations within a larger context. The I-V-I in the first five measures is a progression of this type. While outlining the structure of the measures in question, it also achieves the prolongation of the I which is the first member of the total harmonic framework (Graphs a, c). The bass of the I-V-I progression is the horizontalized expression of one single vertical chord form. ►[Ex. VI]◄

Horizontalization, as pointed out on page 16, results in prolongation. Thus the chords built on B, F♯ and B and their progression create a prolongation of a B-minor chord—a harmonic prolongation because the chords are connected on the basis of harmonic association. ►[Ex. VII]◄

We must, therefore, distinguish between contrapuntal and harmonic chord prolongation. Any chord may be prolonged either in a contrapuntal or harmonic way.[11] In the Schubert Waltz both types occur, contrapuntal prolongation in meas. 9-12 and harmonic prolongation in meas. 1-5, as explained above. Both grow out of the structural harmonic progression I-III-V-I, which represents the progression of the highest structural order. All progressions of voice leading, i.e. all prolongations, show a differentiation between those of lower and those of progressively higher order, comparable to such varying degrees of order as motive-phrase-theme-section, etc. The progression of the highest structural order is the structural framework indicating the composition's basic direction. Throughout this book emphasis is laid on this distinction.

The question has probably arisen in the reader's mind: If I-V-I is a prolongation of a I of a higher structural order, must not the structural progression I-III-V-I also be logically classified as a prolongation of a I of a still higher structural order? It is true that the progression I-III-V-I is *de facto* a prolongation of a B-minor chord. This progression becomes the structural framework because all other prolongations, harmonic or contrapuntal, prove to be offshoots of it in this composition. The B-minor chord is a governing logical fact but it has no structural significance per se. In any piece, the one progression which is of highest structural order must be interpreted as the ultimate structural framework.

The presence of the tonality-indicating chord is only one more proof that chord prolongation is the essence of tonality. The horizontalization of the fundamental chord creates the structural harmonic progression of which all other prolongations, contrapuntal or

---

[11] See Part II, Chapters V and VI, for detailed discussion and application of contrapuntal and harmonic prolongations.

harmonic, are integral parts or, we might say, diminutions. It must become clear that the interpretation of certain chords in a composition as structural or prolonging depends upon whether we are analyzing a phrase, a section or the whole piece. If we analyze three measures of a piece, as in the Bach Prelude, then we separate them from the larger organism of which they are an integral part. They become a structural organism in themselves; therefore we are entitled to call the I-II-V-I progression the structural framework of that phrase because it represents the progression of the highest structural order of those particular measures. In analyzing the whole Prelude, however, the three measures would appear as a small part of the whole; thus the I-II-V-I progression would become a harmonic prolongation of a chord of a higher structural order.

It should be unnecessary to point out that all these explanations in no way indicate the chronological order of composing. This never can be made the subject of a theory of composition; it can never be explained and differs with every composer. The sole purpose of this kind of explanation and the use of the graphs is to show tonal coherence in gradual stages—which is necessary, if we are to explain in a systematic way what we hear.

Prolongation is not only applied to harmonic and structural chords. Any chord in a piece, whether it be harmonic or contrapuntal, diatonic or chromatic, may be prolonged without impairing the tonal stability, if its position and function within the structural framework are clearly defined. For example, if a passing chord is prolonged, it still retains its function as a passing chord although its influence in the phrase has been greatly intensified. In short, whether or not a chord or the progression to that chord is prolonged, its original function remains the same. However, the prolongations may not wander aimlessly or vaguely but must at all times point to the structural chord that follows. This is especially true in large forms in which it is essential for every prolonged chord, regardless of the number of measures it covers, to convey the feeling of direction in moving to its structural goal. Thus form, as an expression of artistic unity, depends on the conception and the working-out of the prolongations.

The development section of the first movement of Mozart's Sonata in A minor is our next example; the first problem is to show its relation to the structure of the exposition. ►[Ex. VIII]◄

The exposition reveals a structural motion from the tonic A-minor to the mediant C-Major chord, in which both of these structural chords

are greatly prolonged, thereby creating subjects 1 and 2.[12] Passing to
the development (starting with meas. 50), we find that the expanded
mediant, after an extended prolongation, reaches the dominant with
the recapitulation beginning on the tonic chord. This indicates that
exposition and development are held together by an underlying I-III-V
progression with the recapitulation starting again on I. We are thus
confronted with a structural progression very much like that of the
Schubert Waltz, but on a much larger scale. In both, the conception of
tonality is the same, but in the Sonata, it is understandable that the prolongations are longer and the ear is forced to hear over greater
distances between structural points. For this reason structural understanding of the Sonata is more difficult than of the Waltz. An illustration of this fact is the wide span between the opening C-Major chord
of the development section and the D-minor chord (meas. 70). Although the emphasis on this D-minor chord at first suggests that it may
be a structural goal, the close of the whole section on a dominant
E-Major chord reveals that the true function of the D-minor chord is
that of a passing chord between the C- and E-Major chords (Graph c).
The space, especially between the C-Major and D-minor, and to a
degree between the D-minor and E-Major chords, is greatly expanded
and enriched by the intervening chords. These prolonging chords in
no way impair the integrity of the structural III-V progression in expressing the A-minor tonality, because they have a clearly defined
function within the motion from III to V. The great prolongation, for
instance, between the III and the vital D-minor passing chord can be
visualized in the following three stages: ►[Ex. IX]◄

Stage a) shows the basic progression of the whole development as a
progression from C (III) via D (passing chord) to E (V).
Stage b) indicates the main prolongation of this progression consisting
in a stepwise movement via B (meas. 58) to A (meas. 66), the
applied dominant chord of D.
Stage c) introduces as a further prolongation an E chord which is part
of a descending fifth progression [13] between the B and A
chords.

Thus the B chord has the function of a passing chord in the motion
from the III to the A-Major applied dominant chord. Furthermore, it

[12] We had to confine ourselves to this summarizing explanation since it is not
possible at this point to present a thorough discussion of this exposition. The
reader, studying the contents of this book, will himself be able at a later stage to
provide a detailed analysis.
[13] For an explanation of this term, see p. 165.

is a remarkable indication of Mozart's dramatic conception of form that the D-minor chord is not prolonged. After the extended prolongation leading up to it, such an expansion might have retarded the drive to V. Instead, the motion from the D-minor chord to the V is prolonged and intensified through inversion from an ascending second (D-E) into a descending seventh (Ex. VIII, Graph a).

It was stated earlier that a chord can have a contrapuntal function within the structural and tonal framework. This implies that contrapuntal function suffices to make a chord a member of the governing key. This point is illustrated by the B-Major chord which belongs to the key of A minor because it serves as passing chord between the III and the applied dominant chord of the D-minor passing chord. The clearly defined function of this passing chord within the framework of the I-III-V-I progression in A minor gives it a rightful place within this key, which its prolongation only intensifies.

Later, many illustrations will be given showing that any chord may be part of any key, provided it has a function to fulfill within the structural framework. In general, whether or not a chord belongs to a key depends on function only, not on degree of harmonic relationship. A chord may be consonant or dissonant, chromatic or diatonic; it may be a triad, a seventh, a ninth chord, etc.; only its function decides whether it belongs to a certain key.

When structural hearing is applied to large forms, it is evident that the relationships between the harmonic framework, the contrapuntal chords and the architectonic elements of chord prolongation which we found in single phrases, are also the factors that provide and maintain the coherence of the larger sections of a piece or even a whole movement. The factors are basically the same; only the dimensions are larger.

It is this type of large dimensional hearing which we must either possess naturally or acquire in order to grasp the unity and coherence fully in any of the larger forms. What insight into the music is offered if we explain the organic motion from the C-Major to the D-minor chord as a series of modulations from the key of C Major to the respective keys of B, E, and A Major, leading to D minor? This last would then be considered as one more key in the chain of modulations. How many other keys will the motion from the D- to the E-Major chord reveal in addition to the return modulation to the key of A minor? Using this analytical method, we start at the beginning of the development and somehow arrive at the dominant of A minor; two or three modulations more or less would hardly have changed the picture. It is surely a more convincing interpretation of the music to hear the development as a motion from III to V, by way of the passing D-minor chord, and to perceive all other tones, chords and passages as integral parts of this widely expanded mediant-dominant progression, than as a row of many tonal entities that split the motion into many different key centers whose function in relation to the whole cannot be explained.

This new conception and explanation of tonality, which has been roughly outlined above, was gradually evolved by Schenker over a period of many years. Just as he sensed that chord grammar failed to differentiate between the diverse functions which chords fulfill, so he realized that to regard only the beginning and end of a work as indicative of the key-signature offered a similar lack of explanation of the status and function of so-called modulatory sections. The concept of modulation, he realized, was incapable of indicating the unity which we perceive aurally.

By clarifying the meaning of tonality, we shall overcome the limitations hitherto attached to its scope and use—limitations that have undermined our capacity for the large dimensional hearing which the masters so clearly presuppose in their works. In fact, it is the narrow conception of tonality and its restricted possibilities that has led many theorists and musicians to believe that tonality is bound up with the so-called harmonic conception of music (with its "perpetual cadential basses"). However, since chord prolongation, contrapuntal or harmonic, is the force which creates tonal coherence, the history of tonality begins *not* with the detection and establishment of harmonic relationships and harmonic chord progressions, but with the first use of contrapuntal chord prolongations in the twelfth century.[14]

The same narrow conception of tonality in connection with music of more recent times has led to the idea that composers use "vagrant" keys in works which, in fact, indicate a structural framework within a single tonality, enriched and intensified by the enormous possibilities of prolongation. This is true of many works often regarded as illustrative of the dissolution of tonality. In these instances the question is of a change in style, not in the fundamental concepts of tonal language.

*

*   *

Progressions based on the fundamental harmonic progression I-V-I are by no means the only types of frameworks in which directed motion finds expression. This is especially true of music from the twelfth to the fifteenth century, in which frameworks of directed motion are very often expressions of a melodic-contrapuntal conception and the

[14] This question will be discussed in more detail in Part III.

chord progressions to which it gives rise. And the same can be said of present-day music with its tendency to avoid the harmonic conception inherent in the tonic-dominant relationship. To illustrate this point the beginning of Hindemith's Third Sonata for Piano is cited. ▶[Ex. X]◀ It is difficult to see how harmonic analysis could explain this passage. One could point to several modulations occurring prior to the entrance of the tonic chord in meas. 10, but this would not explain the meaning of this passage in terms of its inner coherence.

If we listen to it from the standpoint of motion, we find that there is a strong motivating impulse leading from the tonic to the A♭-minor chord (meas. 9), a neighbor-note chord, and on to the final tonic. This outlining framework constitutes a contrapuntal progression and is indicated in Graph e. It expresses the tonality of B♭ and determines the direction of motion. The neighbor-note chord on A♭, a contrapuntal chord, takes on structural significance since it is a member of the structural framework of this particular fragment. (The added label C S means *contrapuntal-structural*.) Practically the entire passage is a large prolongation of the progression from the tonic to the chord on A♭; looking at Graph d, one sees the pivotal points of motion which indicate the nature of the prolongation.

These pivotal points consist of a motion in ascending thirds filling the space of a ninth in the top voice, from B♭ to C♭, a prolongation of a second. The bass also ascends in thirds, the last third (meas. 8-9), however, is expressed as a descending sixth. The composer has used various enharmonic exchanges (see Graphs c and b); for instance, the D♭ in meas. 6 is followed immediately by C♯; instead of an F♭-minor chord, an E-minor chord appears; and instead of a C♭ in meas. 9, a B♮ is employed. We have "corrected" these enharmonic changes in Graph d. It follows that the chords on D♭ (or C♯) and on E (meas. 6 and 8) are passing chords which convincingly lead the ear from the B♭ tonic to the A♭ neighbor-note chord. Once the single direction of this motion, aided by the intermediary pivotal passing chords, becomes clear, the functions of all other tones and chords take on significance. As imaginative prolongations of the main direction, they in no way obscure the motion in its destination to the goal, the A♭ chord. On the contrary, being organic details they create the expressive and aesthetic value of this entire passage. These prolongations are shown in Graphs a and b.

Last but not least, the reader's attention should be drawn to the thematic material, the rhythmic treatment of which so strongly contributes to the persuasiveness of the music's continuity. The first structural tonic and each intermediary point introduce phrases which become progressively shorter and more contracted until the final structural tonic in meas. 10 is reached. We thus find a contracting sequence: first three and a half measures, then two measures and again two measures, then one measure. Finally the A♭ chord appears filling half a measure, followed immediately by the final tonic (see the numbers in Graph b). This contraction with its resulting momentum vitally aids the ear in understanding this passage as directed motion.

F. The implications of structure and prolongation

In the course of this chapter, it has been made clear, in the instances examined, that the concept of structure and prolongation is the outstanding factor on which tonal coherence is based. It will be found that all explanations of tonal coherence can be based on the same conception; this is the reason for the voice-leading graphs and the stage-by-stage explanations which they provide. The recognition of this underlying conception is Schenker's greatest contribution to the evolution of musical understanding. The conclusions which he reached later stemmed from that fundamental discovery.

The conception itself, however, is by no means Schenker's discovery. The idea is not new that mankind's creations, every complex thought or spiritual and artistic product is the elaboration, expansion, individual shaping or, in short, a series of prolongations of a basic underlying idea or structure.

It is an age-old fundamental principle of creative devising and thinking. It has always contributed vitally to the thoughts, actions and creations of mankind. At different periods, only very few have been conscious of it; now, however, as a typical symptom of our time, it has become a very conscious concept. It is so natural to our way of thinking, so much a part of our mental disposition and attitude, that it governs far more than our scientific and artistic planning and thinking; it must be accepted indeed as a universal law of life.

For instance, let us take language, the logical means of expressing our thoughts, and let us think of a very simple example. In the process of listening to a long sentence, a sentence with subordinate clauses and phrases, we unconsciously grasp the gist of what the whole sentence expresses—we grasp the essential outline. This outline appears elaborated and extended by means of the subordinate clauses, the prolongations. Thus the whole sentence appears as the prolongation of a single, structurally organized idea.

In preparing a speech or lecture we are confronted again with that eternal conception. The ever-recurring problems of being too brief or too "long-winded," of "making one's point clear"; the wish to surprise; the necessity to prepare one point, or to stress another one or to recapitulate—all these architectonic principles are dealt with on the basis of structure and prolongation. Only on this basis will the fundamental idea or purpose of the speech stand out in the maze of elaborations and details.

In explaining the contents of a drama we should certainly not begin with the first sentence of the first scene, but from the basic idea the author had in mind; from there we would proceed to the acts and scenes and details in progressive stages. Never to lose contact with the structure of the whole in spite of the most fascinating details, makes all the difference between a clear or confused explanation.

Every novel or play has a structural idea which can be expressed in a few words. The elaboration and prolongation of this idea gives the artistic detail, the deviations and detours with all their tensions and surprises. The more we consciously or unconsciously feel the relations of the prolongations to the structure, the more we have the impression of an organism. In an organism we can practically speak of an interdependence of structure and prolongation. For the structural idea only receives artistic life through its prolongations; on the other hand, the detail alone, without being part of a larger whole, is never an integral part of that larger organism—it has no home, and thus remains a detail, however beautiful or interesting.

The same conception is also an essential element of psychology. Psychology does not explain the actions, characteristics or problems of a person on the basis of "visible" symptoms. It achieves results through penetration into the deep-rooted, unconscious, often long past cause of all the symptoms the person presents. In the coherence between the basic cause and the actual, visible facts—or in our terms, in the coherence between the structure and its prolongations—lies the explanation of a person's character.

Thus, in creating or reproducing an organic whole, on whatever level and in whatever field, whether in speech, teaching, art, science or in the art of living, we are consciously or unconsciously forced to deal with the concept of structure and prolongation.

That this fundamental principle of creative thinking also governs musical creation and thus musical reproduction and explanation seems obvious and convincing, once one has been awakened to its presence. It is so obvious that many musicians quite rightly state that Schenker's writings have clarified what they instinctively feel and that what seems to be a method is in fact the bold systematization of an instinctive tendency to hear and to understand—the inborn tendency for *structural hearing*.

Music is motion in time. What is the musical meaning of that motion? How does it come about that we listen to hundreds of measures presenting rows of tones and chords and still feel instinctively that they form an organic whole? What *is* musical organism?

I readily concede that there is a good deal in music, its development and interpretation, which can be explained in aesthetic, cultural, historical, philosophical, psychological and physiological terms; a complete explanation will never neglect these vital factors. I believe, however, that these factors can only be of real value if they are applied on the basis of a *musical understanding of music*, since, of necessity, this musical understanding will influence those other factors to a very definite degree.

Strange and exaggerated as it may sound, we have been seriously lacking in a musical explanation of music. What we have at our disposal and use constantly are purely *descriptive* types of explanation and teaching. Although it has become only too obvious in many other fields that purely descriptive devices have grave limitations, it does not seem to have struck the majority of musicians that we are still completely in the grip of methods that in most cases do not go below the most obvious surface of "visible" facts. Chord grammar and the theory of modulation are unable to reassemble the fragments into which they dissect a musical work. Similar observations apply to current ways of analyzing melody, rhythm, form and style. Although we shall return to some of these problems in detail later, it ought to be pointed out here that according to customary teaching methods these elements of composition, all of which represent interdependent parts of an organic structure, are channeled off into water-tight theoretical disciplines and more or less separately applied to the organic whole presented by an actual composition. They live their own life apart from the compositions which they are supposed to explain.

There seems no doubt that these inadequate pedagogical methods and concepts have materially contributed to the present crisis in musical thinking. As far as they are concerned, the situation *can* be changed and I believe that the revision of basic musical conceptions would have a great and lasting effect upon all our musical activity. Schenker has opened our ears and minds by penetrating to the significance of musical motion and its most subtle problems of coherence; he has opened the door to the understanding of music as an organic expression of motion. The fact remains, of course, that even the most penetrating musical approach and understanding of all other factors contributing to a piece of musical art will never completely divulge the secret of artistic quality, the secret of great art. There is too much in art that defies reasoning and concrete explanation. It is Heinrich Schenker's work, however, which for the first time has brought the theory of music and composition to a level on which the results of explanation and understanding lead to the fringe of the problems of quality.

P A R T

II

The Pedagogic and Systematic Approach
to Structural Hearing

Part II   Chapter One

The Scope of Elementary Theory

     A thorough familiarity with the fundamentals of music is a prerequisite for understanding the following chapters. Such studies of elementary theory should, however, be preceded by a great deal of listening experience. It is an unfortunate fact that students too often are subjected to theory before they literally have heard music. A sound approach to music will base itself on the naïve enjoyment of listening, since principles and generalizations must be derived from observation rather than from dehydrated abstractions. Thus, acquaintance with actual music cannot possibly be overrated. A continuous contact with music will awaken healthy curiosity, which alone will make the study of structural problems in music one of vital significance.

Since it is not the function of this book to discuss the first steps in theory in detail, a brief outline of its scope may prove helpful.[1]

The Rudiments of Music:

a) Notation; scales; church modes; overtone series.
b) Major, minor, diminished and augmented intervals; triads and seventh chords; non-harmonic tones (neighbor and passing tones, appoggiaturas, suspensions, anticipations); Roman numerals and figured bass numerals.
c) Chord grammar (ability to write and identify any chord).

Listening Approach:

a) Aural recognition of the material listed above.
b) Meter (duple, triple and compound); rhythmic design of melodies.
c) Melodic dictation of folk tunes and themes from instrumental music; two-part dictation as preparation for two-part counterpoint.

[1] The following books are recommended for study of elementary theory: Angela Diller, *First Theory Book.* G. Schirmer, Inc., New York, 1921; Alvin Bauman, *Elementary Musicianship.* Prentice-Hall, Inc., New York, 1947; William J. Mitchell, *Elementary Harmony,* 2nd ed. Prentice-Hall, Inc., New York, 1948.

d) Sight singing, taught with the greatest possible use of music. Exercises should be reduced to a minimum and used only for points requiring special drill. Most of the time allotted to sight singing would be devoted to reading the great works of vocal literature.

e) Analysis of motive, phrase, various cadences, devices such as sequence, imitation, etc.; analysis of form (two- and three-part forms, sonata form, rondo form, dance forms).

Music of the masters, frequently introduced and discussed from many angles, will eventually convey a general knowledge of their styles. This knowledge will be based on the experiencing of a few works rather than a formal course in music history. Through listening assignments, the student will be encouraged to broaden his knowledge of the literature. He should be asked to illustrate each new point with quotations from music with which he is familiar. For this reason a basic facility at the keyboard should be acquired.

On the basis of the four year course now customary in music schools and liberal arts colleges, the material outlined will take up one or two years. During the second year, it will be possible to add the study of Chapters II, III and IV of Part II of this book. Chapters V and VI should be discussed in the third year, whereas Chapters VII and VIII will be the subject of the fourth year of the complete course. It is suggested that Part III be either incorporated into the fourth year studies or left for possible post-graduate work. This outline is by no means meant to constitute a rigid schedule which does not allow for an occasionally more liberal interpretation. For instance, a preliminary glance at the analysis of some of the complete compositions in Chapter VIII may be of value during work on earlier chapters.

Part II   Chapter Two

Musical Direction as an Organizing Force

A.   Problems of musical continuity and synthesis

After having mastered the preliminaries outlined in the preceding chapter, it is essential for the student to acquire an idea as to what music really is, as to the things he is expected to hear and grasp in listening to music. This means that he must now be brought into contact with the problem of constructive musical understanding. So far his mechanical ear has received some training, and he has learned to recognize various chords along with their names and symbols. Important though this is, it does not explain the role these chords play in music, which is conceived as a living motion of tones and voices. It is just at this stage of his training that the student must have revealed to him as clearly as possible the existence of problems of musical structure and musical context. These should be brought forward now, before he studies harmony and counterpoint, for the latter will be meaningless disciplines to him unless he can first gain some idea of their purpose and role in musical construction. This introduction will not relieve him of the necessity of practicing keyboard exercises later on. However, if he has gained some idea of the phenomenon of musical continuity by attentive rather than passive listening, he will not feel that he is being confronted with a deluge of more or less useless exercises. Instead, he will understand why he has to practice certain exercises in written form or at the keyboard, provided of course that they represent the musical techniques of composers, rather than theory for the sake of theory.

But how shall we proceed at this early stage of musical training? Is not a knowledge of harmony, counterpoint, form, etc. required before structural problems can be tackled successfully? Experience proves that it is entirely possible to demonstrate elementary problems of musical structure and continuity even to a student who has not studied harmony and counterpoint, but only the fundamentals of music. Furthermore, the basic significance of these two disciplines and the need for their detailed study later on can be greatly clarified at this stage of the student's training. It is no exaggeration to state that even a superficial realization that problems of musical structure and continuity exist, will make the later study of harmony and counterpoint more meaningful.

The first need, therefore, is to awaken a sense of musical direction. The student must be made aware that when he has labeled each vertical relation of tones or has given names to visible factors of a composition, he has covered important preliminary ground but has not yet touched upon the vital problems of musical construction and continuity. He would hardly think it possible to compose in the same manner in which he has analyzed chords, i.e. by merely adding one chord to another and coupling one melodic idea with another. Since music exists in time, the main problem will certainly be to create musical length. But it must be organic length, which can never be gained simply by adding one chord to another or by any similar procedure. The result would be nothing but an undifferentiated succession of musical facts. Instead, the composer must create an organic whole, in which every chord and motive has its meaning in the construction of the entire organism. A musical masterpiece does not sound like a vague, arbitrary succession of chords and themes, but like an organic whole in which every chord, every melodic event leads convincingly to what follows.

Tonal music of western civilization consists of motion, but not motion for its own sake. It represents motion which has an objective, which from the beginning shows direction to a certain goal. On the way to this goal we find details and detours; we hear chords, tones and passages which give form to those details, and serve to make the way to the objective more interesting and colorful. But such chords and tones have only indirect influence on the principal motion to the goal, which remains intact in its over-all significance. Here then we shall touch upon the problems of structure and prolongation.

In order to make the student aware of these problems, we shall now proceed with the aid of simple and relatively short sections from compositions. In many instances it will soon become apparent that he is instinctively aware of certain problems of musical planning and continuity and only lacks the technical knowledge necessary to understand their implications. Naturally the following discussion will not treat these problems thoroughly and will leave many questions unanswered for the time being; later chapters will provide a fuller and more detailed explanation. But if we have succeeded in giving a glimpse of what is to come, of the problems of constructive listening, and of the principal purpose of the study of counterpoint and harmony, enough has been achieved for the time being. The student will understand for the first time, if only in a rudimentary way, the meaning of constructive and creative listening, which is the precondition for structural hearing.

B.   Musical direction—Structure and prolongation

I.   CHORD GRAMMAR—CHORD SIGNIFICANCE

Let us first examine the beginning of a Bach Chorale. ►[Ex. 1]◄ The reader will certainly be able to label the chords according to their status within the key of F Major. In the course of this procedure he will give two chords more or less the same label (the V^6 of meas. 1 and the V of meas. 2). We may now ask him if these dominant chords are of equal significance within the organic whole of the phrase. The answer will be in the negative. He will readily admit, probably without knowing the reasons, that while these chords bear similar symbols, they have entirely different meanings within the phrase. The significance of the dominant chords can be realized only if the student develops a sense for musical direction.

Composers, like poets, speak in sentences. Just as the contents of a spoken or written phrase are not grasped by describing and labeling the grammatical status of every word, likewise a musical phrase is not comprehended as long as we are content merely to label each chord according to its grammatical status. This labeling does not and cannot take into account the fact that we are confronted with an organic whole. To say that a musical composition is an organic whole or organism means that this composition manifests itself as directed motion. In consequence, the main point of interest for musical understanding must be the part each chord plays as a constituent of this directed motion.

Where does this motion begin and where does it lead to? We now can explain that the dominant in meas. 2 is the intermediary goal of a motion which starts on the tonic of meas. 1 and ends on the tonic of meas. 2 at the fermata. The chords between the first tonic and the dominant of meas. 2 are connecting links between these two chords; the V^6 of meas. 1 belongs to this group and partakes of its passing, moving character. The first tonic, the V in meas. 2 and the final tonic, on the other hand, being stable points, have a stable or structural significance (Graph a).[1] By taking motion and its meaning into considera-

[1] Different note-values in this and the following graphs do not indicate metrical values; they express the different structural significance of tones and chords.

tion for the first time, we realize that the same chord, or chords having the same or similar grammatical status, can serve completely different purposes. The realization, however rudimentary, that these different purposes exist, is the first step towards structural hearing.

Another example which makes clear the different architectonic meanings of chords, is the beginning of Scarlatti's Sonata in D minor. ►[Ex. 2]◄ Chord grammar indicates that three dominant chords are used by Scarlatti. But if we consider the phrase as a whole and do not merely stumble from one vertical relationship to the next, we hear a motion from a tonic chord in meas. 1 to a dominant chord which is reached in meas. 4. This dominant chord, as goal of the whole motion, is next in significance to the first tonic as a structural element. The composer, starting on the tonic, could either pass through other chords to the dominant chord or could go to it immediately. But the latter procedure would not create any musical length. We should only—to make a comparison with a spoken phrase—hear two words, not a fully developed sentence. Adopting the former procedure, the composer may even expand certain points along his way. This is just what happens here on a small and relatively simple scale. First we realize that the starting point, the D-minor tonic chord, seems expanded; that is to say, at the beginning of meas. 2, despite the intervening dominant chord in first inversion, we still find ourselves on the D-minor chord (Graph a); this illustration helps to clarify that expansion. The dominant chord serves only as a support for the tone E which stands as a passing tone between the principal tones D and F, tones of the D-minor chord. The bass neighbor note C♯ stresses the embellishing character of the dominant sixth chord, which thus is clearly subordinated to the tonic. Here, as in the former example, the difference between the two dominant chords is fundamental. In Scarlatti's phrase the dominant in meas. 4, being the goal of the whole phrase, is of structural significance, whereas the dominant in meas. 1 has no structural significance whatsoever, but serves to enrich and expand the tonic.

What about the minor dominant chord in meas. 2? This chord has still another purpose than those just mentioned. It lies on the way from the first structural chord, the I, to the goal, the final V. It is not a structural chord, but serves as a link between I and V. It is a passing chord between two structural chords. The role of the chord on G in meas. 3 will be fully understood later; for the time being it is enough to understand that this chord does not actually interrupt the progression of the bass line, but only forms a slight detour (Graph b).

In summary, we have found the same chord, the chord on the fifth

degree in D minor, in three different capacities; each time this chord
has a very different significance. It is now obvious that these differences in chord significance are so important for the understanding of
this phrase, that the grammatical identity of the three chords in question fades into relative insignificance.

2. MELODY—MELODIC DIRECTION AND COHERENCE

Before continuing with the discussion of additional examples which
will make the new problems still clearer, it will be advisable to concentrate for a short time on melodic problems. We shall find that with
melody tones, as with chords, the differences in significance are great,
and that the moment we take the melody's direction into consideration
we no longer can find satisfaction in the mere differentiation of
principal and dependent, harmonic or non-harmonic tones and other
descriptive methods, which might be summed up as "tone grammar."
Let us take a simple melodic phrase such as ►[Ex. 3]◄. It would prove
entirely misleading to follow the visible successions of tones, because
they are often not indicative of the phrase's direction. For example, the
eighth-note B♭ of the second beat is followed by a quarter-note E♭;
one cannot for this reason assert that B♭ leads to E♭; nor does C lead to
F, the downbeat of meas. 2. Instead the musical ear quite instinctively
makes a larger connection and will register the upward motion of a
third from D via E♭ to F as the actual melodic line—the melodic structure. The eighth-notes C and B♭ and the quarter-note C are embellishments and thus offshoots or prolongations of this melodic line (Graph
a). The melody returns from F to D in a somewhat more complex way,
presenting a downward directed line F-E♭-D. The following illustration shows step by step the inner coherence between the structural
line and its melodic prolongations. ►[Ex. 4]◄ It is important to realize
that structure, as may have been gathered from the examples in Part I,
in its final analysis is arhythmic, and that rhythm is a vital contributing
factor in shaping the prolongations.

Thus, these few measures from the Bagatelle, in their melodic structure, move up and down a third.[2] This structural third pervades the
prolongations (D-B♭, E♭-C), making them organic offshoots. The

---

[2] For the student familiar with this approach, it might be mentioned that, taking
the piece as a whole into consideration, this melody might very well mean a prolongation of D. For pedagogic purposes, however, we may interpret the motion
up and down a third as the structural motion of this melody.

structure thus generates the prolonging thirds in meas. 1 and also, though more veiled, the one in meas. 2.

In listening to a melody's direction we, therefore, have to distinguish between melody tones which represent the basic direction, outline or structure, and those which elaborate or prolong that basic structure. Another very instructive example is presented in a phrase by Schumann. ►[Ex. 5]◄ Again we must realize that the visible ascending or descending motion of a melodic line does not necessarily indicate the direction of its structure. For instance, is the ascending line up to A an indication of the melody's structural direction? Careful listening to the whole melody will reveal a parallelism of ascending thirds, in which the first two tones of the thirds act as upbeats. The tone A (meas. 1) now proves to be an incomplete (unresolved) neighbor note of G, from which tone the structural line descends; the ascending line to A is therefore only a visible continuity of four tones (Graph a).

The ascending thirds are the prolongations of a melodic structure directed downwards from G to C. We realize now that prolongations may also precede the structural tones. In this example the prolongation might be likened to two lower grace notes. In meas. 3, however, the prolongation succeeds the structural note, thus inverting the sequential ascending third into a descending one. This creates a greater intensity of motion, since two structural notes now appear in one measure. The student should also observe how the appearance of the structural tones is varied in each case: The G is followed by its upper neighbor note, F appears as a half-note and the E is represented by two quarter-notes. How dull the melody would be without these delicate shadings! (Ex. 5b)

The Beethoven and Schumann examples suggest that it is the prolongations, melodic and rhythmic, which create the interest and color of a melody. However, the value and character of the prolongations become clear only if we grasp them as organic offshoots of the melody's structure. Consequently the understanding of the structural course of the melody and the role the prolongations play will be of importance in the discussions that follow.

While the structure of the preceding melodies reveals motion from the beginning, we shall find in the next example a totally different problem of melodic direction. ►[Ex. 6]◄ It would seem at first, that the structural line descends immediately from C via B♭ to A♭, these three tones being prolonged by embellishments. However, in meas. 4, the C is reached again; we thus have a return to the starting point which indicates a large-scale embellishment or prolongation of C. This

C, up to meas. 4, acts as the sole structural tone. In its dominating capacity, it retains its structural value and can be classified as a *retained* tone (indicated with a dotted line in Graph a). In meas. 5, the melody makes an attempt to descend structurally to B♭, only to turn again and perform a further prolongation of C to which the melody fleetingly returns once more in meas. 6. Only then does the melody proceed to B♭ and the concluding A♭.

Summing up, we realize that for the greatest part of its course this melody does not move from one structural point to another, but around one structural tone. This gives a lingering and delaying effect until at last the line descends to the tonic.

Finally, let us compare the problems of structure and prolongation in three melodies presented here in the same key. ►[Ex. 7, 8, 9]◄

In the Haydn example the structural line [3] moves from C in meas. 1 to B♭ in meas. 3 (see Ex. 7, Graph a). The composer, instead of going directly from C to B♭, prolongs this progression through embellishing tones. The melody then proceeds directly to A in meas. 4. Throughout meas. 5-8 it will be apparent that basically the melody is moving from G in meas. 5 to the final F in meas. 8. However, these final measures show many embellishing tones, which themselves are ornamented with appoggiaturas. In meas. 5 and 6 the embellishing tones are chord tones of the G-minor chord and pivot around a single tone G, in contrast to meas. 2 and 3, in which the embellishing tones move between two different tones (C and B♭). Since the tone G keeps its structural value throughout two measures, it acts as a retained tone, finally moving to F.

Turning to the folk tune (Ex. 8), a cursory hearing might lead one to consider F as the first structural tone, since the melody moves in meas. 1 entirely within the arpeggiated F chord. Attentive listening, however, does not bear out this initial reaction. The first F helps, rather, to indicate the chordal background of the melody, which drives immediately to C. It is from this tone C that the D (meas. 2) comes as a neighbor note; the intervening F serves merely as an embellishing tone to C, and in no way affects the real direction of the melody. The neighbor note D, in turn, has its own embellishing motion; the melody goes from D to the embellishing tone F, from which it returns immediately to D. The neighbor-note motion is then completed with the return from D to C. We should assume, so far, that C is the first structural tone, since the melody has been circling around that tone throughout the first two measures. Confirmation that C actually is the struc-

[8] The stems connected with the long beam point to the structural tones.

tural tone is given by the fact that the melody takes its continuation from C by moving to B♭, and after an embellishing C, to A, G and finally to F (Graph a).

Our third quotation, a Schumann melody (Ex. 9), is characterized by an extensive prolongation of the tone C (meas. 1 to 4) by leaping up a sixth to A and descending stepwise. Before the C is reached again the melody retards the motion to C by circling for a full measure (3) around D. This relatively extended prolongation of C reduces itself to an expanded neighbor-note motion, C-D-C, after which the line descends via B♭ to A, which in turn is prolonged. The structural line then proceeds to G, where Schumann creates a melodic parallelism with meas. 3 (see brackets). With meas. 8 the structural tonic is reached (Graph a).

The student will have realized by now that these three very different melodies have the same basic direction, the same structural progression: C-B♭-A-G-F. A comparison of the melodies certainly indicates to him that one definite structural line can find its prolonged expression in different ways, and he will intuitively sense that there are many more possibilities beyond the ones indicated. We have only to compare the first two measures of the folk tune with the first four measures of the Schumann passage to realize how differently a neighbor-note motion can be elaborated. Observe, too, how differently the structural progression from C to B♭ is achieved in the Haydn melody and in the other two examples. These examples also illustrate two other significant points: Firstly, that melodic prolongations can occur above or below the structural tones; secondly, that a prolongation may either precede or follow a structural tone to which it is related.

3. RELATIVE SIGNIFICANCE OF MELODIC STRUCTURE AND PROLONGATION

Generally speaking, there are two factors accounting for the differences in appearance and character of the three melodies discussed above: the rhythmical distribution of structural tones and particularly the distribution and nature of the embellishments, detours and elaborations which we call melodic prolongations. We have found that in all preceding examples there is a connection between the tones of the structural progression or line, even though they may be separated by prolongations.

Throughout this discussion of melodic problems it has been necessary to draw the student's attention to structure, since this must be grasped before he can proceed; at the same time the importance of the prolongations cannot be too strongly emphasized. The musical understanding of a melody requires a knowledge of its basic direction or structure, but it requires this knowledge only as a prerequisite for determining the course and characteristics of the prolongations. The structural tones are the spine of the melody; they establish its basic direction. What makes a structural line live, however, are the many different types of prolongation, since they provide the character, rhythmic interest and color of a melody. Consequently, knowledge of structure alone is by no means enough. The mere statement that a melody features a descending fifth as structural outline is fragmentary knowledge. This structural outline becomes of vital interest if we realize the detours and deviations that stem from this basic direction, the possibilities of which are unlimited. This is melodic hearing on the basis of structure and prolongation, and as such closely parallels the situation with respect to chords.

Later explanations will show the student how to differentiate with assurance between structural tones and prolonging tones, so that he will not pick out notes at random and profess to hear them in one capacity or the other. Only further experience and special studies will enable him to proceed from instinctive feeling to certainty based on knowledge. However, the feeling for these problems of musical construction has to be awakened; this has been the purpose of the present section.

4. INTERDEPENDENCE OF MELODY AND CHORD SIGNIFICANCE

Up to this point some examples have been examined from the point of view of chord significance and others from a purely melodic standpoint. However, if we were to continue analyzing melodies, without taking the basses and chords into consideration (or analyzing chords without listening to the melody), we should soon encounter difficulties. We shall be confronted again and again with the fact that to determine the significance of a chord we must grasp the structure of the melody. It frequently happens that the meaning of the melodic outline clarifies the meaning of the supporting chords. On the other hand, the course of the bass often determines which melody tone is structural and which is prolonging.

That these two facts, significance of melody tones and significance of chords, are interdependent in forming a musical organism can be shown in a short example from the slow movement of Beethoven's Sonata, Op 2, No. 2. ►[Ex. 10]◄ The melody embellishes the tone F♯ through a lower neighbor note in meas. 2 and an upper (accented) neighbor note in meas. 3. On the third beat of this measure there is the final return to F♯ which then leads to the goal of the phrase, the tone E. We therefore can state that the melody moves from a prolonged F♯, covering three measures, to E (meas. 4). It is well to keep in mind that a neighbor note may not only embellish but also prolong the value of the main note. It would thus seem completely inadequate to perceive this melodic line by mechanically registering superficial facts which show three movements away from F♯, first to E, then to G and then again to E. Instead, one has to feel a unifying neighbornote motion around F♯ in meas. 1-3, and then the descent from this F♯ to E (Graph a).

The significance of the three dominant chords in meas. 2, 3 and 4 will now be evident. The first two are neighbor-note chords subordinated to an over-all structural tonic chord. The final dominant chord, being the goal of the phrase, is of structural significance. One must realize that in this case, as with the Scarlatti theme (Ex. 2), chords of motion, which comprise not only passing chords but also embellishing chords as well, are used to prolong the value of one structural chord (here by circling around that chord). In such instances the inadequacy of chord grammar lies not only in its neglect of musical direction but also in its inability to indicate the interdependence of melody and chords.

The same feeling of dissatisfaction would prevail if a mere listing of chords were offered as an explanation of the next example. ►[Ex. 11]◄ Here it is primarily the melody and its significance which actually determine the significance of the chords. Graph a indicates a prolongation of the tone A and shows how it is achieved. The melody moves within the interval of A-E (a characteristic interval of the A-Major chord) which appears here horizontalized. The dotted line indicates the structural retention of A up to meas. 3; only then does the melody proceed to B and finally to C♯. As to the significance of the chords, it seems evident from the foregoing that the A chord governs the scene, so to speak, including the first beat of meas. 3 (Graph b). This example has a tendency similar to that found in the preceding Beethoven and Scarlatti examples, although it appears here in a more elaborate and complicated form: several different chords can be subordinated to one dominating chord. The meaning of the melody, moving through a characteristic interval A-E-A of the A chord, unmistakably contributes to the impression of an expansion of the tonic chord. This impression is confirmed by the bass which moves within another interval of the A-Major tonic, A-C♯ (Graph c). As a result of this predominating single-chord outline of melody and bass, the chords on the sixth, third and fourth degrees of the scale take on the character of passing and embellishing chords within the melodic fourth (A-E) and sixth (A-C♯) of the bass, and consequently within the realm of the A chord. In this way the structural value of the tonic chord appears very subtly expanded. We call this phenomenon *chord prolongation*. The final chords, the II, the V and the I, are of structural significance because they support the structural tones B and C♯ of the melody, the structural melodic tones of the whole phrase being A-B-C♯. The progression I-II-V-I thus forms the structural framework within which the other chords move (Graph b).

The discussion thus far, has centered on the difference between tone and chord grammar and between tone and chord significance. The primary purpose of this chapter has been to bring this difference into focus. In summary, since chords of identical grammatical status may have different meanings even within one short phrase, labeling a chord according to its appearance and position within a key becomes insufficient. Chord grammar is essential, but only as a prerequisite, not as an end in itself.

In the examples cited, we encountered chords which had strong structural implications. Such chords serve as pivots. They are the stable points which determine the course of the musical motion on the way to its objective. Expanding this framework, creating the element of motion and connection, and thus achieving color, richness and prolongation, are chords of very different significance. These appear between the structural chords, as passing or embellishing chords. In addition, instead of moving between two structural chords, these chords may move within or around one single chord. In this case, they serve to create an expansion of the value of one structural chord which we have termed chord prolongation. The structural chords determine the direction of the motion; the passing and embellishing chords, which are the chords of prolongation, execute that motion—they constitute the motion itself.

In order to hear the different significance of chords and to evaluate their part in the formation of the phrase, it is essential to develop a sense of musical direction. Whenever we are confronted with musical motion which shows direction to a goal, a full explanation of its meaning will demand the answers to three basic questions: Where does the motion begin? Where does it lead? How does the composer reach the goal? Here the course of the melody is of vital importance. Just as there are chords of structure and chords of prolongation, there are tones in a melody which have structural significance, and others which serve either to embellish these tones or to elaborate their progression. In Ex. 10 and 11, we observed that melody and chords were mutually interdependent; the cooperation there between structural melody tones and structural chords was the strongest possible.

In spite of the complete difference in significance between chords of motion and those of structure, in practice they are inseparable. Together with the melody they form the unity of a phrase, they create an organism. The same applies, generally speaking, to larger sections and to whole pieces. The distances between the structural points are larger, the prolongations are on a much greater scale and the techniques used are more subtle and more complicated, but the principles remain unaltered. To understand and master these techniques the student now needs more "tools" and above all more ear training, both the mechanical and structural kind. In order to find out for himself which chord or tone is of structural significance and which stands for motion, i.e. in order to grasp thoroughly the musical significance of a phrase or a whole piece, the student has to master the characteristics and implications of each group of tones and chords. Up to the present point it has only been possible to give the student a few hints and to suggest the course which he must pursue in order to achieve musical understanding. Now he must gain detailed knowledge which will convince him that structural hearing means more than arbitrarily selecting certain tones and chords as structural, while another person might as easily select others. From now on it is vital for him to acquire exact knowledge in order to fortify his intuitive understanding. At this point counterpoint and harmony enter the picture.

C. The functions of harmony and counterpoint

The reader will have noticed that in the examples given, the structural chords (in root position or inversion) invariably form progressions based upon the fifth relation. These have been called harmonic progressions. A harmonic relation is one that we define in terms of the overtone series, the fundamental physical basis for tone relations. As we know, the first overtone to appear above the fundamental is the octave. The next tone is the perfect fifth, the first tone "foreign" to the fundamental appearing in the series. The relationship of tones a fifth apart is thus established as being the closest possible relationship between two different tones. Upon this fifth relation the entire concept of harmony is based.

All this will be explained more fully in Chapter IV. For the moment, it must be pointed out that I-V-I and its elaboration I-II-V-I (the II having a fifth relation to V) are truly harmonic progressions. I-V is an incomplete harmonic progression, but fulfills a genuinely harmonic function. Only progressions of this kind serve a harmonic purpose within a phrase, and only they should be the concern of the study of harmony. That study should occupy itself solely with the various characteristics, forms and implications of these and similar patterns ultimately based on the fifth relation.

On the other hand the vast majority of chords one encounters in actual compositions belong to an entirely different category. Passing and embellishing chords, which are here called chords of prolongation, and which fulfill varied functions and have no harmonic relationship to each other, appear as the result of the motion of several simultaneously moving voices. These chords represent the vertical result of voice motion. Since they originate in motion and voice leading, they cannot be the concern of harmony; examination of problems of voice leading and voice motion is the task of the discipline of counterpoint.

Counterpoint is not only continuously present but often predominant even in works which have too often been regarded as purely homophonic or harmonic in style. The student should not believe that counterpoint is restricted to so-called linear voice leading, to imitation, canon, fugue and other typical contrapuntal devices. Its manifestations are to be found in every type of composition.

The general curriculum in most music schools provides for training in harmony before counterpoint is studied. After the discussion of triads, chord construction and chord progression usually follow, and this constitutes so-called four-part harmony. Instead, I suggest that, following the study of the fundamentals of music (as outlined in Part II, Chapter I) and after having been introduced to the problems of structure and prolongation, the student take up a thorough study of counterpoint. Then, following completion of two- and three-part counterpoint, he should begin his studies in harmony. Although in some schools counterpoint is studied before harmony, the reasons for doing so are rather different from those presented here. Therefore I find it necessary to explain the reasons, first, for demanding strict separation of harmony and counterpoint, and second, for taking up the study of counterpoint before harmony.

The phrases and sections discussed so far have one fact in common: they represent tonal entities. These organisms show the interlocked relationship of the main elements of composition—factors of motion and prolongation which are elements of counterpoint, and factors of stability and structure which are here called harmonic progressions. Motion is the predominant element in tonal music, but, as indicated in the examples, it may be directed by the structural framework of the harmonic progressions. In spite of this interrelation in composition, it seems logical to say that the student must first learn to differentiate between elements of stability and those of motion and embellishment, i.e. between harmonic and contrapuntal factors in pure form. Most compositions which the student plays show the working of both factors. In consideration of this fact, it should be the prime objective of musical education (after instruction in elementary theory has been completed) to make the student aware of the differentiation between chords or progressions derived from harmony and those derived from counterpoint. For this purpose, the interlocked elements of tonal composition, harmony and counterpoint have, at first, to be separated as strictly as possible.

In the beginning we shall concentrate on the individual characteristics of each of these utterly different and almost contradictory forces. Only after making a study of each of these elements in pure form, shall we take both simultaneously into consideration (in Chapters V, VI and VII) which will enable us to examine fully their cooperation in actual compositions. Of this cooperation the student has already had a glimpse. The combination of two different conceptions of musical construction constitutes one of the greatest achievements in the history of music.

Contrary to the procedure just outlined, our present-day theory very often does not sufficiently separate counterpoint from harmony; there is too much overlapping of the two elements. For instance, before counterpoint is ever mentioned, harmony courses discuss voice-leading principles and the avoidance of parallel octaves and fifths. These principles are essentials of counterpoint and belong only secondarily to harmony. On the other hand, the teaching of counterpoint is often done on a harmonic basis, with discussion of cadences, elements of harmonic relations, etc.[4] When it comes to composition, on the

---

[4] Many books demand the knowledge of harmony as the prerequisite to the study of counterpoint.

other hand, where harmony and counterpoint are really interlocked, each is applied more or less separately. One speaks of pieces or sections in harmonic or homophonic style, or of those written in contrapuntal style, and thus practically denies the intricate interdependence of the elements. The consequences are "harmonic analysis," "contrapuntal-melodic analysis," "form analysis," etc., *separately* applied to products of an art, whose characteristic feature is that no element can be explained without taking the others into consideration. Indeed, the elements influence each other even to the extent that the course of one often determines the course of the other.

In separating harmony from counterpoint, we shall find that harmonic progressions contain a contrapuntal feature, the simultaneous motion of several voices. The converse does not hold true, however, because contrapuntal progressions can be studied in pure form without any interference from harmonic considerations. This appears quite logical if we realize that harmonic progressions came to be used only after great contrapuntal experience had been acquired during the course of several centuries.

These facts alone speak for studying counterpoint before harmony. Quite apart from these considerations, however, the necessity of introducing the study of counterpoint first lies in the overwhelming part it plays in composition. We shall see that, far transcending its generally accepted role in the techniques of independent voice leading, imitation, canon and fugue, it represents the fundamental force of musical motion. The study of counterpoint develops a sense for musical direction, for individual voice leading and for chords created through motion of voices. On the other hand, an early concentration on harmony, especially if based on the present-day method with its perpetual drill in cadences and its indiscriminate labeling of every chord as a harmonic individuality, might so hamper the ear, might make it so cadence-minded, that it would lose its instinctive capacity for motion and direction. Since music *is* motion it seems logical that we must first learn to move in tones, lines, intervals and chords before the organizing power of the harmonic progressions can be really understood. In addition, the procedure of counterpoint corrects the unconscious tendency of some students to hear only from one chord to the next. Since it demands hearing and looking ahead, and planning the motion of voices in advance, counterpoint is highly important and beneficial for ear training and represents the most basic preparation for understanding and devising directed musical motion.

Part II   Chapter Three

The Contrapuntal Concept

A. Introduction

The primary aim in presenting this chapter is to furnish a preparation for the contrapuntal concept as elaborated in Chapters V, VI and VII. For reasons to be enumerated, this concept is most clearly represented within the actual discipline of counterpoint. My secondary aim emerges as a direct consequence of this fact. If we are to work within the framework of the study of counterpoint, full indications must be given as to the pedagogic approach that most clearly brings out the essential meaning of the subject. For this reason, attention will be centered not only upon the discipline of counterpoint as it demonstrates the contrapuntal concept, but in addition upon the pedagogic approach to the subject itself. Insofar as this chapter deals with such an approach to the subject, it is addressed essentially to teachers and students of counterpoint. However, I feel that beyond their pedagogic implications, the coming discussions will serve as an important preparation for the hearing approach presented throughout this book.

The method established by J. J. Fux in his *Gradus ad Parnassum* (1725) still offers the best solution of the basic problems of teaching counterpoint. I believe, however, as did Schenker, that Fux's approach can only be used with decisive modification. Though Fux thought of his *Gradus* as a method of composition based on the works of Palestrina, it should be considered merely as an elementary and preparatory discipline for one of the elements of tonal composition, apart from any problems of style. This viewpoint will demand some explanation.

Whether knowingly or not, Fux had allowed elements of composition of his own time to infiltrate his work so that the *Gradus* does not actually represent sixteenth-century counterpoint in pure form. Knud Jeppesen, in his *Counterpoint*,[1] has produced a more truly representative book on sixteenth-century polyphony. Although using Fux's

---

[1] *Counterpoint* (translated by Glen Haydon). Prentice-Hall, Inc., N.Y., 1939.

method with its division into five species, Jeppesen, with greater insight, has produced a remarkably thorough study approaching in some
ways a theory of composition of sixteenth-century polyphony.

But since the sixteenth century, style has changed—changed, as we
all know, a good deal; yet we still adhere to the same method of teaching counterpoint. This has aroused much doubt and uncertainty. Why
should one learn these rules, why deal with these limitations, if Bach,
Mozart and many others apparently disregarded them? Questions like
these are often answered quite unsatisfactorily. Some theorists try to
make the study of counterpoint more palatable and interesting by introducing stylistic features from compositions of later periods. Others
refer the student to such truisms as "nothing can be achieved without
hard work and strict mental discipline" or "without mastery of the
strict style, one can never expect to write a good free style." But the
question as to where the logical connection between the strict and
the free style lies is not answered at all. Evidently there has to be some
connection, or the strict style would be of no help as prelude to the
free style. In any case, all such vague statements fail entirely to show
the connection, for instance, between an example of third species and
a certain technique used by Chopin. In addition, the rather misleading
term, "strict" counterpoint, has added to the general feeling that this
method is traditionally upheld, merely for the sake of a method.

The way out of this confusion has been shown for the first time by
Heinrich Schenker. From his writings and analyses we can learn that
there is actually no contradiction between a composition by Beethoven
and the theory of so-called strict counterpoint. There is rather a relationship comparable to that of structure and prolongation, or of basic idea
and extension and development. Accordingly, rules and progressions of
counterpoint should not be applied directly in composition. It is
senseless to elevate the rules of counterpoint to those of composition,
senseless because counterpoint does not represent a study verging upon
composition itself, but only the study of one of various elements forming a complex pattern. The average composition written on a tonal
basis includes elements of harmony, counterpoint, form, rhythm, motivic development, melodic prolongation, chromaticism, etc. If we
wish to understand the essence of counterpoint, we must separate it
from this complex pattern and study it in its purest form. For such a
purpose, the Fux method is highly valuable; it is adaptable as a preparatory discipline even for compositions of far later periods. Problems of melodic contour in music of all styles may be approached
through the medium of this contrapuntal discipline. Many contrapun-

tal techniques and progressions found in the compositions of the seventeenth, eighteenth, nineteenth and even twentieth century are based upon the techniques found in Fux, but appear extended and prolonged through other elements of composition.

It is my belief that unless such a connection can be shown between the examples considered in the study of counterpoint and voice leading as it appears in composition, it is correct to call the study of "strict" counterpoint obsolete and to insist upon some more "up-to-date" method. The Fux method, however, far from being obsolete, may be said to represent a quasi-abstraction of counterpoint as a concept. It can be used to demonstrate the contrapuntal way of thinking in its purest form, which finds elaborated application in music of widely separated periods. It is only in this sense, as a study of the most basic principles of voice leading, that we shall employ it. Exclusive study of the *Gradus ad Parnassum* is inadequate, however, for gaining an understanding of the problems of musical direction and continuity. These are the problems which should not be separated from any contrapuntal study, because counterpoint and musical direction are practically interdependent factors. Furthermore, certain changes in method will be necessary if, instead of teaching sixteenth-century counterpoint, we are to teach the elementary contrapuntal techniques of later periods. For instance, the reader will notice a broader application of the dissonant neighbor note as well as a less rigid limitation of melodic outline. Counterpoint will be discussed not on a modal, but on a tonal basis. It must be kept in mind that the study of counterpoint is presented here as a preparatory discipline for understanding works based on the tonal system. This will bring about certain deviations from the style of Palestrina, but certainly does not imply that we shall drift towards harmony in our choice of examples.

This brings us to so-called "harmonic counterpoint." Many theorists have considered it essential that a student have a basic training in harmony preceding his contrapuntal study. The student of two-part counterpoint is then taught to consider each interval in its vertical aspect, to classify it in terms of one chord or another and to deal with it accordingly. In three-part counterpoint the same chordal thinking is further fortified by permitting certain chord successions while prohibiting others. The consequence is that the student's exercises are neither harmony nor counterpoint, nor are they real compositions. The student has learned to produce exercises which, at best, are artificial mixtures of harmony and counterpoint, while he has never had the opportunity to study and understand the functions, characteristics and possibilities of either element.

This intrusion of harmonic considerations into the study of counterpoint is not only unnecessary but actually harmful. Two-part counterpoint results in intervals which are the outcome of a horizontal conception, not of vertical or chordal thinking. It is harmful for the student to have to decide whether or not an interval at which he arrives (E-C, for example) is part of a C-Major chord or of an A-minor chord, because he then considers the connection of intervals as a problem in vertical thinking, not as a result of horizontal motion. Whether or not the series of intervals at which he arrives is satisfactory to the ear must be judged, not on the basis of chord progression, but according to melodic principles. We must never forget that horizontal motion, the building of a fluent melodic line, is the primary consideration. A few sentences from Schenker's book on counterpoint pertinently express his view of the meaning of this study as a whole:

> Counterpoint must be separated from composition if the ideal and practical truth of both are to come into their own right. . . . The discipline of counterpoint is not meant to teach a specific style of composition, but to serve to lead the ear for the first time into the endless sphere of original problems in music. The ear must be led to distinguish the characteristics of the intervals of music . . . and must learn to understand situations in which two, three or four voices are brought together. . . . Counterpoint must restrict itself on the basis of a modest exercise . . . to demonstrating the nature of the problems and their solutions, and should not attempt to be more than a preparation . . . for genuine composition.[2]

In accordance with this conception of the study of counterpoint, the term "pure" seems more adequate than "strict." Since this is a study of the fundamentals of voice leading only, it is necessary to eliminate all elements which might in any way obscure fundamental principles. Many of the known limitations and rules thus have the purpose of creating a basis for the discussion of pure voice-leading problems. What appears later to be "free counterpoint" is not obtained through a sudden, unmotivated disregard of those limitations and rules, but through the addition of other elements of tonal composition. Very often these "freedoms" have their origin, not in counterpoint, but in harmonic, chromatic, rhythmic or motivic influences. All of these in-

[2] *Kontrapunkt.* Universal-Ed., Vienna, 1910, pp. 15-16.

fluences create prolongations or expansions of the pure forms of counterpoint. A distinction between "strict" and "free" counterpoint as two
separate disciplines appears, in that light, to be entirely misleading.

Since this chapter is not intended as a complete textbook on counterpoint, it will not be necessary to deal with all aspects of the subject.
Some elements are intentionally omitted which would otherwise be
vital to the teaching of counterpoint. Because two-part counterpoint
affords the opportunity for a systematic exposition of the present approach to the problems of counterpoint, this study will be taken up in
almost complete detail. Indeed, because I wish simultaneously to demonstrate the contrapuntal concept and what I consider to be a sound
pedagogic approach to the subject itself, this portion of the book will
actually have very much the appearance of a textbook. However, as
most of the problems dealt with in two-part counterpoint repeat themselves in only slightly altered form in three-part counterpoint and in
combined species, discussions of these topics will be far more limited,
and will include only those details which make a definite addition to the
contrapuntal concept and which appear necessary as preparation for
the following chapters.

B. Two-part counterpoint

FIRST SPECIES

The contrapuntal concept embodies all of the principles which concern the simultaneous movement of several voices. Accordingly, the
study of counterpoint deals with the setting of two or more independent voices against each other.

This discipline, divided by Fux into five species according to rhythmic values, employs a given melody called the *cantus firmus*. A counter-
melody or counterpoint is added either above or below this melody.
While the *cantus firmus* appears in whole-notes throughout the different species, the counterpoint appears in first species in whole-notes; in
second species in half-notes; in third species in quarter-notes; in fourth
species in syncopation; and in fifth species in mixed note-values (florid
counterpoint).

This method shows a clear progression from the rhythmically simple
to the complex. Simultaneously, the other elements of contrapuntal
study, notably the use of the dissonance, are presented in a systematic
way. The culminating point is reached in the fifth species, to which the
four preceding species serve as preparation, and in which each of the

species exhibits its true function and significance within a well-balanced whole. Even the fifth species, however, must remain an exercise, since certain elements vital to artistic melody as we know it today are still lacking. This very lack is the virtue of Fux's method, which provides the opportunity for a study of pure contrapuntal and voice-leading problems, entirely removed from other considerations.

If two melodic lines move against each other, the principal question is: What type of motion may we employ between the two voices? There are three possible kinds of motion: parallel motion, in which both voices move in the same direction ►[Ex. 12a]◄; contrary motion, in which the two voices move in opposite directions ►[Ex. 12b]◄; and oblique motion, in which one voice moves while the other voice remains stationary. ►[Ex. 12c]◄ As the *cantus firmi* usually do not exceed 8 to 12 measures, it is important to achieve a fair distribution of all three types of motion throughout the exercise.

The movement of the two melodic lines against each other creates a series of intervals. Although the intervals result from voice leading, it is still necessary to know which intervals may be used.

Intervals are divided into consonances and dissonances. The primary consonances are the unison or prime, the octave, the perfect fifth and the major third. The secondary consonances are the minor third and the major and minor sixths. Seconds, sevenths and all diminished and augmented intervals are dissonances.

Consonances are characterized by their stability, while dissonances tend to move. In reference to this tendency, the fourth, though often classified as a consonance because it is the inversion of the fifth, actually has a dual character. As a vertical interval it is unstable, because it tends to resolve to a third, the upper voice moving downward. In two-part counterpoint the fourth thus acts as a dissonance. On the other hand, when used in three-part counterpoint between the middle and top voices, thus presenting the inversion of the fifth, it acts as a stable interval or consonance.

Just as the element of rhythm is studied in this discipline in progressive stages, likewise the elements of motion, as embodied in successive consonances and dissonances, will be presented in progressive degrees of complexity. Logically then, the first species deals with two melodic lines resulting in intervals of stability; all the intervals will be consonances exclusively. For the horizontal motion of the counterpoint in all species the following skips should be avoided: all augmented and diminished intervals, sevenths of any kind and all intervals greater than the octave.

The shortness of the melodic line imposes certain limitations. Just as it is desirable to achieve variety in the types of motion employed, it is important to distribute the possible intervals evenly. Thus combining two melodies should not result in a succession of more than three identical intervals. This rule applies to all consonant intervals with the exception of the fifth and the octave.

This brings us to the rule forbidding parallel primes, octaves and fifths, a controversial subject which has come under discussion again and again throughout the development of tonal music. Only the origin of this principle and its general voice-leading validity [3] will be treated here.

Regardless of how it is dealt with by individual composers of different periods, the rule forbidding parallel fifths and octaves has a definite justification within the simple setting of pure counterpoint. It must never be forgotten that we are dealing with elementary problems of voice leading in the simplest possible patterns, and that the study of counterpoint affords the opportunity to examine the qualities and characteristics of each interval, both individually and in series. This problem should not be discussed on the basis of "it sounds good" or "it sounds bad," for the aesthetic evaluation of intervals has changed greatly throughout the centuries. The issue is not an aesthetic evaluation of the intervals, but an investigation of their properties in terms of voice leading; it reveals which intervals are best suited for use in parallel motion, and which should only be used singly.

It is fairly obvious why the unison and octave should not be used in parallel motion. One of the basic aims of counterpoint is to develop voice leading which is as independent as possible. Parallel primes and octaves nullify this demand since the two voices use the same tone either in an identical or in a different register.

But why are parallel fifths forbidden, while parallel sixths and thirds are allowed? (These intervals, unlike the prime and the octave, consist of two different tones.) The answer lies in the definitive quality of the fifth; in contrast to the sixth and the third, it is a strongly key-defining interval. D-A, for example, inevitably means the boundary interval of a D chord, whether major or minor. Neither the sixth nor the third has this quality; C-E may be part of a C-Major chord or an A-minor chord. They are neutral intervals. As a result, when the ear hears a succession

---

[3] Brahms himself gave this problem detailed consideration. He compiled and commented on examples of parallel fifths and octaves from a wide range of musical literature. This study has been published, with commentary, by Heinrich Schenker (*Quinten und Oktaven u. a.* Universal-Ed., Vienna, 1933).

of thirds and sixths, it easily perceives the horizontal flow of two melodic lines, proceeding in parallel motion. But when the ear is confronted with parallel fifths, it ceases to hear two horizontally moving voices only; it tends to be distracted by the vertical, key-defining aspect of each fifth. (Likewise, as the second overtone, its dependency on the fundamental is obvious.) To prevent this confusion the principle of avoiding a succession of fifths has been established.

It can be seen that there is an additional objection to a succession of parallel primes or octaves. Since these are intervals consisting essentially of one tone only, they have a natural tendency to suggest the key of that one tone.

In the following examples one may observe the differences in effect between a succession of fifths and octaves or a succession of thirds and sixths, using the same top voice. ►[Ex. 13]◄

In the austere surroundings of pure counterpoint, with its elimination of all other elements of composition, even to approach the fifth and octave in parallel motion has proved to be objectionable. The moment one of these intervals is approached in parallel motion, its vertical, key-defining aspect tends to overshadow the feeling of horizontal continuity. ►[Ex. 14]◄ For this reason one should avoid approaching the fifth and octave in parallel motion. ►[Ex. 15]◄

Before specific examples can be discussed, we must deal with a few other general problems. For beginning a counterpoint above the *cantus firmus*, either the octave or fifth should be employed. Since the first note of the *cantus firmus* will always be the tonic, the octave will represent a doubled stress of the key-note, while the fifth will exhibit its key-defining quality. While the prime would serve as well as the octave in establishing the key, it is usually impractical in the upper counterpoint; since most *cantus firmi* begin with a line ascending from the tonic, free motion between the two voices would be impaired by a unison beginning as the counterpoint would be forced to leap.

A lower counterpoint (i.e. below the *cantus firmus*) should start with the prime or octave. The function of the octave will be exactly as in the upper counterpoint. Precisely because the prime was impractical in the upper counterpoint, it is now an advantageous beginning in the lower, since the counterpoint will be brought into contrary motion with the ascending *cantus firmus*. The interval of a fifth is naturally out of the question in the lower counterpoint, since the tonic of the *cantus firmus* with its lower fifth would yield a beginning out of the key.

The prime is best employed only at the beginning and at the end, since in the course of the exercise the meeting of both voices on one tone, particularly a tonic tone, may create a feeling of finality.

In both upper and lower counterpoints, the melody may end either on the octave or on the prime. Due to the final descending line of the *cantus firmus*, the octave will prove more advantageous in the upper counterpoint, the prime in the lower.

In the next to the last measure, the leading-tone must appear in one of the voices because of its conclusive drive to the tonic.

The student now knows how he may begin and end his exercise in first species, what intervals he may use throughout the exercise and what types of motion he may employ in going from one interval to another. Now he must learn to use his knowledge towards producing a coherent melodic organism.

Actually there are two contrasting aims by which the student must be guided in constructing a satisfactory melodic line. He must always keep in mind the most direct possible connection between two points, while at the same time striving to achieve variety in the melodic line and independence of voice leading. Upon this contrasting pair of principles the entire study of counterpoint is based.

If the tones of a melodic line are to form a coherent organism, they must have direction, which implies that they must have a goal. Every tonal melody has a goal, to which all elements inherent in the complex pattern of composition contribute. As most of these elements are lacking in our contrapuntal study, we must endeavor to create a goal to give contour to the melody. A melody that has no design other than to begin on the tonic and to arrive somehow on the final tonic would achieve little more than an aimless circling of tones or an arbitrary succession of undirected lines whose only object is to fill up space.

To prevent such aimless motion, a natural goal in the form of a climax has come into use, by which the highest tone (or possibly the lowest tone, in the lower counterpoint) serves as an intermediary goal of the melody. In this way arises the possibility of motion directed from the beginning through an intermediary goal (climax) onward toward the goal of the final tonic. It follows then that a repetition of the climactic tone would be undesirable, as tending to disturb the effect of the single intermediary goal. The main criterion of good melodic construction will be how convincingly the melodic line achieves the climax and proceeds from that point to the final tonic.

It is obvious to the student by this time that within the discipline of pure counterpoint he is not endeavoring to study melody writing as a whole, but only certain of its vital elements. These can best be studied and analyzed within the limited means admitted here. It is precisely because of these self-imposed limitations, because of the exclusion of such elements as motive, sequence, chromaticism and so on, that we are able to study the basic principles of melodic construction, unhindered by other considerations. The difference between "melody" as it appears in composition and the melodic line which the student will strive to achieve must always be borne in mind if the student is to understand the advantages gained by the restrictions imposed upon him in this study. For example, in writing in the species, the use of sequences is forbidden, not because the conception of a repeated pattern of tones is incompatible with good melody writing, but because the use of such a device at this stage of study can obscure the main issue, which is straightforward melodic development.

Now as to the student's approach in actually writing an exercise: First of all, he must at no time be allowed to proceed solely from one interval to the next, without taking into consideration the melody as a whole. Though his ear and mind may still be unable to devise the whole melody in advance as a logical entity, one has to train him to keep certain general aims in mind, while always planning specifically three, four or five measures ahead, according to his musical capacity. In general terms he knows now that he must think of a well-directed melodic line, which means he must think primarily of a climax reached and left in a convincing way. This principle he should always keep in mind, be it in the first measure as he begins, or at the point when he has arrived at the climax and is searching for a satisfactory continuation and conclusion of his melody.

PROCEDURE OF CONTRAPUNTAL WRITING

The student may now begin to write an upper counterpoint to a given A-Major *cantus firmus*. ►[Ex. 16]◄

Although the student knows that it is possible to begin on the fifth or on the octave (on E or on A), he must now decide which is the more practical interval for this specific exercise. It is true that with some *cantus firmi* the fifth and the octave are equally satisfactory as a beginning, yet it is equally true that in some cases one of these intervals may be more advantageous than the other as a point from which to initiate a logical motion towards the climax.

Let us consider the possibility of E as a beginning, and proceed through three or four measures. We could arrive at the counterpoint indicated in the next example. ►[Ex. 17]◄ Here we have already come upon a difficulty, for, although the first three measures go along quite well, at the fourth we suddenly find that the *cantus firmus* is on the verge of colliding with the counterpoint. As a result there is nothing for the counterpoint to do but to make a leap parallel to that in the *cantus firmus* in order to get out of the way. But this forced parallel leap destroys the independence of the two melodies; the counterpoint is obviously compelled to employ the tone A, not because this serves its own melodic purposes, but only because it has to get away from the *cantus firmus*. This proves that at the very outset one must closely observe the contours of the *cantus firmus* in order to plan an independent counterpoint.

Keeping this objective in mind, we can now alter the beginning so as to avoid the forced leap. ►[Ex. 18]◄

Now that we have a beginning we must consider the continuation. The first thing we should think of now is the climax. It may occur at any point in the counterpoint, as long as its position is organically reasonable. Let us assume that we would like to reach the climax over A or B, which means at approximately the middle of the *cantus firmus*. As a possibility let us consider E over the *cantus firmus* tone A. We have nearly reached this point and consequently cannot approach the E stepwise. Since we shall reach the climax by a leap, it will prove necessary to leave the climax in stepwise motion so as not to isolate the climactic tone entirely. Let us look at the next counterpoint in the light of this fact. ►[Ex. 19]◄

Two things stand out immediately as detrimental to the melodic line. It is not the skip to the climax as such which is disturbing; with a proper continuation this would be entirely acceptable. It is rather the skip from the smallest possible interval to an interval beyond the average space limit of a tenth that is objectionable. This wide upward skip in the counterpoint comes simultaneously with a wide skip downward in the *cantus firmus*. Despite the fact that the voices proceed in opposite directions, the simultaneous skips make for dependency of motion.

A second objection is far more serious. The continuation indicated completely isolates the tones E and D, a circumstance which, as we have known from the outset, weakens the entire melodic line. In addition, there is a repetitious use of the tones A and G♯ throughout the melody which should be avoided. The following altered version, using the tone D as climax and exchanging G♯ for B in meas. 5, seems much more convincing and eliminates most of the shortcomings of the previous melody. ►[Ex. 20]◄ Because the climax is approached stepwise, the skip away is not only possible but actually preferable, for it comes as a relief from a long stepwise motion. And the one B of meas. 5 suffices to prevent a monotonous repetition of tones.

However, it is still possible to improve this melody, since it shows a tendency towards sequence (see brackets). This shortcoming can be overcome quite easily by a change of only one tone, thus effecting a satisfactory counterpoint. ►[Ex. 21]◄ A beginning of the counterpoint on the tone A, though theoretically possible, would have not only limited the melody's range, but would have again created a repetitious use of this tone. ►[Ex. 22]◄

Further examples in first species are provided. ►[Ex. 23 and 24]◄ The counterpoint above the *cantus firmus* needs no comment, since we have already discussed fully the basis upon which we judge this to be a satisfactory melody. Ex. 24a and b serve as suitable exercises in lower counterpoint. Particularly, they demonstrate the different effects upon the whole melody, especially upon the climax, of beginning the lower counterpoint on the unison or on the octave.

The student's ear training may not be sufficiently advanced to enable him to hear all progressions presented throughout this chapter without the help of the keyboard. In this case he is advised to use the keyboard and to listen carefully to all the different versions, voice-leading problems and exercises. Pure counterpoint must be prevented from becoming a mere written exercise which the student is unable to hear.

SECOND SPECIES

In the second species the counterpoint moves in half-notes against the *cantus firmus;* in this species dissonance is introduced.

All the dissonances of tonal music are based upon three fundamental forms: the dissonance as a passing note, as a neighbor note and in syncopation. Since these forms evolve out of the contrapuntal concept of tonal music, they will be introduced systematically into the discipline of pure counterpoint. This discipline provides the opportunity of making their use abundantly clear, by introducing them separately in successive species. Too often the student makes no clear distinction between a passing note and a neighbor note, although in fact their functions within a melody are distinctly different. To clarify this distinction, the dissonance is introduced in second species as a passing note only. In third species it will be used also as a neighbor note, and in fourth in syncopation. All these possibilities will be combined in fifth species, in order to show how they can be blended.

With the addition of the dissonant second half-note the feeling of motion in the counterpoint is greatly enhanced. ►[Ex. 25]◄ First species would present a motion from one stable interval to another stable interval, as in Ex. 25a. In second species there appears the germ of what will be termed "directed motion." One has the feeling in Ex. 25b of beginning at a stable point and of proceeding through a point of tension on towards the following stable point. In this case the dissonance acts as a bridge between the two consonances, and as such is entirely dependent upon the consonances on each side for clarification of its own meaning. It is in this way only, as a passing note or passing interval between two consonances, that the dissonance may be used in second species. This use of a dissonance within a stepwise progression implies that a voice may not leap either to or from a dissonance, which is a fundamental principle of pure counterpoint.

Since any consonant interval is stable, its function does not need to be clarified by its relationship to any other interval. Consonances may be used freely in second species, on either the first or second beat. They may form passing notes or intervals but also may be approached or left by leap. Although it is not forbidden to leap across the bar line, it is usually better to leap within a measure than from one measure into the following. The reason will become clear when the examples are discussed.

In second, as in first species, parallel fifths and octaves on directly adjacent beats are objectionable. On the whole, parallel fifths or octaves should be used with caution on successive first beats, although in certain instances the second beat can prevent the characteristic impression of parallel intervals. ►[Ex. 26]◄ Although it is clear that the fifths in Ex. 26a will be too strong because they are used in a sequence, the fifths in Ex. 26b are quite admissible, because the melodic line continues in the opposite direction, thus weakening somewhat the effect of the perfect intervals. The same principles hold true in general for parallel octaves, although these intervals should be used less often than the fifths. On the whole, progressions involving the perfect intervals should be used only rarely because of their key-defining quality.

According to the same principles given for first species, the approach to the octave or the fifth in parallel motion should be avoided.

Whereas it is preferable in first species not to use the unison in the course of the melody because it may tend to create the feeling of an ending, it is possible to use this interval in second species, but with certain reservations. Although the use of the unison on the first beat could produce a similar result as in first species, a unison appearing on the second beat does not have the same effect, since the second beat could never cause an impression of ending. It may happen that the unison is approached by a large leap, as a means of gaining a new register or of getting into a more advantageous position. Regardless of how the unison is approached, however, it must be left in such a way as to justify the use of this interval. If the counterpoint leaps away from the unison, the impression is given that there was no actual voice-leading or melodic reason for using this interval. Therefore the counterpoint must leave the unison stepwise. Furthermore, in practically all cases, a more convincing result will be obtained if the counterpoint proceeds in the direction opposite to that by which the unison was approached. ►[Ex. 27]◄

It is possible to begin a melody either with two half-notes in the first measure or with a half-rest followed by a half-note. It is preferable to begin an exercise with a half-rest, since such a beginning accentuates the nature of the species at the outset.

The next to the last measure may contain either two half-notes or a whole-note, as in first species. If two half-notes are used, the second half-note, the one directly before the final tonic, must be the leading-tone. In minor keys this necessitates the elimination of the augmented second by raising the submediant. ►[Ex. 28]◄ Since the species are based on diatonic progressions, the use of the altered sixth and seventh degrees must be restricted to the next to the last measure unless one uses a whole-note for the leading-tone. ►[Ex. 29]◄

Obviously, in this species it is possible for the counterpoint to be more independent of the *cantus firmus* and to achieve a far more fluid melody than in first species. Here, as always, the primary consideration continues to be a well-directed melodic line. This can never be achieved by writing an exercise which in reality consists of a first species melody with a second half-note thrust by force into each measure. The second half-note must be an integral part of a melodic whole, if the study of second species is to be of any value. In general, melodies are desired in which each tone has some real part to play within the motion of the whole. The problem here is to apply this principle within a second-species melody.

Let us consider a possible exercise. ►[Ex. 30]◄ Up to the climax tone E♭, what we actually have is a descent of the interval of a seventh, and an immediate reascent of an octave. Very little is accomplished by this motion, not because the line up to E♭ is bad in itself, but because it is ineffectually used. The melody neither covers this space by a large leap, nor proceeds in a smooth stepwise motion. Instead, the entire line is summed up by the ear as a passing motion up and down a scale, with a few tones arbitrarily omitted here and there.

More or less the same impression is created in the measures immediately following the climax tone. Here the melody proceeds down a sixth by means of small leaps, a motion not objectionable in itself, but which demands a clearly directed continuation in order to explain the purpose of the small leaps. Here the melody continues awkwardly, using an undesired repetition of the tone B♭, so that the entire motion seems to hesitate in its direction.

The next example provides a decided improvement of this counterpoint. ►[Ex. 31]◄ We find now a gradual but almost uninterrupted ascent to the climax tone replacing the two somewhat hurried motions up and down the scale in Ex. 30. The small leaps from the climax are replaced by a direct leap down an octave, which at once establishes the main register and offers melodic relief from the predominantly stepwise motion.

Analyzing the functions of the tones within these melodies, it becomes more clear why in one place (Ex. 30) the impression of indecisive motion is created, and why in another (Ex. 31) this impression is altered. Since in second species the actual motion is carried from the downbeat of one measure to the downbeat of another through an intermediary second beat, the function of the second half-note in carrying this motion is of vital importance. Various treatments of the second half-note are possible, each of which must be discussed in detail.

The role of the second half-notes of meas. 1 and 3 in Ex. 30 is quite clear. These tones serve as passing tones, forming the most direct type of melodic line. The second half-note in meas. 6 of Ex. 31 has what might be called an opposing function, since, instead of forming a direct melodic line, it deliberately breaks that line to go into another register in order to start anew from another point.

But what is the function of the second half-note of meas. 5 in Ex. 30? The skip of a third may hardly be taken in the same sense as the leap of an octave in Ex. 31, which effected a change of register. Indeed, despite the fact that it is reached by a small leap, the D of meas. 5 (Ex. 30) actually serves primarily as part of a passing motion on the way up to E♭. Meas. 5 in its most direct form would show a succession of mixed note-values. ►[Ex. 32]◄ The leap of a third often serves as a passing motion of which one tone is simply omitted. It is merely a variation of what in its most natural form would be a direct stepwise line. This technique of the skipped passing tone is one which will be encountered later on in many instances.

What is the meaning of meas. 2, Ex. 30, where a skip of a fourth appears as part of the motion downward from D to E♭? In a sense it also abbreviates a stepwise passing motion. ►[Ex. 33]◄ On the other hand, the way this leap is applied in Ex. 30 does not appear to be convincing. We must distinguish between leaps abbreviating and contracting step-wise passing motions and those which we may call true leaps. A true leap causes an interruption of the melody and, for the sake of melodic variety, effects a change of register or a change of melodic direction (often a change of register is followed by a change of direction). The leap of a fifth, sixth or octave especially, creates the impression of a true leap and should be used as such. The fourth, on the other hand, being a border interval because of its size, should be used with caution either as a true leap or as an abbreviation of a passing motion; occasionally the fourth seems to act in both ways simultaneously.

Neither of these leaps, however, should be applied as is the fourth in the beginning of Ex. 30. There it appears in the midst of a passing motion which had begun in the preceding measure and which continued afterwards in the same direction. The leap in such cases lacks a clearly defined function and is therefore unconvincing.

It is possible to alter the beginning of Ex. 30 so as to make the leap of a fourth quite acceptable. ►[Ex. 34]◄ The next examples illustrate the effect upon the melodic continuity of various leaps discussed above. ►[Ex. 35]◄

In Ex. 31, meas. 3 and 5, one finds the second half-note serving a different function. Here there is a single step between the successive first beats, and the second half-note serves merely to delay the motion.

It is possible for the second half-note to have still another function. It may be used as a substitution in a progression which in its natural form would contain some voice-leading error.

For instance, a progression containing parallel fifths would be inad-missible. ►[Ex. 36]◄ If A is substituted for C, however, the parallel fifths are eliminated. ►[Ex. 37]◄ We have here, then, a case of melodic substitution in an elementary form. This device may be used not only to improve the voice leading, but also to achieve variation in the melodic line. ►[Ex. 38]◄

We have already pointed out that leaps across the bar line are in most cases inadvisable. It can now be seen more clearly why this is true. ►[Ex. 39]◄ It remains doubtful what purpose has been served by the second half-note of the first measure in each case; it appears at first to be part of a stepwise motion. But instead of continuing stepwise, the mel-ody leaps away, leaving the second half-note without continuation and thus without function and justification. The second half-note, coming on the weaker of the two beats, is always dependent upon the continuation for clarification of its function within the melodic line. It is far better to leap away from the first beat, the stronger of the two beats. ►[Ex. 40]◄

Occasionally it is possible to leap across the bar line, if the melody continues in a direction opposite to that of the leap. In this case the skip of a third serves to bring about a change of direction without actually disrupting the melody in any way. ►[Ex. 41]◄

To recall Ex. 30, two small leaps in the same direction (from E to G) occur in meas. 6 and 7. It was stated that this motion in itself is not objectionable but its continuation there is poor. The aimlessness of the melody in the following measures is at fault.

►[Ex. 42]◄ provides examples of two leaps in the same direction appropriately used. The small leaps are actually understood by the ear as a unit, since they stand for a single large leap; the second half-note subdivides the larger leap into two small ones. In both examples the leaps bring the counterpoint into a favorable position—favorable, because a clearly directed continuation in contrary motion is now possible (change of direction).[4]

The functions of the second half-note in second species can be summarized as follows:

a) as a dissonant passing tone
b) as a consonant passing tone
c) to change register
d) to change direction
e) to subdivide a larger leap
f) to delay melodic progression
g) to improve voice leading (substitution)
h) to achieve melodic variety (substitution)
i) to abbreviate stepwise passing motion (skipped passing tone)

Illustrations of each are given in ►[Ex. 43.]◄

This detailed analysis of the functions of the second half-note in second species will serve to explain what comprises a good melody in this species, and as a means of finding wherein a melody lacks logic and continuity. This list of functions is given as a means of evaluating certain details of a melody, not as a means of conceiving and constructing a melody as a whole. The student must be prevented from taking these examples as formulae by which to construct a counterpoint artificially.

---

[4] It should be understood that the sum of two successive leaps should not outline a dissonant interval or any interval greater than an octave.

There follow two additional examples in second species, which need no comment. ▶[Ex. 44, 45]◀

THIRD SPECIES

In third species the counterpoint moves in quarter-notes. In this species dissonances will be employed not only as passing notes, but as neighbor notes. Here for the first time it is possible not only to progress in a continuous line towards a certain point, but also to interrupt the progression of the melody for a moment to prolong the value of a single note by means of an embellishment.

The simplest form of embellishment is the neighbor note, which may appear either above or below the main note, and either on the accented or the unaccented portion of the measure. ▶[Ex. 46]◀ [5] Not only may the upper and lower neighbor notes be used singly, but they may combine as an embellishment of a single tone. ▶[Ex. 47]◀

Here we find an apparent disregard of one of the fundamental principles of pure counterpoint mentioned before, that a voice may not leap either to or from a dissonance. But actually there is only a visual leap from a dissonance, for the ear hears the entire motion as a contraction of two complete and thoroughly understandable neighbor-note motions, as in Ex. 47b. Actually the D goes, not to B, but to C, of which it is a neighbor. Similarly the B comes, not from D, but from the first C. Each motion is delayed, but with the final tone C the ear hears the connection and comprehends the whole as an embellishment of one tone.

A further prolongation of the neighbor note [6] gives us the following melodic embellishment. ▶[Ex. 48a]◀ This may be expanded even farther, resulting in an embellishment which comprises five tones. ▶[Ex. 48b]◀

In this species we may employ at the same time the two concepts of melodic continuity, namely, melodic progression (motion from one tone to another) and melodic embellishment (the prolongation of a single tone). Each of these types of motion may be used separately within a single measure. ▶[Ex. 49]◀ In addition, melodic progression and melodic embellishment may be combined. ▶[Ex. 50]◀

Progression and embellishment have different effects on the momentum of the melody. As is evident from the illustrations, embellishment

[5] The consonant neighbor-note motion 5-6-5 may also be used now.
[6] All derivative uses of the neighbor note (for example the incomplete neighbor note and the appoggiatura) are not introduced in the species, for we are mostly dealing with elementary forms throughout our study.

always retards, whereas progression always means straightforward motion in a single direction. These differences become evident when one reduces each of the examples to its actual equivalent in half- or whole-notes.

The given progressions, for example, may be reduced to second species; each contains a succession of three tones which give expression to one single tone, C. ►[Ex. 51]◄ There may even be as many as four or five tones which in reality stand for or prolong the value of one tone. Such prolongations are accordingly reduceable to first species, those of five tones being equivalent to oblique motion in first species. ►[Ex. 52]◄ On the other hand, a straightforward progression from one point to another in which each tone progresses to the next, involving no prolongations, is not as satisfactorily reduceable to another species. ►[Ex. 53]◄

One can see immediately that in third species, with all the new possibilities which present themselves, the question is not so much how to bring motion into the counterpoint, as how to gain a logical and fluent combination of the elements of progression and embellishment now at our command.

In third species the same general principles in regard to parallel fifths and octaves are maintained. Now that there are three quarter-notes between successive first beats, there is no longer the danger that octaves or fifths on consecutive first beats will be heard too strongly. Parallel intervals on directly adjacent beats (4 to 1) should, of course, still be avoided. In addition, it will not be good to have either fifths or octaves from third beat to first beat, for the single intervening quarter-note will not have the power to counteract the effect of parallel perfect intervals.

One may begin an exercise in third species either with a measure of four quarter-notes or a quarter-rest and three quarter-notes. The next to the last measure must always contain four quarter-notes, and the last of these must be the leading-tone. Here, as in second species, alterations of the sixth and seventh degree of the minor scale may be used.

Now let us examine an example in third species. ►[Ex. 54]◄ Although the counterpoint is correct in relation to the *cantus firmus*, the melody shows a number of weaknesses. If we examine the ascent to the climax in meas. 5, it is apparent that the melody ascends more or less gradually and logically. But in that process the melody employs the neighbor note in three of the four measures. Since the neighbor note is a device used for prolongation and always tends to retard the motion, the overuse of this device produces an undue effect of "waiting around" from measure to measure, rather than of proceeding from one point to another. In addition, the use of the same embellishment in one measure after another is monotonous, even though the use of the neighbor note is slightly changed each time.

As explained previously, in order to judge whether or not the climax is satisfactory, we must examine how it is approached and how it is left.

If we stopped at the tone F, we should find that there is no objection to the way in which that tone is reached (overlooking, for the moment, the repetition of the neighbor-note motions). But as soon as we examine the continuation we realize that within the melody, taken as a whole, the climax is not organically reached, for it is both approached and left by a leap. Such a motion tends to isolate the tone rather than to accentuate its use as an integral part of the whole. Furthermore, the climax is weakened by its repetition in meas. 7.

The ending suffers from the same difficulty which appeared in the beginning of the exercise, a needless repetition of the same type of movement, this time of straightforward melodic progression. The ending gives an impression merely of repetitious scales which run up and down between two tonics. It should be plain, then, that no motion, neither melodic progression nor embellishment, is good or bad in itself, but will show its real value only in relation to a succession of several measures.

The following counterpoint to the same *cantus firmus* shows certain improvements of the melodic line. ►[Ex. 55]◄ This counterpoint reaches its climax tone in meas. 7. The ascent to this tone is still gradual, but has a far more fluid line than that of Ex. 54. The monotony of the neighbor-note motion is eliminated; this motion is replaced by a line which progresses, recedes and drives onward to the climax. The line has made use of the possibilities of both progression and embellishment, without weakening the organic direction towards the goal. After reaching the climax, the counterpoint moves more gradually towards the end, giving more space for movement, so that the static quality of the last four measures of Ex. 54 is eliminated.

If we examine the functions which tones may have in third species, we will find that in many ways they are similar to those of second species. The possibilities of melodic progression and of melodic embellishment have been discussed quite fully above, but there are new possibilities for melodic substitution.

The motion in Ex. 54, meas. 5, is an example of a substitution. Proceeding directly from F to Bb ►[Ex. 56]◄ would not have been bad in terms of the motion of the melody, since it would have helped to maintain the feeling of the climax tone which had been reached by skips.

But inasmuch as parallel fifths would have resulted between the fourth beat of meas. 5 and the first beat of meas. 6, this progression is out of the question. For this reason a motion down an octave and back up to the Bb was substituted for a direct stepwise motion from F to Bb downward, a device which served to improve the voice leading. As in second species, the device of melodic substitution is equally useful as a means of gaining variety in the melody.

Another counterpoint to part of the same *cantus firmus* furnishes other examples of substitution. ►[Ex. 57]◄ The tones enclosed in brackets substitute for a direct passing motion. In ►[Ex. 58]◄ the passing motion is not substituted for, but the passing tone A appears delayed by embellishment.

In general, it will be found that the forms of melodic substitution or delay occurring in third species represent extensions of forms which appear in a more direct way in second species. The following examples serve as a summary and will be self-explanatory. ►[Ex. 59]◄

Two additional examples of third species counterpoint are presented, one below and one above the *cantus firmus.* ►[Ex. 60, 61]◄

FOURTH SPECIES

After the discussion of dissonance as found in second and third species, the question arises: May not the dissonance appear on the first beat? This brings us to the third fundamental use of dissonance, the dissonant syncopation used in fourth species.

In this species the counterpoint moves in half-notes, with the half-note on the second beat of each measure tied to the half-note on the first beat of the following measure, thus creating a series of syncopations. Whereas in second species, the first half-note had to be consonant, while the second half-note could be dissonant, in this species the second half-note has to be consonant. The first half-note may be dissonant or consonant. Should the first half-note be consonant, we are confronted with a consonant syncopation from which one may proceed up or down, stepwise or by leap to another consonance. If a dissonance appears on the first beat, we speak of a dissonant syncopation; a dissonance in fourth species has to resolve stepwise downwards.

Here we come upon one of those questions to which it seems impossible to give a completely satisfactory answer. Why must the dissonant syncopation always resolve downwards in fourth species?

It must be clear, first of all, that there is a distinction between suspension and syncopation. The suspension appears in isolated cases and may resolve either upwards or downwards according to the specific case. The syncopation, on the other hand, always appears in a series of equal tied or sustained intervals, and in composition, in the majority of instances, it resolves downwards.

There are certain situations in which it seems to me to be unquestionably logical that the dissonance resolves downwards. Such cases are the 7-6, the 4-3 and the 11-10 in the upper counterpoint, and the 2-3 and the 9-10 in the lower counterpoint. In each type, the dissonance resolves to either the sixth or the third, the two intervals which, because of their neutral quality, are best suited to movement in series. ►[Ex. 62]◄ It seems quite understandable that the 7 should not resolve up to 8, and the 4 up to 5 in the upper counterpoint, and similarly that the 9 should not resolve up to 8 in the lower counterpoint, for the latter resolutions would result in perfect intervals which are not always desirable from the standpoint of contrapuntal continuity.

But not all of the resolutions follow this reasoning. Why are the resolutions 9-10 and 2-3 in the upper counterpoint and 4-3 and 7-6 in the lower counterpoint considered objectionable? ►[Ex. 63]◄ From the standpoint of continuity these upward resolutions seem to be quite satisfactory, yet they are forbidden in the discipline of counterpoint. I do not believe that an entirely satisfactory explanation has yet been offered of why the dissonant syncopation in its elementary form should in all cases resolve downwards. On the whole, the principal reason seems to be a pedagogic one. It is quite possible that, because the principal syncopations resolve naturally downwards, as enumerated above, the exceptions to this rule have been sacrificed for the sake of pedagogic consistency.

*
*   *

When the counterpoint lies above the *cantus firmus*, the syncopations 2-1 and 9-8 should not be used in series, as this would automatically create a succession of parallel unisons or octaves. Similarly, the 4-5 and 7-8 syncopations should not be used in series when the counterpoint is in the lower voice.

How then are the 5-6 and the 6-5 syncopations to be treated? To begin with, there is a fundamental distinction between these and the typical fourth species syncopations. Here both of the intervals involved are consonances. This circumstance produces a situation quite in contrast to both second and third species, and to the dissonant syncopation in fourth species. In second species one has the normal stress of strong and weak beat, in which the first is the strong, consonant beat, while the second is the weaker, dissonant beat leading on towards the following first beat. In fourth species there is a reversal of this normal conception of strong and weak beat; the tied note tends to stress the second beat rather than the first. This is especially true if the first beat is a dissonant syncopation and demands a resolution, creating an additional pull towards the second beat.

When the syncopation is consonant, this pull is considerably weakened so that there is practically an equality of beats, although the tie alone is sufficient to give a slight stress to the second beat. In the case of the 5-6, there is no question of one interval resolving into another interval, so that the consonances on the two beats are practically of equal value. However, one hears the sixths more than the fifths because of the ties, so that this syncopation proves to be one of the most useful and frequent devices in composition for avoiding parallel fifths in series. ►[Ex. 64]◄ In the 6-5, on the other hand, the slight stress is upon the fifths; this syncopation should be used with caution (Ex. 64b).

In this connection it must be mentioned that the consonant syncopation, with its possibility to proceed with a skip, presents an opportunity to break the monotony which constant use of dissonant syncopation would threaten. A break in syncopation altogether may be created by moving from the second beat to a new tone, thus reverting for a moment to second species. These devices should be used to bring some flexibility and interest into the melodic line. Pedagogically, however, fourth species presents few problems and it is best taken as a preparation only for the use of syncopation in fifth species.

Finally, an upper and a lower counterpoint in fourth species are presented. ►[Ex. 65]◄

FIFTH SPECIES

Fifth species is the culmination of the study of two-part counterpoint. In the first species the use of the consonance, and in the succeeding species the three fundamental uses of the dissonance have been discussed. The fifth species presents no new problems in the use of dissonance, but instead, combines the four preceding species. However, "combination" does not mean a melody composed of a few measures of second species connected to a few of third species, with one or two syncopations in the middle. Fifth species represents a blending of the most useful features of all species within a logical whole; it offers entirely new possibilities for gaining a musically satisfactory counterpoint. Outstanding among these possibilities is the fact that the melody can now have a definite rhythmic as well as melodic continuity; accordingly, the primary issue in this species will be to investigate the general principles that lead to logical rhythmic continuity.

Each species may be used not only in its pure form within any given measure, but may be used in combination with other species within the same measure. If the melodic line is to possess unity and continuity, each measure must be the natural outcome of the preceding ones, and must at the same time serve as sound preparation for what is to come. There should be no abrupt stops, no single element which interrupts the continuous flow from beginning to end.

The only species which has a restricted use within fifth species is the first. This is understandable since the use of whole-notes in a melody which should feature a continuous melodic and rhythmic flow is not practical, except at the end. It would create an awkward beginning and would inevitably bring the melody to a stop.

The eighth-note can be used in this species, but it has a different function from the other note-values. While the melody is carried forward by the quarter-notes and half-notes, the eighth-notes merely pass within the actual flow of the melody or form a small embellishment. Thus they must always be used stepwise, either as neighbor notes or as part of a passing motion. Occasionally it is possible to jump to an eighth-note, but in such cases the first eighth-note should form the beginning of a short passing motion. In general, they must be used with great caution and with careful observance of their real function. ►[Ex. 66]◄

In the combination of different note-values, the most natural and elementary succession is from the long to the short. It is upon this general principle that the whole conception of rhythmic continuity is based. Of possible combinations of note-values within a measure, some successions are entirely in accordance with this principle, while others are in contradiction to it. ►[Ex. 67]◄ The most natural and therefore appropriate combinations are given in Ex. 67a-d.

The succession, short to long, in any form, creates impressions which are contrary to the aims of pure counterpoint. In the first place, such a succession tends to counteract the normal beat stresses within a measure, since the longer note-value always accentuates the beat upon which it is placed (Ex. 67f and h). Although, in a composition, we may often wish to utilize a displacement of the stress to gain some particular rhythmic, motivic or thematic end, the purpose here is to learn how to move entirely in accordance with the natural laws of rhythmic impulse. Only later when the student is able to utilize a rhythmic figure or peculiarity for motivic purposes should a conscious alteration of the normal succes-

sion be undertaken. Motivic writing, however, is foreign to the principles of pure counterpoint.

The impression gained from Ex. 67e and g, is that of motion which
has been abruptly stopped, rather than of motion which is capable of a
smooth continuation. Obviously this conflicts with the desired uninterrupted flow of motion. It follows, then, that eighth-notes should not be
used on strong beats (that is on either the first or the third beat of the
measure); this immediately suggests that not more than two eighth-
notes should be used in succession.

There is, however, a possibility of altering the objectionable impression given by Ex. 67e and g. For if either of these figures is used in connection with a syncopation, the impression of a jolt no longer remains,
and the possibility of an entirely smooth continuation is gained in the
next measure. ►[Ex. 68]◄ Accordingly, the succession of two quarter-
notes followed by a half-note, or of a quarter-note and two eighth-notes
followed by a half-note, may be used in fifth species, but only if the
half-note is syncopated.

Whereas the syncopation appeared in fourth species in only one form
(in a succession of half-notes), it may appear in this as well as in various other forms in fifth species, as long as the essential nature of the
syncopation remains intact. In fourth species, a consonance on the second beat of one measure is tied to a dissonance on the first beat of the
following measure, which resolves downwards to a consonance on the
second beat of that measure. Any combination of note-values within a
syncopation must clearly follow the basic principles of the fourth
species. For instance, in a succession in which the syncopating half-note
is tied to a quarter- instead of a half-note, the resolution of the dissonance (according to the second half-note in fourth species) must fall
on the third beat rather than upon the quarter-note which immediately
follows the tie. The intervening quarter-note (falling on the second
beat) has no essential function within the syncopation; it merely serves
to delay the arrival of the true resolution until the third beat. As a
purely delaying tone, it should not cause a new element of tension
until the dissonance is resolved. This means that a dissonance must not
be used on the second quarter of the measure, as this would interfere
with the syncopating dissonance and its resolution. On the other hand,
when a consonance is used, the ear can retain as a unit the impression of
the syncopating dissonance and its resolution on the third beat. There
are several possibilities. ►[Ex. 69]◄

In some of these examples there is again a seeming disregard of the
fundamental rule of contrapuntal writing which forbids a leap from a

dissonance. In each of these instances, however, the leap is only visual (as in Ex. 47), since the dissonance proceeds actually not to the second but to the third quarter-note. As in the case of the combined upper and lower neighbor note, the ear is able to hear the essential connection with the true note of resolution.

It is possible to substitute two eighth-notes for the second quarter-note. ▶[Ex. 70]◀ This substitution must be made in accordance with the function of the second quarter-note of the measure and also with the general rules governing the use of eighth-notes. It may be recalled that eighth-notes may only be used stepwise, as part of a passing or of a neighbor-note motion. A leap to the first eighth-note is possible, but only if it forms the beginning of a passing motion (Ex. 70c). In all the above examples, the use of the syncopation is essentially of the fourth species type. However, if a tied quarter-note rather than a tied half-note is used as the beginning of the syncopation, the basic succession is altered in a more fundamental way; the consonance which serves as the beginning of the syncopation now comes on the fourth instead of the third quarter of the measure. ▶[Ex. 71]◀ It is possible to use the tied quarter-note preferably when it is followed in the next measure by a normal syncopation beginning on the third beat. In this way the quarter-note syncopation serves as a preparation for the syncopation to come. But because it represents a divergence from the normal succession, this altered syncopation should be used sparingly, preferably only once in an exercise. ▶[Ex. 72]◀

The relation of the counterpoint to the *cantus firmus* presents no new problems. Each species will maintain exactly the relation to the *cantus firmus* which it has in unmixed form. For this reason there is of course no new problem involved when a measure moves entirely within any one species. Even the mixture of species within one measure and the addition of eighth-notes actually create no new relationship; their use depends solely upon a proper application of the appropriate species in any one case. The eighth-notes will represent either an extension of fourth species, when they appear in connection with a syncopation, or of third species, when they appear in connection with quarter-notes, as previously illustrated.

Not all of the new possibilities which appear in fifth species will be discussed here. The general rule is still that each tone must have some clearly defined function and must be used in accordance with that function. Several possible combinations of a half-note with two quarters within a measure are presented in order to illustrate how one must think in terms of function in a mixture of species. These same ways of thinking may be applied to any problem that arises in a fifth species melody. ►[Ex. 73]◄

The counterpoint in Ex. 73a poses no problem, since both quarternotes are passing tones between the two consonances on the first beats. However, when the figure turns instead of continuing downwards, one must be sure of the functions of the two quarter-notes in the last half of the first measure. In Ex. 73b the tone D which is dissonant is heard as a passing tone between the two consonances in the first and fourth beats of the measure. In Ex. 73c it is the C which is dissonant; the ear, therefore, makes the connection between the two consonant D's in adjacent measures, and the C is heard as a neighbor note to that tone D. But what is the function of the two quarter-notes in Ex. 73d? Here both tones are dissonant; they actually have no function, since they are neither passing tones nor neighbor-note tones. This specific figure, then, is not possible as a counterpoint to the *cantus firmus* tones E and D. Any figure which could arise in the course of a fifth species melody may be evaluated in the manner just indicated. The above, then, covers everything needed to write a perfectly correct counterpoint. But this is no guarantee of a rhythmically and melodically satisfactory line. We must first examine a few measures and later entire melodies, to find out how fifth species can be used to create a unified and coherent whole.

Earlier it was said that the combination of species does not mean short sections of one species followed by another, arbitrarily joined without regard to continuity. The next example shows the effect of such a procedure. ►[Ex. 74]◄ Even though each species is used quite properly, and the melodic line is fairly good, such a combination creates blocks of equal note-values which inevitably give the effect of a lack of continuity.

One might attempt to change the impression of too much third species by the addition of eighth-notes producing an alternative as indicated in ►[Ex. 75.]◄ This alternative does not better the situation; in fact, it tends to accentuate the impression of too much motion in quarter-notes in contrast to too little motion in the beginning, though the eighth-notes are used correctly. The introduction of eighth-notes into a measure never constitutes a change of species; it serves only to intensify a motion consisting of larger note-values. Thus, in Ex. 75 the addition of eighth-notes does not accomplish a change of species, but merely alters the appearance of the third species. Preferably not more than two and a half consecutive measures of one species should be used, and under no circumstances more than three.

►[Ex. 76]◄ shows the overuse of eighth-notes. Here they carry the passing motion upwards from F to E♭. The outline of a seventh is bad, as is the hurried effect of eighth-notes in the passing motion up to E♭. In ►[Ex. 77]◄ the impression of haste is entirely eliminated by the substitution of motion in quarter-notes. Although eighth-notes must always be used with caution, they have their own functions within a melody, and, within proper limits, can be used to real advantage to gain variety in the melodic line.

Syncopations will be exceedingly useful in fifth species, as they will form the actual rhythmic life of the melody. To take full advantage of the syncopations, one should employ them in series. In such a series, it is always important to vary the techniques of resolution. It will be monotonous if eighth-notes are used each time, even if their use is slightly varied, since in pure counterpoint such repetition as a motive is not appropriate. ►[Ex. 78]◄ One should take note of the various possibilities both eighth-notes and quarter-notes offer. ►[Ex. 79]◄

It was evident from Ex. 74 that it would be impossible to gain a satisfactory melody by merely adding one species to another, in whatever order they might appear. Each measure must in some way prepare for what is to follow. In proceeding from second to third species, for example, it is best to prepare for the coming quarter-notes by a measure consisting of a half-note and two quarters, which serves as a connection between the two species. ►[Ex. 80]◄ Similarly, ►[Ex. 81]◄ shows a mixture of note-values which helps to gain a smooth flow of rhythm.

The examples which follow offer some of the possibilities of fifth species. ►[Ex. 82, 83, 84]◄

C.   Three-part counterpoint

Three-part counterpoint is discussed here primarily for its bearing upon the contrapuntal concept, and only secondarily from the pedagogical point of view. Certain aspects of first and second species, and a few facts pertaining to fourth will be discussed. The use of third and fifth species in three parts can be clearly understood from the study of two-part counterpoint and from a knowledge of the general principles of movement in three voices. There are no new methods of work here.

FIRST SPECIES

The study of counterpoint deals with two or more melodic lines which move simultaneously, each line maintaining its own melodic individuality. When there are two such melodic lines, the vertical result is a series of intervals; when there are three, the vertical result is a series of chords.

In three-part, as in two-part counterpoint, the independence of the horizontal lines is of primary consideration. The chords are a result of horizontal, not vertical, thinking. One should not think, "What chord would best follow this chord?" but, "What is the best voice leading for each of the three voices?" This musical conception produces in purest form a succession of chords which come about solely as a result of voice-leading and are thus pure contrapuntal chords.

Exactly the same general principles will be maintained as in two-part work, but with certain adjustments and additions necessitated by the added third voice. In proceeding from two- to three-part counterpoint, the question arises, "Which is the added voice?" Actually it is the middle voice which is added, since the two outer voices in a three-part setting serve precisely the same functions as the two voices of a two-part setting. This introduces for the first time the distinction between outer and inner voices. Although the middle voice need not achieve the same scope and freedom as the top voice and the bass, it must maintain a perfectly satisfactory melodic line. Whatever the scope of the inner voice, under no circumstances should it serve the function of a mere "chord-filler."

The primary adjustment brought about by the addition of a third voice is in the conception of consonance and dissonance. How does this conception, as previously explained, apply to three parts? The consonance in three-part counterpoint is represented by the triad; therefore the consonant triad in a three-part setting is equivalent in conception to the consonant interval in a two-part setting.

It was said at the outset that vertical thinking is to be avoided insofar as possible. Nevertheless, just as it was necessary to discuss the intervals in a two-part setting, so it is necessary here to discuss chords. There is no contradiction in this so long as we keep in mind that the chords are the result of the motion of the voices, not the determining factor in that motion, although they impose certain restrictions upon it.

Since the bass is the strongest tone in any chord, the relation of each tone to the bass is of paramount importance. When both of the tones within the triad are consonant with the bass, we have a consonant triad. When either one of the tones is dissonant with the bass, we have a dissonant triad. The root position of any major or minor triad contains two intervals which are consonant with the bass—the fifth and the third; the triad in root position, therefore, forms a consonant triad. The first inversion of these triads, the sixth chord, also contains two intervals which are consonant with the bass, so that it too represents a consonant triad. But in the second inversion this is not the case. Although the bass forms a consonance with one of the chord tones, it forms a dissonance with the other. Therefore the triad in second inversion is dissonant.

Within the major mode and the natural minor mode there are not only major and minor triads, but one diminished triad. This triad in root position is dissonant, since it contains a diminished fifth in relation to the bass. However, in first inversion this triad is no longer dissonant, since there is no longer a dissonance between either of the voices and the bass. The precedence of the bass is so great that even though an augmented fourth appears between the two upper voices, the triad is still consonant. This triad, like all other triads, is dissonant in second inversion.

In short, the consonant triads include all major and minor triads in root position and in first inversion, and the diminished triad in first inversion. Other triads are dissonant, and accordingly may not be used in first species.

Any of the consonant triads may be used either in open or close form. The student already knows the distinction between open and close form from his study of elementary theory. Not only is open form permissible, but it is preferable; it gives better spacing between the voices than close form, and gives opportunity for better voice leading.

In addition to being used either in open or in close form, the triads may appear either as complete or incomplete triads. More than two incomplete chords should not appear in succession, unless the voice leading warrants it. The incomplete chord containing the fifth and the octave ►[Ex. 85]◄ is best employed at the beginning or the end of an exercise. However, its occasional use in the course of the exercise may be entirely justified.

The unison should be avoided between any two voices except at the beginning and the end of an exercise, since even a momentary appearance of this interval reduces a three-part counterpoint to only two voices.

In the next to the last measure the leading-tone should appear in one of the voices; it is preferable to have a complete chord in this measure.

The reasons which make parallel fifths and octaves unsatisfactory in two-part counterpoint are equally applicable in three-part counterpoint with regard to motion between any two voices. However, in a three-part setting there are instances in which a progression to the fifth or the octave in parallel motion is permissible. If all of the voices proceed in parallel motion, it is better that no two of them should move into an octave or a fifth. However, if one of the voices, especially one of the outer voices, proceeds in contrary motion to the other two voices, the effect of going into a perfect interval in parallel motion is counteracted; therefore such a motion need not be avoided.

Since the primary consideration here continues to be the life and independence of the individual voices, it is clear that the conception of melodic direction remains exactly the same as in two-part counterpoint. Consequently the same approach must be maintained; all work must be done on the basis of thinking ahead logically in terms of voice motion. In two-part counterpoint it was necessary for the student to learn to think ahead in terms of two melodic lines, instead of thinking from interval to interval. Now he must learn to think ahead in terms of three melodic lines, instead of planning from chord to chord. Since the student cannot immediately be expected to achieve the ideal of thinking in terms of three voices simultaneously, it is necessary to give him some indications of how he can best proceed.

If the *cantus firmus* appears either in the bass or in the top voice, it is best to plan the outer voices first for three or four measures, and afterwards to add the middle voice. This certainly does not mean writing two complete voices and putting in an inner voice afterwards wherever it falls by chance. While following the practical expediency of working with two voices a little at a time, the student must at the same time keep in mind his ultimate aim of achieving three independent voices.

If the *cantus firmus* appears in the middle voice, there is more of a problem, since one must actually consider all of the voices almost simultaneously. Preference is given, however, to the bass, since the bass is of crucial importance to the meaning of the chord. At the same time, the third voice cannot be left out of consideration while one is writing the other two, for if it were, it would almost inevitably be weak and would consequently tend to weaken the whole exercise.

An example in three parts, as in two parts, is logical or illogical according to whether the voice leading is logical or illogical. If there is a fault in the counterpoint it will always be found to lie in the voice leading, and not in such a matter as "chord-succession," for example. That being the case, since the principles of melody writing and of voice leading have been discussed in detail in connection with two-part counterpoint, they are not repeated here.

One example in first species, three-part counterpoint is given. It will be apparent that this type of horizontal planning results in a series of contrapuntal chords. ►[Ex. 86]◄

In each subsequent species one voice moves in the species, while the *cantus firmus* and the other voice move in whole-notes. Both the "species" part and the *cantus firmus* may appear in any voice.

SECOND SPECIES

In a two-part setting the second species introduced a passing note and thus a passing interval. Analogously, a three-part setting produces a dissonant or consonant passing chord between the consonant first beats of two consecutive measures. Through the activity of the second half-note there occur, however, not only passing chords, but in addition, chords which have a delaying purpose and chords which improve the voice leading—all of them arrived at exclusively as a result of voice leading. To illustrate how these chords may appear, whether the "species" voice is at the top, in the middle or in the bass, three examples are given. ►[Ex. 87, 88, 89] ◄

In Ex. 87, meas. 2, the tone E♭, and consequently the entire chord which results on the second beat, is used in passing from first beat to first beat. In meas. 6, the B♭ on the second beat serves as a delaying note between the otherwise directly adjacent tones D and C. As a result, the chord itself takes on a delaying character.

These and other uses of the second half-note already cited in second species in two parts, appear in all three of these exercises, regardless of which is the "species" voice. Thus in Ex. 88, meas. 5, the tone G is used as a delaying tone between the chords on B and on C. In Ex. 89 the chords on the second beats of meas. 2 and 3 are passing chords; in this case the main passing motion is in the middle voice.

How such progressions of chords resulting solely from voice motion and voice direction are used in composition will be discussed in detail in Chapters V-VIII.

FOURTH SPECIES

The fourth species presents especially interesting problems if the syncopated half-notes are in the inner voice. Progressions occur which will be encountered later on in elaborated form. ►[Ex. 90] ◄

COMBINED SPECIES

The possibility arises of letting three voices move in different note-values. Practically speaking, this means that the *cantus firmus* is the only voice which proceeds in whole-notes, while each of the other voices moves in another species. Whereas the previous exercises belong to what one may call elementary counterpoint, the combination of species places this study in the field of more advanced counterpoint. It should not be undertaken until the simpler forms are thoroughly mastered.

Any two species can be combined with the *cantus firmus*. As a result, there arise many possibilities of motion and consequently new uses of dissonance. No attempt will be made here to discuss all possibilities of motion which may appear. Certain combinations will be taken up, however, for the purpose of showing how the combination of species broadens and enlarges the contrapuntal concept.

The new possibilities of motion which present themselves do not come, of course, from setting aside any of the principles already learned in elementary counterpoint. New uses of dissonance spring solely from an extension of concepts of voice motion, brought about by the combination of species. This extension of the pure principles of voice leading will result in a further elaboration of the conception of dissonance.

In two-part counterpoint, two such elaborations have already been seen—in third species, when an upper and a lower neighbor note were combined, and in fifth species, in the use of a quarter-note on the second beat of a dissonant syncopation. In each case the ear was expected to understand the use of the dissonance, not on the basis of immediate continuation, but on the basis of its larger connection. These examples show the first germs of contrapuntal prolongation.

Now in combined species there are additional examples of prolonged uses of the dissonance which make this procedure the true beginning of what later will be called "prolonged counterpoint." However, all of the prolongations of combined species will be understandable in terms of voice leading, and voice leading alone. Here, as in the preceding instances, each voice is considered in its relation to the bass and to the *cantus firmus*, and each voice is governed by the same principles as heretofore.

The next example illustrates the use of second and third species in combination with the *cantus firmus*. ►[Ex. 91]◄

This example shows several of the characteristic uses of the dissonance which may arise logically out of the employment of such a combination. As meas. 2 and 4 illustrate, it is possible now, because of the two "species" voices, to arrive frequently at as many as three dissonances in succession, a circumstance which only rarely arises in elementary counterpoint. These three successive dissonances may occur as a result of a combination of a neighbor-note motion in one voice with a passing motion in another (meas. 4), or as a result of passing motion in each of the moving voices (meas. 2).

There are certain interesting problems which present themselves in relation to this combination of species. One must always bear in mind that clarity in this study is dependent upon the provision that the relationship of each voice to the *cantus firmus* and to the bass remains intact. Thus in meas. 6, the leap to C in the bass is good, although this motion appears, visually, to constitute a leap to a dissonance. Actually the D in the middle voice is introduced as an accented passing tone between the consonances E and C, so that the leap to C in the bass is heard in relation to the consonant C on the fourth beat. Conversely, the leap to C in ►[Ex. 92]◄ is not good, although the bass appears to leap to the consonant chord C-C-E. The figure in the middle voice can be understood only as an upper and lower neighbor note of the tone B (it is only on this basis that the significance of the tone A is clear). Accordingly, therefore, the leap to C is made in connection with a dissonant chord C-B-E, and is not good.

Other interesting problems appear with the combination of third and fourth species, in relation to the resolution of the dissonance. ►[Ex. 93]◄

Here the dissonance may resolve to a chord which is consonant on the third beat, in the manner indicated in elementary counterpoint; such a resolution appears in meas. 3. However, it is now possible to delay the resolution until the fourth beat, because of the motion of the quarter-notes. In meas. 9, for example, the resolution is delayed by the dissonant passing note E until the fourth beat, when the chord F-F-D results. Another such delay appears in meas. 10, this time caused by an upper and lower neighbor-note motion.

As in the previous combination of species, one must be careful to take into consideration the true meaning of the tones. Thus it will be found that, although the dissonant tone G in ►[Ex. 94a]◄ moves downwards stepwise, it does not form a resolution with a consonant triad, either on the third or on the fourth beat. ►[Ex. 94b]◄ gives a correct resolution.

In the combination of two fifth species melodies with a *cantus firmus* we reach the culmination of the entire study of pure counterpoint. This combination makes possible the use of elements of imitation, both rhythmic and melodic, affording an excellent opportunity for introducing this important contrapuntal technique. The next example shows some of the possibilities of this combination of species. ►[Ex. 95]◄

D. Summary

In this chapter, horizontal melodic considerations have been predominant. The creation of chords and their connection has not been the main purpose of counterpoint. The chords rather resulted from horizontal devices. Such chords are connected on the basis of voice leading and voice motion only and thus represent the incidental aspect of a three-part horizontal orientation. They are called chords of motion or contrapuntal chords, and progressions of them represent the principles of counterpoint. Thus it follows that a progression of chords per se is not necessarily harmonic, nor does it imply the presence of harmonic principles.

As will be amply illustrated later, the concept of counterpoint as the element of motion remains basically unaltered in actual composition. The basic contrapuntal progressions discussed in the discipline of counterpoint undergo further prolongation, however, and new elements of musical expression are added.

Part II   Chapter Four

The Harmonic Concept

A.   Contrast to contrapuntal concept

In addition to counterpoint and the progressions of chords resulting from counterpoint, music of western civilization has developed chord progressions of very different appearance and significance. These progressions are based on the relationship between certain tones, a concept foreign to the principles of pure counterpoint. Since this relation between tones is a harmonic relationship, the resulting chord progressions are harmonic progressions and the members of these progressions harmonic chords or harmonies.

The relative distribution of contrapuntal and harmonic chords or the predominance of either group within a unit is a decisive factor in the interpretation and understanding of a phrase, a section or a whole piece. Therefore, recognition of the fundamentally contrasting characteristics of harmony and counterpoint is essential. Although more will be said later of the cooperation between contrapuntal and harmonic chords, at the present time emphasis is laid upon their basic differences. These differences may be demonstrated by means of the simplest melodic line, the descending third. This melodic line may be treated contrapuntally. ►[Ex. 96a]◄ If for tonal reasons the bass must conclude on C, it is obvious that D of the melody should be set against B, since the use of D in the bass would cause parallel octaves. In order to create motion in the middle voice and thus avoid retaining G for all three chords, the the G is suspended into the second chord and then proceeds through F to E. In this example the movement and direction of three voices are the primary considerations; the outstanding contrapuntal factor is the progression of the intervals 10-10-8 in the outer voices. Chords are formed as a result of this motion, and their connection has been achieved on a definitely contrapuntal basis.

In the next example, however, although the same chords are used, a very different result is obtained. The setting of the melody is based on a harmonic conception. Finding a satisfactory counterpoint to the descending melodic third is of less concern than finding a "harmony" as chordal support of the melody tone D. In this process of "harmonizing" we shall seek a chord which is closely associated with the C chord. Instinctively we are led to the chord on the fifth degree of the scale as being most closely associated with the fundamental C. ►[Ex. 96b]◄

Composers and musicians of the past have intuitively felt this relationship between tones and chords a fifth apart and have established a system of harmonic progressions based upon it. This instinctively perceived relationship was verified centuries later by the application to theory of the overtone series, a phenomenon that proves the natural origin of the triad. ►[Ex. 97]◄ In a contracted form this chord appeared in the early centuries of polyphonic music as an incomplete chord $\frac{8}{5}$ and later developed into the complete triad. ►[Ex. 98]◄

There is no scientific explanation of the compelling force inherent in the progression I-V-I. It seems, however, that its existence must have some connection with the chord forms just mentioned, since their horizontalized outline constitutes a motion from the fundamental to the closely related fifth and from the fifth to the fundamental. This motion represents the bass tones of the I-V-I progression. ►[Ex. 99]◄ This progression is therefore already established within the earlier incomplete form of the triad; the third was a later addition which proved to be of weaker harmonic relationship to the fundamental than the fifth. It should be added that the impulse to move from V to I is given a greater momentum by a melodic impulse from D to C, and B to C, or D to E (see Ex. 96b, 104, 106a).

B. The fundamental harmonic progression and its elaborations

In Ex. 96b the descending third of the melody was "harmonized" by use of the I-V-I which will be called the *fundamental harmonic progression*. Its notation in a non-rhythmic form is used to indicate the over-all structural significance which it so predominantly demonstrates in tonal music. It should be noted that the V often appears as V⁷. The origin of this V⁷ seems to lie in a contraction of a passing note with the V and thus to be the result of melodic-contrapuntal influence. ►[Ex. 100]◄ In the examples which follow, either the V or V⁷ may be used, the latter often providing for better voice leading.

It might seem to a student who has taken a conventional harmony course that there is very little difference between Ex. 96a and 96b, since both show the succession of a C chord, a G chord and another C chord, with the G chord written in one place in root position, and in the other in first inversion. This may appear to be a minor change which does not actually affect the status of the progression as a harmonic I-V-I progression. Recalling the statements made in Chapter II, I contend that only the grammatical status of the chords is similar, but that their actual significance is very different. In principle there is a decisive difference between a bass featuring neighbor-note motion (a typical melodic-contrapuntal device) and a bass motion which indicates a fifth association (a harmonic relation between tones and their triads). This difference in the basses is significant and underlines the distinction between a purely contrapuntal and a purely harmonic conception. Certainly tonic and dominant chords are used in both cases, but the significance of these chords in the two examples is widely divergent.

The fundamental harmonic progression can be enriched with either the II, the III or the IV. Each of these chords asserts a harmonic association of varying degree with the I and the V—however, only if placed between those two harmonies. They thus elaborate the fundamental harmonic progression, producing the three patterns, I-III-V-I, I-II-V-I and I-IV-V-I. ▶[Ex. 101]◀

The order in which these three progressions are presented indicates their structural significance. Ex. 101a shows the III placed naturally under E of the top voice. The harmonic relationship of this chord to the I, though weaker than the fifth relation, seems evident, since the third is one of the overtones close to the fundamental. The larger implications of this progression I-III-V-I were demonstrated in Part I, Chapter II. As shown there, it can serve as the harmonic framework for a large section or even a whole piece (see Part I, Ex. VIII and V). In an actual composition, the single members of such a progression often appear widely separated. Here, however, the progression is given in a contracted form which may sound unfamiliar. It is therefore necessary to point out the larger implications of such a progression, in order that its true use may be understood.

Ex. 101b presents the II, which has a fifth relationship to V. The harmonic progression I-II-V-I may be set not only to a descending third, but to the elementary melodic progression of a descending fifth, with the tone E appearing necessarily as a passing note.

Finally Ex. 101c introduces the IV, which is the fifth *below* the tonic. The IV thus lacks a natural upper fifth relationship to the I, which considerably weakens its harmonic role. On the other hand, the proximity to V strengthens its driving tendency to this harmony.

Once these progressions were firmly established, it became possible to alter the form of certain chords within a progression without altering the basic meaning of the progression as a whole. It is possible, for example, to use the II in first inversion in the I-II-V-I progression without seriously impairing the harmonic characteristics of the entire progression. ►[Ex. 102]◄

The VI, in contrast to the II, the III and the IV, has no direct harmonic relation either to I or to V. It is likely that this progression has been derived through a process of inversion and imitation in order to achieve more harmonic variety. The progression from I to V which has a natural ascending direction, can be inverted. ►[Ex. 103]◄ This inversion, in turn, gives rise to and makes possible an imitation of the genuine, upward directed harmonic relation I-III, by a motion a third downward, with the resulting pseudo-third relationship I-VI. The artificiality of this process is responsible for the rather ambiguous role the VI frequently plays in tonal music. The harmonic tendency is indicated by the use of the basses of the fundamental harmonic progression introduced in inverted form. On the other hand, the pseudo-third relationship I-VI occasionally makes the VI appear more as a passing chord between I and V, and thus stresses its contrapuntal significance. However, because it is frequently used as a strong point on the way from I to V, the student should add this as a *secondary harmonic progression* to the fundamental progression and its three elaborations. ►[Ex. 104]◄ The downward trend of the bass in the progression I-VI does not prevent the composer from using the lower C at the beginning, as indicated here in parenthesis. Since the bass is descending, the melodic line of a third has been presented in ascending form; a falling melodic line E-D-C would have led to unsatisfactory voice leading. ►[Ex. 105]◄

The fundamental progression, its three elaborations and the secondary harmonic progression demonstrate the harmonic element in music in its most concentrated and purest form. In Ex. 96b through 104, an almost complete separation of harmony and counterpoint has been achieved. Yet, in demonstrating these harmonic progressions, it has proved impossible to completely eliminate counterpoint. Although it is possible to demonstrate counterpoint without any harmonic influence, the harmonic progressions show certain contrapuntal characteristics. For instance, the dissonant passing tone in the middle voice and in the melody (see Ex.100 and 101c) and the simultaneous motion of four voices demand voice-leading considerations to some extent, though these are insignificant in comparison to the underlying harmonic concept dominating these progressions.

C. Exercises

The student must acquire complete mastery of the fundamental progression, its three elaborations and the secondary harmonic progression, not only in written form but above all at the keyboard. For the time being, melodic progressions of a descending and ascending third or a descending fifth should suffice. The significance of these melodic progressions in tonal melodies cannot be fully grasped at this stage. However, the student will readily realize that these progressions fill in the main intervals of the tonic chord and thus form the most elementary and the clearest possible horizontal outline of the tonality. This makes them especially suited to serve as top voices to the harmonic progressions.

In practicing these progressions it is well to distinguish between their written and keyboard forms. This is important because many students are not sufficiently familiar with the piano to play every kind of distribution of the voices between two hands with equal ease. Ex. 100-104 represent therefore the easiest and most practical type of keyboard exercise. It places the top and two middle voices in one hand and only the bass in the left hand, giving the student a clear perception of vitally important bass progressions.

KEYBOARD EXERCISES

1) Play the fundamental, the elaborated and the secondary harmonic progressions as described above.
   a) Practice them in all major keys.
   b) Always think ahead; have the whole progression including top voice clearly in mind before you play. This will prove to be of great help later in prolonging and expanding these elementary progressions.

WRITTEN EXERCISES

The problem of written style should be taken up as soon as the progressions just discussed have been mastered. This should be done in a four-part vocal or, as we may call it, "*chorale style.*" ▶[Ex. 106]◀ The student, who by now is familiar with chord construction and three-part counterpoint, will have no difficulty in writing these progressions satisfactorily.

Ex. 106 shows two versions of the final I, which must be explained. Voice-leading considerations would lead to an incomplete triad on the I, since the leading-tone resolves naturally to the tonic. It should be pointed out, however, that Bach, in his chorales, frequently skips away from the leading-tone when it is an inner voice tone in order to achieve a complete triad. Since both versions are used, there is no justification for an ironclad rule that the leading-tone must always resolve to the tonic.

D. Harmonic progressions in minor keys and the influence of mixture

Turning to harmonic progressions in minor keys, we shall focus our attention on the dominant chord as the strongest harmonic factor. In the natural minor, the dominant appears as a minor chord. However, the strongest harmonic relation between two chords, the fifth, is based on major chords, for the overtone series creates only major chords (see Ex. 96b and 97).

As a solution of this problem—preserving the minor character of the progression on the one hand, and doing justice to the natural relation between chords on the other hand—a compromise has been developed which uses one chord, the dominant, in its major form, thus creating a *mixture* between a major key and its parallel or synonymous minor key.[1] ►[Ex. 107]◄

Today the teaching of the natural minor is often neglected; the harmonic and melodic minor are not taught as the results of mixture between major and parallel minor but explained as two principal minor scales at least equal, if not superior, in value to the natural minor. Consequently the student often tends to alter the fifth of the mediant chord when he is asked to play I-III-V-I in a minor key. ►[Ex. 108]◄ This seems to be an example of theory for theory's sake because in all cases in minor in which composers treat the III as a harmonic chord, it appears as a major chord, according to its status within the natural minor. ►[Ex. 109]◄ The III as a major chord seems perfectly logical, since its loss would rob the minor mode of one of its characteristic features, namely

---

[1] As will be shown later the minor dominant appears quite often within contrapuntal progressions and within so-called harmonic prolongations; it would therefore be very misleading to state that the dominant in a minor key is always a major chord.

the appearance of a major chord on the third degree of the scale in contrast to the minor chord on the third degree in major.[2]

We now come to the progressions I-II-V-I, I-IV-V-I and I-VI-V-I. The progression I-II-V-I is presented in two versions, with II in root position and in first inversion; the latter reduces the effect of the diminished chord. ►[Ex. 110]◄

In summary, harmonic progressions in minor keys, with the exception of the dominant, present the chords of the natural minor scale.

KEYBOARD AND WRITTEN EXERCISES

1) Practice at the keyboard in all minor keys all versions of harmonic progressions with melodic progressions of a descending fifth and a descending or ascending third.

2) Write in chorale style several harmonic progressions in different minor keys. Watch for good voice leading.

There are further possibilities of mixture between major and minor. ►[Ex.111]◄ Here a progression in major has been given a temporary minor coloring by introducing the subdominant of the parallel minor; this is still the procedure seen in Ex. 107. Ex. 111b, however, represents a second type of mixture in which one member of a harmonic progression is mixed with its own major or minor counterpart; in this instance a chord which is originally minor appears as a major chord.

E.   Intensification of the V by a preceding ⁶₄ chord

The dominant of a harmonic progression often appears emphasized and intensified through a preceding ⁶₄ chord. ►[Ex. 112]◄

Why is the ⁶₄ chord, which is plainly the second inversion of a tonic chord, not marked as I⁶₄? It is necessary to recall the distinction made earlier between the grammatical status and the actual significance of a chord. Although this chord is a second inversion of the tonic, its significance lies in the fact that it emphasizes the V. It has the effect of a ⁶₄ chord constructed as a suspension or appoggiatura on the dominant bass tone G and resolving to ⁵₃, rather than of an independent chord; it appears closely linked with the V. Proof of this lies in the fact that in listening to an example such as Ex. 112, an ear uninfluenced by theory will hear the ⁶₄ chord not as a return to the tonic, but as a

[2] The reader is reminded of the I-III-V-I progression in Ex. V, discussed in Part I.

chord belonging to and strengthening the V. The grammatical status of a chord is always the same within one key, but its significance varies according to its function within the tonal unit, phrase or section. I$\begin{smallmatrix}6\\4\end{smallmatrix}$ is the grammatical label of this chord whereas $\underbrace{\begin{smallmatrix}6&5\\4&3\end{smallmatrix}}_{V}$ characterizes

the significance of the $\begin{smallmatrix}6\\4\end{smallmatrix}$ chord in connection with the following dominant. Since chord significance is our primary concern, the label just mentioned will be employed in preference to a purely grammatical label.

F.   The use of seventh chords within the harmonic progressions

Besides the V^7, the II$\begin{smallmatrix}6\\5\end{smallmatrix}$ and IV^7 also appear frequently within the harmonic progressions and provide added color. Here the suspension indicates a slight contrapuntal influence. ►[Ex. 113, 114]◄

It has already been stated that the V^7 aids in achieving satisfactory voice leading. The student should exchange V^7 for V in one of the examples to see the improvement in voice leading brought about by the V^7. This chord may also be used to prevent parallel octaves. ►[Ex. 115]◄

All these examples provide additional evidence of the contrapuntal influence to be found in harmonic progressions. This fact, however, in no way detracts from the overwhelmingly harmonic significance of these progressions.

G.   The use of two harmonic progressions in succession

There are many instances in which a theme or melodic phrase is supported by two successive harmonic progressions. ►[Ex. 116]◄ serves as an illustration of this technique, which may show a succession of various types of harmonic progressions; here the end of the first harmonic progression is simultaneously the beginning of the second.

KEYBOARD AND WRITTEN EXERCISES

1) Add Ex. 112-116 to the repertoire of keyboard exercises. Practice them in all major and minor keys and explain their meaning.
2) Write the same examples in chorale style in several major and minor keys. Observe good voice leading.

H.   Harmonic progressions supporting melodic embellishments

All the harmonic progressions given so far support melodic progressions. Discussion of the harmonic concept would be incomplete, however, without reference to the fact that harmonic progressions often support the other elementary type of melodic motion, the melodic embellishment. As indicated in the preceding chapter, the melodic embellishment, in contrast to the melodic progression, circles around one tone. The next examples show various melodic embellishments supported not by contrapuntal, but by harmonic progressions. ▶[Ex. 117]◀

KEYBOARD AND WRITTEN EXERCISES

1) Practice all examples in Ex. 117 at the keyboard in all major and minor keys.
2) Write the same examples in chorale style in several major and minor keys.

I.   Summary and outlook

The harmonic progressions presented throughout this chapter show the harmonic element in its most concentrated form. When these progressions have been mastered in written form and at the keyboard the study of harmony in its purest form, as a complementary discipline to two- and three-part pure counterpoint, will have been completed.

The essence of counterpoint lies in the flow of horizontal lines. In three-part counterpoint, these lines result vertically in chords which are connected solely on the basis of motion and voice leading. In contrast to this type of chord connection, harmonic progressions are based on chord relationships. A chord has a harmonic function only if it proves to be a member of one of the five harmonic progressions in its complete or incomplete form (the latter is shown in Chapter VI).

It is an interesting fact that, in most cases when the II, III, IV and VI chords are not used as intermediary harmonies between I and V, i.e. if they do not come from I and proceed to V, they then lose their original harmonic significance and become contrapuntal chords. Separated from the progression I-V, these chords have a contrapuntal function eliminating any possible harmonic implication.

All harmonic impulse is basically directed from the I to the V and on to the final I. Even though the III and the IV have a harmonic association with I, this association is superseded by the stronger over-all drive to the V, which causes each intermediary harmony such as the II, III, IV or VI, not to retard but to elaborate that motion to the V. This drive to V, however, would be impaired, if two intermediary harmonies such as II-IV, III-II or VI-II appeared between I and V. One of these intermediary harmonies would offset the impulse of the other in elaborating the drive to the V. It will be observed throughout the book that there is seldom room for doubt as to whether the IV or the II, the III or the II, etc. is the salient harmonic force between the I and V. Once the V has been reached the final I is due; sometimes the V is prolonged to delay the appearance of the I which remains the ultimate goal of a complete harmonic progression.

It will be the purpose of the following chapters to demonstrate the application of the harmonic and contrapuntal concepts to composition.

Part II   Chapter Five

Structure and Prolongation I

In the two preceding chapters, harmony and counterpoint were separated to the greatest possible extent in order to present their fundamental characteristics. It was seen that they originate from very different conceptions and represent very different attitudes towards the problems of musical continuity. While counterpoint and contrapuntal progressions represent the element of motion, harmonic progressions, through the harmonic associations of their members, create stable, but limited musical organisms; they represent musical organization and entity in its most basic and concentrated form. Thus the forces of motion and the forces of stability are brought into juxtaposition.

To a great extent, the problems of tonality and tonal composition (regardless of style) do not result from either harmony or counterpoint alone, but are the outgrowth of a combination of these two contrasting forces. Therefore, it is essential, at this point, to explain how they have been combined for the purpose of creating an artistic whole. While Part III deals with this problem from a historical aspect, in this and the following chapters a very advanced stage of this combination will be discussed. In this advanced stage compositions show varied and clearly defined functions of harmony and counterpoint which result in a few clearly discernible principles of construction.

One of these principles of tonal construction and organization conceives of the harmonic progressions as a framework, which receives its life, color and interest from the contrapuntal-melodic progressions and chords, creating the motion within the framework of harmonic chords.

It has been one of those great and basically inexplicable phenomena in the development of western music that two contrasting musical conceptions have combined in such a way that each has become a part of the other, instead of their being applied alternatively, each living for its own expression. Chapter II touched upon this fact; it will now be explained systematically.

A. Contrapuntal chords or progressions within the harmonic framework

I. PASSING CHORDS—VOICE-LEADING CHORDS

a. Passing chords

In Chapter IV, most bass progressions from I to V or to the intermediary harmonies II⁶ and IV were indicated as ascending motions, because the natural position of V is above I. This procedure, however, in no way indicates that ascending bass motions are more frequently used in composition than descending progressions. If, for instance, the bass descends from I to II⁶, which happens just as often as it ascends, the interval outlined is that of a fifth.

This interval may be filled either with one passing note which creates a motion in thirds, or with several passing notes in stepwise progression. Such bass progressions may generate one or several passing chords within the harmonic framework of I-II⁶-V-I. ►[Ex. 118]◄ The coherent bass motion directed from C to F makes it clear that the above progressions show a drive from I to II⁶ via one or more other chords before proceeding to V and the final I. Concentrating on Ex. 118a, we realize that it is the function of the chord of the submediant to connect the I with the II⁶. Thus the A chord, as a result of voice direction and connection, is a chord derived from a contrapuntal conception; it is a *passing chord*. As such it has a completely different function than the I or the II⁶ which, together with V and the final I, form a harmonic framework. This framework appears slightly prolonged through the insertion of a contrapuntal element in the form of a passing chord. In order to distinguish between harmonic and contrapuntal chords, only harmonic chords will be marked with Roman numerals. A passing motion will be indicated by an arrow.

Whereas Ex. 118b shows a slight intensification of the first progression, the additional passing tones in the top voice as well as in the bass help to create a series of several passing chords (see Ex. 118c). The presence of these passing chords (the sixth chords on B, A and G) increases the contrapuntal factor which in turn heightens the elements of direction and prolongation between I and II⁶. Although this II⁶ is a sixth chord too, its function is completely different from the three preceding chords in first inversion. The fact that the direction of the bass changes right after the II⁶ and the fact that this harmony moves on to V makes the II⁶ not only a pivotal chord but also a member of the harmonic progression I-II⁶-V-I. Again we see (we remind the reader of the first examples of Chapter II) that chords with similar grammatical symbols may have very different functions. The dominant in meas. 3 is a member of the harmonic framework with a structural significance, whereas the dominant sixth chord in meas. 1 is a contrapuntal chord, a passing chord, and thus a chord of prolonging significance.

In summary, it may be stated that the harmonic and the contrapuntal concepts have been combined to create coherent musical progressions.

The next examples ►[Ex. 119, 120]◄ present illustrations closely resembling the progressions of Ex. 118a and b.

Although the passing chords in the above progressions are placed between I and an inversion of II or IIⁱ, it happens frequently that passing chords are found between I and the root position of the supertonic chord. Through inversion of the bass, which by nature moves a second upward, the composer can gain the greater space of a seventh downwards which opens the way for the use of several passing chords. ►[Ex. 121]◄ Here we encounter two triads in root position, the submediant and the subdominant, as passing chords between I and II. To call such a progression a harmonic progression I-VI-IV-II-V-I shows a complete disregard of the various functions chords may fulfill. It is time now to recall one of the statements made in the summary of Chapter IV. It was pointed out there that two intermediate harmonies of equal strength would impair the drive to the V, because each would offset the impulse of the other in elaborating this drive. I believe that the student will recognize without difficulty that in Ex. 121 the II is the one salient harmonic force between I and V, and that neither the VI nor the IV can be classified as an intermediary harmony. Since the bass shows a coherent progression to the II, at which point the direction changes, it is the function of the VI and the IV to connect and prolong this progression. These chords therefore are passing chords on the way from I to II, both of which are members of the harmonic framework I-II-V-I.

An example illustrating passing chords between I and II can be found at the beginning of Bach's Chorale No. 348. ►[Ex. 122]◄ This phrase also serves to show that a harmonic chord may be found on a weak beat, the fourth beat, whereas the subdominant chord which the bass motion indicates to be a passing chord is placed on the stronger third beat. There are even instances in which a passing chord is put on the first beat of a measure as in the Chorale phrase quoted. ►[Ex. 123]◄ In the first measure the I appears expanded; on the fourth beat of this measure the bass starts to move directly from G via E to C where it changes direction by going to D, the bass of the dominant chord, which in turn is followed by the I. Thus the E-minor chord, in spite of its position on the first beat, remains a passing chord between I and II⁶₅; and the V, though set in the weakest possible rhythmic position (the second eighth-note of the second beat), constitutes the V of the harmonic framework I-II⁶₅-V-I. This example illustrates that rhythmic position per se is not indicative of a chord's function. The factor actually determining whether or not a chord has harmonic or contrapuntal function will always be its position within the voice-leading pattern and the purpose it fulfills within that pattern.

Sometimes passing chords require the addition of a specific contrapuntal technique (acquired in pure counterpoint) in order to achieve satisfactory voice leading. If we listen to the progressions in ►[Ex. 124]◄ the passing-chord function of the G⁶ and F⁶ chord is obvious. They would create a succession of parallel fifths, however, if the progression of 7-6 syncopations were not used to provide better voice leading.

EXERCISES I

1) As a review, explain the meaning of all preceding examples in this chapter. In regard to this and all future exercises, it must be emphasized that real understanding is achieved only if the student can define and clarify a problem. For this reason, exercises of this kind are of utmost importance.

2) Practice Ex. 118, 121, 124 at the keyboard in several major and minor keys using either keyboard or chorale style. Always plan the progression in advance and keep in mind which technique is illustrated. To memorize chords without understanding their function will never lead to structural hearing.

3) After doing these exercises it is particularly important for the student to find other passages from the literature, illustrating the techniques discussed so far.

b. Passing chords improving voice leading

In the progressions in Ex. 124 our attention was focused on the achievement of good voice leading. This ever-acute problem presents itself most strikingly whenever the outer voices both move downward starting in the position of an octave or tenth. ►[Ex. 125, 126]◄ The juxtaposition of progressions with good and bad voice leading shows

that in Ex. 125 parallel fifths have been avoided through the use of the
5-6 technique. In Ex. 126 the octaves have been avoided by means of
an 8-10 progression. In minor keys the II, a diminished triad, is often
replaced by the II⁷, the II⁶₅ or the II⁶. ►[Ex. 127]◄ In each of the preceding examples all chords between I and II are passing chords; even
those on the second beats in Ex. 126, where only the top voice participates in the passing motion, can be classified as such because they take
part in carrying the motion downward. However, all chords on the
second beat in all three examples have a voice-leading function in addition to their main function as passing chords; they promote good voice
leading. Chords which fulfill such a function are called *voice-leading
chords*. Thus the chords on the second beats are simultaneously passing
and voice-leading chords. We shall presently return to this latter chord
function.

The student must realize that the power of the contrapuntal element
within the framework of the harmonic progressions has increased considerably. In the above examples the progression from I to II has been
extended or prolonged. This prolongation is made possible by the inversion of a normally ascending second not only in the bass, as seen in
Ex. 121, but also in the top voice. ►[Ex. 128]◄ Such an inversion creates a wider space and makes the introduction of more passing chords
possible. It is these passing chords that carry the motion from I to II.

The combination of contrapuntal with harmonic technique has produced a significant development of the original conception of passing
chords as derived from the principles of pure counterpoint. The instinctive recognition of the coherence existing between members of a harmonic progression makes it possible to separate those members, even
more than has been shown so far, without causing a loosening of their
structural contact. The artistic separation and simultaneous connection
of those members is expressed in terms of musical motion through
counterpoint and contrapuntal progressions. Pure counterpoint tends to
move for the sake of motion. Here, motion and its logical execution, not
motion to a structural goal (excluding purely melodic goals, such as the
highest or lowest note) are the prime objectives. On the other hand,
harmonic chords, with their strong inner coherence, are virtually predestined to establish structural points which in turn give added purpose
to the contrapuntal progressions directed from one of these points to
another. Thus the principles of pure counterpoint are no longer the sole
determining factors for the validity of voice leading. It is the greater
structural power of direction to a structural goal which makes prolongations of pure contrapuntal techniques possible.

EXERCISES II

1) As a review, explain the contents and the meaning of Ex. 125, 126, 127.
2) Practice these progressions in several major and minor keys.

c. Voice-leading chords

We frequently encounter chords which have a voice-leading function without having a passing function at the same time. If, for instance, we want to support the melody of an ascending third with the harmonic progression I-II-V-I, the first inversion of II achieves more satisfactory voice leading. However, should the composer wish to use the II in root position, a contrapuntal device may be employed to improve the voice leading, namely, the insertion of a chord between I and II. For this purpose the subdominant chord or the first inversion of the I, though weaker, are best suited. Examples with several voice-leading chords (6 chords and ⁶₅ chords) are added. ►[Ex. 129]◄

The next progressions show the use of voice-leading chords within the harmonic framework of I-IV-V-I. ►[Ex. 130]◄

EXERCISES III

1) Explain the contents and the meaning of the preceding examples.
2) Practice Ex. 129 and 130 in several major and minor keys. (Omit Ex. 129b in minor keys.)

d. Summary and outlook

The preceding paragraphs have emphasized the passing chord rather than the voice-leading chord, despite the important role played by the latter. The introduction of a passing chord, or even more conspicuously, of a series of such chords into the framework provided by the harmonic progressions proves to be an architectonic idea of far-reaching consequence. It constitutes a most striking factor in the long list of techniques which result from the combination of harmonic and contrapuntal concepts. In order to hear and understand the significance of chords as passing chords and to enable the ear to penetrate to the structural goal of a motion, a sense for musical direction has to be developed. While these problems could only be hinted at in Chapter II for the sake of defining the basic functions of harmony and counterpoint, systematic discussion of them has now been undertaken.

After simple exercises and examples have been shown to the student, the teacher is perfectly justified in presenting more involved passages from the literature. A precondition for the choice of such examples, however, is a clear and definite motion of the bass. As long as the bass gives a definite indication of the over-all direction, such excerpts will be of great value to the student. His sense for musical direction will be strengthened even though some aspects in these passages—such as the structure of the melody, the relation of the top voice to the bass, chromaticism, etc.—have not yet been discussed and explained. In many sections, the course of the bass gives such conclusive indication of the music's direction that an early concentration on it will prove extremely helpful. Three such passages are now cited. The first is taken from Chopin's Waltz in A minor, meas. 17 to 24. ►[Ex. 131]◄

The bass shows a clear, straightforward motion from I to IV, the IV filling two measures before proceeding to V. The chords between I and IV thus appear as passing chords. As far as the melody is concerned the student's attention need only be drawn to the fact that the sequential motion is changed just before the IV is reached. This change heightens the significance of the subdominant and increases the feeling of drive to that point.

At the beginning of the Gavotte from Bach's Fifth French Suite, the first impression might be of a drive from I to V via four passing chords. ►[Ex. 132]◄ More careful listening, however, proves that the bass leads straight downward to the IV, followed by a change of direction by going up to the V. This motion indicates a harmonic framework not of I-V-I, but rather of I-IV-V-I (Graph a). Another example is the opening of Brahms' Sonata, Op 5. ►[Ex. 133]◄

For a more extended passage, the reader is advised to turn to the first twelve measures of Chopin's Prelude No. 4 in E minor. This example will help to prepare him for the large-scale passing motions which will demand his attention in the later portions of this book. It takes the bass ten measures to proceed from the tonic to the V. The ear must be gradually strengthened in order not to lose its way in such a passage and in even larger passages. It is important to keep the starting-point of the motion in mind and not to be distracted by possible temporary stops and delays. This sense of direction is essential in order to follow and understand those broadly conceived ideas of which the literature of music presents such remarkable examples.

The recognition of bass motions and their direction provides highly valuable ear training and the student is now advised to find passages from the literature in which similar types of motion occur.

2.   THE CHORD OF MELODIC EMPHASIS OR COLOR CHORD

Another chord of contrapuntal origin is the chord of melodic emphasis. At present we shall deal only briefly with this chord because its full significance will be better appreciated if it is shown in larger and more complex examples. It is neither a passing chord nor a voice-leading chord; it serves solely to provide a counterpoint and a chordal support to a melody tone, without improving the voice leading or contributing to the phrase's direction. ►[Ex. 134]◄

This chord has no structural necessity, but it enriches the pattern of a phrase and provides color and chordal variety.

3.   THE NEIGHBOR-NOTE CHORD

Next to the passing chord, it is the neighbor-note chord (N) which introduces the strongest contrapuntal factor into composition. We shall begin with the shortest and simplest possible examples which will provide adequate preparation for later and more complex ornamental motions. ►[Ex. 135]◄ In the first example both outer voices perform a neighbor-note motion, thus presenting the most complete form of this ornamental construction. In the second, only the top voice shows a neighbor note while the bass skips; still, because of the top voice and the return of the bass F to C, the function of the F chord as a neighbor-note chord is unchanged.[1]

A great variety of neighbor-note chords is possible and we shall present various examples. The neighbor note may ornament either the root, third or fifth of the triad. By using upper and lower neighbor notes the resulting chords may be triads in root position and in both inversions, seventh chords in all inversions and the diminished seventh chord. ►[Ex. 136, 137]◄

Neighbor-note chords also result if the bass is sustained, producing the so-called pedal point. ►[Ex. 138]◄ Several forms of the neighbor-note chord may arise if the ornamental motion takes place in the middle

---

[1] Such contrapuntal organisms must not be mistaken for the earlier mentioned harmonic treatment of melodic neighbor notes (see Chapter IV, Ex. 117). There is a definite distinction between harmonic and contrapuntal neighbor-note chords.

voices. ►[Ex. 139]◄ [2] The following excerpts are offered to illustrate some of the progressions just discussed. The student should discover for himself which of these progressions have been illustrated. ►[Ex. 140-145]◄

In contrast to the complete neighbor note which returns to the main tone, the incomplete neighbor note follows the main tone but does not return to it. Such a neighbor note supported by a chord produces the *incomplete neighbor-note chord*, indicated by IN. ►[Ex. 146a]◄ In the following practically identical example, the return to the main tone is visible rather than audible because the eighth-note E of the melody is a passing tone between the neighbor note and the following main tone. The subdominant chord thus remains an incomplete neighbor-note chord. ►[Ex. 146b]◄

The beginning of Bach's Little Prelude in C minor offers a good illustration of the incomplete neighbor-note chord supported by a pedal-point bass. ►[Ex. 147]◄

If one of the outer voices presents a neighbor note and the other a passing note, the resulting chord is a *neighbor-passing chord*, which is indicated by $\frac{N}{P}$. ►[Ex. 148]◄ It would be misleading to call such a chord either a neighbor-note chord *or* a passing chord since it exhibits the characteristics of both.

EXERCISES IV

The student is required:

1) to explain the meaning of the terms: complete and incomplete neighbor-note chords, neighbor-passing chords.
2) to practice Ex. 135-139, 146, 147a, 148, in several major and minor keys. In presenting Ex. 135-139 the student, before playing the progressions, should always define the chord which serves as a neighbor-note chord.

*
*   *

The neighbor-note chord, like the passing chord, serves the purpose of motion and prolongation. Whereas the passing chord signifies a motion between two different chords, the neighbor-note chord helps to create an embellishing or ornamental motion around one chord.

---

[2] In progressions showing a skip in the bass to the subdominant, submediant or mediant, their general embellishing quality may be stronger than their specific neighbor-note character. This impression is enhanced if the top voice also shows no direct neighbor-note motion. In such cases these chords may be termed embellishing chords (Em); see Ex. 313.

This brings us to the technique of *chord prolongation* which has already been touched upon and whose significance for the development of western music can hardly be exaggerated. Further demonstrations of the neighbor-note chord are futile until the meaning and implications of chord prolongation have been discussed in detail.

B. Chord prolongation
(Movement around and within one chord)

The roots of chord prolongation lie in pure counterpoint. It is based on the principle revealed in counterpoint that several tones can stand for the one tone that dominates a group of tones. Thus in ►[Ex. 149]◄, whether a neighbor-note motion or a melodic embellishment is used, the tone E or the interval of a tenth is given elaborated expression by use of tones other than E and intervals other than the tenth. Similarly in three-part counterpoint, the fleeting appearance of chords other than the main chord does not weaken the effect of the main chord. ►[Ex. 150]◄

From this melodic-contrapuntal concept probably grew the recognition that the structural value of *one* chord may be prolonged with the help of *several* other chords. Looking back at Ex. 135b, it is now clear that the F-Major chord subordinates itself to the C chord which it helps to prolong. This progression of tonic-subdominant-tonic creates a small organism which prolongs the I in C major, as indicated by the bracket. ►[Ex. 151]◄ This technique is called chord prolongation.

It follows that all examples cited to illustrate the use of the neighbor-note chord also represent chord prolongations or, to be more precise, contrapuntal chord prolongations, since the prolongation is achieved by a contrapuntal progression.

Once the significance of the neighbor-note chord as a chord prolonging factor has been clarified, an additional illustration can now be shown to good advantage. ►[Ex. 152]◄ This excerpt presents neighbor-note chords which cause a broad prolongation of the C chord. In the added voice-leading graph the phrase is traced back to the C chord which the entire phrase so beautifully expresses.

A combination of upper and lower neighbor notes creates the so-called melodic turn. When the melodic turn is supported by a contrapuntal bass, we arrive again at contrapuntal chord progressions which give expression to one single chord (chord prolongation). ►[Ex. 153]◄ The brackets indicate the location of the turn in different voices. Three phrases by C. P. E. Bach, Chopin and Josquin des Prés may serve as illustrations ►[Ex. 154, 155, 156]◄

Often the bass appears in the form of a pedal point. ►[Ex. 157]◄ The beginning of Bach's D-minor Prelude gives an example of the combination of pedal point and turn. ►[Ex. 158]◄

All of these chord prolongations can be characterized as motions around one chord.

The next examples present melodic turns counterpointed with a slightly freer bass motion. ►[Ex. 159]◄ The technique as demonstrated in Ex. a appears more elaborated in a phrase from a Bach Chorale. ►[Ex. 160]◄ The tones D and C of the top voice, meas. 1, are embellishing tones of E. These tones receive their own counterpoint in the bass in the form of a descending third; as parallelism, the next measure also contains a descending third, which in addition provides the counterpoint for the passing tone E of the top voice (Graph a).

Prolongation of the neighbor note leads to the melodic embellishment. Several examples of melodic embellishments with supporting contrapuntal bass progressions and their resulting chords are now presented. ►[Ex. 161]◄ Such progressions may be found often in the literature. ►[Ex. 162 and 163]◄

EXERCISES V

1) Explain the meaning of chord prolongation.
2) Practice Ex. 152a, 153, 157, 159 and 161 in several major and minor keys; explain the contents and characteristics of all examples.

*
*   *

I am of course aware that apart from the concept of chord prolongation, the contrapuntal interpretation of all the progressions given above is at great variance with the orientation of present-day textbooks. I mention this not in order to dwell upon differences of approach but to make the point and the readings presented unequivocally clear. For instance, the question might arise as to why Ex. 152 is regarded as a contrapuntal progression. Why not read a harmonic progression I-II²-V⁶₅-I? It is highly significant that in spite of the actual chord succession of tonic-supertonic-dominant-tonic, the events of the bass motion such as the suspension and the neighbor note completely absorb any harmonic characteristics which one might at first be inclined to acknowledge. The bass has been deprived through contrapuntal melodic devices of its possible harmonic implication. It is a *melodic and not a harmonic bass* that we encounter in this phrase. We are thus confronted with a contrapuntal, not a harmonic progression. One has only to support the right-hand part with a typically "harmonic" bass and compare this bass with the one used by Bach, in order to understand the fundamental difference in conception. ▶[Ex. 164]◀ Version b avoids the typically harmonic bass motion to the V in root position (typical because it is so indicative of the main harmonic characteristic, the fifth relationship). Thus the succession of tonic-supertonic-dominant-tonic, per se, does not always imply a harmonic progression; whether a progression is contrapuntal or harmonic depends first of all on the bass position of the dominant. To deny the importance of this distinction and to assume that the only difference between the two versions of Ex. 164 consists in the difference in chord position (root position or inversion) means sacrificing the vital element of counterpoint to what is wrongly supposed to be an all-powerful and dominating harmonic conception. The differences therefore between both versions are not merely those of chord position but those of conception, the harmonic versus the contrapuntal.

The contrapuntal character of the bass is even more pronounced in a progression such as that presented in Ex. 161b. Such progressions are usually termed harmonic; one interprets the VII⁶ as a substitution for the V [I-IV-VII⁶ (for V)-I]. This substitution is considered a mere exchange of chords with no important implication. Although it is not intended here to rule out the principle of substitution in the construction of musical coherence, this principle can be accepted only when the basic significance of a phrase or progression is not affected by substitution. But the whole meaning of a phrase is certainly affected by interpreting it either harmonically or contrapuntally. ▶[Ex. 165]◀ In b) we hear a melodic connection between F and C in the bass which provides a good counterpoint to the ascending melodic line of the top voice from C to E; the skip from C to F in the bass brings the outer voices into a contrapuntally favorable position insofar as they may proceed from that point in contrary motion; the following chords are a direct result of this contrapuntal contrary motion. Listening to a) one might argue that a I-IV-V-I progression would have caused voice-leading problems (parallel fifths) between IV and V and that, therefore, the V had to be substituted for by a VII⁶. Even granting that this conception was the motivating force which created the bass in Ex. 165b, it still remains an indisputable fact that the substitution of VII⁶ for V eliminates the fundamental harmonic characteristic of the fifth relationship in the form of I-V$\frac{5}{3}$-I, and that in avoiding this harmonic character-istic, the progression becomes contrapuntal. It is therefore entirely mis-leading to cling *à tout prix* to a harmonic conception and to ignore the contrapuntal character of such a bass. The VII[6] implies more than just a substitute for the harmonic V; it implies a contrapuntal conception and not a mere exchange of chords within the same harmonic conception; the VII[6] is always a contrapuntal chord.

It is one of the greatest achievements of western music that the de-velopment of the harmonic concept has not overpowered the contra-puntal concept. The former has been applied instead in such a way as to allow the contrapuntal concept to develop fully its own characteristic function, so that it is even possible for whole phrases and units to be dominated by counterpoint and its progressions.

Within progressions and phrases giving expression to one prolonged chord we have to make a certain distinction between such progressions as Ex. 161e and f on the one hand, and Ex. 161a, b, c, d, on the other hand. The former achieve chord prolongation through a quasi-circling motion *around* the main chord. The latter—through a motion of one of the outer voices outlining and filling an interval of the main chord—give the impression rather of moving *within* the chord. Here a chord interval appears *horizontalized*. ►[Ex. 166]◄

Although it will be shown later that the bass has the power of giving various interpretations to the structure of the top voice we can state that a melody horizontalizing the interval of a chord is particularly suitable as top voice of that chord's prolongation; for, by moving within one chord the melody gives added emphasis to the architectonic idea of a single chord's prolongation. This characteristic of moving within rather than around a chord also appears in chord prolongations where the top voice shows a melodic progression filling one of the chord intervals, thus moving from one tone to another instead of circling around a single tone. ►[Ex. 167]◄ Ex. f shows the combination of a neighbor-note motion and a melodic progression.

To grasp fully the significance of such examples it is important for the student to compare preceding passages such as Ex. 121-125, with Ex. 160, 161, 162, 163, and 167.

In all of these examples a musical organism has been created. In the former group, the harmonic progressions are the unifying power; the direction of the tones and chords is determined by the disposition of the members of a harmonic progression. In the latter group, however, the chord progressions do not lie within a harmonic framework, since not one of these chords is the member of a harmonic progression. Both the architectonic conception of chord prolongation and its realization give meaning and unification to the latter group of examples.

Three excerpts follow which illustrate chord prolongation by movement within a chord. ►[Ex. 168, 169, 170]◄ As far as the first example is concerned, one might have expected a $^6_4$ chord on the first quarter of meas. 2. Bach replaced it with the G⁶ chord which provides for a more melodic bass motion. The student will easily recognize which progressions of Ex. 167 are illustrated by these three excerpts.

EXERCISES VI

1) The student is required to find more examples illustrating the organizing power of harmonic progressions and showing the architectonic idea of chord prolongation.
2) Practice Ex. 167 in several major and minor keys.

Movement within one chord is most clearly defined if both outer voices horizontalize intervals of the prolonged chord. ►[Ex. 171]◄ Whereas these examples are relatively extended, chord prolongations may be extremely brief. ►[Ex. 172]◄

Turning again to the progressions of Ex. 171, it seems evident that the element of motion and direction is greatly intensified, since both outer voices proceed from one tone to another. We are therefore justified in calling the chords between the two tonics passing chords. However, these are passing chords within the framework of one single prolonged chord whereas previously we encountered passing chords connecting two different harmonies. This distinction, as will be shown later, is important for understanding musical direction.

If one outer voice shows an embellishing motion and the other a passing motion, the resulting chords may be called embellishing-passing chords. ►[Ex. 173]◄

EXERCISES VII

1) Explain the difference between Ex. 171a and Ex. 173.
2) Practice Ex. 171, 172, 173 in several major and minor keys.
3) The student is also advised to observe carefully the use of 6, $^6_4$, $^6_5$, $^4_3$ chords throughout this chapter as passing, neighbor-note or embellishing chords.

SUMMARY

In all of the examples from Ex. 135 through Ex. 173 the structural value of one chord has been extended through various techniques of prolongation, summed up under the term "chord prolongation." In chord prolongation, one chord governs a progression of various chords; these different chords are subordinated to that one chord which they help to express and prolong. Two main types of chord prolongation have been accounted for, namely:

1) Chord prolongation through movement *around* one chord, with both outer voices circling around tones of the chord.

2) Chord prolongation through movement *within* one chord, with one or both outer voices horizontalizing or filling in an interval of the chord.

Both types may find their expression in connection with a pedal-point bass.

C.   Application of chord prolongation
(Direct and indirect motion)

Although chord prolongation may constitute the organizing factor of a whole phrase (see Ex. 160), the question arises as to the role this technique plays in connection with the harmonic concept. What is the role of chord prolongation in regard to harmonic progressions and their function as the framework of a phrase or passage?

Several phrases from Bach's Chorales will illustrate how chord prolongation may be combined with harmonic progressions. ►[Ex. 174, 175, 176, 177]◄

Before going into details we must realize that all of these illustrations show one common factor of prime importance. The contrapuntal chord prolongation is the subordinated part of a larger organism which is outlined by the framework of a harmonic progression. In these examples, the I has been prolonged before proceeding to the V, II or IV. Again the harmonic framework is extended by contrapuntal chords.

We now find that these chords are applied in two different ways. Either they enrich and improve the voice leading and fill in the space between two harmonic chords (see Ex. 121-134), or they help to prolong a single harmonic chord as illustrated above.

The two different ways of applying contrapuntal chords imply two kinds of motion, one direct and the other indirect. Contrapuntal chords, especially passing chords, between two harmonic chords indicate direct motion. The music really moves from one point to another; it drives ahead to a new structural point, the stress is thus more on direction than on prolongation.

On the other hand, contrapuntal chords prolonging a single harmonic chord foster a more indirect type of motion. Here the element of direction is weaker, and a delaying effect is apparent. Frequently compositions express these two types very clearly and definitely; quite often, however, we hear passages which show various shadings of motion tending either to the one or to the other type.

Returning now to the four Chorale phrases of Ex. 174-177, we hear first a broadening, lingering effect through the movement around or within the I (indirect motion) before the motion proceeds to other members of the harmonic framework. The student should carefully compare former examples such as those cited in Ex. 121-134 with those of Ex. 174-177. His ear will come gradually to differentiate between the direct motion of the preceding group and the indirect motion of the chord prolongations in the latter group.

If we now compare the chord prolongations of these four excerpts and include in this comparison Ex. II (Part I), it will be found that some chord prolongations present a more self-contained impression than others. The strongest and most self-contained type is represented in Ex. II. The prolongation of the I ends on a strong beat with the main chord in root position, after which the bass leaps to the V. In itself, the prolongation shows no tendency to move to that V. Slightly less self-contained are the prolongations of Ex. 174 and 175; coming as it does on the weak fourth beat, the end of the prolongation is weaker, so that there is a slightly stronger feeling of direction to the following harmony. This impression is also created by phrases like the one in Ex. 176, which shows the I in first inversion at the end of its prolongation. Such prolongations are more "open" and thus have a greater tendency to move on than those in preceding phrases. A definite tendency to move on, in spite of the governing chord prolongation, can be noted in Ex. 177, in which the whole motion within I shows a direct impulse to the IV^7, as the bass drives from D directly to the G of the IV^7; it is this continuing bass motion which considerably weakens the I^6, the end of the chord prolongation.

Thus even within a prolonged chord there may be tendencies of motion of varying degree. These are the "shadings" of motion mentioned above, which may weaken the end of the chord prolongation and so contribute to the organic coherence of the whole phrase. Such subtle but, nonetheless, important characteristics influence the motion and its direction. The student is urged to listen carefully to these fine distinctions.

EXERCISES VIII

The following brief examples illustrate the different meanings of musical motion within a prolonged I. ►[Ex. 178]◄ The top voice in each case prolongs the tone E with an embellishing motion of a descending third before proceeding to D. This top voice motion makes chord prolongation entirely logical; the different shadings of motion within the prolonged I need no further comment.

The student should be able to explain the differences and the similarities between Ex. 174, 175, 176, and 177; he should then proceed to play Ex. 178 in several major and minor keys.

D.   Structure and prolongation

Throughout this chapter, terms such as "harmonic framework," "chord prolongation," "chords of structure and prolongation," and so on, have been used. The illustrations of their meaning in connection with the examples have probably made it clear by now that these terms indicate the existence of additional functions which chords may fulfill beyond those of a harmonic or contrapuntal nature. In fact, the terms imply architectonic functions of tones and chords in regard to the fundamental problem of musical motion, its direction and organization as a whole.

It is thus highly significant that chords may fulfill structural or prolonging functions as well as harmonic or contrapuntal functions. Invariably it has been found in the above excerpts that the members of a harmonic progression have simultaneously a structural significance in relation to the meaning of a phrase as a whole, whereas contrapuntal chords, besides their specific contrapuntal functions, have prolonging implications.

So far, two chord functions, *harmonic-structural* and *contrapuntal-prolonging* have been introduced. The harmonic progressions indicate the structural points of the whole phrase; the various types of contrapuntal chords either expand those points (chord prolongation), connect them or serve voice-leading or embellishing purposes; for these diverse tasks we may use the common denomination of chords of prolongation. In addition it has been seen that the melody cooperates strongly with the chord functions. There is even an interpendency between the functions of melody tones and those of chords. Listening to Ex. 174 and 175, we find that the embellishing and thus prolonging tones around C♯ and F♯ are supported by contrapuntal-prolonging chords. Similarily the structural tones of the melody are supported by harmonic-structural chords.[3]

More and more we will take the melody and its direction into consideration because, as will be seen, problems of analysis and composition are largely based on the relation between melody and bass. A melody may admit of different structural interpretations. It is the bass, and consequently the chords, which can eliminate this possible ambiguity. This points to the interdependency of melody and bass, just mentioned before. For an illustration we may turn to the beginning of a Chorale. ►[Ex. 179]◄

Let us compare this phrase with that of Ex. 177. These examples are different settings of the same melody, except for the omission of the second eighth-note in meas. 1 of the C-minor phrase. Concentrating on the melody (in the D-minor version) we can have no doubt that its basic direction shows a descending fifth, A-G-F-E-D; and whereas there can be no doubt either about the structural tones F-E-D in meas. 2, the question arises as to which A and which G in meas. 1 constitute the structural tones. It will be shown that in this respect two different readings of this same melody are possible. ►[Ex. 180]◄ Graph a demonstrates an embellishment of the tone A by the horizontalization of the third A-F; this reading makes A the structural tone which retains its value until the fourth quarter of meas. 1. After this the direct descent to D takes place.

On the other hand, Graph b shows that the identical melody may be interpreted as starting to descend structurally with the third quarter of meas. 1. This reading makes the descending third at the beginning of meas. 1 a short embellishment of A which moves to G as the next structural tone; the last two eighth-notes of that measure are embellishing notes which embellish the following structural note, F.[4]

Both readings have been used by Bach, the one (a) for the D-minor version, the other (b) for the C-minor version. For the sake of clarity,

[3] The direction of voice leading and the different functions of tones and chords have been and will increasingly be indicated in graphs which we call *voice-leading graphs*. As the ability of writing correct graphs, together with the detailed understanding of their meaning can be expected to develop only gradually, no special rules for their writing are given here. Although more is said about the meaning of the graphs on p. 142 f. of this chapter, and about their terminology in the Glossary of Vol. II, a clear way of indicating the voice leading must grow naturally out of the correct hearing of a musical organism.

[4] See the discussion of embellishing tones above the structural melody tone in Chapter II.

the voice-leading graphs of both versions may now be placed in juxtaposition. ►[Ex. 181]◄

Clearly it is the bass and, consequently, the distribution of harmonic chords and their prolongations in the form of contrapuntal chords, that cause us to read the melody in two different ways in the two versions. For instance the bass—and thus the chord progression of meas. 1 of Ex. 177—indicates a prolongation of the D-minor tonic so definitely that the melody tone A becomes the logical structural top voice tone of that chord. Likewise in Ex. 179, the IV⁶ must be interpreted as a harmonic chord since it comes from I and leads to V; consequently the melody tone F (third quarter-note) receives structural emphasis. The strong $^6_4$ chord on the dominant tone G draws the embellishing tones and their bass tones E♭ and F into its orbit; the resulting embellishing chords prolong the structural value of the $^6_4$ chord.

Finally several excerpts are given showing that two or more small prolongations can be so closely interwoven as to produce one larger chord prolongation before proceeding to the following harmonic chord. The graphs of ►[Ex. 182, 183]◄ explain the interwoven combination of small prolongations under the structural cover of the I which thus appears prolonged. In both examples, particularly in the second, the end of the prolongation is weak so that the feeling of motion and direction to II (Ex. 182) and V (Ex. 183) is intensified.

We come now to a tendency of prolongations to branch off into further details and diminutions. Three examples illustrate this tendency of what appears as a prolongation of the prolongation. In the following illustration, ►[Ex. 184]◄ the neighbor-note chord (Graph b) is prolonged by an embellishing motion of the top voice and a neighbor-note movement of the alto to F which as a further offshoot produces the prolonging F⁶ chord (Graph a).

More complex is the prolongation of the neighbor-note chord in the following phrase. ►[Ex. 185]◄ Comparing graphs c and b the student will realize that the B♭ chord constitutes the main prolongation of the F chord. The B♭ chord itself, however, appears prolonged by its own neighbor-note chord, the C chord. Graph a illustrates additional small prolongations; the incomplete neighbor tone G (meas. 3) has its counterpoint and this creates another neighbor-note chord. The final B♭ chord is prolonged too, which gives added variety and emphasis to the melodic tone F. The Bartók excerpt ►[Ex. 186]◄ shows subtle prolongations of the main prolonging $^4_2$ chord which is indicated in Graph b. The reader should observe (see Graph a) a certain apparent independence of the neighbor-note motions of the left hand part in relation to

the neighbor-note motion of the right hand part, all of which are nevertheless subordinated to the one neighbor-note motion as indicated in
Graph b.

In contrast to the preceding excerpts, these last three examples show
progressions resulting from a contrapuntal conception without any
harmonic influence. Contrapuntal chord prolongation is the essence of
each phrase taken as a whole.

The architectonic idea of structure and prolongation governs all of
these examples; however, far beyond the few illustrations cited so far,
this idea is the leading creative force which makes for tonal coherence
and organization. Its development will be discussed, in its various phases,
throughout this book. It will become more and more clear that this idea
is the unconsciously motivating impulse that makes phrases, themes,
sections and finally complete compositions appear as prolongations of
basic structural progressions. In the relation between the structure and
its prolongation lies the coherence and thus the understanding of the
boldest and most complex passages, sections and complete compositions.

The great majority of illustrations so far presented have shown simple melodic lines in a vocal style. As the student has not yet been introduced to the wide field of melodic-contrapuntal prolongations he could
not be expected to understand the use of chord prolongation and other
techniques in examples with more complex melodic motions. At this
stage of the student's training, however, he can proceed to the four-part
setting of short and simple melodies. By setting melodies himself, he will
have the opportunity to apply harmonic and contrapuntal techniques
based on the conception of structure and prolongation.

E.   Four-part setting of short melodic phrases

The melodies to be used should be carefully devised or selected and
adapted. The main problem is to work out short and very definite
phrases which, in their construction, offer a suitable basis for application of some of the techniques of structure and prolongation so far
discussed. At the end of this section a few phrases of this type will be
provided for which the student should work out one or more versions
in four-part writing based upon the techniques gained so far and upon
those which he will acquire in the following examples.

Before proceeding to set such melodic phrases, it may be advisable to
recall the usage of sixth, $^6_4$ and seventh chords, which, along with the triad
in root position, have been encountered continuously. Harmonic chords

most often are used in root position, although the II frequently appears as II⁶ or II⁶₅. These inversions, however, do not detract from a chord's harmonic significance, provided it comes structurally from I and proceeds to V. The ⁶₄ chord was found in connection with the V, to which it resolved in ⁵₃ position. Seventh chords appeared as V⁷, II ⁶₅ and IV⁷.

These same chords, however, were used to a great extent as contrapuntal chords. Sixth chords appeared as passing chords, as chords of embellishment and as neighbor-note chords; the same could be said of ⁶₄ chords and seventh chords.

A short melodic phrase follows; it should be added that the four-part settings of such melodies are considered as preparation for the four-part settings of chorale melodies. ▶[Ex. 187]◀ In this melody the descending third appears embellished by a neighbor note. Since the harmonic framework is the first factor to consider, we must determine the harmonic setting of the structural tones E–D–D–C. With the progression I–II⁶–V⁷–I used as harmonic support, several versions are possible, using techniques so far discussed and combining them. ▶[Ex. 188]◀ Versions a, b and c show neighbor-note chords creating chord prolongations of the I. We prefer b) and c) because these versions do not anticipate the structural bass tone F as does version a. Versions d and e support the neighbor note with a ᴺ₅ chord. We hear a chord prolongation of the I, but in these settings the element of direction (⟶) is quite obvious. Like some examples previously quoted, these latter versions have a driving-on tendency within the chord prolongation. The student should also observe the difference between those versions which use movement within a chord and those using movement around a chord.

The main difference between d) and e) lies in the direction of the bass line between I and II. Version e represents the inversion of the natural ascending tendency of the bass; this inversion naturally causes different passing chords. Both versions show a II ⁶₅ gained by repetition or suspension of a middle voice tone. In d) a motion to D in the tenor would have created parallel fifths between alto and tenor. Version f demonstrates an interesting prolongation. When the top voice returns to E the bass already appears to be on the move. The resulting A chord is a passing chord between I and II⁶₅; thus this example is a prolongation of Ex. 118a. This prolongation is achieved through interpolation of the G seventh chord which supports the neighbor-note tone F. Thus in this version we are not confronted with a prolongation of I but with a prolongation of the progression from I to II⁶₅.

EXERCISES IX

The student is required:
1) to explain the significance of each version of Ex. 188.
2) to practice all versions in several major and minor keys.

On the basis of the examples just studied, the following melodic phrases and their different settings will be clear without much further explanation. ►[Ex. 189-194]◄ Again the student is advised to decide on the structure of the melody and the harmonic framework to be used before he takes up the different possibilities of prolongation. All versions should be explained in terms of their significance and all of them practiced in different major and minor keys. The prolongation in version d of Ex. 194 is related to version f of Ex. 188 and b of Ex. 190. However, here the motion to the passing chord on G is still further prolonged and delayed by an embellishing chord on the subdominant.

Except for cases in which special versions are indicated as better suited than others for minor keys, all versions may be set and practiced in major and minor keys.

EXERCISES X

On the basis of these studies and of his previously gained experience, the student is required to write one or more four-part versions to the following short melodies. ►[Ex. 195]◄

F. Melodic-contrapuntal prolongations

In the preceding paragraphs and in Chapter II, the student was introduced to the problems of melodic structure and prolongation. At that stage it was impossible to go beyond a general differentiation between structural and prolonging tones. With few exceptions, only melodies which presented a simple and direct outline were chosen for detailed discussion; it was not hard therefore, for the reader to distinguish the basic melodic direction or melodic structure from those tones which we had labeled with the term of prolonging tones.

Listening to the basic direction or structure of tonal melodies, and to the prolongations of that structure, we have found and shall increasingly observe that both melodic structure and prolongation may be expressed in three ways. They appear either in the form of a continuous line connecting two different tones, which we might call an *interval-filling* type of motion, or in the form of a motion around one tone representing the *ornamental* type of motion. In addition, for prolonging purposes only, the composer may use the so-called *interval-outlining* type of motion. This gives us three basic types of melodic motion. ►[Ex. 196]◄

The ornamental type of motion, though based essentially on the neighbor note, covers not only the neighbor-note motions, but all those motions around one tone which we have already encountered. It often appears that the interval-filling and the interval-outlining types of motion combine to create the ornamental type of melodic motion. ►[Ex. 197]◄ In a) and b) such a combination of the interval-outlining and interval-filling type of motion is shown, a combination which produces a movement around one tone.

Although all these statements will find their corroboration in the coming paragraphs and chapters, the student's attention must be drawn to a fact of great significance for the understanding of musical direction. In listening to a melody as a whole, we shall realize that the same types of motion appear on different structural levels of that melody. For instance, whenever the structure of a melody shows an interval-filling motion, other interval-filling motions and the other types of melodic motion may serve the purposes of prolongation. On the other hand, if the melody moves essentially around one tone, then other ornamental motions and the other types of motion may serve to prolong that motion around one tone. Thus, in one melody, interval-filling, interval-outlining and ornamental motions of different structural order may be at work.

The foregoing differentiation of the types of melodic motion and the conception of their use in different structural order within a melody, apply to many of the short melodies thus far quoted. These conceptions also apply to those few melodies (Ex. 131-133) which the student may as yet be unable to understand consciously in regard to their basic melodic direction and its prolongations. With these few exceptions the student is required to review all the melodies of the previous paragraphs and chapters, to observe the different types of motion used and to note how these are applied to express the structural direction and its prolongations. This study will enable him all the better to follow the discussions and explanations of this chapter, which intends to demonstrate in detail the more complex forms of melodic direction, continuity and prolongation. While up to now, melodies in a vocal style have served for most of the illustrations, from now on more instrumental melodies will be

given, since their wider range offers greater opportunity for prolongation.

Melodic prolongations in a polyphonic style of music confront us
with problems of counterpoint. A prolonged melody often demands a
prolonged form of counterpoint; thus we shall encounter prolongations
of those basic principles of voice motion studied in pure counterpoint.
Some techniques discussed in the following sections of this chapter directly extend the possibilities of contrapuntal setting, some affect the
horizontal problems of the melody. All, however, contribute to the
countless possibilities of contrapuntal setting employed in compositions
of the most varied styles.

The following sections 1-4 will deal with prolongations of the
basic melodic direction; section 5 will introduce the subject of prolonged counterpoint.

1. ELEMENTARY INSTRUMENTAL FIGURATION

The figurations so often found in instrumental music belong to the
most elementary forms of melodic prolongation. ►[Ex. 198, 199]◄
Singly used, similar motions around one tone have appeared in some of
the previously cited vocal melodies. Their basis is, clearly, the third
species of two-part counterpoint; since the function of the embellishments in third species have been fully discussed, such figurations demand no further explanation.[5]

Interval-outlining motions lead naturally to *chord-outlining* motions
which represent one of the simplest forms of chord prolongation. Such
chord-outlining motions also form an elementary type of melodic prolongation. ►[Ex. 200]◄ Instead of continuing to use the vague, though
essentially correct, term of figuration when we speak of motion around
one tone, we shall try in the following examples to determine the exact
status of the figurating tones. ►[Ex. 201, 202]◄

We realize that these passages in their chord-outlining motions move
into and out of the inner voice of the chords which they outline. In
Ex. 201, the melody skips into the inner voice of the chord, then proceeds to the inner voice of the following chord and thereafter reaches
the top voice tone of this latter chord. In Ex. 202, the melody, after
having skipped into the inner voice, proceeds upward stepwise to the
top voice tone of the following chord. Although the use of the term
figuration is quite adequate here, the designation of *motion into and*

[5] In this connection, see the chapter on "Tones of figuration" in Mitchell's *Elementary Harmony*.

out of the inner voice (already discernible in these fleeting passages) appears more appropriate for longer and more involved prolongations. Such prolongations give the impression of figurations on a higher structural level.

2.   MOTION INTO AND OUT OF THE INNER VOICE

An excerpt from Mozart's Rondo in A minor serves to illustrate what is here called figuration on a higher structural level .►[Ex. 203]◄ The listener will sense that the tonic chord is prolonged until the end of meas. 3, and only then moves to II^6 and V (meas. 4). As for the melodic events during this prolongation, the turn around E at the beginning with the help of upper and lower neighbor notes is obvious. The following skip to A may be explained as a motion into the inner voice of the governing A-minor chord. From this middle voice tone the melody ascends stepwise (chromatically) to E, thus completing a quasi-semicircle around this tone. While the motion into and out of the inner voice occurs, the E simultaneously acts as a tone retaining its structural value. This characteristic feature of melodic structure has been termed *the retained tone* in Chapter II.

Although motion into and out of the inner voice and the effect of the retained tone are actually created by one voice alone, it appears as if this single voice has split into two parts, one retaining the structural value of E, the other performing the motion into and out of the inner voice of the governing chord. This is characteristic of tonal melodies of the most different styles, and will be encountered from now on increasingly often in these pages. This polyphonic manifestation proves that tonal melody is not based on a purely horizontal conception in spite of all the "linear" tendencies it may demonstrate. Tonal melody participates in the polyphonic texture, and this participation is characterized by the motion into and out of the inner voice. Thus a type of melody has been created whose development is discussed in the course of this book. It may be termed *polyphonic melody*.

Returning once more to the Mozart example, let us compare it with the previously quoted simple figurations. It becomes increasingly clear that Mozart's melodic prolongation in the Rondo is a more elaborate and more broadly conceived version of the same idea, the prolongation of one tone (or chord). The student should carefully examine the indicated motives and phrases. ►[Ex. 204]◄ They all show motion into and out of the inner voice as the melodic prolongation of one tone; thus they appear as figuration, though on different, progressively higher structural levels. For a) the term figuration is completely adequate; b) indicates a continuation of the melody in order to draw the reader's attention to the various degrees of figuration in meas. 1 and 2. Whereas the prolongation of D and C in meas. 2 are just short embellishments, the one seen in meas. 1 covers the whole measure, throughout which the melody remains, as we may say, at a structural standstill. Although the term figuration could still be used for that measure, it becomes wholly inadequate for the melodic prolongation of c). Forming virtually a whole phrase, that prolongation must be characterized by motion into and out of the inner voice. This type of melodic prolongation may appear in a far more extended form, which then makes greater demands on our capacity for structural hearing.

While the last Mozart excerpt illustrates an extended prolongation of one tone, the next example shows the prolongation of a melodic progression. ►[Ex. 205]◄

As the voice-leading graphs indicate, motion into and out of the inner voice prolongs the basic melodic direction moving from D via C to B. In meas. 2 the melody moves from A via B to C. The retained D acts like an incomplete neighbor note to C, comparable to A♯ in the following measure which is an appoggiatura to B. We realize that the prolongation of motion into and out of the inner voice retards the structural progression. While the melody performs that prolonging motion, the structural progression is in suspense; this suspense, even in such simple examples as the present one, gives interest to a melodic progression.

In the preceding examples, the top voice moved into the inner voice of the prevailing chord. It happens just as frequently, however, that from that inner voice the melody then proceeds to the inner voice of the following chord before returning to the realm of the top voice, a feature appearing quite frequently in simple instrumental figuration (see Ex. 201). In the following four examples more elaborate motions into the inner voice of the following chord are presented. ►[Ex. 206, 207, 208, 209]◄ It often occurs, as can be heard in the excerpt from Mozart's Fantasia, that the motion into the inner voice of the following chord overshadows the initial motion into the inner voice of the first chord. Here the melodic stress lies clearly on the inner voice tones C♯ and D.

The first three examples show the neighbor-note technique as the main prolongation. This technique appears further prolonged through these motions into the inner voice, which again illustrates the tendency of prolongations to branch off into further prolongations or diminutions and detours. On the basis of structural hearing we are able to hear these subtle differences between the prolongations. It is their different value in relation to the structure which makes necessary their explanation in different stages (expressed through the graphs).

Whether the music reveals the neighbor-note technique plus motion into and out of the inner voice as in Ex. 206-208 or shows the latter type of prolongation as in Ex. 209, the fact remains that all four passages demonstrate that the same types of prolongation allow for the greatest variety in the rhythmic treatment of the prolonging tones. In the Beethoven example, for instance, the first neighbor note is in a more prominent position than the first structural Ab (upbeat). However, the last neighbor note which, with its new bass, is the stronger of the two, is subdued somewhat by the motion into the inner voice tone E (first beat). Yet in spite of all these deceptive rhythmic facets, the structural outline remains completely clear. In the phrase from the Mozart Fantasia, in addition to the rhythmically stressed inner voice tones C♯ and D (meas. 2 and 4), and the accented passing note D♯ and the appoggiatura G, we find rests which so expressively interrupt the motion on its way from the inner voice back to the top voice. These interruptions create small but very artistic elements of tension.

In many melodies, we witness apparently contrasting aims. One aim seeks to maintain a clear structural direction, the other seeks to obscure that direction by means of the most diversified rhythmic treatment of the prolonging tones and sometimes even of the structural tones, creating those deceptive motions and accents which we constantly encounter in listening to music.[6] The technique, in itself unchanged and unchangeable as a quasi-abstract force, is presented only to let the prolongations appear in their full meaning and to allow possible differences in their treatment to stand out more clearly. Only on the basis of a general technique are we able to appreciate and understand the great variety of expressive possibilities inherent in the prolongations.

Three excerpts are now given, two by Haydn and one by Froberger; they are conceived on a somewhat larger scale than the examples just cited. Although the technique of melodic prolongation is basically the same, its application is strikingly different, thus accounting for the contrasting individuality of these examples.

The first example, the opening measures of Haydn's Sonata No. 35 [7] also represents the first illustration of the harmonic technique using two

[6] Similarly contrasting aims of melody writing were mentioned in connection with the demonstration of the contrapuntal concept.
[7] The numbering used is that of the complete edition (Breitkopf und Härtel).

harmonic progressions (see Chapter IV). As each member of these progressions supports a structural tone of the melody, all of them are harmonic structural chords. The reader should note that the tonic of meas. 5 is simultaneously the end of the first progression and the beginning of the second. ►[Ex. 210]◄ The melody, using chord-outlining motion, moves from the inner voice tone C (on the upbeat) to the first structural tone G. After the repetitions of the tone G, the melody, again using chord-outlining motion, moves rapidly via the inner voice tone C of the tonic into the inner voice tone B of the V⁷. The motion from this inner voice tone upward, however, proceeds deliberately and creates a stop in meas. 4; for a moment the ear is left in doubt as to what will happen next. The following measure with F in the top voice, stressed by an upbeat, gives the answer; that motion out of the inner voice has only now come to an end. We hear a structural connection between G and F, the top voice tones of the I and V⁷ (see graphs). The stop on D in meas. 4 proves to be only a temporary interruption, not a structural stop. This subtle but nonetheless definite interruption is characteristic of this melody and creates a certain amount of tension. The student's ear will by now be able to grasp the structural connection between G and F in spite of the prolongations and their delaying tactics.

After the I has been reached in meas. 5, the melody again moves into the inner voice, thus prolonging that tonic. This short prolongation anticipates the structural descent to C. The E of meas. 5 retains its structural value and moves to the D of meas. 7, supported by II⁶ of the second harmonic progression. Another movement (skip) into the inner voice of the last V⁷ causes a substitution of B for D, thus avoiding the unnecessary repetition of D (Graph c).

While, in this C-major theme, the motion of the melody into the inner voice of the first I had been fleeting and the motion out of the inner voice of V to its top voice had proceeded more deliberately, the following example from the slow movement of Haydn's Sonata No. 19 in distinct contrast, presents a broad well-defined motion into the inner voice of the following II⁶, with an immediate ascent thereafter to the top voice of that harmonic chord. ►[Ex. 211]◄ By the addition of counterpoints to the tones of this deliberate motion into the inner voice tone F♯ of the II⁶, passing and voice-leading chords have been created within the prolonged I. Although the graphs make the contents of this theme clear, the reader's attention should be drawn to the end of this excerpt where, through suspension of the melody tone D and anticipation of the bass tone E (dominant), the normal relationship of the voice leading has been prolonged (Graph c). We might call this a rhythmic, rather than a melodic, prolongation.

A very different passage presenting the same type of melodic prolongation is taken from Froberger's Suite *Auf die Mayerin.* ►[Ex. 212]◄ Here the motions into and out of the inner voice take place within the prolonged I. It is, however, the motion from the inner voice tone E (meas. 3) which attracts special attention. If one plays the melody without Froberger's bass, one hears a motion into the inner voice D of the I, which proceeds to E, the inner voice of the C chord; this C chord acts as a neighbor-note chord to the I and reaches its top voice C on the third quarter of meas. 3. This C, which is the neighbor note coming from B, moves on directly to the following main note B. Although Froberger's bass leaves the neighbor-note function of C intact, it moves via B and A to G, thus preventing a prolongation of the C chord which, according to the top voice, might have been expected.

Direct motion into the inner voice, stepwise or by skips, occurs frequently at the end of phrases, as in Ex. 210. In that excerpt, the melodic tone B, an inner voice tone, substitutes for D. More such motions into the inner voice, but somewhat more elaborately worked out, will be found at the end of the next phrases. ►[Ex. 213, 214, 215]◄ In Ex. 213 and 214 the graphs clearly indicate that the motions into the inner voice substitute for the structural tones F and A, respectively. In Ex. 215, on the other hand, there is a motion into the inner voice tone F♯, but the structural A appears again, after a motion out of the inner voice; therefore, in this latter excerpt no melodic substitution is found. Melodic substitution will be shown later on in a different connection. At this point we should like to recall the origin of substitution in the second species of two-part counterpoint.

3.   SUPERPOSITION OF INNER VOICE

Melodic prolongations which are achieved through movement into and out of the inner voice and which appear as prolongations below the structural tones, are often joined by prolongations above the structural tones. In simple examples such as Ex. 198 and 199 the term figuration serves its purpose for prolongations both above and below the structural tones. However the prolongation above the structural tone in its more elaborated form, and thus on a higher structural level, can best be explained as the *superposition of an inner voice* with the purpose of moving above the structural tone. ►[Ex. 216, 217]◄

The melodic prolongations of the phrase by Chopin are offshoots of a neighbor-note motion which has been illustrated step by step, this time in the direction from the structural background of the chord (Graph a) to the most subtle melodic detail of the phrase. Graph b shows the neighbor note as the main prolongation of the B-Major tonic. Graph c, as a further offshoot, indicates a descending third downwards into the inner voice tone B. This is followed by a shift of the inner voice tone F♯ to the top (superposition) making a second descending third possible as an apparent answer to the third D♯-C♯-B. Finally Graph d, after embellishments of the first descending third, shows another superposition of the inner voice, this time the tone B, which leads via G♯ to F♯. We thus find prolongations below and above the structural tone D♯.

In the Mozart excerpt, the melody begins on the top voice tone C. The following passage in sixteenth-notes moves to the inner voice tone F which, through superposition, is immediately shifted to the top voice region. This F appears above the structural C and moves downward stepwise to D, the upper neighbor note. The melody then moves to the B♭ of meas. 5, before reaching the structural C of meas. 6. The C in meas. 5 is an accented passing tone to B♭, while D in the last measure serves as an appoggiatura to C. Graphs a and b thus indicate a prolonged neighbor-note motion (turn), the most elaborate prolongation taking place between C and D. An important effect within this chord prolongation is obtained by Mozart through an ascending sixth in the middle voice from A to F, which provides a fine counterpoint to the melodic events just mentioned.

While the last excerpts have shown both types of melodic prolongation within one prolonged chord, the two following examples illustrate these techniques within a complete and within an incomplete harmonic progression. ▶[Ex. 218, 219]◀ In the Mendelssohn passage the superposition of the inner voice tone F♯, which appears already in the upbeat, helps to form a wide melodic arc around the structural tone A. When the melody reaches A again (meas. 2), the bass is already on its way to F♯, the bass of the I⁶ chord. The melody then proceeds into the inner voice tone D, which appears covered by the simultaneously reappearing structural tone A (first beat, meas. 3). Here the prolongation of the I is at its end, bass and melody having created passing chords within this prolonged tonic. The structural A then moves once more to the inner voice tone D which leads to E, the inner voice of II⁶₅, substituting for G. From there the melody passes on to F♯, E and the concluding D, thus completing the structural line of a descending fifth.

In the excerpt from *Don Giovanni*, both types of melodic prolongation are effectively used. Graph a, indicating the prolongations, makes further comment unnecessary. The student should study this example carefully and notice the great breadth of the melody which, for the most part, is a remarkable prolongation of an ornamental motion around D. In this connection, the statements about more or less self-contained chord prolongations (see Ex. 178) must be recalled. Although in this Aria the prolongation of the tonic covers 7 measures, it is the bass progression to B (bass of the I⁶ chord) and onward to the IV which imbues the end of the tonic prolongation with a strong tendency of motion. This effect is even heightened by the fact that a new melodic phrase starts in meas. 6, the same measure in which the bass begins to move. We realize again how strong the forces of musical direction may become even within the realm of a single prolonged chord.

In all the above illustrations, motion into the inner voice and superposition of the inner voice are of approximately equal importance.

It happens quite often that superposition of the inner voice constitutes the predominant prolongation in a melody. ►[Ex. 220]◄ As in the example quoted in Ex. 216, the prolongation of the tonic is based on a neighbor-note motion; in the Clementi excerpt, however, with one exception, all prolongations are caused through superposition of inner voice tones either following or preceding the structural tones.[8] At the end we find the only motion into the inner voice. The up and down motions of the melodic prolongations tend to conceal both the structural standstill around E and the structural descent (meas. 3).

The student will now be ready to understand a more subtle phrase, the beginning of Beethoven's Sonata, Op 109. ►[Ex. 221]◄ This phrase is based on the progression as presented in Graph a (see also Ex. 125). Superposition of inner voice tones give rise to the broken thirds which are so characteristic of this melody (see Graph b). It is these thirds which bring the melody to E in the third measure, instead of to B, which would be the normal top voice tone, as the contrapuntal progression of Graph a shows.

4. TRANSFER OF REGISTER

In Ex. 214 we heard the melody being shifted one octave up to B and returning to the original register, all within one measure. Thus the tone B appears prolonged through what we may call a transfer of register.

---

[8] In spite of the two-part pattern the chordal background is understood; although the chords are only hinted at, they nevertheless form the basis of this setting. We encounter here the two-part setting of a three-part progression.

While in this instance the transfer of register creates an ornamental piano passage, in the next excerpt it represents virtually the whole phrase. ►[Ex. 222]◄ Largely by means of interval- and chord-outlining motion, a transfer of the tone D into the lower register and from there back to the original register is effected. Although the top voice, taken by itself, indicates a motion within the B♭ chord until the original position of the top voice tone D has been reached again, Beethoven counterpoints the motion ascending to the original register with a passing motion in the bass from B♭ to F, which causes a motion from I to V. The $^6_4$ chord on F in meas. 4 is therefore achieved through what we might call a structural suspension, which gives us the often-found dominant elaboration $^{6-5}_{4-3}$. The reader should note the two brackets in Graph a which point out an imitation of the top voice by the bass, causing the neighbor-note function of the two dominant chords in meas. 1 and 2. Only at the very end of the phrase does the melody move structurally onward to C. Up to that point it moves within the realm of D. In the light of this melodic stability, one should hear the subtle influence of direction which the bass brings into the otherwise solemn repose of the phrase. Observe also the three different functions of the dominant.

Another kind of transfer of register is achieved through the inversion of a second, giving rise to interval-filling or interval-outlining motions within a seventh. Two examples are cited. ►[Ex. 223, 224]◄ A comparison between the actual music and the voice-leading graphs will reveal the great possibilities inherent in this type of melodic prolongation. Such a comparison also helps us to realize the basic melodic direction and the coherence of such instrumental passages. In order to find that melodic continuity, it is important to determine the actual contrapuntal relationship between top voice and bass.

Ex. 223 demonstrates how through the use of interval inversion, a structurally descending line can appear in the actual music as an ascending motion. On the other hand, in Ex. 224 we find the frequently recurring technique of a structurally ascending third transformed into a descending passage. In both, the space created by the inversion is filled by interval-filling and interval-outlining motions.

Both techniques creating a transfer of register (the *octave shift* and the *interval inversion*) may appear within one melodic phrase. ►[Ex. 225]◄ It is necessary to add that these techniques of melodic prolongation, although found in vocal literature, are more typical of instrumental style, in which it is natural to employ wider ranges of melodic motion.

In addition we offer an excerpt from the Beethoven Sonata, Op 79, which shows that the transfer of register may affect both the structure and the prolongation. ►[Ex. 226]◄ The reader must beware, however, of automatically interpreting every motion of a seventh as a transfer of register of one voice; quite often the two tones outlining that seventh may belong to what are, in effect, different voices of a polyphonically conceived melody. ►[Ex. 227, 228]◄ In the phrase by Handel, the D and the C in the final quarter of the measure do not belong to the same voice, but represent two distinct voices. D is the middle voice of a $^6_5$ chord, while C, a seventh above, is a top voice tone to which the D of the preceding chord has moved. In the Bach example, the voice leading in meas. 2 and 3 shows that the C does not lead to the D, a seventh below, but to the B♭ at the end of the next measure. The D at the beginning of meas. 3, on the other hand, is an inner voice tone which comes from E♭ and which starts a motion out of the inner voice of the B♭ chord, thus delaying the top voice progression from C to B♭. Again we see how important it is to realize the exact voice leading of the whole phrase before jumping to any conclusion.

Before leaving the subject of transfer of register, let us consider the beginning of the last movement of Beethoven's Sonata, Op 14, No. 1. ►[Ex. 229]◄ First we hear a transfer of register through interval inversion in the motion from B up a seventh to A. Then we notice a new technique, for the interval of a second A-G♯ appears expanded to a ninth which is filled in. We thus add *interval expansion* to the previously mentioned techniques creating transfer of register. Apart from its melodic prolongations, this excerpt is characterized by the fact that the structural basses E and B are only reached after the structural melody tones have sounded; the bass line shows a motion out of the inner voice of the I and V downward to the roots of these harmonies.

5. PROLONGED COUNTERPOINT

Recalling the definitions and demonstrations of the pure contrapuntal concept in Chapter III, the student should now concentrate on the contrapuntal settings in the music discussed so far. These voice leadings have been explained in the form of graphs in different stages; it is these graphs which explain how certain pure contrapuntal techniques and progressions appear prolonged and elaborated in the actual composition.

The counterpoint in composition is frequently termed "free" counterpoint. Just as the term, pure counterpoint, has been used instead of strict counterpoint, we intend also to replace the term, "free" counterpoint. This term contributes to the widespread belief that the moment we approach composition we meet an altogether different type of counterpoint. On the basis of this belief a student quite rightly may question the need for a study of "strict" counterpoint. Why be "strict" at first if we may be "free" later on? Why follow rules which are hardly ever obeyed by composers? Why do we not immediately study the "free" counterpoint found in composition? These questions are completely justified as long as teachers fail to explain the reason for and the meaning of so-called strict counterpoint.

The reason for its study and its fundamental significance lies in its relation to the so-called "free setting." This relationship is an established one and cannot be challenged. The preceding paragraphs have already demonstrated it to a certain extent and as we proceed it will become even more obvious. But even at this stage the reader will readily agree that "strict" writing is not replaced by free composition. It is not at all a problem of "strict" versus "free" but the problem of pure or unprolonged counterpoint being enriched and elaborated by the inclusion of new elements, which we call elements of prolongation. The so-called "strict" counterpoint remains the basis of the so-called "free" counterpoint; the two are interrelated on the basis of structure and prolongation. Therefore we speak more precisely of *pure (or unprolonged)* and *prolonged counterpoint;* the latter is a more highly developed off-shoot of the first.

The last paragraphs on interval inversion and expansion have shown how melodic prolongation accounts for the motions of sevenths or ninths. The prolongation expands or modifies but does not fundamentally alter a progression which exhibits the *basic contrapuntal setting* of a particular phrase. It is this setting which is based on the principles of pure counterpoint. In addition, we realize that a melodic prolongation becomes a contrapuntal prolongation by the addition of a counterpoint; this means that by using this or that type of melodic prolongation, the counterpoint may appear in a prolonged state. It must also be kept in mind that pure contrapuntal progressions are now often combined with harmonic progressions, a fact which in itself changes the appearance of pure counterpoint to a certain degree. However, in spite of the harmonic progressions, the main principles of pure counterpoint remain clearly in force.

We shall now investigate the relationship of pure and prolonged counterpoint in greater detail and shall present prolongations of a specifically contrapuntal nature.

The first example shows a small and simple detail of a phrase by Mozart, which illustrates the interdependence of pure and prolonged counterpoint. ►[Ex. 230]◄ Even such a simple case as this one, with the skip from the interval of a seventh, sometimes causes students to doubt the value of studying pure counterpoint; this seems logical, as they are hardly prepared to blame Mozart for "faulty" voice leading. The reader, however, realizing that the melody starts from D and leads to B♭, will probably have no difficulty in hearing an interval progression of 10-5-6 as the contrapuntal progression on which this little phrase is based. The "distance" between that basic contrapuntal progression, the representative of pure counterpoint, and the phrase as it appears in Ex. 230 is explained in Graphs a, b, c. Graph a shows the basic contrapuntal progression. Graph b indicates its prolongation with interval-outlining embellishments and an appoggiatura to B♭. Graph c shifts the top voice tone F from its position above B♭, engendering the figure of three eighth-notes above the bass tone F. We realize that these embellishments of a third (Graph b) cause the appearance of the seventh and the skip away from that interval. The seventh is thus an interval derived through the process of melodic prolongation and is an elaboration of the progression 10-5-6; it has a clear prolonging function within that progression which is its basis. The seventh elaborates and prolongs, but it in no way disturbs or offsets the basic contrapuntal progression.

So-called "free" counterpoint is therefore possible and logical if it appears as a prolongation of a basic contrapuntal setting representing the techniques of pure counterpoint. It is, as will be repeatedly observed, the security of melodic and contrapuntal direction as derived from the underlying progression that makes the boldest designs of counterpoint not only logical but artistically desirable and fascinating.

Another strong factor making prolonged counterpoint possible (sometimes even superseding the power of a basic contrapuntal progression) is the architectonic principle of chord prolongation already demonstrated. In pure counterpoint there was as yet no higher architectonic principle binding a series of intervals or chords organically together. The problems of voice leading and direction were the only active principles; everything was dependent upon clear, unequivocal voice leading. If a progression gives expression to one single chord, however, then there is, beyond the problems of voice leading, a factor of higher structural significance which explains the function of intervals and chords. ►[Ex. 231]◄

The prolongation of the C chord in first inversion is clearly established through the contrary motion between the two sixth chords in different registers; the direction of movement within one chord is so clear that even more than three consecutive dissonances in no way obscure the intended progression. In contrast to pure counterpoint, it is here not so much the voice leading between single intervals and chords but rather the chord prolongation that represents the structural factor to which all intervals (or chords) are subordinated; whether they are consonant or dissonant, their function as passing intervals within the C chord is evident. Under the protection of that governing chord, counterpoint loses its sole responsibility and thus can move in a prolonged form. In a great number of passages, including the one quoted in Ex. 230, a basic contrapuntal progression gives expression to a single chord. This fact imparts added structural meaning and unity to a progression and makes the elaboration and prolongation of pure counterpoint all the more logical. ►[Ex. 232, 233]◄

Founded on the clearly directed, basic contrapuntal motion which gives expression to the A chord (Bach example) and the G chord (Mozart example), the single voices can express their melodic and motivic individuality. In the Bach excerpt, the upward leap of a seventh in the bass for the sake of transfer or register, prolongs but does not obscure the progression from A to G♯. The following dissonant interval F♯-E occurs through the motion of the top voice into the inner voice E, and through the use of the neighbor note F♯ in the bass to fortify G♯; the last seventh is an embellishing seventh. All these prolongations are offshoots of the basic contrapuntal progression of 8-10-10 which, as a whole, expresses the A chord. The prolongations make that progression more interesting but they subordinate themselves to its motivating impulse. In the phrase by Mozart the "independent" voice leading of the third beat is a prolongation of a chord as indicated in the graph, achieved by using complete and incomplete neighbor notes.

The underlying basic contrapuntal progression of a phrase and its direction may receive added emphasis through the harmonic progression within whose framework it moves. It is essential to keep in mind that the clearer the direction and meaning of the basic contrapuntal progression, the more convincing are the elaborations and prolongations of this basic direction. In addition the harmonic framework may contribute to the clarity and purposefulness of the motion's basic direction.

The beginning of Schumann's *Melody* serves as an illustration of this point. ►[Ex. 234]◄ The reader, bearing in mind the principles of pure counterpoint, will immediately question the status of the two "unprepared" or, as they will be more accurately termed, "free-entering" sevenths in meas. 1 and 2. Within the harmonic framework I-II-V-I, the top voice moves from E to A (the inner voice of the II) and reaches C via B (the inner voice of the V); thus the melody, as it appears, presents a prolongation of a descending third E-(D)-C. The tone B on the fourth beat of meas. 1 is a passing tone; the bass tone C, the counterpoint to B, acts like a pedal point retaining the bass of the I; thus the "free-entering" seventh C-B appears within the prolongation of the I as a prolonging seventh. The bass tone C clearly moves to D, the bass of II; this D appears simultaneously as counterpoint of a melodic embellishing-tone C. Thus melodic prolongation creates the second free-entering seventh which adds to the interest and color of the counterpoint but in no way offsets or obscures the basic progression and direction. The harmonic progression I-II-V-I, carrying and framing the basic contrapuntal progression, furnishes the pivotal points.

The reader's attention must now be called to the use of incomplete neighbor notes or appoggiaturas as simple prolongations of pure counterpoint. Sometimes they are used in succession, as may be observed in the next example. ▶[Ex. 235]◀

The use of a complete neighbor note may also introduce prolonged counterpoint, as may be heard in two phrases from Bach Chorales. ▶[Ex. 236, 237]◀ In the first example, the D in the bass is delayed through a neighbor-note motion around C; this delay causes the prolongation of the basic 10-8-6 progression. Similarly, in the second example a neighbor-note motion prolonging the bass causes a succession of two fourths in the outer voices. These fourths are the prolongation of the tenths, which actually represent the basic contrapuntal progression within the tonic.[9]

It thus belongs to the technique of contrapuntal prolongation to shift or displace tones and voices in such a way as to hide their actual pure contrapuntal relationship. Musicians often mistake the results of contrapuntal prolongation for the real relation between the voices. As a logical result, they have come to recognize a discrepancy between "free" and "strict" counterpoint, which, for them, makes teaching the latter of extremely doubtful value.

In the following phrase by Handel, a shift of a tone brings about the prolonged counterpoint of meas. 3. ▶[Ex. 238]◀ The counterpoint of the first two measures, in which the top voice moves from C to D, needs no further comment. The appearance of these tones on the second beat of meas. 1 and 2 respectively, leads the ear to expect an E on the second

[9] The student has been prepared for the voice leadings of both of these examples through the procedure of combined species (see Chapter III).

beat in meas. 3, which would have presented the voice leading as indicated in Graph a.

However, as far as meas. 3 is concerned, Handel shifts the E to the third beat, which puts the tone F as an incomplete neighbor note on the second eighth-note. The second beat, which normally would have brought E, has been filled with an F, serving as an appoggiatura to that E. Thus E, the actual goal of the ascending line beginning on C, appears, not above its true bass tone C, but above the tone F. This shift gives rise to the implied IV⁷ chord which appears at the end of meas. 3 (see Graph b).

A shift of tones is also responsible for the voice leading of the following short phrase from Copland's *Appalachian Spring*. ▶[Ex. 239]◀ The graphs will give a clear indication of the shift of the bass tones E and F. Finally, two excerpts from widely separated periods will be quoted to show that the "presence" of a basic contrapuntal setting makes a greater individuality of the single voices possible. To call such voice leading independent is misleading, since it is still dependent on the basic, unprolonged setting from which it derives its justification. ▶[Ex. 240, 241]◀

The salient point of this discussion has been to show the relation of the so-called strict and free types of counterpoint, or as they are called here, pure or unprolonged and prolonged counterpoint. Pure counterpoint still remains the foundation of contrapuntal progressions as they appear in composition. The principles of pure counterpoint thus do not apply directly to composition, but to its structural background or basis. Through the elaboration and the detours of the basic contrapuntal direction, prolonged counterpoint arises, and, as the term implies, it prolongs but *does not replace* the basic direction.

In trying to understand the actual relationship between pure and prolonged counterpoint we must distinguish between the factor which makes prolonged counterpoint possible (i.e. the factor which creates the precondition for a prolongation and elaboration of pure counterpoint) and those factors which actually effectuate the prolongation of pure counterpoint. The first consists in the clear purpose and direction of a basic underlying contrapuntal progression representing the techniques of pure counterpoint. This clarity of purpose and direction may be created (often, however, only further promoted) by chord prolongation and by the harmonic framework. On the other hand, the forces so far discussed which actually effectuate the prolonged form of counterpoint are the melodic prolongations and the specific contrapuntal prolongations such as the appoggiatura and the shift of tones; others will be taken up later.

G.   Continued use of pure contrapuntal techniques

It is only natural that many techniques and progressions of pure counterpoint should be represented in actual composition in an almost unprolonged form or only slightly figurated. Among the progressions of pure
counterpoint which find direct application in composition are those
from the fourth species. ►[Ex. 242]◄ For the 7-6 technique as found
in a) we find an illustration in William Byrd's *The Earle of Salisbury.*
►[Ex. 243]◄ An excerpt from the first movement of a Mozart Sonata
illustrates this technique used between the outer voices. ►[Ex. 244]◄
The 5-6 technique as given in Ex. 242b is illustrated in a slightly prolonged form (transfer of register) in a passage from an Air by Gottlieb
Muffat. ►[Ex. 245]◄ Bach's Prelude in E minor from the *Well-Tempered Clavier*, Book I, provides a good example of the 9-10 syncopation
technique as given in Ex. 242c. ►[Ex. 246]◄

H.   Recognition of voice leading

Thus far different themes and phrases have been cited to explain diverse
types of prolongation and to show their actual use in composition. In
the great majority of instances, however, they have been chosen for
the purpose of demonstrating the use of specific features and techniques.
The student was told what to look for. If in the following examples he
wishes to sum up his experiences and take stock of what he has gained,
it will prove helpful to him to approach new passages, not with the purpose of looking for one definite technique, but with an open mind and
open ear, so that the music is free to tell its own story. One cannot emphasize too often, even at this relatively early stage, that the student
must beware of forcing his knowledge and conception upon the music.
It is far better to draw no conclusion as to the organization of the music
in question, than to make the composition the testing ground for a half
understood hearing approach.

At the same time new problems may come up, which will receive
consideration for the first time in the following paragraphs. All discussions will remain detailed and in "slow motion." Once the student's
capacity for structural hearing has grown sufficiently, it will be possible
to dispense with many explanations, as he will then be able to hear and
understand the significance of many prolongations as soon as they are
presented.

In attempting to follow the voice leading of a theme, the student often finds that the beginning causes him difficulty. While the harmonic framework and the direction of the bass are usually the first factors to divulge their meaning to the listener, it may be difficult at times to determine the direction of the top voice and its relation to the bass. In particular, the location of the first structural tone of the melody may present some problems. Up to now examples have been carefully chosen to avoid any problem in connection with the entrance of the first structural tone; in fact, the student could not have had any doubt that the first melody tone or the downbeat of the first measure (following a possible upbeat) was also the first structural melodic tone.

However, as pointed out in Chapter II, the first tone of a melody is not always the first structural tone. Before deciding on the structural direction the student must listen carefully to the music as a whole; in many instances he must hear it several times, before drawing any definite conclusions as to the nature of the structure and its prolongations. Whether the first structural melody tone in the following examples enters on the first or on any other beat, these excerpts are not cited for a discussion of that problem alone. They serve, primarily, to sum up the details now mastered as well as to present the ear and mind with new illustrations.

For the first of the examples let us discuss the beginning of Haydn's Sonata No. 21 in C Major. ►[Ex. 247]◄ The factor which must be clear from the outset is the bass line, which indicates a framework of two harmonic progressions. The top voice, however, with its skips and detailed upward and downward motions, might present some problems. The question arises whether the tone G, the first downbeat, or the high C to which the first chord-outlining motion is directed, is the first structural melody tone. Before dealing with this question, it will be necessary to define the first structural top voice tone. It is the tone from which the melody or theme takes its basic direction to the goal. As we already know, the basic direction of a melody, called also the melodic structure, is thus differentiated from the various different directions the prolongations may indicate. This in turn implies that not every up-and-downward motion of the melody is indicative of its basic direction. Turning back to the question as to which tone, G or C, constitutes the first structural tone, it should be emphasized that it is only the continuation of the melody, never the first measure itself, that will answer this question. Since only the melody as a whole can indicate its structural direction, conclusions drawn from concentrating on only one or two measures often prove to be wrong. If at first hearing two solutions present themselves to the student's mind (which in this case means that he would consider C and G as equally possible first structural notes), he should follow through each reading to its logical goal. Such a procedure will show in this case that the melodic structure is very different according to whether he regards C or G as the first structural note.

Even if the reader has decided immediately that one tone and one direction are the only logical choices, it will be advisable for the sake of training his ear and musical judgment to study both readings. Assuming that C is the first structural note, we hear, first, a shift of C an octave upwards to the high C, from which tone the melody leads a ninth downward to B, meas. 3 (expansion of a second). The C is reached again at the end of meas. 4 after embellishments above the main tones B and C (superposition of inner voices). From C (meas. 4) the melodic outline leads to the upper neighbor note D, then again to the lower neighbor note B and finally to the C of meas. 6. This reading as a whole is indicated in the graph; it shows a top voice prolonging a structural motion around C (Graph a).

The question mark points to the fact that the II is the only harmony whose top voice F results from the prolongation of the melodic structure. Although this in itself may occur, one hears in this particular theme a complete correspondence between the structural tones of the melody and the harmonic basses. Above all, the ear registers a melodic motion in meas. 1-2 and 3-4 which presents a definite melodic parallelism completely ignored by the reading indicated above (Graph b). It appears that the parallelism ties the tones G-F-E structurally together. This impression is strengthened by the fact that G is a retained tone from the first beat of meas. 1 and that the E of meas. 4 clearly moves via D downward to the final C, thus presenting a structural line: G-F-E-D-C. This in turn shows that the high C in meas. 1 is a middle voice tone shifted to the top and that the motion to B (meas. 3) starts from F and is a motion into the inner voice of V^7 with F retained as top voice of this chord (Graph c).

The preceding discussions on melodic prolongation make further explanation of the prolongations as indicated in Graph c unnecessary. For those who were in doubt as to the first structural tone a comparison between the two versions will have proved that it is the second reading, interpreting G as the first structural tone, that represents convincingly the structural direction of the theme. Two factors in particular are so compelling as to make this second reading unequivocally the correct version. The first factor is the melodic parallelism between meas.

1-2 and 3-4 creating a stepwise downward motion. The resulting correspondence between harmonic and melodic structure, which gives added emphasis to the descending line G-F-E-D-C, is the other corroborating factor. In comparison, the first reading of Graph a seems forced and artificial. It assumes the high C to be the first structural tone because it is a relatively accented tone. Consequently the parallelism as a vital element of the melody's basic direction has to be ignored and this in turn forces the supertonic in meas. 2 into the role of a quasi-passing chord.

Probably the reader has considered G to be the first structural note from the outset. It is important, however, to be conscious of the reasons which compel us to assume one reading to be right and the other to be wrong. The student should therefore be advised always to weigh every possibility carefully and to give account of the reasons which convince him of his own reading. This will prove helpful in future, more subtle and longer examples.

In the following example from Mozart's G-Major Sonata there probably will not be much doubt that D of meas. 1 is the first structural tone; however, to hear the structural continuation of the melody might present some difficulties. ►[Ex. 248]◄ It will appear clear that the tonic is expanded throughout 4 measures which form a small phrase in themselves. In trying to hear the melodic coherence of these measures we realize that from D the top voice skips into the middle voice tone G which leads to the inner voice tone F♯ of the following seventh chord; the little motive at the end of meas. 2 and the beginning of meas. 3 answers the first motive. But what is its structural significance? Listening further we hear the descent from C to the B which concludes this little phrase. Now we understand that F♯ is the inner voice of a dominant seventh chord of which the top voice is the C of meas. 3, leading on to B. Thus, the little motive just mentioned is an inner voice shifted to the top (superposition). All this is illustrated in Graph a. One only has to play the little motive A-F♯-A in its "original" position to realize how much more graceful Mozart's prolongation of superposition has made this phrase; this motive also delays and thus increases the interest of the progression from D to C.

Continuing on, we find that the first structural top voice tone D appears again in meas. 6 and is retained until meas. 8. The C chord with E in the top voice (meas. 5) appears as a neighbor-note chord of the prolonged G-Major chord (meas. 1-4); thus the prolongation of the tonic with D in the top voice goes further than we thought in the beginning; it extends to meas. 8. From there a prolonged descent of the top voice D-C-B-A-G supported by I-IV⁶-V-I seems obvious. We thus arrive at the voice-leading graphs of the whole (Graphs b and c). The first four measures now appear as a prolongation subordinated to the main prolongation (compare the two graphs). The melodic motion of a third is a motion into the inner voice; this third is subtly answered by an embellishing third preceding the neighbor note E of meas. 5. Observe also the prolongation of the descending structural line through transfer of register (meas. 8 and 9).

Although the branching off of prolongations into smaller ones has already been observed, this theme presents a rather intricate example which makes definite demands on our capacity for structural hearing.

A general characteristic of tonal melody, its polyphonic manifestation, may be found in Bach's melodies especially. The characteristic ruggedness of their contours is caused by those constant skips or stepwise motions into and out of the inner voice. The beginning of the next example may be cited in this connection. ►[Ex. 249]◄

Before discussing this theme as a whole let us concentrate for a moment on the first two measures, as they show the polyphonic conception of a melody very distinctly. After two skips in meas. 1, from E♭ to G and from D to F, motions into the inner voice, the D (third quarter) finds a continuation in the last eighth-note, C, of meas. 2, thus completing a descending third E-D-C. However, while this occurs, the inner voice creates a diminution of a descending third (Graph a). This is not so much a prolongation *of* a prolongation but literally a prolongation *within* a prolongation. It is all one melody, but its motions into the region of the inner voice of the implied chords, together with the parallelism of descending thirds in, as it were, two different parts show again that such melodies are not the result of a purely horizontal conception. The following measures prove that the descending third, in regard to the whole, is a motion into the inner voice while the E♭ is retained as a structural tone. This E♭ moves to D, supported by II⁶ (meas. 3), from which another descending third branches off leading into the inner voice B of the V. In the course of further diminution the melody continues to move one more third downwards to G, before returning to the structural tone D. The V then proceeds to I with E♭ as the top voice tone. The A♮ in the bass (meas. 2) preventing a repetition of C, provides for additional color in this phrase; the resulting A♮ seventh chord serves as a passing chord between I and II⁶. Of great interest also is the polyphonic expression of the melody in meas. 3. The first F is an inner voice tone, the E♭ appears to be an appoggiatura to the structural tone D, the tones F and A♭ represent superpositions of inner voice tones of the II⁶ and C, the last note of that measure, is part of the inner voice motion from D via C to B (see Graphs b, c, d).

The question now might arise as to why we have not interpreted the C on the first beat of meas. 1 as the first structural note (Graph e).

The reader will agree that this reading ignores several important factors which all point to the Eb as the first structural tone. Firstly, it ignores the parallelism of two descending thirds from Eb and from D, both of these tones being placed on the second beats of their respective measures; secondly, it ignores the small prolongation of Eb-D-C in meas. 2 which stresses the Eb; lastly, the eighth-note Eb of meas. 3, which appears as an appoggiatura to D, is a kind of reminder that it is the Eb from which the D comes. We thus are justified in reading Eb as the first structural tone of the melody which, unlike the first structural tones of previous examples, appears on the second beat. One cannot stress too often how imperative it is for the student not to approach music with a preconceived idea as to its probable structure. Even if structure and prolongations seem to be very clear, the weighing of different readings is good training for structural hearing.

In the excerpt from Chopin's Mazurka, Op 41, No. 4, for instance, it is important for the student to be able to explain why Ab on the first beat is not the first structural tone. ►[Ex. 250]◄ We find that there is no continuation from that Ab, since the melodic course does not take up Ab any more. Actually this Ab is an inner voice tone which moves to G, then back to Ab and remains in the inner voice region, alternating with G throughout those eight measures. Comparable to the upbeat of Ex. 247, the Mazurka shows an ascent out of the inner voice to the first structural tone, which is Eb entering on the second beat of meas. 1.

The student should be able on the basis of previous explanations to understand these voice-leading graphs and the nature of the melodic prolongations.[10] Interesting details occur in meas. 7, 8 and 9; it seems at first that the melody returns to the starting-point Eb; however, if we hear the whole phrase up to the downbeat of meas. 9, the Eb appears only as a superimposed inner voice tone which immediately afterwards is put into its real position of an inner voice. The structural melodic connection thus goes from Bb (meas. 7) to Ab (meas. 9). There is also an interesting symmetrical succession in the prolongations. The first two measures show the placing of the prolongations below the structural tones, while in the following two measures they appear above the structural Db; then again we find the prolongations for two measures

[10] The function of chords like the one in meas. 4 will be explained in Chapter VI.

below the structural Db and C, until in the last measures the prolonging notes are above *and* below Bb and Ab. This symmetrical arrangement of the prolongations gives an impression of swaying, though the melody as a whole is clearly directed downwards from Eb to Ab.

A similar instance may be found in Chopin's Etude in E minor. ►[Ex. 251]◄ Here the motion of meas. 1 consists again of an ascent out of the inner voice to the first structural top voice tone G, from which the melody with small prolongations descends to E.

Although such short delays of the entrance of the first structural tone usually cause the student little trouble, the reading is more complicated if this tone of the melody appears in the second or third measure or even several measures later. In such cases we are still confronted, technically, with the same kind of motion from the inner voice to the top voice, but instead of appearing as quasi-upbeats, such wider prolongations give the impression of an architectonic principle of delay. Such larger prolongations are termed *postponements of the first structural tone.*

In their simplest form these postponements are so easy to hear and understand that they need little explanation. ►[Ex. 252]◄ The pedal-point technique leaves not the slightest doubt about the prolongation of the I. In addition the rapid ascent to D, fortified by an embellishment, makes it quite clear that this D is the first structural tone from which the structural line descends to G.

In this connection Ex. II and III of Part I, Chapter II may be recalled. The initial ascending lines of those excerpts are too important a part of the melodies to give the impression of prolonged upbeats. The question thus may arise as to why we have indicated these ascending lines as motions to the first structural tones instead of just speaking, in regard to the whole, of a melodic structure showing an ascending *and* a descending third. If we listen to these Chorale phrases in a completely linear way (i.e. with no regard to harmony, counterpoint or chord prolongation), then there would be absolutely no difference in structural value between the ascending and descending lines. But these melodies have hardly been conceived in a purely horizontal or linear way; at any rate, in the above examples they are supported by counterpoint and harmony. In both examples, the ascending thirds to D and to C are the melodic lines of prolonged chords. Any triad may be prolonged and will have either the root, third or fifth as a top voice tone. Just as one chord in its vertical position can only have one top voice tone, a chord in its prolonged form will also have only one structural top voice tone. Therefore, if several melody tones move within a chord and thus help to prolong that chord, only one of them will be of structural value. In the B-minor phrase, the first structural top voice tone can only be B or D and in the A-minor phrase only A or C. The reasons for reading D and C as the first structural tones of these two phrases are twofold. Firstly, the motion leads strongly to those tones, and secondly, it is these tones which lead to the top voice tones of the next structural chords—the V in the B-minor phrase and the II $\frac{6}{5}$ in the A-minor phrase. Thus a structural connection exists between D and C♯ in the B-minor phrase and between C and B in the A-minor Chorale; the arrows in both examples indicate the postponement of the first structural tone by means of an ascent out of the region of the inner voice. ►[Ex. 253]◄

Finally let us consider the beginning of Beethoven's Sonata, Op 14, No. 2, which will give an indication of how extended and elaborated such postponements may be. ►[Ex. 254]◄ Here each tone of the ascending third leading to the first structural tone B appears prolonged, either by means of inner voice tones shifted to the top or (as happens in meas. 5 and 6) by using the technique of transfer of register. This particular part of the entire prolongation has been illustrated in a separate graph, because it constitutes a very instructive example of melodic prolongation. In looking back once more at the two examples from Part I and the Beethoven theme just mentioned, we realize that the structural motion of these melodies is directed downwards. And yet, motions which are structurally moving downwards may feature strong upward tendencies, especially in the beginning.

Although the full meaning of this type of prolongation will only be completely understood after the reader has analyzed larger sections, its significance warrants separate treatment from the other melodic prolongations even at this stage of the student's training.

I. Voice-leading graphs as the systematic expression of structure and prolongation

The intricate relationship between structure and prolongation has found its systematic expression in the so-called voice-leading graphs, whose significance the student by now can fully understand. He will have recognized above all that they symbolize the processes of structural hearing. In looking over the voice-leading graphs which have been presented so far we are able now to arrive at an explanation and definition of these processes.

It will have occurred to the student throughout these discussions that he has been instinctively aware of certain facts of musical coherence and direction. I definitely believe that most persons deeply interested in music have, in varying degrees to be sure, an inborn ability and capacity for structural hearing. It is the aim of this book and its many graphs to make conscious, develop and promote this ability.

As will become increasingly clear, the whole realm of tonal music shows the perpetual interrelationship and interdependence of two architectonic factors:

STRUCTURE	and	PROLONGATION
The music's basic direction		Its shaping and individual treatment through elaboration, expansion and detour

Structural hearing divulges the very existence of structure and prolongation and their individual tasks in creating an organic musical whole. Since they present the essential problems for musical understanding, recognition of them should form a significant goal of musical education.

Although it is believed that the graphs so far presented will have conveyed to the student the exact meaning of the symbols, note-values, slurs, etc., for the sake of complete clarity, the main signs and their significance are explained in the Glossary in Vol. 2. The voice-leading graphs have the ultimate purpose of explaining the coherence of a musical unit in a systematic way. However, they in no way indicate how a composer proceeds from his first idea to the final form of his work. Nothing of this kind is implied, either in the foregoing or in later discussions. Nor is any suggestion intended as to the possible order in the successive phases of creative work. I do not believe in any "method" of composition and should consider it a fatal misunderstanding if the reader thought that organic musical works could be created by prolonging a simple progression. However, I do believe strongly that structural hearing strengthens the creative and interpretative ear and mind to an unusual degree, and that an understanding of structural hearing brings about a penetration into the problems of musical composition and architecture, of value for the musician, whether he is a composer, performer or teacher.

J.   Exercises in prolongation—Structural ear training

In the course of what may be called *structural ear training and plan-ning*, it appears important for the student to play and explain the voice-leading graphs in sequence from the basic structure to the actual composition. Before or while playing each successive stage, he should try to explain every type of prolongation in its significance and in its relation to the unit as a whole.

In requiring this work we have two goals in mind. The one is to lead from the basic structure to the finished composition in successive stages, a study which provides useful ear training. The structure and its first prolongation—let us think for instance of Ex. 219, Graph b—may be played without putting them into a definite rhythmic form. However, the graph most closely approximating the actual composition (Graph a) should be played so as to suggest more definitely the rhythm of the actual composition. Our second goal is to bring out the general nature of the prolongations as techniques of composition. We thus stress their general value, apart from their use in particular phases.

In order to further his understanding of problems of musical direc-tion, the student should acquire the capacity not only for hearing but also for planning both small and large musical units. It is here that exercises in prolongation will prove to be of help. A beginning in such exercises has already been made in many of the keyboard exercises thus far given. Further exercises will now be indicated, taking into con-sideration the student's experiences in melodic prolongation. Some of the following exercises have been influenced by certain excerpts dis-cussed so far, but the rhythmic patterns chosen to demonstrate prolon-gations have been freely formed. This was necessary in order to create exercises through "de-individualisation" of real music. Such exercises, in contrast to the ones previously given, are meant to be technical abstractions from prolongations found in compositions. It is therefore not advisable to follow them up by the actual excerpt we may have had in mind, since the impression might be created that out of the exercise develops the composition, a completely erroneous and misleading as-sumption. Such exercises serve as structural planning only and are in no sense attempts in composition. They constitute certain techniques of prolongation brought into rhythmic form and are no more compositions than are finger exercises. If, however—and this happens quite often—these exercises stimulate first attempts in improvisation or composition, they have served a double purpose: understanding of existing techniques of prolongation, on the one hand, and encouragement of creative work, on the other.

Several exercises are now offered for the purpose of structural planning. First the basic chord or the basic structural progression is given, followed by several prolongations in the form of short phrases. These prolongations and their exact status should be explained and defined by the student. All exercises should be played in different keys. ►[Ex. 255-263]◄

K. The technique of interruption

So far all phrases, themes and units presented have been undivided. The following paragraphs will show that, by means of a special architectonic device which will be called "interruption," a structural unit may be expressed in the form of two distinct parts or periods.

Although this architectonic device actually belongs to the chapter on form (Chapter VIII) where its implications will be fully understood, it must be mentioned here because it may affect even the small parts of a composition with which we are dealing at the present. Let us, before considering any illustrations, examine that process of dividing a structural unit. ►[Ex. 264]◄ Graph a shows a very simple structural progression, which in Graph b is subdivided into two structural progressions through the process of interruption. The melody proceeds to the tone above the fundamental, and the bass to the V at which point both are interrupted instead of immediately moving on to the tonic. Subsequently the melodic line and the harmonic progression begin once more and follow through to their conclusion. The (D) under the V at the point of interruption is an abbreviation of the term, divider or dividing dominant; for this dominant, in contrast to the following one, helps to bring about the division of the harmonic structure.

It is characteristic of every theme showing interruption that the melody's structure proceeds to the supertonic tone, at which point the bass reaches the V, called the divider. These motions are interdependent; the fact, for instance, that a phrase leads to the dominant is in itself not indicative of the special technique of interruption. It is furthermore of importance to realize that the first melodic movement to the supertonic (2) does not create a motion to a neighbor note D. With the melodic tone D a motion comes to a stop even if only temporarily; when the motion starts again with the tone E, the second structural line begins. Thus there is no neighbor-note connection between the D that creates the interruption and the second beginning on E. Instead, interruption performs a division of a structural unit into two distinct structural periods or parts. The fact, however, that the period following the interruption completes what has been initiated in the first period, makes for the interdependency of the two periods as parts of a whole of a higher structural order. We shall call these periods *pre-interruption and post-interruption period*. Turning to the literature we find a straightforward example of interruption at the beginning of the second movement of Beethoven's Piano Sonata, Op 14, No. 1. ►[Ex. 265]◄

We now refer the reader back to the phrase by Mozart cited in Ex. 183 of this chapter. This phrase represents the pre-interruption period of a theme divided through interruption, and no difficulty will arise in analyzing the post-interruption period. Whereas in the first period the subdominant chord is a contrapuntal chord, this same chord in the post-interruption period appears as a harmony coming from I and proceeding to V.

It often occurs that the melody of the pre-interruption period moves into the inner voice of the dividing dominant; this characteristic is illustrated by a passage from the last movement of Haydn's Symphony No. 100 in G Major. ►[Ex. 266]◄

I should like to stress that the recognition of a specific technique is only the basis for the appreciation of its many possibilities of application. In the case of interruption the possibilities for varied treatment are truly manifold. An example is chosen to show that wide melodic differences between pre- and post-interruption periods may occur although the structure proves that the technique of interruption is adhered to. ►[Ex. 267]◄ The differences between the two periods are striking, although the parallelism of the ascending prolonging melodic line in both periods contributes much to their organic coherence. On the other hand, the second period appears as an intensification of the first, the melody driving up to G, which tone in its ultimate analysis is a prolongation of a neighbor note E♭ and is supported by a IV (compare Graphs a and b). Basically the first period also shows the characteristic of a neighbor-note chord, but appearing in a contrapuntal connection. A transfer of register of F, placing the E♭ in the inner voice is substituted for the melodic neighbor-note motion (see Graph a). It is this prolongation which creates the rugged contour of this very intense melody.

Finally, for an example from an earlier period we turn to a *Basse Danse* from the sixteenth century. ►[Ex. 268]◄ The voice leading in general, the ascent to the structural melody tone A (meas. 2) and the prolongation of that tone, supported by the tonic, appear so self-evident that we shall dispense with a voice-leading graph.

While studying the following chapters more examples of interruption with their diversified treatment and elaborations will divulge their meaning to the student.

Part II   Chapter Six

Structure and Prolongation II

The growth and intensification of tonal coherence throughout music history, the constant urge to increase the scope and the architectonic possibilities of musical organization, have made it impossible to limit harmonic chords to structural purposes and contrapuntal chords to the task of prolongation. This natural desire to enrich and extend accounts for the composer's instinctive action in creating new chord functions in addition to the two functions discussed in the preceding chapter. And so we approach a group of chords and chord progressions whose significance shows that both harmony and counterpoint may interchange their structural and prolonging functions. This means that harmonic chords may take on not only a structural but also a prolonging status, and there are many occasions when contrapuntal chords have a structural significance.

Hence, in addition to the progressions mentioned in Chapter V which were harmonic-structural and contrapuntal-prolonging, we frequently encounter chord progressions which have a harmonic-prolonging and a contrapuntal-structural function. The former will be discussed in the following paragraphs; they are summed up under the term of *harmonic prolongations* and occur whenever a complete or incomplete harmonic progression appears subordinated to a harmonic progression of higher order. The latter will be discussed later.

A.   Harmonic prolongations

The study of musical organisms, whether small or large, reveals that a harmonic progression can fulfill two different functions. Firstly, it may outline and determine the basic direction of a musical organism, as seen in Chapter V, and thus has a structural function. Secondly, a harmonic progression appears subordinated to a harmonic progression of higher order. In expanding one single chord it serves a prolonging purpose in regard to the whole. It is an offshoot of the progression of structural function and creates a harmonic prolongation of that one single chord. This possibility of dual function of harmonic progressions lies in the nature of a harmonic progression itself. We had remarked in Chapter IV that the progression I-V-I may be conceived as the horizontalized outline of the chord-form $\begin{smallmatrix} 8 \\ 5 \end{smallmatrix}$ (Ex. 99). Hence inherent in a triad is its own harmonic progression, which may be used to give expression to that one triad. On the other hand, a harmonic progression (see Chapter V) has a tendency to create tonal organization. In the first instance it acts as a prolongation, in the second instance as a structural framework.

We will observe in the following examples that two harmonic progressions of different structural order may take place within one organism. Examining the literature and taking into consideration the fact that any triad may be prolonged in a harmonic as well as a contrapuntal way, the question arises as to the position of such harmonic prolongations within the structural harmonic framework of a unit as a whole. First we shall approach the problem of how the tonic of a structural harmonic progression may be prolonged harmonically.

I. HARMONIC PROLONGATION OF THE TONIC

a. *Complete harmonic progression as prolongation of the tonic*

In ►[Ex. 269]◄ the Chorale phrase reveals a structural difference between two harmonic progressions. The first two measures prolong (harmonically) the tonic which then proceeds to the V.[1]

We thus are confronted with a structural harmonic progression of I-V which includes as an organic offshoot a prolongation of I in the form of another harmonic progression (I-II-V-I). The larger and smaller type of Roman numerals used indicate the different structural value of these progressions. The harmonic prolongation is a subordinated part of the harmonic progression of a higher structural order. Within one phrase, then, harmonic progressions may demonstrate a structural and a prolonging function.

In order to make the difference between a harmonic and a contrapuntal prolongation very clear the harmonic prolongation has been transformed into a contrapuntal one. ►[Ex. 270]◄

The harmonic prolongation of a tonic should not be confused with

---

[1] The chord preceding the V is a prolonged applied dominant, a chord function which we shall soon discuss.

the very different technique of the two succeeding structural harmonic progressions, as discussed in Chapter V. This technique, as we recall, shows two harmonic progressions next to each other, each supporting part of the melodic structure with neither serving to prolong a single harmony. Neither one is the offshoot of the other. On the other hand, the harmonic prolongation as presented above shows a subordinated I-II-V-I as organic offshoot of a harmonic progression of a higher structural order; the tonic of this harmonic progression has been prolonged in a harmonic way.

The use of a prolonging I-V-I progression may be found in a piece by Orlando Gibbons; here the student has a good opportunity to study three different functions of a dominant. Observe also the melodic and contrapuntal differences between the pre- and post-interruption periods. ►[Ex. 271]◄

The next two excerpts present the new type of prolongation within larger units. The first is taken from the last movement of Haydn's Sonata in E♭, No. 52. ►[Ex. 272]◄

The reader will readily grasp the phenomenon of harmonic prolongation in the form of a prolonging I-II-V-I; notice also the magnificent rhetorical use of rests and fermatas. Here we have a striking example of the advantage that structural hearing presents. These dramatic rests appear all the more interesting and meaningful if the musical coherence of the measures is fully understood. Haydn creates artistic tension on the basis of logical musical coherence.

A highly interesting harmonic prolongation is to be found in an *Ave Maria* by Josquin des Prés. ►[Ex. 273]◄ The student should observe the motion into and out of the inner voice, the latter motion supported by a prolonging V which itself is contrapuntally prolonged. This excerpt provides an excellent example of contrapuntal chords resulting from motion of the outer voices (meas. 2-5). In Graph a only the main chords of these measures have been indicated as complete chords and with stems. The same graph also shows the penetration of the structural third of the melody into the smallest melodic prolongations. Interestingly, in this example, the contrapuntal treatment, especially of the inner voices, never prevents the melody from developing its wide arc. The composer has achieved a wonderful balance of contrapuntal-melodic and harmonic writing. The harmonic progressions are only regulating factors in a freely flowing contrapuntal texture.

In contrast to this example by Josquin the next excerpt from a Mass by Pierre Cléreau, shows a far greater emphasis on the harmonic element in presenting three harmonic progressions of different structural order. ►[Ex. 274]◄

EXERCISES I

  1) On the basis of these examples the student should define and explain the term "harmonic prolongation of the tonic."
  2) The following keyboard exercises should be explained before being played and practiced in several keys. ►[Ex. 275]◄

Recognizing that harmonic progressions are prolongations of one single harmony, a student might argue that every structural harmonic framework itself constitutes a prolongation of a single chord and that this statement can serve as a form of explanation. Although every harmonic progression finds its final explanation as the prolongation of a single chord, this final single chord does not serve in any way as a structural explanation, since it does not affect the motion and direction of the theme or phrase to the slightest extent. Therefore, as soon as the framework-creating harmonic progression of the whole unit under discussion has been established, we have arrived at the final harmonic-structural explanation of such a unit. Since all prolongations are off-shoots of this one progression, it is then the progression of the highest structural order.

Let us for example recall such instances as Ex. 174-177 in Chapter V, or the Bach phrase, Ex. 269. To mention the one harmony which those harmonic frameworks fundamentally express would be of no value for a structural explanation of the musical motion of those particular phrases. The realization that such small phrases constitute the harmonic prolongation of a single over-all structural harmony is of value only when these phrases appear as parts of a larger whole. When trying to hear the detail in relation to the whole, much may be gained by the knowledge that the detail is the prolongation of a chord or harmony of higher structural order.

Let us return once more to the technique of harmonic prolongation in general. In presenting harmonic progressions of different structural value, it seems that the main problem for the listener is not to lose contact with the over-all structural direction of the theme or phrase. This was relatively easy in the phrases cited in the preceding chapter, where harmonic progressions were solely used for creating the structural framework. Now, however, with the appearance of subordinated and prolonging harmonic progressions, the task of structural hearing may often appear to be somewhat more complex due to the necessity of discriminating between harmonic progressions of different structural order.

b. Incomplete harmonic progression as prolongation of the tonic

Although a progression like I-II-V-I or I-V-I is the most complete harmonic prolongation of a I of a higher structural order, there are several other means of prolonging a chord harmonically. Sometimes, for example, a prolonging harmonic progression may not have a final tonic. This gives the whole prolongation an unsettled, less self-contained character. ►[Ex. 276]◄ Since the harmonic prolongation of the I is not completed, a different effect of prolongation is created. While in the preceding examples the final I of the prolonging progression leads on harmonically to the next structural harmony, we find in this Chorale phrase that the prolonging IV and V have a harmonic relation only in backward reference to the structural I; this relation has been indicated with an arrow. In regard to the coming structural II, there is only a contrapuntal connection, but no harmonic relationship, between the prolonging V and this II. The latter is a harmonic dependent of the preceding I only. Thus we are confronted not so much with a movement *within* a I but rather with a prolonging progression *attached to* the structural I. The principle of harmonic prolongation is the same, but the effect the prolongation causes is different. The task of structural hearing is to establish contact between the I and the II (meas. 2), and thus to interpret the IV and V as harmonic dependents of the structural I. It is this hearing and reading which prevents the purely descriptive and mechanical registering of an unorganized succession such as I-IV-V-VI-V⁶-II-V-I.

Another illustration of the incomplete harmonic progression as a prolongation of the I may be found in the beginning of Mozart's Sonata in D Major, K. 576. ►[Ex. 277]◄ This theme appears subdivided into two phrases, the first phrase containing the tonic and its attached prolongation in the form of the incomplete progression I-II-V, the second containing the II-V-I of the structural progression. It is essential upon reaching the II (meas. 5) to grasp its derivation from the structural I; this structural coherence is underlined by the use of the same motive for both members of the harmonic framework .

EXERCISES II

1) The progression given should be used as a keyboard exercise
   and practiced in different major and minor keys. ►[Ex. 278]◄
   We deem it important for the student first to play the progression as indicated in a) and then to explain how the I is to
   be prolonged. Finally he should proceed to the prolonged version as indicated in b).

2) Find examples from the literature illustrating prolonging complete and incomplete harmonic progressions.

c.   Dominant prolongation of the tonic (the prolonging V)

The same type of prolongation, only somewhat simpler, is created if
a prolonging V alone is added to the structural I; we shall call this a
dominant prolongation of the tonic. Two short examples are given.
►[Ex. 279, 280]◄ In Ex. 279, the sixth A-F♯ of the inner voices at the
end of meas. 1 is an anticipation of the chord tones A-F♯ of the coming
IV⁶₅. This anticipation, however, in no way affects the status of the
prolonging V.

In the phrase from the Bach Prelude the use of the prolonging V is
more elaborate. Here the top voice with its embellishing tone contributes to the prolonging effect of that dominant. Subsequently the top
voice A♭ appears as the structural continuation of B♭, as indicated in
the graph.

EXERCISES III

The progressions given in ►[Ex. 281]◄ should be used as keyboard
exercises and practiced in several keys.

d.   Dominant prolongation and incomplete harmonic progres-
sion preceding the structural tonic

A very different result is created if the prolonging dominant or the
incomplete harmonic progression precedes the structural tonic. Many
pieces begin in this way. The drive to the I becomes the main effect of
this type of harmonic prolongation; the impression is that of an introduction to the I rather than of an expansion of the I. ►[Ex. 282, 283,
284]◄ While in previous examples the second tonic of a harmonic prolongation was omitted, here the first tonic of a progression is missing.

The harmonic relation is now between the prolonging V and the following tonic which thus gathers momentum. The third example is especially interesting as the dominant itself is prolonged by a $^6_4$ chord acting as neighbor-note chord, and by the top voice tone D♭, representing an appoggiatura to C.

Such examples, however, must not be mistaken for similar ones with different meaning. ►[Ex. 285]◄ If the upbeat tone is a chord tone of the I, we are still confronted with a complete I-V-I even if the first I is only hinted at and thus appears considerably weakened.[2]

The impression of introduction is intensified if an incomplete harmonic progression has preceded the structural tonic. The first two examples quoted are from songs by Schumann. ►[Ex. 286, 287]◄

This fascinating technique of prolongation creates a certain amount of tension, since the meaning of the prolonging chords is revealed only after the appearance of the I to which the other chords are subordinated. Ex. 287 is particularly interesting. The melodic line B-C♯-D would normally be harmonized by I-V-I (see Graph b). However, the support of B with the II[7] creates an indefinable feeling of tension, so well suited to the inner excitement of the poem (Graph a).

The beginning of the first movement of Beethoven's Sonata, Op 31, No. 3 with its extended motion from the II$^6_5$ via V to the structural I (which is not reached until meas. 8) shows the architectonic possibilities of this kind of prolongation in a most beautiful way. ►[Ex. 288]◄ The chromatic passing chord and its accented treatment certainly heighten the impression of suspense so characteristic of this phrase.

The next example is even more chromatic, but the student will be able to understand this very dramatic prolongation by closely studying the graphs. ►[Ex. 289]◄ They indicate that the melodic motion from A♭ down to D is a motion into the inner voice of the dominant. The counterpoint of the bass moves stepwise downward and with the tone F, reaches, for its part, the inner voice of the dominant. The continuing bass motion contributes to the prolongation of the V[7] with a progression moving out of the inner voice of that harmony, while the top voice moves out of the inner voice tone D to the top voice B♭. Graph a shows how the chromatic tones and the small skips from the inner voice intensify the motion to the V[7].

A similar principle of harmonic prolongation, although in a different style, can be found at the beginning of Ravel's *Rigaudon* from *Le Tombeau de Couperin.* ►[Ex. 290]◄ We find here chords sometimes labeled II[11] and V[13] chords although the voice-leading devices of suspen-

[2] See also the *Romanze* from Schumann's *Faschingsschwank.*

sion and anticipation are the chord-creating factors. The meaning of the II in parenthesis will be explained later.

EXERCISES IV

1) The student is required to compare carefully and explain the different results of harmonic prolongation, depending on whether the prolongation precedes or follows the structural I.

2) The keyboard exercises given should be played in several major and minor keys. ►[Ex. 291]◄

*

*   *

Complete harmonic progressions form the most unequivocal and straightforward type of harmonic prolongation. On the other hand, the dominant prolongation and the incomplete harmonic progression, whether they precede or succeed the tonic, are on a slightly more complicated structural level and may make somewhat greater demands on the listener's capacity for structural hearing. The missing tonic, either at the beginning or at the end of the prolongation, gives these passages an air of uncertainty and an unsettled quality which may contribute much, not only to the structural but also to the emotional interest of a composition.

2. HARMONIC PROLONGATIONS OF OTHER HARMONIC CHORDS

Before considering the harmonic prolongations of other members of the harmonic framework it will be necessary to stress once more that any triad, and therefore any member of the harmonic framework, carries within itself the possibility of harmonic prolongation. Since the task for structural hearing becomes more complicated when the prolongations of these harmonies grow more elaborate, we shall now begin with the shortest and simplest type of prolongation of a harmony other than tonic.

a. The applied dominant chord

If a harmony other than the tonic is preceded or followed by its own dominant, then we have applied the fifth relationship existing between chords to a non-tonic harmony. ►[Ex. 292]◄ This dominant is related solely to the following II, which it stresses and prolongs. It belongs only to the II and has no harmonic relationship either to the preceding I or to the following V; it will be termed *applied dominant*.

An example is found in the beginning of a Waltz by Schubert. ►[Ex. 293]◄ It will be clear from the above illustration that the applied dominant has no effect on the structural harmonic framework; it is therefore a chord of prolongation—of harmonic prolongation through the application of the fifth relationship.

In a harmonic progression I-III-V-I, the III is usually preceded by its own dominant. In view of this fact, no illustration of a I-III-V-I progression was given in Chapter V which dealt only with contrapuntal prolongations. ►[Ex. 294, 295]◄

The applied dominant to the IV is a tonic chord with a lowered seventh; therefore this seventh is often added to the tonic which thus is easily transformed into an applied dominant. If we look back to Ex. 250 of Chapter V, we realize that the dominant seventh chord in meas. 2 is an applied dominant chord to the following IV. Another illustration can be found in Schumann's *Humoreske*. ►[Ex. 296]◄ Here the applied dominant chord in meas. 2 is embellished by a neighbor note C♭.

It must be noted that applied dominants by no means always appear as chords in root position. Inversions are used frequently, although the appearance of the root elsewhere than in the bass weakens the harmonic impulse, an interesting fact to which we shall return later on.

The applied dominant chord to the V is a major supertonic. ►[Ex. 297, 298, 299]◄ It is also possible that such an applied dominant may be preceded by its own dominant, thus intensifying the harmonic element in a phrase. ►[Ex. 300]◄ Occasionally in larger units, a major supertonic chord, preceding the V, acts in a relatively structural capacity. In such cases this chord must be interpreted not as an applied dominant but as a member of the harmonic framework achieved through mixture. The discussion of Chopin's Nocturne in F♯ minor, Op 48, No. 2, in Chapter VII will illustrate this fact.

EXERCISES V

First play the elaborated and secondary harmonic progressions as indicated in Chapter IV; then prolong these progressions with the help of the applied dominants of II, III, IV and VI as shown in ►[Ex. 301]◄. Also practice in minor the progressions indicated in b), c), d).[3]

---

[3] Since the II in minor is a diminished chord it does not have an applied dominant —the relationship of tonic-dominant being based on a perfect fifth. Instead composers have used a major chord whose origin and function will be discussed later (section F, 1).

The diminished seventh chord

Although it does not belong to the chords or progressions creating harmonic prolongation, the diminished seventh chord must be mentioned in this connection because it may act in a capacity similar to that of the applied dominant chord.

Its capacity is similar in that it shows a tendency to drive to the following chord, which it thus emphasizes. But unlike the applied dominant which has a harmonic tendency (fifth relationship) to the following chord, the diminished seventh chord through the half-tone progression in the bass and top voice has a melodic-contrapuntal tendency to the following chord, which makes it often appear as an incomplete neighbor-note or appoggiatura chord. ►[Ex. 302]◄ To distinguish between the two different chords acting in a similar prolonging and emphasizing capacity, the sign °7 is added to the curved arrow. ►[Ex. 303]◄

b.   An incomplete harmonic progression as prolongation of a harmonic chord

Members of the harmonic framework other than the tonic may receive a further prolongation and emphasis if they are preceded by an incomplete harmonic progression, i.e. if they are preceded not only by their own V but by II-V, by IV-V, etc. ►[Ex. 304, 305]◄ The graphs show clearly the function of these incomplete harmonic progressions preceding and prolonging a III and a V. The second example at the same time presents a good illustration of interruption. Observe especially the melodic intensification at the beginning of the post-interruption phrase.

The incomplete harmonic progressions refer only to the following harmony, which they thus stress and prolong. They have no relation to the preceding harmony but intensify the direction to the following harmony.

EXERCISES VI

1) Explain the meaning of the preceding type of harmonic prolongation.
2) Practice the given keyboard exercises in several major and minor keys. ►[Ex. 306]◄ Omit c) in minor keys.

c. *A complete harmonic progression as prolongation of a harmonic chord*

The student, having grasped the principle of harmonic prolongation, will have no difficulty in correctly evaluating the following prolongation of a IV and of a III in the form of a complete harmonic progression. ►[Ex. 307, 308]◄

As new demands are made on our capacity for structural hearing, it is more than ever essential not to lose contact with the progression of higher structural order and to keep the phrase or unit as a whole in mind. This, of course, is possible only if a feeling for musical direction has been firmly established. Being able to hear the organism as a whole will prevent the student from "stumbling" over the detail; the harmonic prolongations of the IV and of the III in the last examples present just such details and it is vital to appraise them correctly as offshoots of the progressions of higher structural order. Thus, in spite of their harmonic prolongations, the IV or the III remain members of the harmonic framework expressing E minor and F♯ Major respectively.

Certainly, the examples discussed above are short and relatively simple. But only with the help of such short and straightforward conceptions can the student at this time be expected to hear the connection between two structural harmonies in spite of the delay and the detour created by the harmonic prolongations.

In its large elaborations, which will be explained later on, this type of harmonic prolongation in the form of complete harmonic progressions represents one of the boldest conceptions of artistic retard and detour. And yet every prolongation, whether small or large, constitutes a detail in relation to the motion as a whole. Taking the detail as a main structural event by losing contact with the structural framework, is the surest way of missing the architectonic conception of the phrase or the piece as a whole. Through such wrong evaluation the listener becomes unable to perceive the tonal tension within the structural progression.

EXERCISES VII

1) As a summary the student should explain systematically the different types of harmonic prolongation, starting with the applied dominant and arriving at the complete harmonic progression. Their significance, especially within the structural harmonic framework, must be completely understood if any

benefit is to be derived from future discussion of complete pieces.

2) The following progressions may serve as keyboard exercises of complete harmonic prolongations. In these exercises it is important to play first the structure and then to proceed to the prolongations. ►[Ex. 309]◄

3.   HARMONIC PROLONGATION OF A CONTRAPUNTAL CHORD

Just as any harmony carries within itself the possibility of harmonic prolongation, contrapuntal chords of various functions also may appear harmonically prolonged. As a first illustration of this possibility let us listen to the beginning of Schumann's song, *Auf dem Rhein*. Here a passing chord between I and II$_5^6$ is harmonically prolonged. ►[Ex. 310]◄

Simultaneously with the harmonic prolongation, a melodic motion into the inner voice of the passing chord takes place which adds to the prolonging quality of the D-minor chord. It is essential here to realize that the character of the D-minor chord as a passing chord in no way is offset by its harmonic prolongation. In the structure of the whole phrase, the D-minor chord remains a passing chord whether it is prolonged or not. The prolongation, however, creates an artistic tension, since the ear is compelled, in spite of the additional burden created through the prolongation, to proceed to the II$_5^6$, which in turn it must perceive as coming from the I. This kind of hearing will prevent losing contact with the structural framework.

Very often harmonic prolongations of contrapuntal chords appear as part of a contrapuntal prolongation of a higher order. A very simple example is given. ►[Ex. 311]◄ Here, the subdominant, a passing chord within a prolonged I, is prolonged by its applied dominant.

Two examples from Chorales by Bach will now be presented, the first showing the prolongation of an embellishing chord, the second, the prolongation of a neighbor-note chord, both in the form of different harmonic progressions. The reader should observe how subtly interwoven these harmonic prolongations appear within the completely contrapuntal prolongation of the I. ►[Ex. 312, 313]◄

EXERCISES VIII

The progressions given may be used as keyboard exercises illustrating the harmonic prolongation of contrapuntal chords. ►[Ex. 314]◄

4.   THE CHORD OF HARMONIC EMPHASIS

A supertonic chord frequently is inserted between III and V of the harmonic progression I-III-V-I. This supertonic is a chord of prolongation. Since it appears as a minor chord it does not act as an applied dominant but still exercises a certain harmonic influence through being the chord a fifth above the V. We shall call this chord a chord of harmonic emphasis, because it emphasizes harmonically the coming V in spite of its not being as strong as an applied dominant. This chord will be labeled with a small Roman numeral in parenthesis indicating both its harmonic and its prolonging role within the structural harmonic progression I-III-V-I. ►[Ex. 315]◄ We do not call this chord merely an embellishing chord, because the fifth relationship to the V makes its harmonic prolonging character far more outstanding than its contrapuntal significance.

The supertonic may also act as a chord of harmonic emphasis within a structural I-IV-V-I progression. ►[Ex. 316]◄ In meas. 12 a supertonic harmonically emphasizes the following V within a I-IV-V-I progression. In regard to the piece as a whole it should be noted that at the end of section I (meas. 8), one is still in doubt as to which tone of the B♭ chord forms the first structural melody tone. Only in meas. 9-11 does the F emerge definitely as the initial structural tone from which the melody descends to the tonic. The indefinite swaying between the chord-tones D, F and B♭ in the first section and the definite motion of the second are the characteristics of this dance. Only after hearing section II, therefore, can one conclude that F is the first structural melody tone.

Not only the supertonic, but also occasionally the submediant may serve as a chord of harmonic emphasis. In such cases it emphasizes the following II within a progression I-II-V-I. An example will be found in Ex. 351.

EXERCISES IX

The following progressions may serve as a keyboard exercise and as an exercise in prolongation. ►[Ex. 317]◄

B.   Contrapuntal chords assuming structural significance

While the preceding paragraphs showed that harmonic chords and progressions may not only fulfill structural functions, but may also serve the purposes of prolongation, it will now be seen that chords whose status is clearly contrapuntal may assume structural significance. If a contrapuntal chord is used to support a structural tone in the melody, it has the significance of a structural chord. Therefore, harmonic and contrapuntal chords may both fulfill either a structural or a prolonging function. In the following examples the neighbor-note chord becomes a structural chord (CS, which means *contrapuntal-structural*) and thus is on equal level with the harmonic-structural chords. The neighbor-note chord appears here as a triad in root position, a $^6_5$ chord and a diminished seventh chord. ►[Ex. 318, 319, 320, 321]◄ The excerpt from *Dido and Aeneas* is a particularly beautiful example of the expressive power of baroque music. In these 12 measures the intention to veil all structural punctuation is very clearly felt. The C-minor chords of meas. 4 and 10, structurally so significant, appear inconspicuously within the general course of the voice leading. Note also the expressive voice leading of meas. 8-10 and the superposition of the inner voice in meas. 6, preventing a later transfer of register of structural top voice tones.

To completely clarify the meaning of this new type of structural progression, let us concentrate on the juxtaposition of the following two progressions. ►[Ex. 322]◄ Both examples have the same bass; yet the significance of the same chord on E is different in both cases. The reason lies in the top voice. In a) the neighbor note B♭ is a prolonging tone which in turn causes the bass E and the resulting neighbor-note chord to be prolonging. On the other hand, in b) the neighbor-note chord is a structural chord because it supports a structural tone of the melody. No prolongation in the top voice occurs; therefore the neighbor-note chord has given up any possible prolonging implication and is of the same structural order as a harmonic-structural chord.

In reference to the examples cited above and in regard to all other examples discussed, it should now be evident that a structural progression of the melody may be supported not only by one or two harmonic progressions but also by a combination of a contrapuntal and a harmonic progression. I-CS-I is combined for instance with I-II-V-I.

A slightly different combination of contrapuntal and harmonic structure can be found in Couperin's *La Bandoline.* ►[Ex. 323]◄ The difference lies in the use of the first inversion for the second tonic chord. This increases the contrapuntal element and proportionately decreases the harmonic character of the structural progression taken as a whole.[4]

The fact that contrapuntal chords may take on a structural signifi-

---

[4] For a further example of CS chords, see Ex. 331.

cance opens up the possibility of entirely contrapuntal structures about which we shall hear more in Chapters VII and VIII.

EXERCISES X

1) The student should define the term "contrapuntal-structural chords."
2) Find themes or sections of compositions which show the use of this chord function.
3) The progressions in Ex. 318-323 should serve as keyboard exercises.

*

*   *

The question may arise as to whether every tone of the melodic structure must be supported by a chord. The answer is that occasionally a structural tone of the melody is not supported by a new chord and, as a structural passing tone, still belongs to the preceding chord. A later example already mentioned, Ex. 351, serves as a good illustration.

SUMMARY

In Chapter V all chords found in the illustrations showed either a harmonic-structural or a contrapuntal-prolonging function. In the present chapter it has been shown that harmonic chords may also serve the purposes of prolongation, whereas contrapuntal chords may assume structural significance. This gives us, all in all, four different chord functions·

1. Harmonic-structural
2. Harmonic-prolonging
3. Contrapuntal-prolonging
4. Contrapuntal-structural

C. Double function of chords

Chord functions result when structural and prolonging forces are combined with the musical concepts of harmony and counterpoint. Each of these two "pairs" contains contrasting conceptions: structure contrasts with prolongation, harmony with counterpoint.

So far each chord has been either harmonic *or* contrapuntal, and at the same time it has been either structural *or* prolonging, giving us the four chord-functions listed at the end of the preceding section. It is an indication of tonality's expressive possibilities that in addition chords may be used whose functions show a fusion or overlapping of two contrasting elements. Chords, for instance, may be harmonic-structural but at the same time have a prolonging implication.

I.   HARMONIC-STRUCTURAL CHORDS WITH ADDED PROLONGING SIGNIFICANCE

This type of double function appears in the following excerpt from Chopin's Nocturne, Op 9, No. 2. The II of the structural-harmonic progression is stressed by its applied dominant. The top voice tone of this II, however, is an incomplete neighbor note, a prolonging tone of the melodic structure G-F-E♭. ►[Ex. 324]◄ The student should observe how the double function of the F-minor chord is indicated in the graphs. The quarter-note for the top voice A♭ indicates its prolonging status whereas the half-note F of the bass stresses the chord's structural role. In addition, the label DF is suggested. The reader should now take note of the melodic prolongations. The melodic structure of a descending third finds its diminution in prolonging motions of a third; one descending from G, the second taking place between the incomplete neighbor note and the following F, the last one (comparable in significance to the first) descending from that F. This last descending third, a motion into the inner voice of the V, is contrapuntally supported by a circling motion around B♭, by means of upper and lower neighbor notes. The resulting chords create a contrapuntal prolongation of the V.

Another example is the main theme from the first movement of Schumann's Piano Concerto. Here a chord of double function is created by an incomplete neighbor note [5] supported by IV of the harmonic framework I-IV-V-I. ►[Ex. 325]◄ A main point of interest in this theme is the broad contrapuntal prolongation of the double function chord, the IV. The gist of that prolongation is the motion to the A $^6_3$ chord as neighbor-passing chord while the melody and bass move into the inner voice of this chord. Had the upward motion of the bass continued right into meas. 5, we should have been confronted with a

---

[5] Although the neighbor note is prolonged, it still remains incomplete because the following C is a passing tone and thus may not be interpreted as a main tone (see Ex. 146 b).

harmonic prolongation of that IV, because then the bass of the prolongation would have been D-A-D. After the third quarter of meas. 4, however, the bass changes direction and reaches C♯, which causes the prolongation of the IV to be contrapuntal.

EXERCISES XI

The student is required:
1) to explain the significance of a double function chord.
2) to use as keyboard illustrations the exercises given in ►[Ex. 326.]◄

2. HARMONIC-PROLONGING CHORDS WITH ADDED STRUCTURAL SIGNIFICANCE

The preceding examples showed that a clash of the contrasting functions of structure and prolongation may occur through a prolonging tone of the top voice being supported by a structural bass. Thus the prolonging element appeared in the top voice whereas the bass presented the structural factor. The following example, however, will show that the opposite is possible: A structural tone of the top voice may be supported by an applied dominant which is a harmonic-prolonging chord.[6] ►[Ex. 327]◄ In this specific example the applied dominant follows the structural III and supports the structural tone B of the top voice.

3. HARMONIC-PROLONGING CHORDS WITH CONTRAPUNTAL IMPLICATIONS

While the preceding example showed an overlapping of structural and prolonging functions, the reader will now be introduced to harmonic-prolonging chords which simultaneously have a contrapuntal implication. This results in overlapping or double function between harmony and counterpoint.

a. The chord of harmonic emphasis as voice-leading chord

In the following passage from a Chorale by Bach the chord on the fourth beat is simultaneously a chord of harmonic emphasis and a voice-leading chord. Therefore an overlapping of harmonic and con-

[6] This technique can be found within the exposition of movements in sonata form; see Chapters VII and VIII.

trapuntal functions is apparent. ►[Ex. 328]◄ It should be stated that it makes no difference as to which of the two functions the reader considers to be of greater significance as long as the double or overlapping function is clearly understood.

b.   Descending fifths in sequence

We may find that on the basis of the harmonic fifth relationship, descending fifths in support of a melodic sequence combine to prolong either the progression between two chords or harmonies or to prolong a single chord. This type of prolongation would have been mentioned under the heading of harmonic prolongations had it not been for the fact that in most cases these harmonic-prolonging chords simultaneously show a definite contrapuntal significance.

The first 12 measures of a *Courante* by Handel present a particularly interesting application of the descending fifth technique. ►[Ex. 329]◄ The beginning will cause no great difficulties. The harmonic prolongation of the I lasts for four measures; the melody moves into and out of the inner voice while the D retains its structural value. With the C chord in meas. 5, a descending fifth passage begins and the problem arises as to how far it goes and which chord is the next member of the harmonic framework.

If one's ear were to perceive only the fact that there are chords a fifth apart, one would probably assume that the descending fifth progression starts in meas. 5 and extends to meas. 11. However, the melody in general and the motivic events in particular have to be taken into consideration. The melody shows that after the four measures which prolong the I there appears another group of four measures, which is formed by a new motivic idea and ushers in the descending fifths. With the appearance of the structural tone C of the melody in meas. 9, the motive changes once more, both voices now proceeding in eighth-notes. Consequently meas. 9 is interpreted as introducing the structural II of the first harmonic progression. One must beware of reading the descending fifth technique indiscriminately and of ignoring the possibility that the sequence of chords so related may reach an end even though followed by one or two chords a fifth apart; for these chords may be members of the harmonic structure.

We realize that the technique of descending fifths further prolongs and elaborates the contrapuntal prolongation between I and II. The harmonic implication of this technique seems obvious. It must be stressed, however, that the F♯ and E chords of meas. 6 and 8 have in addition the significance of voice-leading chords since they improve the voice-leading, which would otherwise threaten parallel fifths. Thus we recognize an overlapping of harmonic and contrapuntal elements.

In the following example by Schubert there is no motivic change, but the appearance of the melodic-structural tone A♭ elevates the supporting chord of the supertonic to a member of the structural harmonic framework. ►[Ex. 330]◄

A passage from Vaughan-Williams' Fifth Symphony shows that the technique under discussion appears also in more modern works. Here the descending fifths are between the I and a CS chord. ►[Ex. 331]◄ At the end an interesting example of prolonged counterpoint occurs; the specific technique employed is the shift of tones discussed in Chapter V. The connecting lines in Graph a indicate the "displacement" of the voice leading. In these last two excerpts the descending fifths have again demonstrated an added contrapuntal implication.

Finally a phrase from a Mozart Rondo is quoted. ►[Ex. 332]◄ In such passages the descending fifths show their original status as a progression having a harmonic prolonging function only, without an implied contrapuntal role, for we realize that the 7-6 progression (see Graph b) would not need the descending fifths for voice-leading purposes. They certainly add much to the color and interest of the passage, but they have no contrapuntal significance.

c. Ascending fifths

Rarer than a sequence of descending fifths is the technique of ascending fifths. Occasionally we find ascending fifths expressed as descending fourths. In the next example, from a Schubert Waltz, the bass tones F-C-G-D form a series of descending fourths expressing a progression from F to D. The last fourth appears as an ascending fifth, to prevent the bass from going into too low a register. However, the pattern of motion from the F to the D chord is maintained. The B♭ chord of meas. 5 substitutes D for B♭ in the bass, for voice-leading reasons. Basically, the D-minor chord of meas. 4 is a passing chord between I and IV, which, however, appears as IV⁶. ►[Ex. 333]◄

EXERCISES XII

As an exercise for descending fifths in particular, and for prolongation in general, the student should explain and play in different keys the graphs of Ex. 329-332. This should be done proceeding in the direction from the structure to the prolongations.

d. Applied dominants as passing chords
(Transition to chromaticism)

Applied dominant chords, as we know, are harmonic-prolonging chords. Often, however, they have an even stronger contrapuntal significance. The applied dominant to the VI at the beginning of Schubert's song, *Täuschung*, belongs in this category. ▶[Ex. 334]◀ We now recall the statement made earlier that the harmonic character of an applied dominant is weakened by putting that chord in inversion. In the last example, however, there is not only the question of weakened harmonic effect, but even a serious challenge to the harmonic role of that chord. The contrapuntal function is so strong that one may speak of a *chromatic-passing chord*.

An interesting example showing the double function of applied dominant chords may be found in Weber's Overture to *Der Freischütz*.[7] ▶[Ex. 335]◀ From previous explanations it will appear clear that we are confronted with a contrapuntal chord prolongation of the C-minor chord with a transfer of register in the top voice. The Eb-Major, G-minor, Bb-Major chords and the diminished seventh chord are passing chords within the governing C-minor chord. In addition the preceding applied dominant chords also serve as passing chords, because their top voice tones are passing tones.

e. Applied dominants as voice-leading chords

Applied dominants with additional voice-leading significance may be found in a passage from Haydn's String Quartet, Op 76, No. 4. ▶[Ex. 336]◀ The contrapuntal as well as harmonic significance of the $^6_5$ chords and the last sixth chord seems evident; the sixth chord of meas. 2, however, has only contrapuntal significance, since the following diminished chord has no dominant of its own.

Towards the end of the first movement of Schubert's Bb-Major Sonata we find a fascinating passage in the form of a series of applied dominants in root position with an added voice-leading implication. ▶[Ex. 337]◀ The reader will realize how the applied dominants improve the voice leading between the passing chords within the main motion from I to IV. In order to make the progression clear the constant change of register has been omitted in the graphs; it does not

[7] In her book, *Challenge to Musical Tradition* (Alfred A. Knopf, New York, 1946) Adele T. Katz has quoted this example in connection with the discussion on tonality.

affect the main direction of the progression, although contributing greatly to the color and interest of the passage. Note also the chromaticism of the top voice and the bass, which creates the D♭-minor chord, a chromatic-passing chord. The transfer of register and the fermata must not be permitted to deter the ear from hearing the progression in its drive from I to IV, for it is the underlying feeling or knowledge that the progression is directed toward the IV that makes the fermata, the rests and the changes of register the more artistic and exciting at the same time.

EXERCISES XIII

The graphs of Ex. 334, 335, 336, 337 should be used as exercises in prolongation in general and in double function chords in particular.

In reference to Ex. 334:

1) Play the progression I-VI-V-I with an ascending fourth in the melody.
2) Prolong with an applied dominant to the VI in $\frac{4}{3}$ position and explain its predominantly contrapuntal function.
3) Practice the resulting progression in different keys.

In reference to Ex. 335:

1) Explain in general the characteristics of the prolongation.
2) Proceed to Graph a and define clearly the function of each chord.

In reference to Ex. 337:

Explain the prolongations indicated in Graph a and play it in different keys.

In addition the keyboard exercises offered in the next example should be practiced in several keys. ►[Ex. 338]◄

Ex. 338a shows a passing chord which is simultaneously an applied dominant to an embellishing-passing chord within the prolonged C-Major chord

Ex. 338b shows an applied dominant to V which also serves as a voice-leading chord.

Ex. 338c and d are elaborations of Ex. 126 of Chapter V. The student should first play that example and then elaborate it with the applied dominants as indicated.

f. *Elimination of the harmonic element*

Passing and voice-leading functions of certain chromatic chords may be so predominant that any possible harmonic implication is completely absorbed by their contrapuntal significance. ►[Ex. 339]◄

EXERCISES XIV

In the following exercise the harmonic significance of the applied dominants is lost in the passing motion from I to II⁶. ►[Ex. 340a]◄

The same can be said of the next exercise in which the chromatic passing motion of the alto stresses the contrapuntal significance of the chord prolongation (Ex. 340b).

Whenever we are confronted with a series of applied dominants in inversion forming a chromatic bass progression, these applied dominants tend to lose their harmonic significance and become part of a contrapuntal passing motion (Ex. 340c).

D. Additional versions to four-part settings

It will now be possible to add more versions to the previously demonstrated four-part settings of short melodies. The following versions, employing some of the newly discussed techniques, are suggested for the melodies of Ex. 189, 190, 191, 193, 194 of Chapter V. ►[Ex. 341, 342, 343, 344, 345]◄

EXERCISES XV

Write one or more four-part settings for the following melodic phrases. ►[Ex. 346]◄

*

*　　　　　　　　　*

Such exercises pave the way for the setting of chorale melodies. The student is advised to study carefully the Bach-style of chorale-setting before proceeding to his own settings.[8] It is also possible from here on

---

[8] We refer again to the Chapter "Tones of Figuration" in W. J. Mitchell's *Elementary Harmony*.

to take up the writing of melodies to given instrumental basses (not figured), or the piano accompaniment type of setting of given melodies of different styles, etc.

We believe that an earlier inclusion of the piano accompaniment settings would have been premature. The student must have a firm grasp of what is harmonic or contrapuntal, structural or prolonging and a clear understanding of musical direction before such semi-creative work will be of any benefit.

E. Chromaticism

Applied dominants with their use of the leading tone have given rise to chromatic progressions. Chromaticism as such, however, is a melodic-contrapuntal element of prolongation and intensification. Therefore, the discussion of it belongs, to a considerable degree, to the realm of counterpoint. Although one finds specific chords appearing repeatedly within chromatic motions, it is the voice-leading problems which demand primary consideration. For it appears that these chords are the result of voice leading and voice direction.

I.   THE DIMINISHED SEVENTH CHORD, THE DOMINANT SEVENTH
     CHORD, THE SIXTH AND $^6_4$ CHORD IN THE SERVICE OF CHRO-
     MATICISM

In Chapter V the diminished seventh chord's role as a neighbor-note chord was mentioned and in the present chapter its emphasizing role, similar to that of the applied dominant, has been noted. Its emphasis of the chord to which it resolves, makes its use as a passing chord very logical. In the following two short Chorale phrases the diminished seventh chord serves as a passing chord between II$^6_5$ and the $^6_4$ chord and between IV and V. ►[Ex. 347, 348]◄

Two diminished seventh chords as passing chords between chords which are not harmonic are to be found in a passage from the slow movement of Haydn's String Quartet, Op 76, No. 1. ►[Ex. 349]◄ The first of these seventh chords is a passing chord, but also emphasizes the following A-minor chord; the second appears as a chromatic-passing chord. It should be observed that the chromatic character is maintained regardless of whether the chromatic tones are in the top voice or in the bass.

Another characteristic use of the diminished seventh chord appears in the Mazurka, Op 24, No. 3 by Chopin. ▶[Ex. 350]◀ The chords in question strengthen the following chords and also serve as voice-leading chords. According to the top voice in meas. 2 and the inner voice in meas. 2 and 3, these chords could in addition be labeled as passing chords.

Diminished seventh chords as passing and as voice-leading chords occur at the beginning of Hugo Wolf's song, *Schlafendes Jesuskind*. ▶[Ex. 351]◀

EXERCISES XVI

Although more passages showing the use of the diminished seventh chord will be quoted later on, the exercises in ▶[Ex. 352]◀ deal with the most frequently encountered applications of that chord.

1) Exercises a and b show this chord in the emphasizing role already mentioned; in the second progression it is also a chromatic-passing chord.

2) Exercise c presents the diminished seventh chord as a passing chord. As the outer voices have passing tones, the passing character supersedes the emphasizing role of the chord.

3) Exercise d reveals the diminished seventh chord as a combined voice-leading and passing chord.

▶[Ex. 353 and 354]◀ are exercises in prolongation. The student should explain the exercises from their basic to their prolonged form and describe the nature of the prolongation as well as the function of the diminished seventh chords.

▶[Ex. 355 and 356]◀ present the diminished seventh chords interwoven into contrapuntal chord prolongations.

*

*   *

Chromaticism is often expressed by a series of dominant seventh chords; a remarkable example is taken from Chopin's Mazurka, Op 30, No. 4. ▶[Ex. 357]◀ The seventh chords in succession cause parallel fifths in the outer voices. If Chopin had proceeded in meas. 6 as he had done in meas. 5, we would be confronted with a 5-6 progression. The elimination of the sixth through the use of contraction gives rise to the successive prolonging fifths of this passage (see section *Octaves and fifths* in Chapter VII, page 197).

In the excerpt from Schumann's second *Novelette* diminished seventh and sixth chords contribute to the chromatic character of the passage. ►[Ex. 358]◄

While in the preceding example the bass motion of the prolongation led into the middle voice of the tonic, we now hear the bass motion taking its start from the middle voice, for the bass B♭ (meas. 1) is derived as neighbor note from an A within the D-Major tonic. Note also the transfer of register of the top voice tone F♯.

2. CONTRAPUNTAL TEXTURE IN CHROMATIC PASSAGES

Since many chords within a chromatic passage are derived solely through special contrapuntal devices such as anticipation, suspension or through added chromaticism of middle voices, it is in many instances a mere waste of time for the student to attempt to give a grammatical label to each chord resulting from chromatic-contrapuntal prolongation. Although augmented and altered chords which play an important role in chromatic voice leading will be presented, the mere knowledge of those chord names, including those already discussed, will hardly explain the only factors of importance, the direction of the chromatic voice leading and the forces contributing to it.

Recognition of the voice leading is essential to the understanding of chromaticism. The direction of voice leading may show for instance that the basic contrapuntal setting is diatonic or that it consists of a series of diminished seventh chords. Such progressions may be prolonged by the contrapuntal devices which have been mentioned before.

Let us listen for instance to a passage from Chopin's Mazurka, Op 17, No. 4. ►[Ex. 359]◄ The chromatic motion is clearly based on a progression of diminished seventh chords between the tonic and the D-minor chord. The chord in meas. 3, however, arises out of an anticipation of F (the bass of the coming diminished seventh chord), while the other tones of the preceding diminished chord are sustained. Similarly the chord in meas. 5 is created by an anticipation of an inner voice tone of the next diminished seventh chord and the suspension of the former chord tones.

Whether chord grammar is able to label such chords or not is irrelevant as long as the chord-creating contrapuntal force is clear. In this connection let us consider a passage from Wagner's *Götterdämmerung.* ►[Ex. 360]◄ It is vital to recognize the underlying diatonic contrary motion performing a transfer of register (Graph a). This contrary motion and the chromatic intensification of outer and inner voices are the forces which create the dissonant chromatic-passing chords within a prolonged F chord. A further labeling of single chords would be superfluous, as it would in no way contribute to the understanding of this passage.

In order to make clear in detail the contrapuntal forces which determine the meaning of a chromatic passage, two excerpts from Chopin's Mazurkas are presented. The first is taken from the Mazurka, Op 7, No. 2. ►[Ex. 361]◄ The similarity in structural outline with the preceding Chopin example is obvious; both these passages show a chromatic prolongation of the A-minor chord in which the main event is the motion into the inner voice of the subdominant chord. This chord in Op 17, No. 4 was a passing chord while in this passage it represents a neighbor-note chord (Graphs a and b). A main difference, however, lies first of all in the bass; while the chromatic bass motion of the preceding passage started from the inner voice region, it starts in the latter passage from the tonic A. This passage shows also greater complication in the detail of the chromatic prolongations.

Now to Graph c, which shows that the initial chromatic top voice tone Eb is the continuation from E natural, the structural top voice tone of the preceding meas. 1-16. The chromatic prolongation is mainly based on a progression of diminished seventh chords. In this graph the melodic tones D and Bb appear unsupported by new bass tones, since there are more chromatic tones in the top voice than in the bass. In Graph d we find the chords as they appear in the composition; the new chords, not included in the preceding graph, arise from anticipations and suspensions. At the beginning we realize how the suspension of the bass Ab provides the bass for the melodic tone D (meas. 20). The student will recognize how these anticipations and suspensions help to create the chords which intensify the chromaticism and which appear without stems. Stemless notes are used to distinguish the structural value of these chords from that of the chords which are the actual executors of the basic chromatic motion (see Graph c).

While Ex. 359 and 361 showed certain similarities, the next quotation from the first Mazurka is entirely different in outline and detail. ►[Ex. 362]◄ The reader will find that, after a prolongation of the I, Chopin proceeds to the III via its applied dominant. The chromatic progression which follows constitutes an extended prolongation of the progression from III to V. Instead of a third upward Chopin moves a sixth chromatically downwards. This chromatic prolongation and its "history" will now be studied in detail. The basis of the passage is a diatonic progression of tenths prolonged with 7-6 syncopations (Graph a). As a result of chromaticism in the top and inner voices the following progression arises (Graph b). An added fourth voice engenders the progression shown in Graph c. Through introduction of chromaticism in the bass and syncopation in the top voice we approach Chopin's progression more closely (Graph d). Finally syncopation of the bass causes a rhythmic shift of the bass tones and this brings us to the chord succession as it appears in Chopin's Mazurka (Graph e).

It should be understood that this exact description in successive stages of the music's coherence serves primarily to make clear the importance of the contrapuntal element in chromatic passages. Voice leading creates this type of chord progression; its thorough understanding must be the student's primary objective. In chromatic passages, as in other progressions, chord grammar is unable to bring the listener any closer to the music and the direction of its motion. Certainly the student can afford later on—once those problems have been grasped—to be satisfied with the mere recognition of a chromatic passing motion between III and V. At this stage, however, a thorough insight into the essence and the procedure of chromaticism appears indispensable.

Finally let us listen to a section from Schumann's *Novelette* No. 8 which, apart from chromaticism, presents highly interesting structural problems. ►[Ex. 363]◄ The section as a whole represents a three-part form (A-B-A¹) and is the most involved example yet presented.

We shall first discuss meas. 1-8. Careful listening reveals that the upward motion of the bass combined with a transfer of register in the top voice, creates a prolongation of a B♭-Major chord proceeding in tenths (Graph a). The next stage of prolongation introduces a chromatic bass and the resulting interpolated diminished seventh chords and the single ⁶₅ chord; the top voice contains a motive indicated by a bracket (Graph b). The following graph indicates the voice leading of the actual composition (Graph c).

The first part ends on V; the melodic-structural tone D moves to C; the melodic motion to F is a motion into the inner voice with C acting as a retained tone. This brings us to the middle part. This section represents an extended prolongation of the V. First the bass moves down to B♭; when this B♭ is reached, the top voice has moved a minor second up from F to G♭; from there in the following measures the top voice proceeds to A♭, B♭ and C, the counterpoint moving in sixths. Therefore, the whole passage is based on the indicated progression (Graph d). Within this progression the initial downward motion replaces an upward motion which would show that the bass B♭ comes out of the inner voice A of the V (Graph e).

The progression of Graph d appears further prolonged through chromaticism in the inner voice which creates the augmented chords (Graph f). At the end of the middle section, the structural C is brought down into the original register of the beginning after which the third section starts and develops. Because of its correspondence with the first form section, the exact voice leading is offered only starting from meas. 21 following which changes occur (Graphs g, h).

Taking account of what occurs in this section as a whole, we realize that the technique of interruption, mentioned in Chapter V, is the form-making factor. It even makes possible a three-part form through the prolongation of the V, the dividing dominant, which constitutes the middle part. All these problems of form will be dealt with in detail in Chapter VIII; however, to complete the discussion a graph demonstrating the three-part form as a whole is presented (Graph i).

In conclusion it must be emphasized that this section of the *Novelette* clearly shows prolonged counterpoint and its relation to pure counterpoint (we recall the progression of tenths and the 6-5 progression). It hardly seems possible that the motion and coherence in this example could be explained on the basis of chord grammar or by an entirely harmonic approach.

EXERCISES XVII

1) Play the given exercise in different keys and explain the meaning of the prolongations, proceeding from the structure to the final prolongation. ►[Ex. 364]◄

2) Then proceed to the Chopin and Schumann examples and use them for similar exercises in prolongation.

3.   ALTERED CHORDS

Some of the chords that have occurred in the Chopin and Schumann excerpts will now be studied in detail. They are shown after chromatic examples have been discussed, in order to demonstrate that such examples from the literature may be understood even if certain chord labels are unknown.

a.   *The augmented triad*

This chord results from the contraction of a triad and a passing tone. ►[Ex. 365]◄ This chord appears frequently as a contrapuntal chord (passing chord, neighbor-note or embellishing chord, appoggiatura chord) but may also be used as an augmented I of a harmonic progression. ►[Ex. 366, 367]◄ In the first example the augmented tonic creates a colorful accent. In the phrase from *Götterdämmerung* the second inversion of an augmented triad is a passing chord within a prolonged F-Major chord. Through contraction, the bass, instead of jumping from F to C and then proceeding to C♯, skips immediately to C♯ thus increasing the impetus of the following upward motion.

b. The augmented sixth chord

A similar contraction creates the augmented sixth chord. ►[Ex. 368]◄ This chord is used as a contrapuntal chord and is sometimes known as the Italian Sixth.

c. The augmented dominant seventh chord

The element of contraction is also discernible in the augmented dominant seventh. In the following two examples ►[Ex. 369]◄ this chord serves as an applied dominant and a chromatic-passing chord (double function).

d. The altered chord of the supertonic
(root position and inversion)

The main characteristic of this chord in root position is a diminished third between the third and fifth of the chord. In the following example this altered chord is an altered applied dominant. ►[Ex. 370]◄ In Ex. 370b this chord has an additional passing implication (A-A♭-G). Most frequently, however, this chord appears in second inversion as a $\frac{6}{3}$ chord, often called the French Sixth (Ex. 370c). In this example the French Sixth acts as a voice-leading chord. A famous illustration of this altered $\frac{6}{3}$ chord appears at the beginning of the Prelude to Wagner's *Tristan und Isolde.*[9] ►[Ex. 371]◄

e. The altered chord of the subdominant
(root position and inversion)

In this chord the diminished third lies between the root and the third of the chord. ►[Ex. 372]◄ As in the case of the altered supertonic, this chord is most often used in inversion, usually in first inversion as a $\frac{6}{3}$

[9] For a detailed analysis of the opening section see the chapter on Wagner in Adele T. Katz, op. cit.

chord, sometimes called the German Sixth. ►[Ex. 373]◄ In both of these progressions, the altered subdominant appears as a passing chord.

The student should be able to explain the meaning of all of the preceding illustrations of augmented and altered chords. In addition he should practice them at the keyboard in different keys.

F. Mixture

In Chapter IV the process of mixture between major and minor and its influence on the harmonic progressions was mentioned. The student's attention should now be called to a specific chord of mixture which frequently appears in music.

1.   THE NEAPOLITAN SIXTH OR THE PHRYGIAN II

There is one instance in tonal music where a mixture occurs not between major and minor but between minor and the Phrygian mode. We know that the II in minor is a diminished chord. In order to obtain a perfect triad with its greater harmonic possibilities, composers have been led to the II of the Phrygian mode, which is a major chord. For instance, in A minor the II comprises the tones B-D-F; using the II of A-Phrygian we obtain the Bb-Major chord. ►[Ex. 374]◄ This II-Phrygian appears in the majority of cases in first inversion and is called the Neapolitan Sixth. The designation of II will be retained here, however, in order to emphasize that this chord has the function of a supertonic. In the beginning of Beethoven's Sonata, Op 27, No. 2, we find a Neapolitan Sixth or II⁶-Phrygian. ►[Ex. 375]◄ The II-Phrygian here is a chord of double function.

For another example the G♯-minor passage in the A-Major Duet from Weber's *Der Freischütz* (Act II) may be cited. ►[Ex. 376]◄ As we are taking this passage out of context and are thus treating it as an isolated unit, we may discuss the harmonic progression I-II⁶-Phrygian-V-I as a structural harmonic progression.

An illustration of a Phrygian II in root position from Strauss's *Ariadne auf Naxos* follows. The Phrygian II appears here within a harmonic prolongation of a II of a higher structural order. ►[Ex. 377]◄

Whereas in the preceding examples the Phrygian supertonic was used as a harmonic chord, it also may appear interwoven into the voice leading of a contrapuntal chord prolongation. The following illustration shows the chord as a passing chord within a prolonged tonic (pedal point) and the quotation as a whole presents an example of a mediant as an embellishing chord. ►[Ex. 378]◄

EXERCISES XVIII

In addition to using the graphs of Ex. 375-378 as exercises in prolongation, Ex. 374 should be practiced in different keys. This exercise may be prolonged by using the applied dominant of the II-Phrygian. ►[Ex. 379]◄.

2. VARIOUS USES OF MIXTURE

The reader's attention is drawn to the following passage from Prokofieff's Gavotte, Op 77, No. 4. The III in Eb Major would be diatonically a G-minor chord; Prokofieff however uses the Gb-Major chord, the III of Eb minor. ►[Ex. 380]◄

Besides the III, the VI very frequently shows the use of mixture. Strauss's *Don Juan* opens with a very effective mixture of the VI. The C-Major chord is the VI of E minor and these opening measures as a whole form an incomplete harmonic prolongation of the I. ►[Ex. 381]◄

Before proceeding to the following excerpts it must be stressed again that the discussion of them, in addition to illustrating a special technique, must be considered an exercise in structural hearing in general.

A mixed VI within a complete harmonic progression in which the progression from I to VI proves to be highly interesting, may be found within the first 12 measures of Hugo Wolf's song, *In dem Schatten meiner Locken.* ►[Ex. 382]◄ The VI is reached by a motion in skips from Bb via D to Gb; the D chord, meas. 5, is thus a passing chord between I and VI and, through mixture, appears as a D-Major chord. An interesting expansion of this progression is achieved by prolonging the I with the dominant which itself appears prolonged by its own incomplete harmonic progression (see Graph a). This prolongation of the I takes up the first four measures. It is essential, in order to hear the whole motion as an organism, not to be unduly diverted by that prolongation, and to be able to hear the following D-Major chord as a passing chord between the I and the VI which is preceded by its own applied dominant. The melodic events, however, present some problems. Graphs a and b will help to indicate the melodic cooperation between the voice part and the top voice of the piano accompaniment. In the beginning, the piano introduces the first structural tone D while the voice moves out of the inner voice. In meas. 4 the inner voice F appears superimposed upon the C in the piano part. The piano proceeds with a transfer of register upwards to reach the high D♭ in meas. 9 while the voice keeps the original register (meas. 7 and 8) and moves in the same meas. (9) to D♭. It is this D♭ which in meas. 11 in the piano part goes back to D♮; the high B♭ in meas. 10 is thus a superimposed inner voice. Although the singing voice has retained the register of the structural progression, it is the piano which now, in giving up the high register which it had attained, ends the whole phrase. It is typical of Hugo Wolf that the piano appears as the main executor of the melodic prolongations.

It frequently occurs that in addition to the VI, the first I of a harmonic framework appears mixed with its parallel minor. An illustration is the middle part of the slow movement of Beethoven's Sonata, Op 13. The first part ends in meas. 36 on the A♭-Major I and, with the following meas. (37), the middle section begins on the A♭-minor I. ►[Ex. 383]◄ Starting from the top voice tone A♭ there develops a motion down a sixth to the middle C (meas. 51), the starting point of the third form section (see Graphs a and b). This motion of a sixth is set to a harmonic framework of I-VI-V-I, the first two harmonies appearing as a result of mixture with A♭ minor (note the enharmonic change of F♭ to E♮). Meas. 42 and 43 show a prolongation of the applied dominant of the mixed VI which is especially effective through the superposition and transfer of register, which Graph a illustrates.

Another bold and complex example of a mixed I-VI-V-I may be found at the end of the slow movement of Schubert's Sonata in C minor. ►[Ex. 384]◄ In a motion similar to that in the Wolf excerpt, the progression to the VI moves in two major thirds (Graph a). However, the thirds are filled and this makes for a great difference in the detailed prolongations. The first third is expressed through inversion as a sixth down. The C chord, completing the first step of the progression from I to VI, appears through mixture as a C-Major chord. The second third is filled with chromatic passing tones which give rise to D♭ Major and D-Major chords and the detailed voice leading indicated in Graph b. It is important for the student not to be disturbed and distracted by the fermatas on the passing chords and by the transfer of register. These chords still remain passing chords, and the motivic sequence helps to keep the whole motion together until the VI is reached, where the first structural stop is created. The preceding A-Major chord is a passing chord which brings the top voice to B♮ (C♭). The tonic chord following the VI has the function of a voice-leading chord between VI and V.

As the application of mixture is so very characteristic of Schubert's technique of composition, another illustration from his works will be presented, the song, *Pause*. ►[Ex. 385]◄ As a whole, this section presents bold prolongations of a I-II-V-I progression. The graphs point to two prolongations, one between I and II, the other between II and V. Although the second prolongation shows chords of mixture (the chords on A♭ and G♭), we first have to concentrate on the progression from I to II. Instead of a second up from B♭ to C, Schubert moves in thirds downwards, so to speak, filling the space of a seventh. We say "so to speak" because in the actual composition the starting point of the bass motion is not the higher B♭; nevertheless the meaning of the motion from B♭ to C is that of a seventh downwards (see Graph b). The top voice shows motions into and out of the inner voice until the II is reached, ushering in the upper neighbor-note E♭; thus the II is a double function chord. The following sudden entry of the A♭-Major chord (mixture with B♭-minor) is baffling until we realize that the passing motion in thirds is taken up again. The last third from A♭ to F, the dominant, is filled with another chord of mixture, the chord on G♭. The progression from A♭ to the chord on G♭ is in itself prolonged (see Graph a) through two chords, which are the result of a further process of mixture which we may call "*double mixture*." The A♭-Major chord had been derived from a simple mixture. This chord through further mixture becomes an A♭-minor chord (meas. 63) which also explains the following F♭ chord in first inversion. This latter chord improves and colorfully enriches the voice leading. It can not be denied that double mixture offers an expansion of tonality's expressive possibilities.

In surveying this colorful and rather complex section once more we believe that its correct understanding depends on never losing contact with the starting point. This is imperative if we are not merely to register visible facts without inner connection. Of course the full meaning of this section, beyond the purely musical understanding, is very dependent on a consideration of the words. However, a discussion of the relation of words and music would take us too far afield from our immediate objective. One minor but significant detail may be pointed out. In meas. 54, after the diminished seventh chord and in view of the coming C-minor chord, one would expect a C chord in first inversion. At this point, it appears, the word *bange* (anxious) demanded a special color; and this coloring is provided subtly by the use of an A♭ chord in second inversion which, however, does not affect the general voice-leading direction.

The relation of words and music on the basis of structural hearing presents a host of new and important problems and could open up a special field for many theses and dissertations. In this connection I should like to quote a highly expressive use of mixture, both in melody and harmony, in a phrase from Mahler's *Das Lied von der Erde*. ►[Ex. 386]◄

And now to the last example, a passage from Chopin's last Mazurka (posth.) in F minor, Op 68, No. 4 which presents a further illustration of double mixture. ►[Ex. 387]◄ As a result of mixture with F major the III would appear as an A-minor chord; by a second process of mixture this chord appears as an A-Major chord. This harmony of double mixture creates a neighbor note in the top voice, and is reached by a chromatic drive from I to its applied dominant.

EXERCISES XIX

1) The preceding graphs should be used as exercises in prolongation.

2) The student is required to find additional examples illustrating various uses of mixture.

G.   The role of the submediant

In passages outlined by two harmonic progressions it frequently happens that the tonic, which simultaneously constitutes the end of the first and the beginning of the second harmonic progression, is replaced by a submediant. This submediant thus becomes part of the harmonic framework. ►[Ex. 388, 389]◄ Once a substitution is desired, the choice of the VI is convincing, since from the point of view of voice leading it presents the most satisfactory chord. It achieves not only suspense and chordal variety, but also, through the instability of the first harmonic progression, a heightened feeling of urge towards the final dominant and tonic.

It would, however, be misleading to interpret the submediant in the following two excerpts in the same way. ►[Ex. 390, 391]◄ Although the submediant again acts in substituting capacity, it simultaneously becomes a passing chord—in one example to the II⁶, and in the other, to the Ab neighbor-passing chord. Consequently, in regard to the passages as a whole the contrapuntal function outranks the "local" harmonic implications, and the result is a fascinating overlapping of contrapuntal and harmonic elements with greater emphasis on the contrapuntal.

This use of the submediant chord can be traced back to a progression shown in Ex. 126, Chapter V. The function, for instance, of tonic-dominant-submediant chords at the beginning of the progression is very similar to the use of these chords in the last two excerpts. In all three, the submediant is a passing chord; however, this function stands out more strikingly in the keyboard progression (Ex. 126) as a result of the sequential passing motion.

To sum up, the difference between the submediant in Ex. 388, 389 and the submediant in Ex. 390, 391 lies in the fact that in the former passages the submediant substitutes for the I of a structural harmonic progression and in this way becomes, so to speak, an end in itself. In Ex. 390, 391, however, the submediant is predominantly a contrapuntal chord (a passing chord) and therefore only a means to an end, which is arriving at a chord of higher structural order.

Conventional harmony calls these uses of the submediant indiscriminately "deceptive cadences." It seems that this term has some justification when applied to passages similar to those shown in Ex. 388, 389. It becomes rather misleading in the other excerpts, because hearing a cadence, even a deceptive cadence, may cause the reader to miss the eminent contrapuntal function of the submediant. To be sure, in all these passages a dominant moves to a submediant, but that in itself is not more than a description of chords and leaves problems of chord function entirely unsolved.

H. Expansion of units—The relation of structure and prolongation in larger units

In discussing themes, phrases and small sections of pieces, the aim has been to prepare the student for progressively larger and more complex units, leading to the discussion of entire compositions. In this chapter we have already taken a few larger units into consideration as the student's ability to hear structurally has enabled him to follow their organic coherence.

It now becomes increasingly important to clarify the problems and relations of structure and prolongation in larger units. If, for instance, we put a small phrase back into the larger framework from which we have temporarily separated it, the evaluation of what represents structure and what represents prolongation will change. A progression which was interpreted as being structural because it formed the structure of a particular isolated phrase under discussion, will have the function of a prolonging progression the moment that passage is analyzed as part of a larger whole. It must become very clear to the student that the determination of structural and prolonging factors depends entirely on whether he analyzes a phrase or a theme as a unit in itself or as part of a larger whole.

Let us recall for instance the Chorale phrase of Ex. 276. The two measures showed, as a separate unit, a harmonic structural framework of I-II-V-I and a descending third D-C-B as structural line of the top voice. If we now listen to the following phrase, we shall realize that the two phrases together form a unit of a higher structural order, making the phrase of Ex. 276 part of a larger whole. ►[Ex. 392]◄

Listening to those four measures as an entity, we realize that the top voice, having descended to B (meas. 2), ascends to D again in meas. 3. We understand now that in relation to the whole, the melodic motions of the first phrase are a motion into the inner voice and—again in relation to the whole—the supporting harmonic progression is a harmonic-prolonging progression which is followed by a short contrapuntal prolongation of the G chord. Thus the prolongation of the tonic is subdivided into a harmonic prolongation as a support for the motion into the inner voice, and a contrapuntal prolongation as a counterpoint of the melodic ascent back to the structural tone D. After this return has been accomplished, the structural progression of the melody descends to G and is harmonized by IV-V-I.

Since the phrase quoted in Ex. 276 appears now as a prolongation, it is logical to change the structural note-values. The tones C and B and their supporting bass tones A, D and G which were indicated by half-notes will now be written as quarter-notes.

Another phrase we discussed as an isolated structural unit was the beginning of Chopin's Waltz in C♯ minor (see Ex. 297). We shall now put these measures back into a larger framework of 16 measures. Meas. 1-4 will now appear only as part of a larger prolongation of the structural I. The top voice shows a motion into and out of the inner voice. ►[Ex. 393]◄

We shall now embark on the discussion of the largest section which we have taken so far and shall explain its coherence. Meas. 1-44 from the first movement of Schubert's Sonata in B♭ Major will prove to be a valuable testing ground for our ability to understand a larger musical

organism. ►[Ex. 394]◄ After listening to this section (which represents the broadly conceived first theme of that movement), we realize
that it leads to the V. In addition we grasp that it is constructed in itself
as a three-part form A-B-A¹, with a section prolonging the Gb-Major
chord as the middle part. Recalling what has been learned from the
two preceding examples, it will be apparent that the 18 measures forming the first part represent in their relation to the whole an extended
prolongation of the tonic. This should be kept in mind even if we are
unable as yet to provide a more precise explanation. The bass tone Bb,
the structural bass for these 18 measures, moves to Gb, a result of mixture (meas. 20-35) and then in meas. 35 to F, which is the dominant of
Bb Major. In meas. 39 this dominant moves to the I. If we now take the
bass motion as a whole we obtain Bb-Gb-F-Bb which are the bass tones
of a harmonic progression I-VI-V-I. ►[Ex. 395]◄ This bass outline
gives the first clue to the coherence of our example; this emphasizes
that for structural hearing on a large scale the recognition of the bass
outline will prove to be indispensable.

We may now proceed to the detailed hearing of the first 18 measures. It should be kept in mind that the determination of what is structural and what is prolonging depends entirely on the point of view
we take. If, for instance, we isolate the first four measures, they present a structural I-V-I progression, supporting a descending third in
the top voice. ►[Ex. 396]◄

In its relation to the group of measures up to meas. 7, however, that
progression is a subordinated prolongation. In meas. 7 the dominant,
supporting the supertonic of the top voice, is reached. This fact plus
the following re-entry of the same melodic material and the conclusion on the tonic in meas. 18 show us that the first part is subdivided
through interruption. ►[Ex. 397]◄

Since this section is not to be dealt with alone, but in relation to the
complete section of 44 measures, structural half-notes (except for the
first tonic) have not been used in the final graph of this section (Graph
b). The interruption forms—we must keep this in mind—only the first
18 measures, which in relation to the whole shows a motion into the
inner voice supported by a harmonic prolongation of I. The reader
will note also the different use of the neighbor note Eb in the pre- and
post-interruption period; observe also the penetration of the melodic
descending third into the smallest prolongations.

In undertaking to discuss the middle part, we realize first of all that
the trill on Gb in meas. 8 proves to be a very expressive anticipation of
the Gb of the middle section. This alone is an indication of synthesis

which, however, is overshadowed by the fact that the melody built on the Gb chord up to meas. 25 is closely related to the melodic events of meas. 10-18. This makes for organic coherence of seemingly contrasting sections and should be studied carefully by comparing the next graph with Ex. 397, Graph b. ►[Ex. 398]◄ This new graph gives a clear explanation of the melodic events on the basis of a Gb pedal point. We see the whole section as a contrapuntally prolonged VI which in meas. 35 moves to the V.

And now for the most fascinating synthesis of the whole section. Instead of using the V $^6_4$ $^5_3$ at the end of the middle section, which would have caused the third section (A¹) to start with the tonic, as one might expect, Schubert, although still on the $^6_4$ suspension of the V, nevertheless begins with the motive of the first theme. While the top voice thus shows a regular recapitulation, the bass, during the first four measures, is still in the process of completing the harmonic progression started previously. This not only creates a very original synthesis of the form sections but also makes possible a prolongation of the dominant which is structurally so significant. ►[Ex. 399]◄

All three form sections can now be presented in a series of graphs which will give a clear picture of these 44 measures as a whole. As the details have been shown in the previous graphs, some of the smaller prolongations are now omitted in order to facilitate the presentation of the complete unit. ►[Ex. 400]◄

The first 18 measures appear as a wide harmonic prolongation of the I, with the tone D as the structural top voice tone; the I moves to VI which supports the neighbor note Db and, in contrast to the tonic, is prolonged contrapuntally. The completion of the harmonic progression with V-I in meas. 36-39, overlapping with the entry of the third form section, will now appear completely clear.

In relation to the structure of these 44 measures as a whole, however, this harmonic progression I-VI-V-I represents a harmonic prolongation of a I of still higher structural order which moves to V.

The student is now required to move from Graph c "backwards" to the composition and to clarify each prolongation, finally taking into account the first detailed graphs.

Part II   Chapter Seven

Structure and Prolongation III

From here on, every example quoted should first be approached and analyzed as independently as possible from the explanations offered in the graphs. These should then be compared with the results of the reader's own investigations.

As it is frequently both awkward and difficult to express in words all the facts and complexities of tonal direction and organization, the graphs will tend increasingly to replace the written word. They deal, as we have already experienced, with all aspects of musical organization in fully revealing just how the smallest detail plays its definite part within the whole. Thus the graphs accomplish the function of explanation much more concisely, accurately and, certainly, more "musically" than written comments. Nevertheless such comments will be added if specific problems appear to make them necessary.

Furthermore, the reader will observe that we are not offering any more special exercises except towards the end of this chapter. We deem them just as necessary as before but believe that the student is now capable of formulating exercises himself from the progressions indicated in the graphs; as before, playing the graphs and transposing the progressions into different keys will prove to be of great value.

A.   Problems of structural orientation
(Examples of complex variants)

At the end of Chapter IV it was stated that within the drive from I to V, two equally strong harmonic chords will offset the impulse to the V. Surveying the examples in Chapters V and VI, there was little doubt as to which chord was the salient harmonic factor on the way from I to V. There are times, however, as was shown in the discussion of the chord of harmonic emphasis, when two intermediary harmonies occur; at first hearing they may occasionally seem to be of equal structural value. In such cases it is essential to compare the relative functions of these chords in the phrase and their respective motivic and rhythmic significance. We must weigh carefully their individual function in relation to the progression from tonic to dominant in order to determine which one, through stronger harmonic and structural impulse, is the actual member of the harmonic framework. The student will have learned from the preceding chapters how necessary it is for purposes of structural orientation to recognize the harmonic framework. This knowledge provides an indication of the music's direction and helps to determine the function of the prolongations. It is of even greater significance when, as shall soon be seen, we approach more complex examples of wide stylistic variety.

Problems in determining the harmonic framework occur in music of very different styles. Let us listen, for instance, to the beginning of the slow movement from Haydn's String Quartet, Op 20, No. 5. ►[Ex. 401]◄ Between the tonic (meas. 1) and the dominant (meas. 8) lie the VI (meas. 5 and 6), the IV and the II (meas. 7). In order to grasp the harmonic framework, the functions of these intervening chords have to be clear to the listener. Their significance has been indicated in the graphs.

In relation to the phrase as a whole, the submediant appears as a prolonged passing chord between I and IV, whereas the II constitutes a chord of harmonic emphasis between IV and V. Two factors contribute to the evaluation of the IV as the outstanding harmonic function between I and V. The first is the rests in meas. 6, following the bass motion F-E-D, which give the coming IV added emphasis. The second is a melodic factor inasmuch as the IV supports the incomplete neighbor note D, which derives from the structural tone C and thus is a tone of higher order than the preceding F (see Graph b).

Going back to literature of the sixteenth century we cite the opening section of a Motet by Orlando di Lasso. ►[Ex. 402]◄ The activity of voice leading lies mainly in the bass and in the inner voices, whereas the top voice is confined to neighbor-note motions of various structural order. This undoubtedly contributes to the quiet flow and the serenity of this passage. In terms of musical direction it appears important to hear through to the VI of the harmonic framework. Once the reader hears the VI as a structural chord, the preceding D and F chords appear as passing chords. Observe the subtle prolongation of the VI and the colorful effect of the voice-leading chord on E♭ (meas. 12).

Several excerpts are now presented in which melodic sequences play different roles in relation to the structure. The first is taken from sixteenth-century music, the beginning of a *Balletto* by Gastoldi.▶[Ex. 403]◀ First hearing gives the impression of three short sequential phrases plus a short closing phrase. The reading of the underlying harmonic framework does not seem to present any serious difficulties. But how are we to explain the significance of the F-Major chord of meas. 6? Closer investigation divulges that, despite the sequence, the passage as a whole appears divided into 2 times 4 measures (see Graph b). The first group of four measures shows two melodic descending thirds in sequence; the second group presents an augmentation and elaboration of a third motion of a third downward, thus interweaving the closing phrase with the organism of the whole. Graph a demonstrates the organization of the bass and the complete structure of this passage. The F chord in meas. 6 is a $\frac{N}{P}$ chord within the prolongation of the V.

Proceeding to music of the second half of the nineteenth century, two passages are presented, one by Wagner, the other by César Franck. The Wagner passage is taken from the end of the second act of *Tristan und Isolde.* ▶[Ex. 404]◀ The motion clearly leads to the V in the eighth measure; in addition a progression to the III (meas. 4) seems significant. However, the A-minor chord (meas. 5) appears at first to be confusing, for the sequential reentry of the first motive a half-tone above A♭ may create the impression that in a structural sense the A♭ chord moves to the A-minor chord, from which chord a second phrase starts, practically of the same significance as the first. This, however, would leave the III unexplained. Likewise, the function of the A chord on the way to V is not clear if we conceive it as coming from the A♭ tonic.

It is important here—as in the example by Gastoldi—not to be misled by the sequence. A motivic parallelism between two phrases certainly exists, which, however, is counteracted by their basses having different goals. In addition, we cannot neglect the significance of the III and may thus realize that the bass A♮ can be heard as coming from C♭ (the bass of the III). This reading appears to be convincing since the bass leads down to E♭, the V, filling a space from III to V. It now appears that the A-minor chord has no structural connection with the tonic, in spite of the fact that it supports the opening motive. It is rather the first step of a passing motion between the III and the V.

All this influences the interpretation in a definite way. A certain stress must be laid on the III, to which the motion drives determinedly. The following meas. 5 should not be played like the beginning of a new phrase, but rather the drive from III to V must be developed, the goal being prepared by the *ritenuto*.

Wagner has often been accused of using his motives in a too obviously sequential manner, applying them, so to speak, in terraces. The passage just quoted would serve as an example for this statement. It must be said, however, that here as in many other instances, Wagner —almost in spite of the motivic sequence—creates an organic whole which gives the sequential repetition of the motive a more subtle meaning than the above-mentioned view would have us believe. Superficial hearing registers two phrases of equal length starting with the same motive and is incapable of explaining these eight measures as an integral whole expressing a I-III-V progression in A♭.

We turn now to the Prelude from the *Prelude, Aria and Finale* by César Franck. ►[Ex. 405]◄ In this passage the abundance of passing motions makes recognition of the structural points at first rather difficult. What alleviates our problem, however, is the fact that Franck treats the sequences as definite architectonic factors. In the excerpt from the Gastoldi *Balletto* a certain structural tension was created through prolongation of a structural point while the sequence was still continuing. In the Wagner example the sequence is used as a purely melodic parallelism which ingeniously feints structural dependency between the beginning and the reappearance of the motive. Thus in both of these examples the sequences are in a sense artistically "misleading." In the passage by Franck, however, the starting point or the end of the sequences indicate significant points in the harmonic and contrapuntal organization of the whole, thus giving the ear definite aid.

The student's knowledge will now permit him to approach the brilliant and subtle techniques of prolongation found in the music of Richard Strauss. Both examples to be cited are from the Quintet of the Comedians from this composer's opera, *Ariadne auf Naxos* and are typical of his individual style. The first excerpt contains a very interesting prolongation of the V. ►[Ex. 406]◄

In carrying out this prolongation Strauss proceeds upward from the bass tone C in minor thirds to the higher C. When, however, the top voice in its motion downwards has reached the structural tone G, the bass has already moved a third up to E♭, the first station on the progression of upward moving thirds. Thus the structural bass tone C does not coincide with the structural top voice tone G, both having begun their upward motion in thirds on different beats. This presents an interesting overlapping of voice motions and contributes to the original character of the passage.

The second excerpt is from a later section of the same Quintet and presents a charming and witty prolongation of a I-III-V-I progression, making subtle use of mixture and embellishing chords. ►[Ex. 407]◄

The literature abounds in pieces which start with prolonging dominants or incomplete harmonic progressions as prolongations of the tonic. The student is herewith encouraged to find additional and more complex examples than those presented in Chapter VI. An exceptionally fascinating example is the opening section of the *Seguidilla* from Bizet's opera, *Carmen*. ►[Ex. 408]◄ Of special interest here is the gradual movement from the prolonging dominant to the tonic. This motion is, in fact, halting with its artistically "misleading" motion to the D and the following G- and C-Major chords. All this heightens the tonal tension which finds its solution in the exuberant confirmation of the tonic (meas. 25-29). In its playful hedging about the actual tonality, the whole section remarkably expresses Carmen's mood at this particular moment.

The following example, the opening section of Chopin's Polonaise-Fantasy, is amazing in the manner in which tonal coherence is achieved. In its complexity it reveals, in the most concentrated form, the refinement and breadth of the late works of this composer. ►[Ex. 409]◄ The theme of the actual Polonaise starts in meas. 24. In meas. 26 and 27 (see Graph e) we hear a motivically characteristic descending octave subdivided into a fifth plus a fourth. The four measures 24-27 convey the impression of conclusion and beginning simultaneously. In fact they are not only the beginning of the actual Polonaise but also the end of a large-scale introduction starting with meas. 1. This introduction contains an incredible feat of musical ingenuity. The above-mentioned descending octave appears anticipated not only in the melodic outline of all twenty-seven measures, but also in the main prolongation between meas. 1 and 19. (Compare the three brackets of Graph d.) Hence the Polonaise theme is introduced and prepared.

Only after these intricate parallelisms have become clear to the reader should he proceed to Graphs b and c which deal with the first nineteen measures as a separate structural unit. This unit shows an elaborate expansion of the progression from I to II by means of a rhapsodic prolongation of the I coupled with a top voice motion from E♭ to D♭ (C♯), a seventh up. Graph a finally presents the prolongations of the detail and gives us an idea of the fantastic boldness of this tonal conception.

The student will have realized that our reading interpreted the tone E♭ as the first structural tone of the top voice. It may be instructive to make a graph starting the top voice from A♭ (see Graph f). He will find, that, although a voice-leading and a harmonic continuity results, it shows hardly any relation to the thematic and motivic design. Thus the introductory and preparatory character of the first nineteen measures, so strongly felt even at first hearing, finds no explanation through this reading.

B. Developments in prolongation of counterpoint and melody

I. PROLONGED COUNTERPOINT

The studies made in Chapter V on the difference between unprolonged and prolonged counterpoint should be continued by the student. Many examples which have been subsequently discussed will give him ample opportunity for research in the wide field of prolonged counterpoint, of which chromatic counterpoint (introduced in Chapter VI) is one phase. The student should now find additional material from the literature and analyze the settings in order to observe some of the great possibilities of this concept of prolonged counterpoint.

a.   *"Independent" voice leading*

In the course of the development of prolonged counterpoint various possibilities for dissonant voice leading occur. These are often referred to, especially in relation to music of the twentieth century, as "independent or linear voice leading"; it is claimed (as we believe, erroneously) that this different type of counterpoint makes exercises on the basis of Fux's method of purely academic value only and hence obsolete. Some techniques of this "independence" have already been pointed out in Chapter V, illustrating their perfect logic as prolongations of a direct or unprolonged contrapuntal setting which hovers in the background of the passage and determines the direction of voice leading. It was shown that the technique of chord prolongation makes possible a greater freedom and elasticity of voice leading. Furthermore, we encountered the shift or displacement of tones, one of the main techniques of prolonged counterpoint. We also emphasized that the clear direction of voice leading makes a greater individuality of the single voices possible without interfering with the all-important continuity of the basic, unprolonged contrapuntal progression. Since the twentieth century has further expanded these inherent possibilities of prolongation we shall now turn to various examples from this period. The first excerpt is a passage from the second movement of Hindemith's Second Piano Sonata. ►[Ex. 410]◄

In this example the voice leading shows a very interesting canonic prolongation of a motion in tenths. This progression in tenths is further prolonged by transfer of register. The term "independent or linear" voice leading for such contrapuntal writing seems very misleading and contradictory since all tones function as prolongations of directed voice leading, i.e. voice leading with a common goal for all voices concerned. Certainly, the concept of consonance and dissonance has undergone radical changes in the course of this century. The distinction between consonance and dissonance appears replaced by a distinction between dissonances of lesser or greater intensity. This, however, in no way precludes the possibility of directed and prolonged counterpoint. The continued power and, above all, the elasticity of the unprolonged voice leading make it possible for the composer to convey the music's direction in spite of all the detours, modifications and dissonant clashes, unknown to eighteenth- and nineteenth-century music.

The idioms of modern music are very varied; as a contrasting but nevertheless characteristic stylistic expression, we quote the expressive beginning of the second movement of Bohuslav Martinů's Second Cello Sonata, which shows the increased use of neighbor and embellishing motions reflecting a characteristic facet of today's voice leading. ►[Ex. 411]◄ Although the graphs will provide the necessary explanation we should like to draw the reader's attention to the gradually developing neighbor-note motion with the climactic entry of E♯ followed by an expressive melodic prolongation.

The following example from Aaron Copland's music to *Our Town* (No. 1 of Three Excerpts for Piano, meas. 17-26) with its use of so-called *polychords* gives us insight into a specific contemporary idiom strongly affecting the contrapuntal setting. ►[Ex. 412]◄ At the beginning of this passage, a subdominant as a quasi-appoggiatura appears with the tonic G chord. In meas. 19 an F chord forms the chord basis, but the subdominant and tonic chords sound simultaneously. In lieu of a better term we are going to use the term polychord, although we do not consider it accurate or indicative. For the chord built on the bass will always be the stronger one, and it is the bass and its chord which will determine the chord grammatical status of the whole chord cluster. Polychord thus would be an adequate denomination only if both (or in this case three) chords would amalgamate on equal terms, which seems hardly possible. Nevertheless, the term will be used temporarily and it thus follows that we shall label the first chord of meas. 19 an F-polychord. The graph shows that the contrapuntal use of this type of chord influences not only the neighbor-note motions of meas. 17-22 but also the interesting voice leading of meas. 23, 24 and 25. The clearly directed outer voice motion between the VI and the V creates and convincingly determines the dissonant voice leading of these measures.

As in previous times, chord prolongation constitutes the great organizing force of many types of modern music. Two relatively short examples will serve as preliminary illustrations. For instance, the clearly directed voice leading in the *Ciacona* theme by Bernard Wagenaar expresses the D chord and makes the dissonances entirely logical. ►[Ex. 413]◄ To give names to these chords would be a futile procedure; they derive their meaning, as the graphs show, from a directed and organized motion around and within the D chord. Of interest is the melodic parallelism indicated in Graph c which shows a gradual approach to D, which, when it finally occurs in meas. 3, constitutes an inner voice tone shifted to the region of the top voice.

The second example is from the slow movement of Martinu's Second Violin Sonata. ►[Ex. 414]◄ The choice of the outer voices largely determines the voice leading of the inner voices and the resulting chords. The progression shows a shift of the inner voice tone B♭ to the top and from there a progression in major thirds back into the inner voice B♭ while the melodic tone F retains its value. The bass tone G is also derived from the inner voice B♭ and proceeds down in minor thirds until it, too, lands in the region of the inner voice. The ensuing counterpoint would make a triad possible between G and B♭ only; the two other outer voice intervals make a triad impossible. Polychords result logically and the chord on G for reasons of stylistic homogeneity also appears as a polychord.

While in these last two examples it has been triads which have been prolonged with new voice-leading techniques, we must now mention one of the outstanding revolutionary achievements of contemporary music: the contrapuntal prolongation of dissonant chords, especially polychords. This development, which seems to have started with the French impressionist school opens up new and far reaching possibilities. Their full meaning for the future development of music can only be gradually evaluated.

The first excerpt is the beginning of Ravel's *Jeux d'Eau*. ►[Ex. 415]◄ The whole section is typical of French impressionistic style insofar as the triad, as an architectonic factor of structure as well as of prolongation, is replaced by seventh chords and altered chords. The melodic line, though in existence, is veiled by the instrumental figurations and the contrapuntal chord progressions. It is worth mentioning that in meas. 4 the altered chords are embellished by the neighbor notes C, A, F♯, D♮ (see Graph e). On the basis of this new achievement (the prolongation of dissonant chords), contrapuntal motion within polychords became a real possibility, as the following examples by Copland and Stravinsky will demonstrate.

We turn to the final pages from the first movement of Copland's Piano Sonata. ►[Ex. 416]◄ Our attention will be focused on the prolongation of a polychordal F chord which contains the B♭ tonic in its outline and which governs practically the whole section (see Graph d). The bass moves from F into the inner voice tone D♭; the top voice moves from F into the inner voice tone C (see Graphs c and b). It is characteristic for polychords that C and D♭ can be called with justification inner voice tones of an F chord. The student should now realize that the structural tonic B♭ chords are also polychords containing in turn the F chord in their outline. From the point of view of chord grammar a fusion of tonic and dominant chords has taken place. Although in regard to the bass a structural I-V-I progression takes place, the polychord and the fact that the tonic and the quasi-dominant chord contain the same tones caused us to put the V in parenthesis.

Finally we draw the reader's attention to the opening measures of Stravinsky's Symphony in Three Movements.[1] The prolongation of the polychord on G with the D♭ chord as a secondary chord of fusion will be clarified through the graphs. ►[Ex. 417]◄

b. Color chords

We mentioned in Chapter V that a contrapuntal chord, the chord of melodic emphasis, constitutes in effect a color chord, since it has no other function than that of giving emphasis and color to the melody or to the setting in general. The question may arise whether certain

---

[1] We will return later on (Ex. 472) to this example in its relation to a large section of the first movement.

chord structures in modern music, such as the polychords, do not result from a desire to create a definite color pattern. We do not deny the role which the aspect of color must have played in the device of polychords and other dissonant chords. The literature, however, proves that we must distinguish between chords whose only function is to provide color and those which have a voice-leading or structural function with an added effect of color. Pure color chords occur in the following two examples by Bartók and Richard Strauss. ►[Ex. 418, 419]◄ If Bartók bases a phrase on triads and then sets the same melody with seventh and ninth chords, these chords have undoubtedly been chosen for the sake of color only. The same holds true for the polychordal effect of the Strauss excerpt. Such chords are neither the result of voice leading nor are they contrapuntally used for purposes of prolongation. On the other hand, the polychords in the examples by Copland, Stravinsky and Martinů cited previously, apart from their coloristic effect, are integral parts of the voice leading, style and pattern. The chords in question represent the basic chords or chords resulting from voice leading.

To a certain degree this distinction between color chords can be made in the examples quoted towards the end of Chapter VI. Whenever the submediant turns out to be a passing chord, as in Ex. 390, 391, the functional use overshadows the color which represents merely an added effect. If, however, the VI substitutes for a structural I, the color effect and the artistic purpose of enriching the pattern seems to have been conscious to the composer. In this connection we should mention one of the most fascinating substitutions of the entire literature appearing within the opening theme of Beethoven's Piano Concerto in G Major. ►[Ex. 420]◄ The whole passage appears as a most imaginative prolongation of interruption, the post-interruption phrase starting with a B-Major chord boldly substituting for the tonic. In addition, this post-interruption phrase introduces a very interesting melodic parallelism in form of an augmentation of the end of the pre-interruption phrase one step higher, which the brackets attempt to outline.

c. "Harmonic" counterpoint

"Harmonic counterpoint" appears to be a term with an ambiguous meaning. To be sure, contrapuntal settings with some harmonic implications occur frequently. We recall, for instance, the passage from Weber's Overture to *Der Freischütz* (Ex. 335), where we found a contrapuntal chord prolongation enriched with harmonic elements. However, even where there is a definite harmonic influence, as in this passage, the term "harmonic counterpoint" is misleading. For the setting is *de facto* contrapuntal and the harmonic element only a contributing factor. That counterpoint gives expression to one single chord in no way makes the voice leading per se subject to harmonic influence. It may show that influence (as in Weber's passage) or it may not, as we have had ample opportunity to observe.

It would be more logical if one changed the term to "chordal counterpoint," meaning counterpoint moving within a chord or even contrapuntal motion between two different chords. But since music of the most divergent styles and periods shows counterpoint moving within consonant and dissonant chords or from one chord to another, even this more accurate term becomes superfluous.

Before concluding the discussion of this topic we should like to draw the student's attention to a simple type of prolongation, which in this context warrants special mention. ►[Ex. 421]◄ Such progressions are of course familiar to the student. The juxtaposition of direct and prolonged versions shows that the diminished fifth or fourth are the result of prolongation and therefore not a matter of pure or direct counterpoint. In a) and b) the skip in the bass, which offsets the stepwise passing motion of the outer voices, proportionately suggests a certain harmonic influence. In c) the prolongation has contrapuntal meaning only because the diminished seventh chord is invariably a contrapuntal chord.

Nevertheless, all these versions would be classified indiscriminately as harmonic progressions by conventional theory, the diminished seventh chord being accepted as substitution for a dominant, and hence as an expression of "harmony." Augmented and diminished intervals are usually considered to belong either to "free" or "harmonic" counterpoint.

There seems hardly any doubt that the same conception would be applied to the following progressions. ►[Ex. 422]◄ We have recognized throughout these chapters, however, that the fundamental harmonic relationship, that of a fifth, asserts itself only if the dominant is in root position. The use of the first inversion (unless it functions as an applied dominant) robs the progression of its harmonic significance and, with the neighbor-note motion in the bass, stresses its contrapuntal character. We therefore interpret both progressions as contrapuntal progressions, the second having been enriched by an applied dominant.

The first constitutes a contraction of two neighbor-note motions with their resulting chords. ►[Ex. 423]◄

d. Octaves and fifths

The problem of parallel octaves and fifths is present throughout many centuries of tonal music's development. It has occupied the minds not only of musicians and theorists but also of great composers —for instance Brahms, as already mentioned in Chapter III. We cannot go into the history of this voice-leading principle here. It is possible, however, to discern roughly three phases within which this principle was conceived and dealt with in different ways. First there was a time, previous to the fourteenth century, in which parallel octaves and fifths were desired or at least were felt to be a natural form of contrapuntal progression. From approximately the fifteenth century on, these progressions were considered as faulty voice leading; trespassings of this "law" were felt to be exceptions. However, for quite some time, many have found that this principle is an outmoded academic rule and it is claimed that the trespassings, which become more frequent towards the end of the nineteenth century, prove its futility. In teaching counterpoint, the ruling on octaves and fifths is often accepted only within the study of sixteenth-century counterpoint or "strict" counterpoint.

It will not be surprising to the student to find that this voice-leading problem has to be investigated on the basis of structure and prolongation. One of the results of structural hearing has been the recognition of the difference between intervals derived from prolongation and those intervals which constitute the basic contrapuntal direction. This means that it is prolongation which creates many intervals and chords, and to these the principles of pure counterpoint do not necessarily apply. Thus some parallel fifths and octaves which are thought to demonstrate the deviation from the rule are those "misleading" intervals of prolongation which do not represent the intervals of the unprolonged voice leading. Two brief examples are given. ►[Ex. 424, 425]◄ The technique causing the prolonging octaves in the first passage is the one called shifting of tones, already mentioned in Chapter V. The fifths in the second example are caused by anticipation of the melody tone C♯.

However, the student should not overlook passages from the literature which avoid threatened parallel fifths or octaves by the use of various techniques, for example the interpolation of the voice-leading chords (see Chapter V) and the 5-6 or 5-8 technique. These latter techniques can be observed in the following passages. ▶[Ex. 426, 427]◀

We return now to passages from music of the nineteenth century containing parallel fifths, which still are in no way contradictory to the principle of pure counterpoint which calls for their avoidance. We must always remember that the concept of pure counterpoint deals, as the term "pure" indicates, with elementary and direct voice leading, isolated from all other elements of composition such as harmony, chromaticism, prolongations like the shift of tones and chord prolongation, etc. In this kind of contrapuntal concept, the key-defining quality of the fifth is so strong that the succession of fifths was felt to impede the most characteristic feature of counterpoint, that of flowing motion.

If those other elements are combined with the procedures of direct, unprolonged voice leading, some of them may be offset or superseded. It thus happens, for instance, that the definite framework given by means of a harmonic progression or a chord prolongation overcomes the static quality of parallel fifths. Let us look back at Ex. 357. The movement within the C♯-minor chord (in the form of a I-V-I harmonic prolongation) in general, and the tendency from V to I in particular appear so definite and unequivocal that the executing voice leading can afford to move in fifths which appear to lose their primary quality. In addition the ear perceives them as the result of a contracted 5-6 progression. Pure counterpoint knows no harmonic influence, no chord prolongation or contraction; therefore Chopin's fifths are not the fifths of pure counterpoint; they belong, in essence, to prolonged counterpoint, made possible through these additional elements of musical architecture.

In this connection a passage from Moussorgsky's *Pictures from an Exhibition* is cited. ▶[Ex. 428]◀ These fifths are not fifths of the basic voice leading, but those of prolongation within a prolonged C chord. In addition they function as a kind of doubling to gain a specifically desired sonority. A famous passage from Verdi's *Requiem* is also appropriate here. ▶[Ex. 429]◀ Instead of doubling the melodic embellishing tones F♯-E-F♯ with thirds over a pedal point C♯, a voice-leading effect from music of the Middle Ages is imitated by having the lower fifths go in parallel motion as a kind of doubling.

Approximately from the end of the nineteenth century on, the problem of parallel fifths or octaves ceases to exist. Parallel fifths, for instance, are desired progressions in impressionistic music (see Debussy and Ravel). The original meaning of this voice-leading principle has been lost or is purposely ignored; fifths appear in structural as well as in prolonging progressions.

2.   TRANSFER OF REGISTER THROUGH SEQUENTIAL SUPERPOSITION
     OF INNER VOICE

We have encountered the transfer of register in various examples and have also demonstrated that melodic prolongation may be achieved through the superposition of inner voice tones. Both types may co-operate in creating interesting and expressive prolongations.

The introduction to the last movement of the *Waldstein* Sonata constitutes a very expressive example. ▶[Ex. 430]◀ Graph b indicates the voice leading without the transfer of register; i.e. a motion in tenths, the melody going into the inner voice E of the dominant seventh (meas. 6) before reaching the D-minor passing chord. In Graph a we have shown how the transfer of register affects this motion into the inner voice and how sequential superpositions are applied to promote that broadly conceived change of register between the structural tones of the top voice. The sequential technique with the expressive use of rests in this almost *recitativo* style contributes a great deal to a feeling of tonal tension which finally is resolved.

Another example is the beginning of the *Meno mosso* section of Chopin's First Polonaise. ▶[Ex. 431]◀ A study of the graphs shows that between meas. 4 and 8, four voices provide an interesting contra-puntal texture. The bass moves from D♭ to E♭ (the applied dominant), the tenor proceeds from D♭ to E♭ (a seventh down for a second up), the alto starting from F moves a sixth up to D♭ (for a third down) and finally the expressive melodic top voice is achieved through superposi-tion of inner voice tones causing a transfer of register.

The student is now required to look back at Ex. VIII (Part I), where this kind of transfer of register appears within a larger form section.

Finally we turn to a rather complex passage from Chopin's Mazurka, Op 59, No. 2 (meas. 77-89). ▶[Ex. 432]◀ The passage has defied con-ventional harmonic analysis for some time, and the reader will readily acknowledge that on the basis of the chord grammar approach not more than a display of "chromatic harmony" can be described. The harmonic framework and the prolongation of the VI (mixture) will probably be the first factors to become clear. The meaning of the top voice, how-ever, is more hidden. Graph b shows what the direction of the top voice would be, had no superposition of the inner voice taken place.

The neighbor note Cb (B♮) would then have appeared as the top voice tone of the Fb (E) chord. Only thereafter does a transfer of register to the lower Cb occur. This tone Cb when it occurs first in the passage is completely obscured by the superposition of inner voice tones which drive the melody up to Ab (G♯)—see Graph a. Thus the climactic tone is a middle voice tone. It is obvious that all this contributes to the iridescent quality of this imaginative passage.

3. SETTING A POSTPONED FIRST STRUCTURAL MELODY TONE
   WITH A NON-TONIC CHORD

Towards the end of Chapter V a technique of melodic prolongation was discussed wherein a melody could gradually progress to its first structural tone which is delayed. We recall here the beginning of Beethoven's G-Major Sonata, Op 14 (see Ex. 254).

On the basis of this technique, composers have developed a very subtle and original prolongation which is used to great effect in the beginning of Chopin's A-Major Polonaise, Op 40. ►[Ex. 433]◄ The melody moves in a space-outlining motion up to C♯, the first structural melody tone. The moment C♯ is reached, however, Chopin stresses the III (not the I) with an applied dominant. It is as though the bass did not want to wait until the top voice had reached C♯, and thus had started prematurely. What actually occurs, therefore, is a contraction of the structural top voice tone of the I with the III of the harmonic framework. ►[Ex. 434]◄

The following passage from a composition by Giles Farnaby is somewhat problematic from the point of view of melodic structure. ►[Ex. 435]◄ We have indicated here a postponement of the first structural tone, similar to the preceding example, because we hear E on the first beat of meas. 1 not as the first structural tone, but as a middle voice tone. In addition we feel the stress always to be on the second and third tone of the sequence(see brackets).

4. POSSIBILITIES WITHIN PASSING MOTIONS

As the student has already realized, the construction of passing motions may vary considerably. For example, it has been seen that they were not always stepwise. Passing tones or chords are skipped frequently; we recall passing motions proceeding in thirds. Occasionally they do not even proceed in regular patterns although they are clearly directed. ►[Ex. 436]◄

In excerpts from first movements of Sonatas by Schubert the student will have no difficulty locating the skipped passing tones. The colorful effect of these passages lies in the sudden succession of chords having no harmonic relation whatsoever, but which nevertheless appear very meaningful and logical through their contrapuntal role. ►[Ex. 437, 438]◄

In both examples the stress laid on passing chords of a whole or a half-step below the I, and the skipped passing tones produce highly original prolongations of a I-V progression. The colorful effect of the chords cannot be denied. But on the basis of our analysis it would appear misleading to speak about Schubert's harmonic boldness as conventional theory does in regard to similar phrases. It is the non-harmonic, stepwise succession of triads which constitutes the bold coloristic effect.

5. THE SIGNIFICANCE OF MELODIC ANALYSIS
    (Studies of melodic prolongation)

Our discussions have pointed to the need of taking the melody's structure and its prolongation into account, in order to gain complete understanding of the music's direction. Although concentration on the bass often gives us the main clues for grasping the organic coherence of a composition, it is just as often the hearing of melodic direction which leads to the understanding of the whole. The student will also have been impressed by the fact that melodic analysis presents greater problems for structural hearing. We shall therefore at this stage discuss various excerpts mainly from the melodic angle. We say "mainly" because a purely horizontal analysis of "polyphonic melody" would have serious limitations.

One of the problems of melodic analysis is found in melodies which, by the use of interval-outlining motions, present a rugged contour. The question as to which tones constitute the melodic continuity is especially acute in such instances. The beginning of Schumann's Piano Quintet (meas 1-9) and the opening theme from Beethoven's Sonata Op 31, No. 1 (meas. 1-26) serve as examples. ►[Ex. 439, 440]◄ In the Beethoven Sonata we find a descending line moving to the first structural tone. This proves that descending melodic progressions do not always indicate motions into the inner voice.

And now to three excerpts which deal with the problem of the highest tones in a melody. It cannot be emphasized enough that the highest tone may be and often is a prolonging rather than a structural tone. Let us never forget that the prolongations provide the tension, color and interest of a melody. They are therefore the natural place for climactic tones, often so expressive in the course of a melody, and they in no way conflict with the structural direction of the melody. The three examples are the beginnings of one of the 10 Easy Pieces for Piano by Bartók and of the slow movements of Beethoven's Sonatas, Op 2, No. 1 and Op 10, No. 1. ►[Ex. 441, 442, 443]◄

Such wonderful motivic and thematic parallelisms bring us to the question of the coherence of phrases or groups of measures which at first hearing seem to offer no melodic parallelisms. The first example is from Mozart's Sonata, K. 279 (first movement, meas. 1-16). We apparently hear new melodic material from meas. 5 on. The student is now asked whether he hears a relation between meas. 1-4 and meas. 5-12. ►[Ex. 444]◄ It appears that meas. 1-4 have a preparatory function for the second phrase which presents the outline of the first four measures in an enlarged and elaborated form.

Without any help the student should now try to determine the melodic relationship between the introduction and the main theme from Mozart's D-minor Fantasy (K. 397).

Turning again to more modern music we find a most intricate thematic parallelism in the first of the *Kindertotenlieder* by Gustav Mahler. ►[Ex. 445]◄ The end of the short introduction is taken up in an enlarged and very expressive form by the voice. The two introductory measures thus prepare the melodic outline of the following measures. Observe the brackets which frame the descending third, embellished with a neighbor-note, and the ascending third. The first of these two melodic motions constitutes practically the complete melodic outline of the entire section. Such subtle relations contribute so much to the tonal organization and expressive possibilities of music.

*

*   *

The student will realize that he has constantly come across melodic structures or prolongations outlining and filling in the intervals of a fifth and a third. Melodic motions of an octave, however, have been found only as prolongations. As melodic patterns of a high structural order, such motions appear rather infrequently. This is probably due to the fact that melodic lines of an octave are likely to have a prolonging implication by presenting a transfer of register of a single tone or by appearing like a prolongation of a neighbor-note motion. ►[Ex. 446]◄ It should be added that the amount of structural melody tones

in a descending octave makes it difficult to achieve an entirely harmonic structural bass.

Nevertheless, what we might call genuine octave motions of a high
structural order do occur. Two examples from very different stylistic
periods are quoted; in both CS chords play a vital part. ►[Ex. 447,
448]◄

We should like, however, to warn the student of melodic passages
which seem to move within the octave but in reality are following a
different course. A chorus from Rameau's opera, *Castor et Pollux*
offers a good example of such a "deceptive" octave. ►[Ex. 449]◄
The greater structural emphasis is clearly on C; therefore, the descent
from F to C in the first four measures constitutes a prolongation not
unlike the beginning of Beethoven's Op 31, No. 1 (see Ex. 440).

We have said that the melodic progression of an octave in structural
capacity is found relatively seldom. Even more seldom are ascending
structural lines. Although we have until now discussed almost exclusively sections from pieces, we can already state that the vast majority
of melodies, if they are not of the embellishing type, move in their
last analysis downward to the tonic. The reason for this may lie in
the natural position of the non-tonic tones in a chord. Their natural
position is above the tonic. Thus, for instance, when in a melody
in C Major the tone G moves structurally to C, the melodic line will
fall to the tonic below rather than ascend to the upper C. In addition,
the fifth and the third are stronger intervals than their inversions, the
fourth and the sixth.

One of those infrequent structural ascending lines may be found
in the Waltz in C Major, Op 50, No. 2 by Schubert which shows an
ascending fourth G-A-B-C.

*

*   *

In concluding these discussions on melody the student's attention
must be drawn again to the fundamental principle of all analysis, i.e.
never to draw conclusions before all factors of musical construction
have been carefully weighed. Just as we have witnessed before that
descending melodic lines at the beginning are not necessarily motions
into the inner voice, so we must be careful in interpreting ascending
melodic lines at the beginning of a phrase. These, we have found, are
often motions out of the inner-voice region towards the first structural
melody tone. The opening theme from Beethoven's Sonata, Op 90

(first movement) proves clearly that this is by no means always the case. ►[Ex. 450]◄

Graph a intends to show that the last sequential entry of the motive appears boldly modified and enlarged. It seems hardly possible that Beethoven was completely unaware of this daring augmentation. How otherwise could he have reached the E in meas. 16 with such definiteness, even emphasizing this tone in a high register and resuming at this point the original rhythmic motive?

C.   Completely contrapuntal structure

The beginning of Hindemith's Third Piano Sonata (see Ex. X, Part I) presented a contrapuntal progression as the framework-making progression of highest order. From this we readily see that there is a possibility for contrapuntal structure. Just as harmonic progressions may serve in a prolonging or structural capacity, so also have contrapuntal progressions the inherent possibility of fulfilling either function.

The progressions of Part II so far termed as structural (i.e. progressions of relatively highest order) were either harmonic or a combination of harmonic and contrapuntal. They indicated and defined the basic direction as well as the tonality of the whole. However, the literature, especially of the last decades, proves conclusively that contrapuntal progressions in regard to larger organisms can be key defining and capable of assuming structural significance.

It must be stated that the following examples demonstrate structural progressions only as long as they are analyzed as temporarily independent units. They become prolongations of various order if the composition is discussed as a whole. Since progressions similar to those to be offered may function as structures of complete pieces, we believe—just as it was the case with harmonic progressions—to be justified in discussing them as structural units.

It will hardly surprise us that contrapuntal structures mostly make use of motions around a chord in order to define tonality. Whereas a harmonic structure permits the motion within a framework-making I-V-I progression with its space outlining and filling possibilities, the elimination of the harmonic principle quite naturally brought about the increased use of neighbor and embellishing chords as chords of structure.

Three excerpts by Prokofieff, Bartók and Hindemith are now presented. Although their structural frameworks are entirely contrapuntal, two of them show the harmonic element still represented in the prolongations. In the Prokofieff section, a harmonic progression constitutes the main prolongation of the tonic; in the Bartók example, a harmonic progression is used for a prolongation of lower order. In the Hindemith excerpt, on the other hand, no harmonic influence whatsoever can be detected. ►[Ex. 451, 452, 453]◄

In the Prokofieff example the mediant, since it does not proceed to the V, becomes a contrapuntal chord, in this case a contrapuntal-structural chord. Here the melodic and chordal parallelisms are of outstanding interest. The first measure with its motion to E♮ appears enlarged within the first phrase (meas. 1-5). This tone E turns out to be a neighbor note of the neighbor note E♭ of higher order. A parallelism occurs in meas. 6-9, only that here the motion does not go beyond the main neighbor note E♭.

The whole section shows a row of expressive transfers of register and great contrapuntal activity of the middle voices, both of which make the structural understanding of this music rather difficult at first. In addition we mention the bass, which shows equally interesting parallelisms; in both phrases it moves with a half-tone step to tones which become inner voice tones of chords (the dominant of meas. 4 and the mediant of meas. 8).

In the section from Bartók's Fifth String Quartet, considered here as a structural unit, the pivotal points C♯-D-C♯ represent the structural bass.[2]

The coherence of this section may at first appear as rather problematical; therefore the student is advised—after having become familiar with the sonorities—to work in the direction from Graph d, indicating the basic direction of the whole, to Graph a which gives expression to the fascinating details of prolongation. The highly impressionistic chord prolongations of meas. 1-4 and 5-10 reveal entirely new possibilities of this technique. Their understanding depends largely on the correct hearing of the neighbor-note motions of a second up and down. Sometimes the first, sometimes the second tone is of significance for the melodic continuity. The whole section is pervaded by neighbor-note motions of various structural levels and only after careful and repeated listening does the actual coherence become clear.

[2] The reader may be interested to note that the composition taken as a whole moves finally to D so that the complete organism expresses a motion C♯-D, constituting a much enlarged appoggiatura of D. Within the harmonic orbit this would compare to an incomplete harmonic progression outlining the basic motion of a complete composition.

Listen for instance to the C chord prolongation from meas. 10-19 and specifically to the mysterious and rhapsodic utterances of the first violin. On the basis of superficial hearing they probably will be taken as merely coloristic effects. In reality, however, they are interwoven in the melodic continuity of the whole. The melodic events here are so varied that we have stemmed one type of appoggiatura upwards, the other downwards. The tones stemmed upwards contribute especially towards pushing the melodic line up to the prolonging C. Finally, a word regarding the end of this fascinating organism. Into the D chord the first violin brings the tone G♯ as an anticipation of the C♯ chord. This presents a baffling effect, which is clarified in meas. 25.

Whereas both of the sections just discussed, especially the second one, have impressionistic tendencies, the final one from Hindemith's First Piano Sonata is an example of imaginative musical architecture. The very original voice leading is definitely directed without any trace of impressionistic veiling. We believe that the reader—after having concentrated on the music and then on Graphs b and c—will be able to understand the prolongations as indicated in Graph a without further explanations on our part.

In conclusion it should be noted that none of these sections cited employ polychords, which further indicates the variety of possibilities within modern tonality.

D. Procedures of structural hearing

In trying to explain the actual procedure of structural hearing in "slow motion," we shall find that it operates through two processes, comparable in many ways to those known in the field of philosophy as deduction and induction. Both are at work in structural hearing, though the emphasis is sometimes more on one than on the other.

The deductive process attempts to establish the goal of the musical motion and the direction it takes to attain this goal. For this purpose it determines the music's voice leading, and in so doing separates the embellishments and prolongations from those tones and progressions which carry the motion in a direct way to its goal and which form the structure. It is deduction which represents the first process of structural hearing and which may find its expression in successive graphs. The prolongations are eliminated in progressive stages or immediately—depending on the complexity of the prolongations and the capacity of the listener; thus the graph is reached illustrating the basic direction or structure of the composition under discussion. The process of deduction has brought the listener to the harmonic or contrapuntal basis of the music.

The student will understand by now that we are not searching for the basic direction for the sake of finding that direction alone. Establishing and understanding the structural basis, however interesting and revealing, cannot in itself be considered the real explanation of a musical organism. We thus come to the more important of the processes of structural hearing, the process of induction.

In this phase we look back from the structure to the composition; we move in reverse order from structure to the completed composition. It is now that we realize the "distance" between the structure and the actual music; the perception of this distance first of all shows that the composition appears as an elaboration or prolongation of the structural progression. The "distance" between a composition and its structure finds expression in the graphs which only now receive their definite shape. For within this process of structural hearing each tone and each progression reveals its significance as an organic offshoot of the basic progression and its individual share in forming the tonal organism in its entirety.

Thus the inductive process explains the meaning and impact of the prolongations which create the color, interest and tension of the music.

In summary, the procedure of structural hearing operates in two directions: from the composition to its structure (deduction) and from the structure to its prolongation which is the actual composition (induction).

In this connection it must be stressed again that the systematic development of the student's ability to hear structurally entails the pedagogic necessity of making conscious the unconsciously felt tendencies and events in composition and of dwelling at some length even on the smallest details. Structural hearing bears fruit only after many of these technical details of tonal organization become an unconscious part of the student's musical equipment. This partial regaining of the instinctive stage of musical understanding can be accomplished after the student has passed through a period of systematic training. Even the smallest problems of composition have to become unmistakably clear in order that they may be absorbed completely; only then will understanding or applying them creatively become the natural expression of a student's musical capacity.

However, the more the student advances the more he will realize that both the deductive and the inductive processes do not any longer function to an equal degree as the conscious techniques of analysis which they most certainly did in the earlier stages of Chapters V and VI. For, if the student concentrates on larger and more complex sections and finally on complete compositions, it will become evident how necessary it is to acquire a sort of large dimensional hearing. This can be achieved by developing the deductive process to a quickly functioning ability and technique. One must learn to spot the structure for reasons of structural orientation, to penetrate as rapidly as possible to the pivotal points of the motion taken as a whole. If there is no understanding of the large dimensional goals, how can the study of the detail, the offshoot of the main motion, be of any real value? It was for this reason that in some previous examples we urged the reader to concentrate first on the graphs demonstrating progressions of higher order. Once the deductive process has been accomplished it will always be the all-important inductive process which will have to follow, if we are not to remain on the surface of the composition.

Thus a most rapid completion of the deductive process is imperative and experience proves that this can be accomplished. We see, therefore, that the two processes of structural hearing do not work in the same "tempo" and at the same degree of consciousness.

However rapidly a student may grasp the structural direction of a composition, the graphs (with few exceptions) will continue to be presented in the direction from the prolongations to the structure and not vice versa. As hearing of the structure always emanates from the composition as a whole, the detailed graph of the whole has to come first in any presentation of musical coherence. Regardless of the form of presentation of the following examples, the student should try on his own to hear and determine in large outline the intermediate and final goals of motion before a detailed study of the prolongations is undertaken.

E. Preparation for large dimensional hearing and planning

I. EXTENDED NEIGHBOR-NOTE AND PASSING MOTIONS

Neighbor-note or embellishing motions and passing motions are, as we know, fundamental types of musical motion. Separately or in combination they not only govern small passages, but may also form the contents of large sections. The study of musical literature proves that the recognition of these motions around one point or from one point to the other constitutes the clue to the directional understanding of many large sections. We therefore present a few examples which in addition to their interest per se may also function as a study towards structural hearing of complete pieces of any possible length.

a. Brahms. Sextet in G Major, Op 36. First movement, meas. 1-53. ►[Ex. 454]◄

Neighbor-note and embellishing motions dominate the first 32 measures. To hear these as one single extended prolongation of the tonic demands large dimensional hearing. Neighbor-note motions also play a considerable role in meas. 32-53, whose main contents are the continuation of the structural progression. Note that the neighbor-note motion D-E♭-D of the first large group of measures is now answered by a neighbor note, E♮; this juxtaposition has a beautiful coloristic effect. In fact there are two melodic motions at work in the second group of measures; one constitutes the structural descent, the other a prolonging motion which leaves the tone D (prolonged through the neighbor note E♮) as a quasi-retained tone hovering above the descending line.

b. Debussy. *Prélude à l'après-midi d'un faune.* meas. 1-30. ►[Ex. 455]◄

Here neighbor-note and embellishing motions are used in a stylistically different vein. Although they frequently occur in Brahms' works, they are not particularly characteristic for his music. They are typical, however, of Debussy's individual style and French impressionism in general.

First a thorough understanding of the improvisatory first measures (the flute solo) appears necessary. The melodic events are: the appoggiatura C♯-B (the latter being the structural tone of the melody), the motion into the inner voice G♯ and G♮, then the return to B which is followed by a prolongation of the initial C♯-B. These motions are presented by the composer in a series of variation-like and highly imaginative repetitions (see the brackets in Graphs a and b). They develop on the basis of a widely prolonged tonic which at the end moves to V via its applied dominant. These quasi-variations contribute strongly to the coherence and simultaneously to the accumulating tension which so convincingly finds its release in the final motion to the V.

It is noteworthy that the melodic motion to G♮, although occurring repeatedly in the prolongations of lower order, appears only once (see meas. 21-25) within the prolonging repetitions of higher order. Thus, in a manner similar to the opening theme, the motion as a whole first goes to G♯ (which motion is repeated); thereafter Debussy, within the the third "variation," proceeds to G♮ (meas. 21-25). Finally we hear, comparable to meas. 1-3, a prolongation of C♯-B through five measures.

*

*   *

With regard to passing motions, again two very contrasting examples are chosen. The student should carefully examine and compare the differences of technique and their application.

a. Chopin. Nocturne in F♯ minor, Op 48, No. 2. meas. 1-30. ▶[Ex. 456]◀

A passing motion from I to II is conceived here as an upwards motion of a ninth subdivided into thirds (see the bass). Note the role of the applied dominants and especially the prolongation of the last applied dominant, the D♯ chord, which creates an ingenious structural retard and a preparation for the entry of the II. This latter chord is regarded as a structural chord, achieved through mixture, and not as an applied dominant to the V, because it is not treated as an auxiliary chord. On the contrary, with its own harmonic prolongation, it acts as an intermediary goal of motion.

b. Prokofieff. Piano Sonata No. 3. meas. 27-59. ▶[Ex. 457]◀

A chromatic passing motion of high order holds this whole section together and appears prolonged through the technique of descending fourths (or ascending fifths). This creates a large-scale passing motion of double function because of the strong harmonic influence exercised by the descending fourths. The activity of this excerpt taken as a whole lies predominantly in the bass and the chordal progression. In such instances even the recognition of the direction of the bass alone gives a clear indication of the music's direction and coherence.

2.   THE DEVELOPMENT SECTION OF SONATA FORM
      (Large-scale prolongations) ·

The development sections of movements in sonata form are particularly suited to demonstrating the necessity for large dimensional hearing. It may be said that among these sections can be found most daring and imaginative conceptions of musical architecture and that musical tension and drive have hardly ever found more convincing expression.

In some ways the following discussion will anticipate Chapter VIII which deals with the problems of form. These developments, however, are such pertinent examples of large-scale prolongations (and thus for the concept of tonality) that their presentation at this point is to be preferred.

We shall learn that it is the structural task of the development to carry the composition from the end of the exposition to the beginning of the recapitulation, i.e. from the prolonged chord constituting and supporting the second theme of the exposition to the dominant which immediately precedes the recapitulation.[3] If the second theme expresses the dominant, then the development presents another large-scale prolongation of this dominant (the end of which leads into the recapitulation). If, however, the second theme constitutes a prolongation of a mediant, then the development has the task of prolonging the progression from the mediant to the dominant.

Hence, the development section is ultimately a section of transitional motion. This fact makes it necessary for the motion—whether it expresses the prolongation of the V or the progression from III to V—to demonstrate an unusual degree of direction in its drive towards the recapitulation. On the other hand, the structural demand to prolong one single chord or one short progression for the purpose of achieving an adequate formal section, engenders an element of expanse and retard. The artistic struggle between these two contrasting factors of dramatic drive and expansion creates the tension so characteristic for the development sections of pieces in sonata form, and which furthermore explains why the entry of the recapitulation in a good sonata movement has an effect of release following accumulated tension.

In the course of the following demonstrations the readings of the top voice structure may appear to some less convincing than the analysis of the bass. Such problems will receive their final clarification in Chapter VIII. In the meantime it should be kept in mind that the need for large-scale tonal planning and understanding is the main purpose of the following examples from sonata and symphonic literature. They present examples of the extraordinary elasticity of tonal direction and architecture.

To understand extended tonal sections is largely a problem of orientation. Thus the knowledge of the pivotal points of motion appears indispensable. Although the graphs of the following analyses appear in the usual order, i.e. in the direction from the prolongations to the structure, the reader is again advised to use the inductive process first. This

[3] This holds true for works based on a harmonic framework.

means he should start with the last graph and from there work to the prolongations shown in Graph a. By this procedure the listener will be enabled to keep in mind the main single progression and its direction, which in turn offers him the possibility to abandon himself to the fascinating play of the prolongations.

We now turn to the many developments which show large-scale prolongations of the dominant. Although in such works the ultimate structural problem is the same, the prolongations with their practically endless possibilities have given composers the opportunity to create sections of greatest variety and, at the same time, of greatest cohesion.

As our first example we mention the first movement of Beethoven's Sonata in D Major, Op 10, No. 3. ►[Ex. 458]◄ The whole section is under the dominance of a neighbor-note motion A-B♭-A as prolongation of the V. The tone B♭ serves as bass for a B♭-Major chord and for an altered chord supporting the lower melodic neighbor note G♯ (see Graph b). Graph a shows that the two neighbor-note chords with the identical bass tone B♭ are conceived by Beethoven as outlining the space of an octave. The chords of lower order on G (meas. 148), E♭ (meas. 157) and D (meas. 163) serve as passing chords carrying the motion from one neighbor-note chord to the other.

In contrast to B♭, the tone B♮ is the governing neighbor note of the development of another work in D Major, the first movement of Haydn's Symphony No. 104. ►[Ex. 459]◄ The neighbor-note chord on B with F♯ in the top voice is harmonically prolonged by a complete harmonic progression I-IV-V-I (Graph c). In Graph b we find the B chord further prolonged, first through a contrapuntal prolongation (meas. 125-137) and then through an interesting and rather complex passing motion to the applied dominant of the IV (meas. 137-155). This passing motion shows great melodic activity of inner voice tones and reveals the use of a 7-6 progression whose upper voice leads out of the inner voice of the B chord into the inner voice tone G♯ of the IV. ►[Ex. 460]◄ Turning back to Ex. 459 and Graph a specifically, the inner voice progression starting from B is stemmed downward and connected with a beam. From this tone B still another melodic line branches off which, through shifting to the top, becomes the melodic top voice of the whole passage. In their ultimate analysis, however, both of these melodic lines are results of inner voice activity and thus subordinated to the melodic progression of higher order leading from F♯ to G♯.

Furthermore, Graph a presents a detailed outline of another prolongation, the prolongation of the IV, which the student will now have no difficulty in understanding. Both of these prolongations, the latter and the one between meas. 137 and 155, are instrumental in establishing the dramatic style of this development. In expanding the space between the pivotal points, while at the same time provoking a strong driving tendency through passing motions, a definite degree of tonal tension is created.

Although in the development from the first movement of Beethoven's Piano Sonata, Op 22 ►[Ex. 461]◄ the final analysis (Graph c) again shows a neighbor note, this technique is apparent in the top voice only, whereas the bass is governed by an extended passing motion between the prolonging I and V (see Graphs b and a).

Passing motions of various structural order dominate the development section in the first movement of Beethoven's Symphony No. 7. ►[Ex. 462]◄ This development uses a very different technique. The V is prolonged but only up to meas. 217; from there the motion as a whole constitutes a passing motion leading into the tonic of the recapitulation (see Graphs c and b). Here, therefore, there is no V immediately preceding the recapitulation. We must marvel at this outstanding example of symphonic and tonal architecture. After the prolongation of the dominant, the passing motion of higher order is slow in developing. This gradual build-up is caused by two widely conceived prolongations between the V (meas. 217) and the first passing chord on D (meas. 254). Graph a explains the first of these prolongations as an elaborate passing motion to the applied dominant of the D chord, and the second as equally elaborate passing motion within this applied dominant chord itself. The tension thus created mounts until, with meas. 254, the motion bursts out into the D-minor passing chord and from here the whole proceeds rapidly to the beginning of the recapitulation. More than any of the other developments this section is conceived as a true section of transition.

*

*   *

We now approach a group of development sections which show a greatly prolonged motion from III to V. Here, too, the masters have created sections of the most fantastic variety on the basis of the same structural outline. There could be, for instance, no greater contrast between two developments than there exists between the first movements of the Piano Sonatas, Op 10, No. 1 and Op 57 by Beethoven, although both move from III to V.

The development from Op 10, No. 1 is completely dominated by passing motions. ►[Ex. 463]◄ Branching off from the main prolongation (see Graph d) is a large prolonging passing motion which conceives the second from F to G as a seventh down, spread over a wide range (see first Graphs c and b, and then Graph a). The passing motion itself moves in thirds and fourths, some of the passing chords being prolonged, which heightens the tonal tension even more.

And now to the development of Beethoven's Op 57. ►[Ex. 464]◄ The characteristic of this section lies in the neighbor-note motion D♭-C which runs as a motto through the whole movement and which even determines the bass of the development. No passing motion of high structural order occurs here. After the III has been prolonged (note the change from minor to major), a D♭ chord is reached in meas. 109 by changing the III into an applied dominant to D♭. It is D♭ which ultimately is designed to lead to C, the bass of V. Immediately preceding this dominant, however, an appoggiatura chord on D♭ appears which we have indicated in Graphs b and c with an eighth-note stem. It follows that the motion between meas. 109 and 123 presents a passing motion between two chords constructed on the same bass D♭ (we recall a similar situation in Ex. 458). Thus a neighbor-note motion D♭-C is greatly expanded. Not all details of the top voice are presented, for instance the many characteristic transfers of register and the neighbor-note motions of the inner voice within the prolonged E-Major chord at the beginning of the development. Our main point of concentration is the bass which is so indicative of tonal direction in particular and tonal architecture in general. We should like, however, to draw the reader's attention to the splitting of the top voice into two voices. One leads from A♭ via G♭ to F and from there via G♭ to the final G♮ (a third down and a second up). The other shows a motion from A♭ into the inner voice E of the V.

The main significance of this development, however, lies in the tonal tension caused by the bold and imaginative prolongation of the incomplete bass neighbor note D♭ supporting two chords.

*

*   *

Within the analytical study of complete pieces, Chapter VIII will present more development sections which the student at this time should at least study in their outline. Some of these developments confront us with new and ingenious techniques. We are thinking here, for instance, of a work of the beginning of this century, the development from the first movement of Ravel's Sonatina. Although here again we find a passing motion from III to V as the main progression, the treatment of the voice leading in general and the more detailed prolongations in particular are highly original (Ex. 498). In order to make clear the subtle voice-leading texture, we have given in Graph c an indication of how the outer voices move in their final analysis. The ultimate voice-leading problem is the movement of a sixth in the bass against a ninth in the top voice which partly explains the suspension of E in the bass (meas. 40-53). The principal detours and retards within the passing motion from III to V are first the prolonged progression from F♯ to E and then the transfer of register from E to C in the top voice (meas. 40-49), with the subsequent dissonant movement of the inner voice to G♯ (see Graphs b and a). As far as the first prolongation is concerned, the B-minor chord and the following voice leadings arise out of the inner voice C♯ of the F♯-Major chord. This inner voice motion continues until it virtually melts into the inner voice of the E chord. The transfer of register of the following prolongation already mentioned moves in two sevenths (subdivided into fourths) to the high C♮; and now starts the interesting motion of the inner voice from F to G♯ which is followed by F♯, both tones preparing the characteristic entry of the recapitulation, G♯-F♯. This entry of the third form section is of great interest too, but will be taken up in Chapter VIII which contains a graph of the whole movement.

Another interesting example is the first movement of Schubert's *Unfinished* Symphony (see Ex. 497). Here the second theme is supported by a VI (not a III!). The development thus has the task of moving from VI to V. This progression is expanded in a most unusual and original way by a widely prolonged embellishing chord, the E-minor chord.[4]

The reader should turn now to the first movement from Brahms' Symphony No. 3 (Ex. 503). This development does not move to the dominant, and the reader will notice from the graphs that the A-Major chord, supporting the second theme of the exposition, is a contrapuntal and not a harmonic chord. Coming events are casting their shadows before. The revolutionary meaning of the technique employed by Brahms is mentioned in Chapter VIII and will be fully grasped if we turn to Ex. 480 and 505 which present major works by Bartók and Hindemith. These developments show contrapuntal prolongations within contrapuntal structures. It is fascinating to realize, however,

---

[4] In its last analysis this chord has the additional function of a voice-leading chord between VI and V.

that in these works of our times the development, despite all the revolutionary changes in contrapuntal language, has maintained its original meaning by constituting a dramatic section of transitional motion.

3. EXERCISES IN LARGE DIMENSIONAL PLANNING

The student is again reminded of the necessity of playing all graphs at the keyboard. This should be done in successive stages in the direction from the structure to the prolongations. He thus will train and equip his mind and his ear for the understanding of the many broadly devised organisms of western music as well as for structural planning which may be of special significance for the young composer. By enlarging a simple progression in various stages using various techniques, the ear receives valuable training. The examples from the sonata form developments present especially suitable material for such keyboard exercises.

In continuation of the exercises in prolongation given throughout Chapters V and VI, bass progressions in various stages will now be presented which, in addition to their value per se, are intended to indicate how sections from compositions already analyzed can be used for making up exercises in tonal planning. ▶[Ex. 465-470]◀

4. TWO PROLONGATIONS OF EXCEPTIONAL EXPANSION

As a conclusion to the detailed demonstration of partial musical organisms which started in Chapter V, we shall discuss two extraordinary conceptions of musical architecture. One is taken from Wagner's *Parsifal*, the other from Stravinsky's Symphony in Three Movements.

The example by Wagner is from Act I of *Parsifal;* it is the music which symbolizes and expresses the spiritual and emotional climax in connection with Gurnemanz's and Parsifal's approach to the castle of the Grail. The section starts in A Major, one measure before Gurnemanz's words, "*Vom Bade kehrt der König heim,*" and reaches C Major 78 measures later. ▶[Ex. 471]◀ The contents of this amazing music will have to be explained in several stages, moving from the over-all plan to the detail, and later to a survey of the whole.

1) General plan: Motion of a third from A to C, conceived as a sixth down (Graph a).

2) This sixth is subdivided into two major thirds and a half step. The end of the first third, the tone F, is reached only in meas. 65; from

there the motion proceeds relatively directly to D♭ and C (Graph b).

3) That first third (A to F) is inverted into an upwards moving sixth, subdivided into two major thirds (Graph c).

This explains the D♭ of meas. 33. This measure is the halfway mark of the whole prolongation moving from A to F.

4) This progression of a sixth in itself appears greatly prolonged (Graphs d and e).

Each third of the motion A-D♭-F is organized into a progression of a half-tone step plus a minor third (Graph d). Highly interesting is the further elaboration of the first third A to D♭ (see Graph e). The kind of prolongation Wagner devised to prolong the initial half-tone step from A to B♭ is the following: Two minor thirds, then a half-tone step and again two minor thirds. Thus the half-tone step and the thirds of higher order are anticipated and prepared in this prolongation of lower order. In regard to this preparatory half-tone step from E♭ to E♮ it should be mentioned that in the music it appears prolonged between meas. 7 and 19.

Graph f shows that in all main points of this section the top voice moves in octaves with the bass.

We are now prepared for Graph g. This graph, because of the great dimensions of this music, omits a detailed explanation of the prolonged D♭ chord (meas. 33-51) and D♮ chord (meas. 55-62) and presents in outline only the prolongation between E♭ and E♮ (meas. 7-19). As it is our main purpose to concentrate on the plan of tonal organization, the student is required to make detailed studies of these prolongations only after he has grasped the significance of this graph.

This brings us to the over-all meaning and the implications of this great architectonic conception. In spite of the detailed evolutions and the length of the prolongations, the F chord (meas. 65) and the following 13 measures moving to D♭ and finally to C, appear as the climax of the whole motion. Everything builds up and drives to these measures which execute the actual motion from A to C, the ultimate musical progression. Although the motive of "*Heilesbusse*" has already appeared for the first time in meas. 51, the conductor must endeavor to create the maximum sonorities when this motive reappears in meas. 65.

One cannot help marvelling at the incredible correlation between drama and music, and at the fact that the music so strikingly expresses the spiritual and emotional contents of the drama. The passing motions from A to D♭ (meas. 1-33) seem to express symbolically Gurnemanz's and Parsifal's wandering to the mighty hall of the Grail.

After this passing motion has come to an end, it appears that the proximity of the castle is expressed with the poignant passages of the Db-Major prolongation. This prolongation effectively broadens and retards the motion up to F, taken as a whole, and thus prepares so convincingly for the climax (meas. 65 ff.). The nearer they get to the Grail, the more retarded is the passing motion to F. Furthermore, the fact that the end of the dialogue between Gurnemanz and Parsifal coincides with the end of the first elaborate passing motion to Db throws considerable light on the text's meaning: Parsifal: *"Ich schreite kaum, doch waehn' ich mich schon weit."* Gurnemanz: *"Du siehst, mein Sohn, zum Raum wird hier die Zeit."* [5]

Do not these words correspond amazingly with the impression the music is creating, the impression of wandering through wide spaces, from A in many thirds until Db is reached, which fundamentally constitutes a small space of a major third and which only is part of a bigger motion to C, symbolizing the final arrival in the castle?

The Stravinsky excerpt comprises 147 measures (from the beginning through rehearsal number 37) and constitutes the first form section of the first movement. ►[Ex. 472]◄

This is perhaps one of the most convincing examples of modern polychordal tonality. Recalling our earlier statements, we should like to stress again that the use of so-called polychords in no way implies two tonalities which would be contradictory to the unity creating essence of tonality, regardless of style. The student has already studied the voice leading of the opening measures and may now wish to learn more about the role of these measures within a larger organism. The expansion of this organism in addition to the rather unfamiliar idiom of polychordal voice leading may warrant, at first, a concentration on the condensed contents as presented in Graphs c and d. Until immediately preceding No. 29, that is through 108 measures, a prolongation of G governs all motions. This main prolongation is subdivided into three prolongations of lower order. The first drives the melody up a third from G to Bb while the bass proceeds to the neighbor note A. The second prolongation pushes the melody a further halftone step up to B♮, the bass reaching the embellishing tone C. Finally the third prolongation, once more starting on G, goes through the space of a third, already outlined before, and drives the melody upwards to D. There is an irresistible consequence in these three melodic outlining motions

[5] Parsifal: I hardly stir, and yet I move apace. Gurnemanz: Thou seest, my son, here time is one with space (tr. by Ernest Newman).

becoming larger until the final top voice tone D of the G prolongation of high order is reached. On the whole, the melody has moved up a fifth. Observe that each of the three prolongations of lower order starts on the unison G or on a G triad (incomplete and complete).

From No. 29 on, the bass descends to B and then rises to D. This amounts to a progression from G via B to D, the first third being expressed as a descending sixth. As a counterpoint to this progression of the bass, the top voice rises one more fifth and reaches A.

Let us look back once more at the gigantic prolongation of G. Although at the beginning of each of the three sub-prolongations the tone G or its triad is pronounced without polychordal combination, this is by no means the case at the end of the first two prolongations. Only the last one, which brings the music to the preliminary melodic goal D, supports this tone with a simple triad on G (one meas. after No. 26).

The reader should now proceed to the study of Graph b and then of Graph a. Graph a and the score reveal Stravinsky's technique of repeating and circling around a chord in lieu of thematic development within chord prolongations. This results in a technique of creating chord blocks. Note, for example, the sections from No. 7 to No. 13 and from No. 16 to No. 19. In this latter section the trumpet part (see in Graph a the notes of the upper staff stemmed downwards) is significant for the continuity of the middle voice. It moves from B♭ to C♯ from where, through a motion of a seventh up, it reaches the top voice tone B♮.

*

*   *

The musical contents of works such as this Symphony by Stravinsky and the different techniques of tonal coherence in works by Hindemith and Bartók point to the great possibilities for a revitalized and, in every respect, contemporary expression of tonality. In spite of all the vast changes which this language has undergone, these works seem to indicate that tonality—in the broad sense outlined in this book, especially in this and the following chapter—may have a definite future.

Part II   Chapter Eight

The Concept of Tonality

A.   The complete composition—Its tonal and formal organization

I.   INTRODUCTION

The overwhelming number of examples cited thus far consisted of phrases, passages, themes and sections of compositions, which have been used to demonstrate in gradual stages the processes and possibilities of structural planning and hearing. This is altogether a new type of ear training, which demands first the study and understanding of the small and simple organism. For, how can the student be expected to grasp the musical direction and coherence of large sections or whole pieces, if he has not first learned to hear the organization of a short unit? The preliminary study of a single phrase or detail appears all the more necessary and logical, since the same characteristics of structure and prolongation prevail in a large section or a complete piece as in the single phrase. In principle the detail is constructed like the whole. In the latter, however, the proportions are different and the dimensions are larger.

The analysis and synthesis of several complete pieces of different style, length and complexity will now be the natural consequence and outgrowth of the preceding chapters. The detailed and large-dimensional approach, as well as the most divergent techniques of tonal continuity and coherence, are now familiar to the student; he is able, furthermore, to hear the detail of the most extended piece of music in proper relation to the meaning of the whole.[1] In the course of our discussion it will have become clear to the reader that whatever appears as structural in the analysis of a detail removed from its context becomes a prolongation the moment this detail is put back into the larger

[1] For the teacher, we should like to add that in individual cases it is pedagogically justifiable to demonstrate tonal coherence of complete compositions at an earlier stage. The musical capacity or experience of a student may warrant such a procedure.

organism. This becomes a guiding principle in our endeavor to explain the coherence of a complete piece.

Although we stated towards the end of Chapter VII the paramount need for structural orientation, we cannot and do not wish to give rules and rigid directions as to what to do first and what to do next in analyzing a complete composition. To a very definite degree the hearing of musical direction and coherence depends on intuition. Furthermore, among different musicians the actual procedure may vary, even within an accepted approach to the problems of musical continuity. Most students, however, will find that the points of structural significance will divulge their meaning first, allowing for the gradual unfolding of the prolongation's significance. Whatever the individual approach, any composition to be analyzed should be completely familiar to the student before any conclusions can be drawn as to the architectonic meaning of the musical contents. All knowledge must naturally grow out of this familiarity with the sonorities, atmosphere and style of the composition. If, in the coming analysis of complete compositions, the graphs are given in the direction from the most detailed prolongation to the fundamental structure, it is because this way of presentation seems the most satisfactory one and not because we in any way suggest a definite chronology of analytical procedure.

In order to survey tonality and its potentialities the analysis of eight strongly contrasting compositions of different stylistic periods will now be presented. The choice of pieces was determined by their variety in style and contents, but not by a wish to present a systematic approach from easier to more difficult works. Nevertheless, the order in which the analyses will be given approximately represents a graded order of their complexity. In concluding, we should like to encourage the reader, before studying the following graphs, to work on these compositions as independently as possible.[2]

2.   COMPOSITIONS BASED ON HARMONIC STRUCTURE
   AND ON COMBINED HARMONIC AND CONTRAPUNTAL STRUCTURE

The first four examples are based on entirely harmonic structures. This means that all motions of the detail, all harmonic and contrapuntal prolongations show their ultimate coherence in a melodic struc-

[2] The reader will find that a number of less complex compositions are either mentioned or analyzed in section B of this chapter. We suggest, therefore, that, in case of difficulties, he postpone a detailed analysis of certain of these eight works until the end of section B, at which time he will have gained more experience.

tural line, supported by a harmonic progression. The fifth example is based on two structural progressions, of which the first is contrapuntal, while the second progression is harmonic. It will now be realized what was meant by the earlier statement that the same characteristics appear within a complete piece as occur in single passages or sections. The structures of the following five compositions could just as well furnish the basic progressions of prolongations. Just as a theme or section constitutes the prolongation of an underlying progression of higher order (showing its basic direction), so a complete composition represents a large-scale, widely ramified prolongation of the structure, the progression of highest order. ►[Ex. 473-477]◄

3. COMPOSITIONS BASED ON CONTRAPUNTAL STRUCTURE

Musical direction and coherence is definitely not dependent on the existence of a harmonic framework. The contrapuntal progressions underlying themes and sections presented in several instances (we recall the examples in Chapter VII, section C) give sufficient indication that even a complete piece may be based on a contrapuntal progression. Looking ahead at the structural graphs of the three following compositions we will notice that no harmonic trait is evident. Thus, in comparison to the five pieces previously quoted the difference in tonal style is obvious, in spite of an adherence to the same principles of structure and prolongation. The structure for the Gesualdo Madrigal is a modal progression. Changing it to its harmonic counterpart presents an instructive example of the difference between the harmonic and the contrapuntal concept. The top voice would be G-F♯-E, supported by a I-V-I progression. The structure of the movement by Bartók with its two bass progressions is the contrapuntal equivalent to the technique of two harmonic progressions, familiar to us by now.

Tonal coherence in regard to a complete piece can thus be expressed in three ways, either through a contrapuntal structure or a harmonic structure or a combination of both. All three may be prolonged harmonically and contrapuntally. Here now are the graphs of three widely contrasting compositions which nevertheless adhere to the same principle of contrapuntal structure. ►[Ex. 478, 479, 480]◄

The reader will be able, by his own experience, to analyze successfully most of the contents of these eight compositions. We, therefore, will refrain from any extended comment. Regarding the Prelude by Debussy, attention should be given to the ingenuity with which the composer deals with the variants of the melodic neighbor-note motion, creating fascinating melodic parallelisms. As far as the Schubert *Lied* and the Madrigal by Gesualdo are concerned, their complete understanding presupposes a knowledge of the poems, since the relation of word and music is very significant in these extremely contrasting works. Notice, for instance, that in the *Lied* the important third stanza is set to music with the structurally highly important motion from the A-minor chord to the prolonged B-Major chord (the III). In the wide prolongation between the initial I and the III, the A-minor chord is the most significant passing chord. In fact, all motion from the beginning on is directed to this chord which ushers in the important third stanza.

There are, however, two factors which need more detailed discussion and explanation, because of their importance for the understanding of any composition—the factors of form and tonality. We shall take up form first, because its problems to a large extent have not been touched upon as yet. It was probably noted though that the formal organization had been indicated by capital letters in the graphs of a number of examples. The concept of tonality was demonstrated throughout Chapters V, VI and VII, but only in relation to passages and sections. The concentration on complete compositions makes a special discussion on tonality equally necessary.

4.   FORM AND STRUCTURE

a.   *Outer form, inner form and design*

We must distinguish three factors in composition which, though closely interlocked and interdependent, may still be defined singly.

The first, discussed throughout these pages, is the functions of structure and prolongation. They need no further definition at this point beyond a summarizing statement that structure indicates the unity and coherence of a composition. The second factor is form which may be defined as a principle of architectonic organization of the structure. In discussing large and small sections from compositions, we were in fact already dealing with the problem of form, for each theme or section may have its own organization, its own form. This formal organization manifests itself in subdivisions or segmentations and various types of repetition. We recall the many instances of parallelism, often veiled, or the structural enlargements or diminutions, all coming under the general term of repetition.

From the point of view of the total composition, however, the form of the detail will subordinate itself to the form of the total organism.

In other words, the various forms of the detail or *inner form* will become organic offshoots of the form of the whole, the *outer form*.

Similar to the relation between structure and prolongation is one between the various stages of inner form and the over-all governing feature of the outer form; there are formal organizations of a lower order and those of a higher order. In stating that the form of a composition is through-composed, two part or three part, one actually implies the formal organization of the highest order. Just as the prolongations are in their last analysis organic offshoots of the structure, so are all details of inner form the organic evolutions of the outer form.

And now to the third factor which may be called *design*. Design is the organization of the composition's motivic, thematic and rhythmic material through which the functions of form and structure are made clear. Design is instrumental in bringing about the formal subdivisions and repetitions and in shaping the prolongations into sections, themes and phrases. These subdivisions, specifically, may be accomplished through various techniques developed in past centuries, such as: thematic repetition, cadences (harmonic as well as contrapuntal), caesuras, change of tempo, rhythm or texture, etc.

All three factors, structure and form on the one hand and design on the other, are completely interdependent. One without the other is unable to create artistic interest and quality. Structure is the organization of the tonal course into a coherent pattern; it is design which gives this pattern shape and profile, which makes it living music. Design without structural direction and coherence is an empty play with motivic or rhythmic material. And the boldest prolongations of structural progressions without convincing thematic and rhythmic design will never be an expression of living art.

b.   Relation of outer form to structure.
Structure-form—Prolongation-form

Having discussed inner form throughout Chapters I-VII it will now be necessary to go into the problems of outer form. We shall see that the principle of repetition is as of paramount importance in the outer form as it was found to be in the inner form and its design. It is further joined by a technique of division of which we shall hear more from now on. Division and repetition—both are the two basic outer-form principles of western music.

It appears that outer form is in significance practically on a par with structure; it is a composition's organization of the highest order because it represents the formal organization of the structural progression. We suggest the reader make a comparison between the structural graphs (with their indications of form) of all eight previously quoted compositions. This will show most clearly the effect of outer form on the course of the structural progression.

Let us concentrate first on the *Lied* by Schubert since it shows a form technique already known to us from the end of Chapter V. Through the dividing and repeating technique of interruption, the structure has been divided into two, interdependent, structural progressions. As each progression constitutes one form section, a two-part form is created.

The Ayre by Dowland is likewise a two-part form but its organization is based on a different principle. Unlike the Schubert *Lied*, in which each part, in its final analysis, is made up of a partial structural progression, the design of the work by Dowland shows a prolongation of I, representing the first form section.

In the Schubert *Lied* it is the structure which is divided, whereas in the Ayre it is the prolongation of the structure which is divided; in the latter, therefore, prolongation is utilized to create a section of the total form.

By stating that prolongation is utilized for the outer-form organization we imply that one structural chord alone, *without* its prolongation, can never create form. This means that one single chord cannot outline and determine structural motion. Yet only motion creates a form section, because form is organized motion. Thus, if in the Ayre the formal division is to be drawn after the first tonic, structure alone would not provide for the necessary motion with which to build a first section. It is only the prolongation of I which, with the help of design, makes the form possible.

This difference in formal organization also applies to three-part forms. In the movement from the Mozart Sonata, as well as in the Bartók Concerto, outer form has organized the structure by subdividing it into three structural progressions; again the motion of each form section is determined by a structural progression. In the Intermezzo by Brahms and the Prelude by Debussy, on the other hand, the organizing subdivision of the outer form is not applied to the structure, but to the prolongation of the structure. Not the structure itself, but prolongations are used to outline one or more form sections.

We now turn to outer form and its relation to structure in the Madrigal by Gesualdo and the Fugue by Bach. The reader will have noticed that in these compositions no formal subdivisions occur. Neither the structure nor the prolonged structure is divided. Thus the undivided structure and the undivided prolonged structure coincide with the undivided outer form.

All this means that we must draw a definite distinction between outer-form types. There is one category which solves form problems by means of the structure itself, i.e. by either stressing the uninterrupted flow of the structure and its prolongations, thus creating a one-part form, or by subdividing the structure into two or three partial structural progressions, thus creating a two- or a three-part form. A second category solves the form problem by use and adaptation of the main prolongation, i.e. by subdividing the prolongation of the structure.

The first type will be called *structure-form*, the second *prolongation-form*. To understand fully the difference between both categories one has to realize that structure-form bases its organizing power completely on the structure. Structure itself provides the means for its own organization. Structure-forms, therefore, are the most natural forms. Prolongation-forms, on the other hand, though equally convincing, are more contrived. They give the impression of a formal design projected on to the unity of structure, rather than of a naturally grown division.

Summing up we can state that the Bach Fugue and the Gesualdo Madrigal are one-part structure-forms. As every one-part form is by necessity a structure-form, from now on we shall call such forms one-part or through-composed forms. The Schubert *Lied* shows a two-part structure-form, whereas the Ayre by Dowland represents a two-part prolongation-form. The movements by Mozart and Bartók are in a three-part structure-form. Finally the Intermezzo by Brahms and the Prelude by Debussy offer examples of three-part prolongation-form.

This was a preliminary discussion on form concentrating on the compositions quoted before. More on this subject of form will be found in section B where additional form types will be shown and where more illustrations of complete works will be offered.

5.   SIGNIFICANCE AND RANGE OF TONALITY

Structural hearing, based on the principle of structure and prolongation, leads to a concept of tonality which, in view of the average present-day approach, is a new concept. Throughout Chapters V, VI and VII, while studying the techniques of structural planning and hearing we were dealing directly or by implication with the problem of tonality. In a most general definition, tonality is the expression of tonal unity and coherence based on the principle of structure and prolongation. Thus, structural coherence and tonal coherence are, in their ultimate analysis, the same.

In recognizing that a certain passage or section of a composition, if separated from the total organism, has its own basic direction or structure, we at the same time acknowledge that it has its individual tonal unity and coherence, i.e. it has its own tonality. This passage, when linked up again with the complete composition and heard in relation to the whole, loses any individual status and becomes a prolongation of an organism of higher order. This means that it subordinates its own basic direction to the one single basic direction of the piece, the structural framework. Simultaneously it subordinates its individual tonality to the one tonality determined by the structural framework or progression. Individual tonalities or keys thus become prolongations or tonal phases of a single tonality.

The structural framework, in addition to indicating the basic direction, determines and outlines the one tonality of the whole composition. Tonality may thus be defined as *prolonged motion within the framework of a single key-determining progression,* constituting the ultimate structural framework of the whole piece. As long as all details of the composition are organic prolongations of such structural and tonal frameworks, as long as every detail has a function to fulfill within the progression of the framework, it contributes to the expression of the one tonality of the framework. It follows, therefore, that any chord whatsoever, be it consonant or dissonant, diatonic or chromatic may appear within any given tonal framework. The sole deciding factor justifying its presence is whether its function within the framework is clearly defined as an integral part of the whole.

We believe that the eight compositions and all the many sections and passages discussed (if we conceive them as parts of a larger whole) corroborate this definition. Let us glance back at meas. 18-31 of the Schubert *Lied.* In itself, separated from the organic whole, this section has its own tonality, C Major. This "individual" tonality, however, it asserts only if analyzed on its own merits. As part of the complete composition these same measures represent a prolongation, constituting a prolonged C passing chord.

This terminology defines the function of this passage, the function within the tonality-determining, structural framework of the whole piece. And this function makes it a prolongation and therefore a member of the one tonality of G Major. For another example we recall the Intermezzo by Brahms. Meas. 17-31, if analyzed independently, have the tonality of D Major. In relation to the complete piece of which they are an organic part, these measures represent a prolonged embellishing chord within the single tonality of the composition which is B minor. Another fundamental type of prolongation shows progressions from one chord to another. They too are expressions of tonal coherence. Let us, for instance, recall the Concerto by Bartók and specifically the section from meas. 68-105. If taken out of its context, it constitutes a motion from the tonality of G to the tonality of F♯ which would represent a modulation. In relation to the whole organism of the movement, however, these measures represent a prolongation again: not the prolongation of one chord, but the prolongation of a progression from one structural chord to another, both being members of the structural framework which express the one tonality of the entire movement.

In regard to the structural framework itself, it would be wrong to assume that only triads can be used, in the belief that only they are key defining. This is by no means the case. The examples by Copland and Stravinsky, in the preceding chapter, made it clear that polychords, for instance, not only constitute no contradiction to the essence of tonality, but have enhanced its potentialities to a degree which today cannot yet be correctly evaluated. The reason for this structural possibility of polychords lies in the fact that the lower triad of this chord combination, the one erected on the bass tone, is definitely the dominating factor. It is the strength of this triad which enables a polychord to act in a key-defining capacity.

Tonality thus is a complex, but highly organized web resulting from the multiple ramifications of the key-determining structural progression. The key-determining progression of the highest order presents the single tonality or key of the composition. The other so-called keys and the "modulations" are prolonged chords and prolonged progressions, all within the framework of that one tonality. They are organic phases of one single tonality.

In complete contrast to these new definitions concerning a single key or tonality, the average present-day concept of tonality implies a multitude of keys and modulations, which at best can be explained as a system of references. The moment a chord cannot be labeled and referred to a certain key according to a most narrow harmonic approach (as a dominant of the dominant, the sub-dominant of the relative minor, etc., etc.) conventional theory assumes the existence of a modulation to a new key. The consequence of this approach is the theoretical assumption that a tonal composition constitutes a row of many keys, appearing in the form of large or small passages, thus presenting a row of details, whose function and inner coherence, however, is not explained. The assumption of many keys is responsible for the widely held belief that a composition is in C, for example, if it starts in C, proceeds then to many other keys and ultimately returns to the initial key of C. Thus the many so-called keys often far outweigh the main key or tonality. Why a composition constructed according to such a conception is called a piece in *one* key, does not seem logical at all. It should be termed a piece in *many* keys.

What is actually achieved by stating that a certain passage of a piece in C major is in F♯ minor if we are unable to explain the function of this F♯-minor passage? Here we touch on the main disadvantage of the old concept: It is unable to explain the function of those many keys as being parts and offshoots of a single organic whole.

The attempt has been made to get out of this impasse by adopting a conception of many keys versus one tonality. A composition is supposed to show a row of many keys and modulations to these keys, but still is believed to represent one tonality. This author does not know of a single instance, however, in which the dependency of these so-called keys on the one tonality, or the fact that the keys are organic parts of a whole, have been demonstrated. The use of the term tonality as distinct from key proves that the difference between a whole and its organic offshoots is not understood. For there exists no definable difference between tonality and key. They are too close in meaning and therefore, according to this terminology, one just has to believe that many tonalities or keys can appear within one tonality or key. It seems that this strange contradiction demands clarification. If the so-called tonality is effective and in force throughout the composition, how can one explain a simultaneous coexistence of many other keys?

How important it is to understand the direction of motion and its significance and how little is gained by the mere listing of "keys" could be gathered from the discussion of the development sections at the end of Chapter VII. It is usually said that the development is the place where the composer works contrapuntally on the thematic material of the exposition by modulating through many different keys until the dominant of the main key is reached; often a list of all those keys is given. But what does the knowledge of this list explain to the musician, eager to know what the significance of the development section actually is? We have realized the enormous tonal tensions which can be created by those dramatically prolonged progressions full of detours, lyrical details and deceiving motions which, however, have definite functions within a clearly conceived whole. Thus the list of keys is at best nothing more than a description of single facts whose function within the motion of the development remains unexplained.

A narrow harmonic approach together with a purely descriptive and cataloging type of analysis have resulted in an extremely limited concept of tonality. Its limits are narrowly drawn and have to be trespassed constantly by the composer in order to achieve movement and variety, indeed, to achieve musical length at all. This may explain the fact that compositions of the most different periods present a concept of tonality at variance with that expounded in many books on theory and analysis.

As structural hearing shows a single tonality with all details in the form of themes, passages, motives, chords etc., as organic expansions of this one tonality, the term modulation to a new key and the resulting conception of themes and passages in different keys become meaningless. Instead of modulation, for instance from F Major to A Major, one should correctly say, "progression (or directed motion) from the F Major to the A-Major chord." If this A-Major chord appears prolonged it should, instead of passage in A Major, be termed, "the passage prolonging the A-Major chord" or, in short, the A chord prolongation. Once, however, this new concept has become familiar to musicians, even the old term "passage in A Major" would be correctly understood, i.e. one would know that no new key in the conventional sense is meant. For all terminology depends on the concept from which it originates.

The crux of the whole difference in the conception of tonality lies in the fact that harmonic analysis, in contrast to structural hearing, cannot conceive or explain artistic variety on the basis of artistic unity. Composers have achieved this unity through a consciously or unconciously felt organic concept of tonality. Harmonic analysis or the old concept of tonality, on the other hand, draws an inorganic picture of a truly organic piece of art. It seems only too natural that this narrow, descriptive concept has contributed greatly to the crisis of tonality out of which we now seem to emerge.

*

*   *

In order to give final clarification to the intricate cooperation between structure and prolongation and the resulting phenomenon of tonality, a diagram is offered. ▶[Ex. 481]◀

Although it has been said earlier in a different connection, we wish to stress again that no chronological order of the creative processes is suggested by this diagram. It rather represents an attempt to demonstrate graphically the "distance" and at the same time the inner connection between the most remote, quasi-abstract, musical factors (such as a tone and its resulting chord) and the finished product of composition. After having investigated musical planning and hearing from the detailed prolongations back to the structure, and from the structure to the details of complete compositions (indicated in the diagram by arrows pointing in opposite directions), we are now in a position to realize the significance and the "place" of all creative phases discussed and illustrated throughout the preceding pages.

In explanation of the diagram it appears possible to go even beyond our definition of tonality and to arrive at a definition of higher order, so to speak. The so-called pre-creative stage indicates the completely unconscious process leading to the structural framework of a composition. In this pre-creative, quasi-abstract stage there occurs a process of prolongation, a kind of "primordial" prolongation, which creates the structural progression. Since all key-determining progressions are *de facto* chord prolongations, the reader may for some time have concluded that the structural frameworks themselves are in their last analysis chord-prolongations. This, as we called it, primordial prolongation must, however, be distinguished from the concrete prolongations of the creative stage; it is more like a logical conclusion at which we arrive, than a technique of composition. One may question the seeming contradiction: How can the structural progression be at the same time a prolongation? The answer to this possible question would be, first, that the structural progression rightfully carries its name because all prolongations of higher and lower order (the prolongations of the creative stage) prove to be offshoots of this one progression. Music is motion and the structural progression is the motion of highest order. However, just as a prolongation of lower order, to be understood, must always be referred to the one of next higher order (which is its structure), so also can the structural framework be referred further back to the tonality-indicating fundamental chord of which it logically is a harmonic or contrapuntal prolongation.

Both stages, the creative and the pre-creative, can now be clearly surveyed. All prolongations of the creative stage reduce themselves to two categories. Either we encounter the prolongation of a progression or the prolongation of a chord (both of which include all types of melodic prolongation). Both categories develop and execute tonality's rich possibilities. They are superseded and governed by the tonality-outlining, structural progression which in its last analysis appears as the primordial prolongation of the tonality-indicating fundamental chord. We therefore come to an ultimate definition of tonality. Since all prolongations (chord prolongations and prolongations of progressions) lead up to the structure which itself is a pre-creative chord prolongation outlining and determining the tonality of a piece, it is correct to say: *Tonality is synonymous with chord prolongation.*

This definition in no way upsets our first definition. It merely indicates that the earlier one covers the creative stage (from the tonal or structural framework to the finished composition) whereas the latter definition covers the total organism of a composition and therefore applies to both stages of creation. Whether one explains tonality as prolongation of the key-determining structural progression or as a chord prolongation—both definitions are correct. They are more or less equivalent since they complement each other. Whether one uses one or the other to define the meaning of tonality depends on how far one's analysis penetrates into the conscious and unconscious processes of composing. Because the key-determining structural progression in its last analysis represents motion within or around the chord (chord prolongation) we are justified in calling the second definition a definition of a higher order.

B.   Various types of form and their use in composition

The problems of outer-form organization will now be investigated more in detail and new form types will be illustrated with examples. For these purposes it would be necessary merely to offer, first the structural graph of a composition and then the graph showing the structure's formal organization. However, as we are interested in a composition for more reasons than form only, we have presented several compositions in more detailed analysis. Whenever, on the other hand, we have merely indicated the structure and the prolongations of high order, the student is required to furnish a more detailed explanation by means of elaborate graphs. In this way the following section will help—beyond its significance regarding the study of form—to provide for more experience in the analysis of complete works, in turn creating a more thorough understanding of tonality's wide range.

I.   ONE-PART OR THROUGH-COMPOSED FORM

In one part-form there occurs no division of structure but a complete conforming with or supporting of the unified course of the prolonged structure. Any possible urge to an outer-form division or repetition is subordinated to the mutual goal of all organizing factors concerned—the creation of a single undivided and unrepeated motion. The unity achieved through a coherent structure and its prolongations dominates the composition. The structure not only represents the harmonic and melodic framework, but simultaneously the framework of outer form.

It appears that, in this "through-composed" form type (see the Fugue by Bach), the various techniques of repetition are confined to the design of the detail, large or small, but do not act as the form determining power in regard to the piece as a whole. Nevertheless, their task in regard to inner form is of no less significance and importance in view of the over-all goal: the creation of a musical organism.

Before dealing with two masterpieces from vocal literature we should like to advise the reader to make further studies of one-part instrumental compositions, taking his examples from Bach's Preludes from the *Well-Tempered Clavier* and from the Inventions, or from Chopin's Preludes, including the fascinating, though complicated Prelude No. 9 in E Major.

The two vocal compositions are Marenzio's five-part Madrigal *Io piango* and Pamina's Aria from Mozart's *The Magic Flute*. The choice of these compositions was dictated by the fact that two so very divergent pieces dealt with the same form problem. In both works the all-important relation between word, tone and form offers extraordinary examples of artistic ingenuity.

Although motivic and thematic repetition had not yet been developed to a degree comparable to the achievements of the eighteenth century, it is amazing how the sixteenth-century madrigalists, for instance Luca Marenzio, have solved the intricate problems of the one-part form. This type has a tendency to drive on constantly with consequent change of its motivic contents, which tendency, however, could conceivably prevent unity, integration and coherence. This potential danger appears nonexistent in Marenzio's madrigal which succeeds in drawing an integrated and coherent tone picture.

The student is advised first to read the poem and then, while studying the graphs, to investigate at which points of musical context the single words and sentences are placed. ►[Ex. 482]◄ The text is the final stanza from a *canzone* by Petrarca. It is subdivided into two sentences. The first and longer one concludes with the words *"ch'i sassi romper ponno,"* the emotional climax of the whole. The unity of this first sentence is musically expressed through a single extended prolongation of the structural I (meas. 1-35), the subdivisions of the sentence corresponding with subdivisions of the prolongation. The second and shorter sentence, describing the fading away of the imaginary appearance of the beloved one and the end of the dream, is musically underlined by the continuation and end of the structural progression. This, in short, outlines the combined organization of text and music.

Now to the imaginative details. Tonal tension is created by the motion in octaves up to the dominant; step by step this progression pushes the context of word and music to the climactic, *"ch'i sassi . . . ,* etc."* Within this motion to the V (meas. 26), note the increase of musical intensity. The first phrase of the poem is repeated and the music accordingly repeats the motion to the A chord which the second time, however, is reached more definitely (compare meas. 7 and 8 with meas. 16 and 17). This A chord which so far has been a neighbor or neighbor-passing chord, becomes, from meas. 17 on, a prolonged passing chord on the way to the V. Now a speed up occurs: The B♭ chord is held for just one measure; and then, within four measures in rapid succession, the music moves upwards (fifths in the bass) and reaches the V and the ensuing I in meas. 26 and 27. Measure- and phrase-rhythm add much to the persuasiveness of this music. In regard to B♭, its choice instead of B♮ appears to have two reasons. First, a diminished chord would have hardly been musically satisfactory since Marenzio planned the motion from I to V (meas. 1-26) to be based on major chords. In addition the word *dolcemente* seems to demand the soft color of B♭.[3] In these four measures of increasing drive, melodic ascending motions of fifths come into play adding with their imitations to the drive and confirming as parallelisms the one melodic ascending fifth of a higher structural order (meas. 1-26). The last fifth has not even completed its course when the soprano in a "new" motive (upward skip of a fifth) breaks in with the dramatic, *"ch'i sassi."* There follows this motive's inversion which, in its strongly imitative use, seems to illustrate the piercing of rocks. The climactic passage reaches its greatest density and intensity just before the tonic appears again in meas. 33.

---

[3] The top voice tone B♭ is placed in the inner voice. This obscuring of the top voice adds to the expressiveness of this measure.

From there on (meas. 33 to 35), the tension slackens. The large-scale prolongation of the I, which brought the whole motion to a climax and sustained it for a while, comes to its end. And now in a very contrasting setting the music proceeds to the C chord (CS), and from there to the I, the V and the final I while the line very gradually descends to the tonic. Short ascending and descending lines of fifths once more appear in simple imitation, but the excitement of the preceding passage is over and the Madrigal ends calmly, practically in the vein of a folk tune. This setting is a most convincing portrayal of the vanishing dream.

This Madrigal gives the impression of a truly through-composed form, with one large motion constantly driving on to its conclusion. Note how effectively the principle of repetition is used and how it aids in sustaining a coherent musical flow (see the brackets and parenthesis in Graph a).

Let us turn now to Mozart's Aria, a great example of one-part form. ►[Ex. 483]◄ The piece is based on a most original organization of the structural progression, which has its explanation largely in the dramatic situation. Pamina, not believing any more in Tamino's love, seeks death. Mozart, in one of his greatest inspirations and with purely musical means, greatly intensifies this dramatic situation. The result is such a moving and realistic account of Pamina's agony, that the words of the libretto give not much more than a hint of what Mozart so dramatically expresses in his music. The composition moves in one coherent flow to the words, "In death alone." With these words the music has reached what appears to be the final V with a structural A in the top voice. The beginning of meas. 27 is logically expected to conclude the Aria. As if Pamina were shuddering back from the final and fatal decision, the E♭ chord suddenly appears instead of the expected ending on the tonic G. The top voice now moves once more to D, while the vocal part, with a repetition of the words, "If for love thou dost not languish," attains its most dramatic intensity. The V with D in the top voice is reached in meas. 30 and again the structure starts to descend. But once more the final step is not taken as the V leads to a neighbor-note chord. This time the suspending of the structural motion is less violent and the music immediately following is shorter. It hovers around the neighbor-note chord and is practically at a standstill. The tonic appears finally in meas. 36 without any further resistance. It is as if Pamina were now resigned to death. The cadence is repeated twice to the words "In death alone." And finally the orchestra, in a moving postlude, sums up the whole musical structure in one final short and concentrated lament.

In twice not completing the structural descent, the music seems to hesitate to touch the tonic G, which in this aria appears to be the symbol of finality, of death. All this is expressed within a one-part form; it is all like one big sentence which only haltingly finds its completion. It is important to realize that these partial repeats of the structural progression, which are so strikingly tied to the dramatic situation, in no way create an outer-form division. Like all other repetitions and parallelisms of the detail (the inner form), they are subordinated to the one governing organization which is the one-part outer form of this Aria. It will be a highly rewarding task for the student to work out a detailed analysis of this masterpiece.

2.   TWO-PART STRUCTURE-FORM

There are three possible ways to create a two-part structure-form: through a modified repetition of the structure, through the division of structure or through the technique of interruption which combines the features of repetition and division.

a.   Repetition of structure

Whenever an entire composition consists in its ultimate analysis of a structural progression and its modified but complete repetition, this latter technical device creates the form of the composition. To preclude any misunderstanding it should be stressed that repetition is not considered form determining if it is applied to single parts, such as the sections of a suite movement or the exposition in sonata form. In these instances, repetition satisfies the urge to emphasize or the need for symmetry. Hence we must distinguish this latter use from its possible form-creating function, now under discussion.

Repetition is such a genuine tool for the creation of musical design that composers were naturally drawn to the possibility of basing the form of a whole piece on this fundamental principle. It cannot be denied, however, that this kind of form treatment entails the danger of being too primitive, for it tends to create monotony rather than formal interest. This possible danger was averted through the application of changes in the repeated section. These deviations run all the way from minor changes to bold and subtle prolongations, which nevertheless in no way deny the existence of the "model" and thus allow the principle of repetition to assert itself strongly. We shall list two compositions from the sixteenth and the beginning of the seventeenth century, in which period this form type was used quite extensively. The first is a *Branle* by Praetorius to be found in J. Wolf's *Music of Earlier Times* (No. 59). It shows only very slight changes in the second part. The second work is a Ballet by Thomas Morley, *My bonny lass*, quoted as No. 159 in the *Historical Anthology of Music* (Vol. 1). Here the differences between the form sections are obvious. On a higher level of formal construction is a *Corrente* by Frescobaldi. The second part is an augmented and interestingly varied repetition of the first part. ►[Ex. 484]◄ The changes should be carefully studied; they will give a clue to the developing technique of variation, so strongly based on the principle of repetition. The second part, in reality, is a variation of the first.

That this kind of two-part form was not unknown to the nineteenth century will now be demonstrated by quoting Brahms' song, *Feldeinsamkeit*. A poem of two stanzas gives rise here to a two-part form based on repetition of structure. This is an excellent example of how the principle of repetition has taken hold of both the inner and outer form. The large-scale repeat, creating the form sections, branches off into the minutest parallelisms of the detailed voice leading. ►[Ex. 485]◄

b.   Division of structure

1.   DIVISION OF BASS STRUCTURE

In addition to repetition, composers have applied a principle of division in order to get a natural specimen of two-part form. A division of a single organism into two partial organisms is a very logical procedure. In other words, a single structure can be divided into two interdependent structural progressions without making one of these progressions a prolongation of the other. Since by this dividing process one achieves a two-part structure, a so-called two-part structure-form is created.

The harmonic concept proved to be a major achievement not only because it led to the structural harmonic framework and its possibilities of harmonic prolongation, but also because it entails strongly form-creating implications. A harmonic framework carries within itself the possibility of division. For instance, the progression from I via the III to the V and on to the I proved to be very suitable for division into two parts:

A	B
I III	III . . . V I

The reason why the division is applied after a III rather than a II, IV or VI may lie in the fact that the III is halfway between the I and the V. As an illustration for two-part form through harmonic division, the reader is advised to look back to Ex. V (Part I) of this book. Here we find that with the help of design a two-part form has been created through division of the harmonic structure. This forming technique can also be found in *La Frescobalda* by Frescobaldi. ►[Ex. 486]◄ For a longer example expressing the same technique the student should make a thorough study of the D-minor Sonata (L. 413) by Domenico Scarlatti.

2. DIVISION OF MELODIC STRUCTURE

Less frequent is the creation of form through a division of the melodic structure. An illustration of this technique may be found in the *Allemande* already quoted from Wolf's *Music of Earlier Times* (No. 39) (see Ex. 447). The forming process here is achieved by the melody which, through division of one octave, creates a descending fourth as melodic structure for the first part and a descending fifth for the second part. In comparison to the top voice the structural bass appears of secondary significance. It constitutes mainly a counterpoint to the top voice, the latter showing the process of form division.

3. DIVISION OF BASS AND MELODIC STRUCTURE

Whereas in the previous examples the form-determining division was applied either to the bass or the top voice, it happens that both melody and bass structure appear divided to create a two-part structure-form. A Sonata in G Major by Domenico Scarlatti presents an interesting example. ►[Ex. 487]◄

The reader is aware that structural progressions may be contrapuntal or harmonic or may show a combination of both elements. Contrapuntal structures occur most frequently in our times and earlier periods up to approximately the middle of the sixteenth century, whereas harmonic structures are characteristic for the seventeenth, eighteenth and nineteenth centuries. There exist, however, compositions which, in this structural aspect, do not follow the prevalent trends of their own time although the style of voice leading and thematic design is "contemporaneous."

Two such interesting examples will be presented, both of which show a correlated division of bass and melody structure. The first is a song by Hugo Wolf, *In der Frühe*. It shows the division of an entirely contrapuntal structure, although otherwise it is very characteristic for its period. ►[Ex. 488]◄

Each of the two stanzas represents one form section. The motion from I to the CS chord makes up the first part, the motion from the CS chord (now major) to the I (major) constitutes the second part. Through division each form part outlines a structural progression; we, therefore, are entitled to speak of a two-part structure-form. The second example is the *Interludium* (Pastorale) between Fugue 2 and 3 from the *Ludus Tonalis* by Hindemith. ►[Ex. 489]◄ In this composition of unmistakably modern contrapuntal style, the first part moves clearly to the dominant and the second part from the dominant to the tonic. In such cases the dominant is simultaneously the end of the first part and the beginning of the second part, both of which overlap.[4] Beyond the aspect of form this composition presents a very interesting example for parallelisms and for modern tonal organization in general. Compare the melodic motions in thirds indicated in Graph c with their elaborations expressed in Graph b and finally in Graph a. Of interest are also the prolonged leading-tone chords at the end of each form part, which seem to replace the old technique using the diminished seventh chord.

c. Interruption

The technique of interruption combines the basic form-creating principles of repetition and division. This kind of melodic and harmonic division, as we know, is very special inasmuch as the element of repetition plays such a varied role. In its straightforward form the post-interruption section (or the second form section) starts again with the tonic, and repeats, at least in its beginning, the motivic material of the pre-interruption section, thus aiding in the establishment of a relationship between both form sections. It must be stressed, however, that composers have found ingenious ways to change the motivic appearance of the post-interruption section while satisfying the urge of repetition by adhering closely to the structure and frequently even to the outline of the prolongation of the pre-interruption section. Thus the contrasting principles of repetition and variety have been brought into balance. We recall the example from Mozart's *Don Giovanni* (Ex. 267). For another example of inner form through interruption, we draw the

---

[4] A similar situation exists in movements in sonata form where the development must be considered to move within the V or from III to V, even if the first chord of the actual development section is neither V nor III.

student's attention to the first part of Donna Anna's Aria in D Major, which itself is formed through interruption with an abbreviated post-interruption section. As in the former example the repetition is not motivic but structural.

The ability to change the motivic appearance while adhering to the structural outline offered the possibility for the so-called character variation of the nineteenth century, a factor which until Schenker had been entirely overlooked.

Turning to the use of interruption as outer form one may find striking thematic changes in the post-interruption section. One also comes across compositions in which interruption creates symmetric or near-symmetric form sections, and those in which interruption gives rise to an asymmetric form treatment.

A relatively simple example is the Third Prelude by Chopin. This composition presents a fairly symmetric two-part form through interruption and repeats the motivic material at the beginning of the post-interruption section. A coda concludes the Prelude. The student should make a detailed study of this work.

The Earle of Salisbury Pavane by William Byrd is an interesting composition, although too presenting a symmetric form construction. ►[Ex. 490]◄ The post-interruption section, despite parallelisms, makes a motivically "new" appearance. A contributing factor is the rather unusual beginning of this part with a C chord, a passing chord between the dividing V and the tonic. This is an original attempt to connect the two form sections with the effect that the entry of the structural tonic in the post-interruption section appears delayed.

A combination of structural and thematic delay occurs in the theme of the variation movement from Beethoven's Quartet, Op 18, No. 5. ►[Ex. 491]◄ Through a prolongation of I which supports an augmentation of the initial outlined interval of a sixth, the reentry of the structural top voice line and the initial motive is delayed.

Turning now to asymmetric two-part forms based on interruption one may recall that Schubert's song, *Liebesbotschaft* presented exactly such a characteristic. The post-interruption section, which is the music to the fourth stanza, is much shorter than the first part which constitutes the music up to the end of the third stanza (see Ex. 476).

Finally Chopin's First Prelude is presented, which from every point of view constitutes an extraordinary composition. It is characterized through a very short pre-interruption part and a highly dramatic and extended post-interruption section followed by a coda. ►[Ex. 492]◄

All these examples intended to prove that the forming technique of interruption allows for the most diversified treatment. There is a wide stylistic and expressive range between "normal" constructions like Chopin's Third Prelude and a piece with such tonal concentration and such an interesting second part as the Pavane by Byrd; or between the Schubert song which masters the form problem by molding four stanzas into a three plus one stanza, two-part form, and the dramatic sweep of Chopin's First Prelude with its very asymmetric outer form which nevertheless shows the characteristics of interruption.

3. TWO-PART PROLONGATION-FORM

As the difference between structure-form and prolongation-form has been explained above, it will now suffice to recall that prolongation-form does not emanate from the structure's possible subdivision, but is derived by a process of adapting a prolongation with the help of design for form-creating purposes.

Three forming techniques are most frequently used. The complete main prolongation or a segment of it may constitute the first form part. Or it may happen, as in the Ayre by Dowland (Ex. 473), that a complete prolongation, which in relation to the whole piece is of secondary order, represents the first form part. In all three cases the continuation and conclusion of the structural progression takes place in the second form section. As the third type has been illustrated already with the work by Dowland we shall now turn to a few examples illustrating the first two techniques.

a. *The main prolongation as a form section*

We find this technique in Schubert's German Dance No. 7 which we have quoted already in Chapter VI (see Ex. 316). The prolongation of the I takes up eight measures and constitutes the first form section.

In numerous pieces it is the motion to a prolonging V, the dominant prolongation of the tonic, which is the main prolongation and which can be used for form-making purposes. We present two examples, a little Prelude in G Minor by Bach and the Waltz, Op 39, No. 8 in Bb Major by Brahms. ►[Ex. 493, 494]◄

b. *Segment of main prolongation as a form section*

This technique which shows a division of prolongation can be found in the second Minuet of Bach's First Partita. ►[Ex. 495]◄ Here the progression between I and IV is prolonged through a motion into the middle voice (D-C-B♭). The B♭ is supported by a G-minor chord which acts as a passing chord between the I and the IV. Design divides this prolongation from I to IV in such a way that the motion from I to its prolonging V, supporting C, makes up the first form part.

There can be no doubt that such form constructions offer a very strong synthesis of the single form parts because the unity of the main prolongation in a way counterbalances the dividing elements of form and design.

4.   THREE-PART FORMS

The reader is requested to look back at the graphs explaining Mozart's slow movement from K.280 (Ex. 475). He will realize that this type of three-part form has been developed out of a two-part structure-form and the technique of interruption. In order to understand this process of form development more clearly, it should be realized that the most natural outer form is either the one- or the two-part structure-form. The one-part form stresses the unity of structure by adhering to the undivided course of the structural progression. In the two-part structure-form there occurs an application of the fundamental organizing factors, such as division and repetition, to the structural progression. As division and repetition actually result in two parts, the three-part form, per se, is a contrived construction, a real product of artistic planning. Under these circumstances it seems logical that composers attempted to develop this form as much as possible out of the more natural two-part form organization. Thus it came about that certain three-part types are related to the two-part form of interruption.

More specifically, two main form types were developed out of interruption, one showing a three-part structure-form (as in the Mozart movement) and the other a three-part prolongation-form. ►[Ex. 496]◄ In both types the origin from interruption is obvious. In the structure-form (Graph a) the actual interruption takes place at the end of part B. Thus, through a further forming process of division, two sections have been created out of a single one, i.e. the pre-interruption section consists now of two form sections. The prolongation-form (Graph b) shows the other possibility of creating a three-part form out of interruption. If the pre-interruption section is to constitute a single section as in two-part form, then it seemed natural to create a middle part through the help of prolongation, specifically by prolonging the dividing dominant.

It would be erroneous to believe that these two types are the only ones to be found in the literature of three-part forms. There are several other possibilities within the realm of prolongation-form based on interruption which we shall discuss later on. And then there are three-part prolongation-forms which are genuine three-part forms, i.e. showing no descendancy from any type of two-part form.

a.   *Three-part structure-form (originating in interruption)*

This three-part form type resulting from interruption is especially suitable for the forming organization called sonata form. The intermediary III is as if predestined to support the second theme of the exposition whereas the development, in its final analysis, has the structural task of bringing the musical motion from the III to V. It is this purposeful motion whose frequently highly imaginative prolongations give meaning to all the motivic and thematic work that the middle section of sonata form may present. Towards the end of Chapter VII we have shown the formidable tonal constructions of the development section. As far as the recapitulation is concerned it has a much deeper meaning than this common term might suggest. Apart from satisfying the principle and the demands of repetition, it represents the section bringing the fulfillment of a three-part form. This statement will hardly be surprising to the reader as he is familiar by now with the real significance of interruption.

In looking back at the sonata development sections we believe it now possible for the reader to completely understand all of their aspects, including those of the structural top voice. The influence of interruption will explain the fact that we indicated the melodic supertonic at the end of several developments as the tone of melodic structure which, however, may be covered by superimposed inner-voice tones. An illustration is the development section from Mozart's Piano Sonata in A minor (see Ex. VIII). The superimposed inner voice tone E at the end of the development veils the structural B to which the structural C has moved. The student will recall that we repeatedly have observed motions into the inner voice at the end of pre-interruption sections. The resulting prolongation helped to obscure the ending on the supertonic tone of the top voice, thus preventing a possible monotonous effect which stereotyped endings on this tone might cause. Superimposed inner voice tones, as just observed, may serve the same purpose of variety as motions into the inner voice.

The student is now equipped to make a thorough study of complete movements in sonata form. The first movements of the following sonatas should be analyzed in detail: Mozart, Sonata in A minor; Beethoven, Sonatas in F minor, Op 57 and in C minor, Op 10, No. 1.

We intend to conclude this section by presenting a structural interpretation of two first movements, one from Schubert's Symphony in B minor ("Unfinished") the other from Ravel's Sonatina for Piano. ►[Ex. 497, 498]◄

In regard to Schubert's work we recognize the fact that a three-part structure-form based on interruption may be based on a structural motion from I via VI to V, organically connecting the exposition with the development. We already mentioned in Chapter VII the fantastically prolonged embellishing chord filling the development section and now urge the reader to concentrate on the form and tonality problems of exposition versus recapitulation.

In the formal organization of the Sonatina, Ravel interestingly combines trends of former periods with those of his own times. The treatment of the exposition for instance is reminiscent of the rudimentary early sonata forms by C. P. E. Bach; we think here of the first movement of the Third Prussian Sonata by this composer in which no real second theme occurs but only an expanded cadence on the dominant. Only towards the end of the exposition does Ravel turn to the III which, however, supports no second theme. Instead the mediant finds expression only in a short neighbor-note passage which concludes the exposition.

In contrast, the dominant at the end of the development is used by Ravel in such a way as to foreshadow techniques of more recent times. In most works in sonata form of the eighteenth and nineteenth centuries the dominant constituted the climactic end point of the development section. The way it is introduced in the Sonatina at the end of the development shows a distinct digression from the classical conception inasmuch as it appears like a chord virtually forming the beginning of the recapitulation. Thus, end of development and beginning of recapitulation overlap in meas. 56, and the dominant loses much of its form-creating power of division which is true to modern trends weakening or eliminating the harmonic concept.

Nevertheless this movement presents a three-part structure-form based on interruption. Quite apart from the problem of form, however, this work should be analyzed as a fascinating style study showing all the characteristics of Ravel's impressionistic but at the same time exceedingly coherent texture.

b.   Three-part prolongation-form (originating in interruption)

The difference between the preceding three-part structure-form and the following possibilities within a three-part prolongation-form, although all are based on interruption, is conditioned by the place within the structural framework at which the actual interruption occurs. This brings us to the second form type indicated in Ex. 496b, discussed earlier. We gather from this little graph that the point of interruption is placed in such a way as to make prolongation necessary in order to create a three-part form. As an illustration the student should now analyze the Trio from the third movement of Beethoven's Piano Sonata, Op 2, No. 1.

This type of form is used not only for works in normal three-part song form but for many movements in sonata form, thus representing the second outer-form type of the eighteenth- and nineteenth-century sonata form. In the exposition of this latter type the second theme is built on the basis of the dividing dominant. The development, though constituting a further prolongation of the dividing dominant presents a completely contrasting forward driving, and often highly dramatic type of prolongation. The recapitulation, as in the first type, is the equivalent of the post-interruption section.

The study of movements in sonata form should now be continued with the following works using the second form type just discussed: the first movements of Beethoven's Sonata, Op 10, No. 3 and Seventh Symphony, and of Haydn's Symphony No. 104. As an example not previously touched upon the student may turn to Haydn's Piano Sonata in F Major, No. 23.

If the point of interruption is placed at the end of the middle section more possibilities within three-part prolongation-form are gained. The Mazurka, Op 17, No. 2 and the Nocturne, Op 9, No. 2 by Chopin will be offered as examples. In the Mazurka, prolongation makes up the first part, whereas in the Nocturne the first and the second form sections constitute prolongations of the I and the V respectively. ▶[Ex. 499, 500] ◀

Concerning the Nocturne the reader should not attach undue significance to the figurated repetitions of each form section; they are not form making. A coda starts in meas. 25 which has not been included in the graphs because it too does not affect the form construction. It will be seen from the graphs of both works that in a structural sense we have interpreted the first form sections differently from the third form sections, although the music in both is largely or completely the same.

The structural reading of a section may be different depending on whether it represents the first or the third form section. For instance, the first section of the Nocturne is followed by the structural V with F in the top voice; that makes the preceding motion of the first section a prolonging motion. After the end of the third form section, however, nothing structural follows. Therefore the descending third and the harmonic progression of this third form section are structural.

This concludes the discussion of three-part structure- and three-part prolongation-form, both originating in interruption. It was our intention to point to the great role interruption may play in three-part forms which as a consequence turn out to be expanded and modified two-part forms. We now approach the third category of three-part forms, the one which presents no influence of interruption, but instead a division of prolongation as the form-making force.

c.   *Genuine three-part prolongation-form*

The literature shows a type of prolongation-form which is more three-part, in the literal sense, than the preceding organizations because no trait of a two-part form, i.e. interruption, can be detected. Nevertheless, in spite of the absence of this means of formal synthesis, the instinctively felt dependency of organic form on the unity of structure and prolongation have, as will be seen, achieved highly organized and very convincing form constructions. The reader should keep in mind that "three parts" does not imply that these sections are just added one to another; rather they constitute coherent parts of a single organic whole of higher structural order. This coherence, however, is not achieved by the fact alone that the A^1-part repeats the thematic material of the A-part. There exists in all well-devised compositions a much greater and deeper cohesion of the sections and thus a greater relation between structure and form than purely thematic repetition or motivic design could ever be expected to provide.

In this connection it is fascinating to observe that such compositions in three parts, viewed as a whole, present a striking similarity to the construction of simple themes and sections, the single cells of the whole. We recall, for instance, a characteristic feature of many passages, showing a relatively large prolongation of the tonic which only towards the end is followed by the continuation and conclusion of the structural progression in comparatively rapid succession. Even in small units this prolongation of the tonic proves to be a cohesive and unifying factor of the first order.

In listening to certain three-part works as a whole, one can in large dimensions hear the same characteristics witnessed while analyzing the detail: The main prolongation of the tonic constitutes the greatest part of the composition and is followed, often practically at the end only, by the continuation and conclusion of the structural framework. It is this large-scale prolongation, harmonic or contrapuntal, which holds three form sections together and which thus acts as the unifying factor in regard to the form of the whole composition.

We recall the Intermezzo, Op 119, No. 1 by Brahms (Ex. 477) and find in general that secondary prolongations (i.e. prolongations of the main prolongation) are used more often in three-part than in two-part compositions to create single form sections.

In the Intermezzo, for instance, the motion to the prolonging V, which is an offshoot of the main prolongation I-Em-I, constitutes the first form section. Regarding the third section we should like to stress again, that with its continuation and conclusion of the structural progression, it represents the crowning section of the whole piece rather than a mere repetition, or a section for the sake of symmetry.[5]

Three compositions will be presented now, featuring highly imaginative treatments of basically the same form problem. ▶[Ex. 501, 502, 503]◀

The Madrigal by Monteverdi shows an interesting motion in fifths up to the II of the main prolongation of the structural tonic. Although the graphs are self-explanatory, we should like to mention the prolonging dominant at the beginning of the composition, which, when appearing in part A¹, becomes a member of the main prolongation of the tonic. The change of function is caused by the G chord. This chord, as goal of the middle section, is structurally stronger then an applied dominant and thus has the function of a II, achieved through mixture. This II in turn elevates the following dominant—which at the beginning of the piece acted as dominant prolongation of the tonic—to a member of the main harmonic prolongation of the tonic.[6]

The works by Schubert and Brahms are fascinating through their treatment of form in its relation to tonal organization. Schubert boldly subdivides a passing motion to the V by ending the first form section on the applied dominant to the first passing chord on F♯! A relatively ex-

---

[5] The student should make a complete analysis of two compositions which show a genuine three-part prolongation-form: The Trio from the third movement of Beethoven's Sonata, Op 2, No. 3 and *Hasche Mann* from Schumann's *Scenes from Childhood*, Op 15.

[6] For a similar use of a prolonging dominant see Chopin's Mazurka in A♭ Major, Op 24.

tended prolongation of this chord provides for tonal tension which is relieved only with the continuation of the passing motion to V.

In the movement from the symphony, Brahms subdivides the contrapuntal main prolongation in such a way that the development section ends on E♭, a prolonged passing chord driving to the tonic F. Thus three form sections are held together by one gigantic contrapuntal prolongation of the I. The use of this technique within the sonata form is prophetic in its anticipation of future tonal concepts. In contrast to such concepts, however, Brahms uses this particular tonal organization to save the dominant up to meas. 183 when it enters with overpowering effect.

In summary we may say that in compositions using this latter type of genuine three-part form, form is achieved not through division of structure but through division of the structure's prolongations. The possibilities within this basic technique of form construction are manifold.

d.   *Three-part prolongation-form* (*contrapuntal structure*)

The reader will recall that Debussy's Prelude *Bruyères* (Ex. 478) offered an illustration of this form type. Although the structure was contrapuntal, the prolongations were partly harmonic. In a work of more recent times, the *Bourrée* from Bartók's *Mikrokosmos*, Vol. IV, the harmonic element, even in the prolongations, appears still further reduced. ►[Ex. 504]◄ We continue this section on contrapuntal three-part forms with the discussion of a composition which is a remarkable example of a present-day conception of form and structure, the first movement of Hindemith's Piano Sonata No. 2. This movement, because of its unusual interest in representing modern sonata form, will be analyzed in detail. For the sake of clarity the graphs should be studied in the direction from the structure to the prolongations. The student is required first to familiarize himself as thoroughly as possible with this work, otherwise the following comments will be only of very limited value. ►[Ex. 505]◄

Graphs e and d show the structure and its outer-form organization; Graph e divulges the possibility for the use of sonata form. In Graph d this form type is fully outlined. The second theme of the exposition prolongs an F chord as a contrapuntal-structural chord. In the recapitulation the second theme is based on the C chord as a contrapuntal-structural chord. The development constitutes a large prolonging motion from F to F♯ which in turn proceeds to G, the beginning of the recapitulation. At the end of the composition a descending line in the melody occurs; however this descending melody does not represent a structural progression. The counterpoint and, above all, the pedal point of the bass G make this progression into a prolongation while the D of the top voice is held as a retained tone. Now to Graphs c and b, which should be carefully compared and studied simultaneously. The I in the beginning of the piece is obscured by inner voice motions; only at the beginning of the recapitulation is the G chord clearly established. This original idea produces a remarkable effect. The passing motion in the bass from I into the inner voice D of the tonic (meas. 1-17) achieves great significance in the recapitulation, where it reappears in augmented form to constitute the bass of the big progression from I to CS and on to the I (inner voice). When D is reached (meas. 130), one might expect it to be the bass of a V and thus a member of a harmonic progression I-IV-V-I. However the D turns out to be an inner voice tone of the tonic and not the bass of the dominant chord; therefore the bass progression, like the one in meas. 1 to 17, indicates a contrapuntal progression.

The student should carefully study the voice leading in general and the parallelism between first and second theme in the exposition in particular. Also observe the important part transfer of register plays in the transition section as well as within the second theme. Proceeding now to the development we realize it to be the most complex and daring section of this sonata movement. Basically the motion leads from F to F♯ in bass and top voice. (In regard to structure the F in the top voice is a middle voice tone—see Graphs d and c.) This motion is very originally prolonged by two motions of a sixth upward. The one (observe the stemmed-up notes) proceeds from an inner voice tone A♭ upward to the top voice tone F♯; the other (see the stemmed-down notes) moves from the implied inner voice tone C to an inner voice tone A of the following diminished chord on F♯. Both lines proceed largely chromatically, but do not "work together," the emphasis being on independence between these two ascending motions. To complicate matters further the F♯ in the bass appears too soon, i.e. at a point where the two other voices, just mentioned, have not yet reached the final tones F♯ and A. And when they reach these tones in meas. 80 and 81, the bass, while waiting for them, has embarked on a prolongation of its own.[7] So it happens that both motions out of the inner voice have reached their goals when the bass is in the midst of a prolongation. Therefore the

[7] This prolongation greatly enlarges a melodic motive of meas. 75 (Graph f).

constant motive repetition from meas. 80 and 81 on, while the bass is still occupied with its prolongation. Finally in meas. 89, all voices join forces to express in unison the common goal, the F♯ diminished chord. Then, similarly to the end of the transition passage in the exposition where F is established before the second theme starts, the tonic is established from meas. 92 on, three measures before the entry of the recapitulation.

The whole development, a section of rare structural originality, is an extremely realistic battle for tones which the clearly directed voices want to reach; it constitutes a fight for F♯ and the diminished chord on this tone for which all three voices are aiming. The greatest contrapuntal "confusion" is reached in meas. 74 to 80 where the bass prematurely reaches the F♯ and the second motion of a sixth has not yet clearly established its final tone A. The only stable voice in this passage is the upper motion of a sixth which clearly moves to E and F and to F♯ in meas. 81. From here on the two upper voices are finally established, but the bass reaches F♯ only in meas. 89. It is like a relief after this struggle when all voices in unison perform the climactic sixteenth-note passage which leads into the recapitulation.

And now the student is sufficiently prepared to grasp the details of this fascinating composition as presented in Graph a. Here we let the tones speak for themselves; therefore further written comments will be omitted. The playing of all the graphs and the use of the prominent prolongations for keyboard work are strongly recommended.

*

*   *

It does not seem necessary to discuss the rondo form in this book. With the experiences gained the student will have no difficulty in analyzing pieces in this form. In its last analysis the rondo is a three-part form.

Rondo: A   B   A¹   C   A² B¹ A³
          ‿‿‿‿‿‿‿‿‿‿   ‿   ‿‿‿‿‿‿‿‿‿
               A   B   A¹

The first three sections combine to make up the first form section (which in itself thus is a three-part form). The section indicated with the letter C constitutes the middle part whereas A² B¹ A³ indicate the A¹ section of a large three-part form.

5.   INDIVIDUAL FORMS AND THE FANTASY

The literature offers compositions which are highly organized in regard to outer form but do not express one of the conventional form patterns. The composer in such cases creates an individual outer-form organization to suit his particular artistic purposes and the formal needs of his musical material.

Such a composition is Chopin's Nocturne in D♭, Op 27, No. 2. ►[Ex. 506]◄ Practically the same structural contents are repeated three times (A B C) in varied versions which become progressively shorter. The first section has 25 measures, the second 20 measures and the third 17 measures. They are followed by a coda. However, this is not a conventional three-part form, because each section says in essence the same as the preceding one. We witness a principle of variation rather than any similarity with average three-part forms. The third section, as the last, brings the descent of the structural top voice, which for so long had been held in suspense, and allows the V, which had been the goal of the two preceding sections, to resolve to the tonic.

This Nocturne, therefore, is composed in three sections but is not in a three-part form. And yet there can be no doubt about a highly organic work of art filled with great dramatic intensity.

Rather different from the preceding outer-form organization is the so-called Fantasy. With the following example, Mozart's Fantasia in C minor, K. 475, we approach one of the boldest musical conceptions in the entire literature. ►[Ex. 507]◄

Mozart's Fantasia presents a highly complex picture of musical synthesis. One can easily register different sections in different keys indicated by various tempo changes: *Adagio, Allegro, Andantino, Più Allegro, Adagio*. One can also feel the presence of a kind of three-part form because of the return of the C-minor section in meas. 166. But these are facts of superficial value only; they do not even touch on the precondition for musical understanding—the problem of musical direction and continuity. As long as this problem is not solved, the sections, their tempo changes and the return of the *Adagio* have not much meaning. We therefore suggest that the student first study Graph c. A startling fact and important clue to structural interpretation is the enormous prolongation of I up to meas. 166. Within this prolongation the movement in four fifths down to the VI (A♭) takes up the great majority of measures. The top voice to the VI is A♭, a neighbor note of the structural G. Once the continuity as expressed in the above graph is clear we may proceed to Graph b. Within the progression of the first fifth down, that is up to meas. 62, lie the main difficulties for musical analysis. We realize now that the third fifth is not the only one to be subdivided; the first fifth also is subdivided into two thirds, the second of which is expressed as a sixth up, organized into a motion of thirds. This is a bold idea in itself, but the way it is expressed in the actual music can be truly termed fantastic. Mozart's genius can afford to dwell through ten measures on a prolonging dominant of a passing chord (the B-Major chord) and to indulge in lyricisms such as the D-Major section—all of which still enables the listener to penetrate to the goal of these 61 measures, the F chord. It is important to recognize that, after the Ab of meas. 6 has been reached, the motion as a whole ascends. B♮ is the first of the consecutive steps in thirds; it is prolonged by its dominant, already mentioned. Only in meas. 26 does Mozart reach the second third D which is prolonged up to meas. 40, using small three-part forms as inner-form organization. Then, for the last third, as if to make up for lost time, the tempo changes to *Allegro* and F is finally reached in meas. 62. The student should realize that, in regard to the whole prolongation of I, only the first step, i.e. the first fifth down, has been as yet accomplished. What a wealth of ideas within this one descending fifth!

The second descending fifth consists mainly of an elaborate passing motion which leads from the F triad two octaves down to a dominant seventh on F, as applied dominant of the coming Bb-Major chord. This Bb chord, the starting-point of the third descending fifth, is broadly prolonged (*Andantino*) and followed by a short transition to G (subdividing the fifth, Bb-Eb). The chord on Eb is reached in meas. 139 in the midst of the *Più allegro* section and a few measures later the temporary goal is attained, the VI on Ab (meas. 143).

After the continuity of the top voice has been studied, the reader should turn to Graph a.

It is only now that the structural meaning of the tempo changes can be appreciated. These changes help to bring out a definite pattern in regard to the progression of descending fifths from C to Ab. Within the first and third fifth a change from a slow to a fast tempo takes place, whereas the second and fourth motions of a fifth down occur in a fast tempo. Together, they therefore give a pattern of slow-fast for the first two fifths which is repeated in a more accelerated way for the third and fourth progression of a fifth. Observe that *Adagio* turns to *Andantino* and *Allegro* becomes *Più Allegro*. We realize, furthermore, that the second pair of fifths from meas. 91 on takes up a smaller number of measures than the first pair to accomplish its mission. All this definitely contributes not only to organization and direction but also to the intensity of musical expression.

The VI is followed by a voice-leading chord leading to the dominant which is stressed with great intensity. (Observe the reiterated exclamation Ab-G.) And so the *Adagio* returns with the C-minor tonic constituting the end of the large prolongation. After all the tonal drama and tension, after all the elaborated and complex prolongations, a strong confirmation of the tonality appears practically as an artistic necessity and so it is only logical that the descent of the structural line and the structural harmonic progression are repeated twice.

In spite of the absence of any set form pattern and the impression of constant change due to the intensely working element of improvisation, we marvel at this most amazing picture of musical planning and organization.

In conclusion, we should consider the difference between a so-called individual form, such as the Nocturne by Chopin, and the Fantasy. In the Nocturne, despite the absence of a conventional three-part form, a definite division into sections in quasi-variation form can be found. The sections are definitely form making. In the Fantasy on the other hand, the sections in no sense contribute to a special division of form. They characterize and enliven the inner form, but they are not form making in regard to outer form. Actually the Fantasy is nearer to the one-part form than any other outer-form type. What distinguishes it from the ordinary one-part form is an element of improvisation. This element implies the use of complex and large-scale prolongations which are organized so as to give the impression that the expected is to be avoided and that any effect of oneness or of one long sentence shall be eliminated. While the one-part form, in spite of the greatest possible variety, constantly stresses the unified structural motion, the Fantasy employs all creative means to stress change and variety in spite of an underlying structural framework. The Fantasy is organized improvisation.

EPILOGUE

In briefly summarizing the experiences gained throughout these chapters, one may state that listening to the direction of music makes us first aware of the difference between chord grammar and chord function. To understand musical direction we need the knowledge of tone and chord function. This was acquired through recognition of the most outstanding and original organizing principle, the principle of structure and prolongation.

This principle and its consequences leads us to a conscious awareness of music's continuity and coherence, and from there to a new, and as it seems to me, much wider and more comprehensive conception of tonality. In addition to previously quoted examples, all compositions analyzed in section B of this chapter, regardless of style, have borne out the explanation of tonality given in section A. Tonality indeed appeared determined by a structural progression. Branching off from this structural progression are the multitude of prolongations, which, from the main prolongation down to the smallest detail, from the prolongations of higher to those of lower order, unfold the *one tonality* of the structure in the most varied and imaginative ways.

The voice-leading graphs proved that all chords in a piece in A, for instance, whether they are consonant or dissonant, diatonic or chromatic, belong to the single key or tonality of A, provided that they are organic offshoots of the structural framework, expressing the tonality of A.

Thus tonality, although dependent on the relation of each seemingly remote detail to the fundamental tonal meaning of the whole, has an enormous range of architectonic and expressive possibilities. We believe that only a concept that takes all these characteristics and possibilities into account is able to explain the contents and the coherence of compositions of the most divergent styles, whether they be by Gesualdo, Byrd, Haydn, Schubert, Debussy, Hindemith or Bartók. Their works express outstanding characteristics of western music, such as wealth of expression, structural imagination, color and variety, all of which is nevertheless governed by a principle of unity in the form of directed motion within structural frameworks.

In conclusion I want to stress as strongly as I can, that finding the structural framework is only the very beginning of creative analysis. It remains futile knowledge, unless we recognize the directed motion within the framework with its limitless possibilities of variety, detours and delays. It is the intricate interplay between the inflexibility of the structural framework and the elasticity and reproductive activity of the prolongations which has given the western world this complex and kaleidoscopic, but highly organic phenomenon, the phenomenon of tonality.

Part III   Chapter One

A.   Implications and consequences of structural hearing

Heinrich Schenker once said that his approach could be characterized as the *Sicherstellung* of the musical instinct.[1] To the reader of the foregoing pages it will have become evident that his ideas make conscious the instinctive perceptions of the musical mind and ear. In fact, structural hearing develops the innate, although unconscious tendency of many musical people to follow the music's motion and direction. The task of clarifying and strengthening this propensity of musical instinct and imagination makes it necessary to systematize the processes of structural hearing in order to gain a workable and practical approach. If intelligently and musically applied, this approach always follows the course of the composition and does not try to impose any preconceived ideas. Structural hearing does not establish any hard and fast rules, the trespassing of which would cause real embarrassments similar to those encountered in some of the current methods of harmony and harmonic analysis.

The ability to follow the music's direction leads to a proper evaluation of the single motives, chords, phrases and sections of a composition, thus preventing the ear from losing itself in a maze of the work's details and enabling it to grasp the motion's continuity. Structural hearing, though allowing for concentration on the impact and interest of the detail, maintains a steady contact with the meaning of the musical whole. This constant evaluation and appreciation of single factors in their relation to the whole has brought about definitions of harmony, counterpoint and analysis and their functions in composition at variance with the definitions of present-day theory. The consequence has been a new concept of tonality.

Within the processes of structural hearing the voice-leading graphs prove very helpful to the understanding of the music's direction and motion. Once the student understands their meaning and necessity he

[1] *Sicherstellung* cannot be translated literally; it implies a combination of several characteristics such as fortifying, securing, guiding, protecting.

will realize that, far from being mere lifeless schemata of the music, they simultaneously delineate the differences between and the mutual dependence of structure and prolongation. They demonstrate step by step the subtle relation between the direct and the indirect phases of motion, explaining all the detours, retards and hidden parallelisms, summarized under the elastic term of prolongation. Thus the graphs strongly point beyond absolute musical facts to the spiritual and emotional qualities compositions so persuasively convey to the listener. Such qualities, for example as tension, surprise, excitement, repose, wistful or lingering moments, vagueness, dramatic drive, etc., may emanate from and thus depend on the musical characteristics of the motion. And it is the meaning of this motion which is clarified, almost in perspective, by the graphs.

Nevertheless, structural hearing in no way represents a static method which is just learned and then applied. In spite of all systematization and in spite of the fact that it can be taught to a large extent, the student must possess a natural inclination for its characteristics and above all a vivid interest in structural problems of music in general. It is at all times the ear which has to decide. As we had ample opportunity to realize, the ear must be enabled to hear the coherence and unity of a composition; it must be trained to perceive the goal of motion through the often fantastic texture of elaborations and prolongations. After ample experience in the detailed approach of structural hearing has been acquired, the student in many instances can afford to omit the written work of the detailed graphs, since the motion conveys its meaning and coherence to the trained ear. On the other hand, the detailed approach proves to be of real necessity in those many instances where even the best musician cannot rely on instinct alone, and when nothing else will help but complete understanding of the music's direction and coherence.

Thus musical direction and structural coherence, as can be seen in the graphs, may be heard in varying degrees of detail and from different perspectives. It is actually up to the listener to decide at which stage or graph his desire for musical understanding appears satisfied. Often the knowledge of the bass motion leads to an adequate explanation; at other times it is the coordination between top voice and bass which must be investigated in order to grasp the significance of the music.

From the discussions of Part II the student will logically deduct that the new approach has its definite bearings on the problems of interpretation. To preclude any misunderstanding, let me state that neither structural hearing nor any other approach can ever be expected to teach a student without imagination how to interpret a piece. The real musician will arrive by various forms of approach and largely by instinct at the interpretation which he and many others feel to be the correct one. The art of interpretation is so very dependent on talent, personality and imagination, in short on so many "unlearnable" qualities that it seems impossible to give detailed indications as to the solution of its problems. Although I believe, of course, that much can be achieved in the rapport between teacher and student, the written word on this subject is apt to lead the student to misunderstandings, the most dangerous of which is exaggerated and purely intellectual interpretation. So we shall only briefly remind the reader of how often the knowledge of musical direction and coherence, and real musical understanding, increase the feeling of conviction and security in matters of interpretation. Especially in those doubtful moments which any conscientious musician encounters only too often, recognition of the musical direction and of its goal proves to be vital. Without exaggeration it can be stated that this kind of musical understanding may often in itself lead to the right interpretation. It must also be kept in mind that the study of structural hearing, the penetration of the music's meaning, raises certain problems of interpretation of which the untrained musical person is not even aware. Thus structural hearing creates not only a high degree of responsibility in regard to the composition to be performed, but at the same time achieves such strengthening of the student's musical capacity and instinct in general that his interpretative capacities likewise cannot fail to increase.

In addition this approach to musical understanding may be of great help in memorizing a composition. Experience shows that the exact knowledge of where one stands in the course of the music's motion, and the possibility of thinking of a composition as one organism, can be of invaluable aid.

By constantly considering the significance of a tone, chord, motive or phrase in relation to the whole, structural hearing not only draws our attention to the techniques of composition but provides the musical mind with a high degree of discriminating ability. It raises new standards in regard to musical architecture and coherence and trains the ear to distinguish between structurally bold, complex, average or weak compositions and to recognize the existence of problematic ones. At best, structural hearing can solve these problems; at the very least, it proves how far we can understand the music's motion and exactly why a certain work or passage remains unclear or enigmatic. In contrast to these possibilities, harmonic analysis and other descriptive methods are merely cataloging devices which largely fail to train the ear and to make it a strong discriminating instrument of musical understanding and appreciation. These methods can be readily applied to any piece, whether it is structurally clear or confused, persuasive or dull, as long as the chords and other features can be labeled. Their results, therefore, usually boil down to a description of almost visible facts, not even touching upon the problem of artistic quality.

This does not imply that structural clarity, interest or even boldness in themselves mean great art, because greatness in musical art depends not only on purely musical, but on other, hardly definable factors. The lack of musical direction, however, or of all the artistic characteristics within the wide orbit of tonal expression as defined in Part II, does imply beyond any doubt a definite weakness in a composition. Thus, through the ability to judge the musical continuity and coherence of compositions, on this basis at least, a heretofore unknown possibility of musical judgment has been achieved, a capacity to judge beyond the often doubtful and flimsy arguments of personal taste and predilection.

*

*   *

In the course of our discussion two problems may from time to time have occupied the student's mind and we believe that they have to be aired and investigated at this point. One concerns the question of whether two readings of a musical organism may be equally correct. The other concerns those pieces, just mentioned, where the explanation seems to be problematic. To deal with such problems demands above all open-mindedness. The necessity of approaching every piece without any preconceived idea and without any wish to imply or impose our knowledge can hardly be overstressed. To this end it would seem almost imperative to forget certain frequently occurring techniques of musical construction whenever one attempts to clarify the contents of a composition, paradoxical as this might sound. We must always try to follow the music, otherwise we shall run the grave danger of providing an explanation of what we want to hear rather than of what the piece actually conveys.

To the experienced student and listener, many compositions yield their musical direction in an unequivocal manner; there appears to be no doubt as to their meaning. But sometimes one arrives at two equally plausible readings. It is only after careful weighing of these possibilities that one reaches a final decision. After repeated playing or listening, one of the two versions almost always turns out to be more convincing than the other. Occasionally, however, if seldom, it happens that two versions are equally correct; which means that it cannot be proven by any technique of analysis that one is more convincing than the other. One listener may decide for one version because it seems to him personally more adequate, the other may decide for the other reading because it has just as many points in its favor.

B.   Problematic compositions

All the examples mentioned in Part II have received a structural explanation. However, the analysis of unclear or at least problematic pieces should also be considered, for it hardly seems plausible that the endless possibilities of prolongation would not have tempted the composer's mind to experiment, thus creating works which pose definite questions for the listener. Such compositions exist and can be found in any period of music history. Of course, what is considered problematic varies according to the way music theory and analysis are approached. Structural hearing on the one hand and harmonic analysis on the other are based on such divergent ideas that what each considers unclear or problematic will of necessity be very different. We shall now present two compositions, which, from our point of view, are problematic.

First we turn to a composition by Chopin, the Nocturne in G Major, Op 37, No. 2. Two graphs are presented indicating the bass outline of the whole piece. ►[Ex. 508]◄ These bass motions considerably tax our ability to hear them as organized progressions. The wide dispersal and separation of the structural points makes comprehending the tonal coherence a hard task. But it is above all the motion within the pivotal points, with its constant use of the technique of interval expansion, which makes it rather difficult to hear a coherent motion. Nevertheless, the will of the composer to create an organism of large dimensions is convincingly evident, and as far as form and prolonged musical direction are concerned, the treatment, though complex, is of the utmost virtuosity. We might mention that form sections B, A¹ and A² start earlier, from the point of view of thematic design, than the progression of the harmonic and contrapuntal chords seems to demand. There occurs thus an interesting overlapping of voice leading and of thematic design (indicated by arrows and dotted lines in the graphs), creating a strong connection between the various form sections.

In trying to hear melodic coherence, however, the problematic factors of this strange work are evident. Although an organic bass motion and, therefore, the musical direction of the whole can be grasped, the melodic events resist an equally satisfactory explanation. To preclude any misunderstanding—the melodic direction of single groups of measures and even of some sections appears quite clear. However, the overall melodic continuity and structure, and especially the correspondence between bass and melody (so regularly found in Chopin's other works) are somewhat lacking. It would almost seem as if Chopin had been so absorbed by the creation of these large and colorful progressions, chord prolongations and passing motions, that the melody somehow could not be made to participate as an equal partner. It appears reduced to a secondary place in spite of its fascinating details. I believe that this lack of large-scale melodic organization contributes much to the kaleidoscopic impression of this Nocturne, although its tonal plan is convincing.

We now turn to a very contrasting style of music, the beginning of a composition by Orlando di Lasso. ►[Ex. 509]◄ As an example of sixteenth-century chromaticism, it is certainly possible to describe this music's style, to detect the composer's intention to write something extraordinarily colorful and expressive and to describe or label the chords. But just what is their meaning and what is this music's direction? In trying to answer these questions we are really at a loss since the problems confronting us here are far more fundamental than the ones encountered in the Chopin Nocturne. We might be told that this music simply has no direction and thus no structure, and that its musical value lies in the colorful effect of the chord progressions. But then we may ask: What is the constructive principle underlying these "colorful" progressions? Is it just color for the sake of color? To speak about colorful progressions without being able to explain their musical meaning seems tantamount to an admission of complete failure to understand the music's structure and significance. This author readily concedes his inability to understand this music. (Naturally the listener is free to be or not to be impressed by this work, to like it or not. Personal taste is altogether another thing and should not be allowed to interfere with such fundamental questions as musical continuity and structure.)

It would be wrong to assume that all chromatic compositions of this period are equally unclear. To substantiate this we remind the reader of the discussion of Gesualdo's *Io pur respiro* (Ex. 479). It can hardly be denied that here too color effects are created and the expressive qualities of this music are at least as obvious as those of the previously presented passage. But there is a fundamental difference between both compositions. Unlike Lasso's section, the music of Gesualdo conveys a distinct impression of musical direction. We, therefore, are confronted with a problem: Either both pieces are based on a different structural conception, or Lasso's composition is an experiment in chromaticism without direction and structure, while Gesualdo's Madrigal is a bold expression of structure and prolongation. This perception may lead to a higher evaluation of this particular composition by Gesualdo, although the author admits that more research will have to be done before definite answers to problems of such scope can be found.

Whatever the answer may be, one fact can hardly be disputed; current methods of style-analysis hardly offer any solution to the problem. They place both examples more or less in the same stylistic category, since both show the influence of chromatic tendencies which developed during the sixteenth century. Structural hearing at least can show the musical direction and coherence in Gesualdo's work. Through this possibility it may, in time, after more experience has been gained, prove the lack of or the superior quality of any two tonal compositions.

Part III   Chapter Two

The Historical Development of Tonal Coherence

From all the music discussed so far, we are able to deduce that composers as different as Josquin, Chopin, Marenzio or Prokofieff adhere to the same basic principles of musical continuity and structure, which they express, however, in the most divergent styles. It was the continuity of these principles and their apparently inexhaustible possibilities of prolongation which we wished to demonstrate in choosing compositions of many different styles. Thus the similarities on a structural level were presented rather than the characteristic differences of their stylistic appearance.

This procedure does not mean to imply that the author in any way underrates the importance of style-analysis or style-criticism. On the contrary, there can be no doubt that all factors which contribute to the existence and to the value of a piece of music must be taken into consideration if we are to understand music in all its facets. Nevertheless, even here in the field of style-criticism, structural hearing has much to contribute. As a subject of further research it will be very rewarding to show that certain prolongations are used in different periods in different ways. However, in regard to the processes of structural hearing an important distinction has to be made concerning the voice-leading graphs. While those graphs which, figuratively speaking, are more remote from the composition indicate the composition's basic language, the ones closest to the piece, which are more detailed, have direct bearing on style-analysis. It is these graphs which help to reveal characteristics of a specific style and will clarify problems belonging to the wide field of style-criticism.

Cultural, sociological, philosophical and similar facets of style-analysis are without doubt of great significance in gaining knowledge of a composition's place within the historical development of music. Style-analysis becomes all the more significant, the further back we go in the history of music, into periods where instinctive musical understanding cannot be relied on as implicitly as in works of the last century. It is not necessary here to dwell at length on the subject of musicology's accomplishments. It should be mentioned, however, that by now the distinctive characteristics and mannerisms of schools and individual composers have been recognized and established. Types of setting and form and their historical development have been investigated and categorized. Rhythmic problems and problems of notation have been solved or are in the process of being clarified, at least as thoroughly as possible. Last, but not least, great and gratifying results have been achieved in showing parallelisms of musical style development with contemporaneous trends in the other arts, in philosophy, in religion, etc.

Yet most of these accomplishments, although vital for further historical investigation, represent only the end of the beginning. We believe this to be so, because with very few exceptions the problems of musical continuity and coherence have not yet been made one of the chief concerns of musicology. And it appears to us that any knowledge of a composition is at best fragmentary if it does not include the ability to follow the music's motion and to grasp its coherence.

The tasks for musicology are therefore twofold, the fulfillment of the first being a precondition for the achievement of the second. The first task—the development of musicological methods and their application to the musical legacy of past centuries—is on the way to fulfillment and has already yielded a rich harvest of vital knowledge. The second, the recognition of musical direction and coherence, has not yet been tackled sufficiently and should now become one of the main subjects of musicological investigation. I believe also that some of the results of style-analysis may have to be revised after this problem has been clarified.

In our endeavor to understand music of the Middle Ages we are severely handicapped. No scientific or historical method of research, no objective attitude, however sincerely believed in, can hide the fact that ears which have gone through the long and intricate development of western music are often incapable of grasping the musical conceptions of the thirteenth and fourteenth centuries, for example. We are hardly able to understand the musical contents of many a composition from these centuries although we can explain their style and place within the historical development, which, however important, does not necessarily imply musical understanding. Every musician, provided he is not indulging in wishful thinking, is confronted with problems which seem to defy any solution. These problems become especially acute as soon as we go beyond the customary methods of musicology. The moment we do not describe and categorize according to style-analysis and ask instead for the actual course of the music's direction and its meaning, our shortcomings become a painful reality.

It is structural hearing which points to the problems presented by music of the Middle Ages that need solution. I am quite convinced though that, in spite of our inevitable shortcomings, structural hearing in time will point the way to a solution of many of those problems which constitute the second and still unfulfilled task of musicology.

The reader should not expect the following discussion to offer anything resembling a concise history of musical developments. We are at a complete beginning and shall be able only to give hints and to present some of the highlights of music of earlier times; whatever the results of our discussion may be, they are in no way meant to substitute for current methods of musicology, but are intended to take the initiative towards the study of the historical development of the techniques of tonal direction and coherence.

*

*   *

Although the early organum represents the actual beginning of polyphonic development, this type of setting constitutes a procedure still lacking the essential characteristics of polyphony. For the added voice, in being confined to a strictly parallel motion, presents the same Gregorian chant as the principal voice, merely taking its course from another tone. The principles of musical construction are therefore exactly the same as those of the Gregorian chant. A less rigid type of this parallel organum shows the two parts starting and ending in unison. This development makes a second type of motion possible, that of oblique motion, and represents a definite step forward.

It was the so-called free organum, however, with its use of predominantly contrary motion, which established the third type of motion and which freed the voice leading from any compulsory motion. Thus with the beginning of the eleventh century the precondition for real polyphonic development had been fulfilled. Three examples in the *Historical Anthology of Music* [1] are vivid illustrations of the free organum and its accomplishments. We reprint the third excerpt. ►[Ex. 510]◄ This music, however, hardly affords the impression of coherent direction. The following problems seem to have governed the planning: The choice of motion (parallel, oblique or contrary), the choice of intervals, the range between the voice parts and the opening and closing tones, which were of course largely determined by the mode and the

[1] Vol. I, No. 26, a, b, c.

constructive principles of Gregorian chant. It is obvious that the proposition of letting two voices sing more or less independently—which means one voice not depending on the motion of the other—was alone bound to completely absorb the attention of the anonymous composer. One can well imagine that contrapuntal motion resulting in the succession of different intervals, as achieved for instance in the beginning of our example, proved to be an accomplishment of the first magnitude. It is therefore only logical that the principles of construction and motion that are involved here do not in themselves lead to the expression of a structural principle of musical direction. We are confronted with motion for the sake of motion and counterpoint for the sake of counterpoint.

Although it appears to be impossible to give an exact date, it seems that the organa of the School of St. Martial contain the first examples demonstrating definite characteristics of structural planning and hearing. Thus approximately the first half of the 12th century presents an event of utmost significance: The birth of structural polyphony with its all-pervading consequences for the development of western music. ►[Ex. 511]◄

In describing the stylistic characteristics of this period, Gustave Reese in his *Music in the Middle Ages*,[2] distinguishes between two styles, a note-against-note style and a sustained-tone style. On the basis of these stylistic distinctions we find that the actual significance of the sustained-tone style lies in the introduction of an element of stabilization and organization into the predominantly horizontal flow of early polyphony. From a purely visual and descriptive point of view, one might deduce that the two voice parts in the example just mentioned had reached their greatest possible independence. Careful listening, however, proves that this independence is just a rhythmic one which has no bearing on the fact that the two voices show an astonishing degree of correlation and a common structural purpose. We have the definite impression of directed polyphony, directed within the horizontalized D chord, and there is hardly any doubt that we are confronted here with probably one of the earliest forms of chord prolongation. The gradual unfolding of the melody within the octave D-D is indicated in the graphs and the reader will observe the small parallelisms of the melodic construction which require no further comment. Above all, however, he will agree that the difference from the previously quoted excerpt (Ex. 510) goes beyond the scope of customary stylistic differences. The recognition of these is highly important, but it is not

[2] W. W. Norton & Co., New York, 1940.

enough. There is more to the music and its meaning than purely stylistic observation would lead us to believe.

It is interesting to observe that polyphonic writing even in a less melismatic, practically note-against-note style demonstrates distinct attempts to gain polyphonic direction and organization. An excerpt from the School of Compostela is presented as illustration. ►[Ex. 512]◄ [3] This example appears subdivided into two short phrases, the contents of which the graph explains. A principle of repetition is at work here which, as is known, attained such importance in regard to design and form and results, in this excerpt, in subtle parallelisms and variants.

Several points of interest stand out clearly. Whether the composition shows the sustained-tone style or a predominantly or completely note-against-note style, the movement within or around a chord is clearly expressed. Furthermore, both voices of the two-part setting, in spite of their own individual melodic life, work together in view of a third and superior factor of structural significance—the unity-creating basic chord.

From the few quoted excerpts alone one may deduce how wrong it would be to believe that chord prolongation hampers the individuality of the single parts. The birth of chord prolongation means the creation of a stable factor within the basic tendency of counterpoint to move for the sake of motion; it regulates but at the same time allows for individual treatment of the single part. At the same time it should be emphasized—although the reader of the foregoing chapters will have drawn the same conclusion—that chord prolongation by no means indicates the introduction of a harmonic aspect or conception. These and further examples are thoroughly and exclusively contrapuntal and are still remote from any harmonic influence or concept. Nevertheless, polyphony, with the help of the architectonic idea of chord prolongation, achieves structural direction and tonal coherence. And it is this fundamental organizing idea which, as we know, expresses the essence of tonality. Thus the foregoing illustrations represent examples of what seem to be the earliest expressions of structural music and of tonality as tonal coherence.

It would, however, be erroneous to believe that this early type of structural polyphony immediately replaces the interval conscious, but structurally undirected style of polyphonic writing as presented in Ex. 510. Within this older style we have to distinguish between two categories. The first is characterized by passages which defy any con-

[3] The reader should keep in mind that there is still much doubt and controversy about the rhythmic setting of this and even later music.

vincing musical explanation. Such compositions occur in the music of the Middle Ages but they gradually become less frequent. To be sure, one can describe such polyphonic works according to their style, one can furnish them with technical terms and trace some of the melodies back to their origins, etc., but all this does not provide an explanation of the music taken as a whole and of its meaning and coherence.

The other category is of special interest as it forms a kind of intermediate stage between structural and non-structural polyphony. For one encounters sections and passages in which an attempt to organize the polyphonic setting is discernible, insofar as it seems to move around the $\frac{8}{5}$ chord-form. However, the exact contrapuntal relation of the voices, the basic contrapuntal setting, seems to elude us, at least for the time being.

An example of this intermediate stage is given in ► [Ex. 513.] ◄ Apart from an apparent lack of organization in the top voice's direction, it is a real problem whether one is justified in reading a prolongation of C within an over-all structural G chord.

Returning to the development of directed and organized polyphony, we find that the second half of the twelfth and the entire thirteenth century not only show a further spreading and confirmation of structural principles but also the first great artistic accomplishments of western polyphony.

In much of this music, one can ascertain a marked elaboration of the detail on the basis of the principle of repetition, mentioned earlier. The end of Leoninus' two-voice organum *Alleluia Pascha* will serve as an illustration. ► [Ex. 514] ◄ The quotation as a whole presents an extended prolongation of C after which a motion to G takes place. The section in C is subdivided into four phrases indicated by brackets. The first is an ornamented descent of a fourth within the chord-form $\frac{8}{5}$; the following three are variations of this melodic descent with corresponding repetitions of the tenor.

The end of this example leads clearly from C to G. We come into contact here with the earliest forms of contrapuntal progressions between two different points (chords), which the reader of the preceding chapters so often has encountered. Next to chord prolongation, these progressions constitute the most important principle of tonal organization. It is in such examples that the later appearing technique of expressing musical direction by way of passing intervals or chords shows its first stages of development.

Certain characteristic features of twelfth- and thirteenth-century music should now be mentioned. The melody frequently moves around one tone with neighbor notes or more elaborate embellishments. Just as frequently one encounters melodic motions of a fourth and, less often, those of a fifth and octave, representing motions into and out of the inner voice of the prevalent chord-form $\frac{8}{5}$ (the third occurring mostly as a passing note). Although only two-voice settings have been discussed so far, they frequently seem to imply three-voice chords.

Also characteristic for the period under discussion is the predominant use of fourths, fifths and octaves moving in parallel motion. These intervals are used not only in the basic contrapuntal setting, but also in the prolongations. Hence they play a part similar to that of thirds, sixths or tenths in music of later periods. Mention should also be made of the dissonant impression of the voice leading caused by the frequent use of seconds appearing either within passing motions or as appoggiaturas.

Turning now to three-voice compositions of the Notre Dame School, it will hardly be surprising that similar voice-leading principles are to be found in these settings. Two excerpts will be presented. The first is rather straightforward and the two graphs presented need no further comment. ▶[Ex. 515]◀

Before taking up the second example, we should like to stress the necessity for adopting large dimensional hearing for this type of music. Allowing for all differences in style and musical conception existing between this period and the sixteenth or eighteenth century, there is no reason whatsoever to hear only from one breve to the following one, just as there is no justification for hearing in later music from one measure to the next only. Although it is correct from a purely descriptive point of view to say that in much of thirteenth-century music the three voices start from the consonances 5 and 8 and move through occasional dissonances to the next consonance, this knowledge promotes no understanding of the music's meaning nor of the composer's unconscious conception of musical continuity. The theory of the period certainly implies a hearing from breve to breve, but this would only be one of the many instances where contemporary theoretical treatises contribute very little to the music's understanding. Whatever the problems of musical synthesis and construction may be, whatever uncertainty might exist as to how far a certain unit, phrase or section may be understood to reach, a procedure from breve to breve would be an approach comparable to the limited methods of chord grammar or harmonic analysis in music of a later period.

Definitely more complex than the preceding excerpt is a large fragment from an organum triplum by Perotinus. ▶[Ex. 516]◀ This section, taken as a whole, presents first a motion from A to G and then on to F at which point the quotation ends. It is the prolongation of the first two structural points which gives rise to problems for the listener. The contrapuntal setting shows overlapping voice leading between duplum and triplum, both of which seem to complement each other in creating the melodic structure and its prolongations.

Although study of the graphs will answer possible questions as to the musical significance of these tone successions, a few points of special interest are mentioned. The organization of the A-chord prolongation may seem problematic at first, especially because of the partial prolongation of C. Here large dimensional hearing is absolutely essential. Otherwise one would fail to grasp the main prolongation as a whole and would merely acknowledge a flow of lines and a succession of intervals. An astonishing feature, furthermore, are the parallelisms created by the melodic prolongations. These factors of musical organization have been indicated by brackets.

Finally the student is advised to analyze Perotinus' organum quadruplum *Sederunt*. Although the fourth voice makes for density of texture, the same structural principles and the same complementary cooperation between the single voices in creating definite tone organisms will be found to function. This work shows a succession of relatively short, then again quite extended chord prolongations, as well as progressions directed from one sonority to another. Many significant factors of musical coherence and continuity can be recognized. So far, however, we are unable to make any conclusive statements as to the outer form of such large works.

*

*   *

One of the main genres of the thirteenth century is the three-part motet, a highly interesting style of polyphonic writing. The previously mentioned analytical approach from breve to breve is often applied to this kind of setting. In fact, it is still a widely held view that the anonymous composer, in setting these three voice parts, had only to be careful to reach a consonant chord at the beginning of each "measure." The motion within the "measures" is thought to be of less concern, which supposedly explains the dissonant character of this style. The music of the Codex Bamberg (transcribed by Pierre Aubry in *Cent Motets du XIII* *siècle*) indicates, however, that this point of view is justified only in regard to a relatively small number of motets. The majority of them demonstrate a remarkable development of structural polyphony in showing strong correlation of the single voice parts towards the creation of musical organisms. Although the diversity of texts is certainly a stylistic characteristic of great significance, it does not influence the individual voices in this polyphonic texture to adopt independent voice leading (in the most literal sense of the term) and to abandon the gains already made in structural polyphony.

It is true, of course, that a style which combines three melodic lines with different texts is indicative of an urge to combine the most divergent and contrasting elements. Nevertheless, whatever the composers may have wanted to express, the result is what counts and it may be said in general that the motet, in spite of its non-structural outward appearance, has materially contributed to the development of structural music.

Hence the first problem for analysis should be the meaning of the total effect of the interesting voice combinations. It is all very well to describe the origin and characteristics of each voice, and to list stylistic features of this certainly strange principle of setting. But as long as the meaning of the voice leading, taken as a whole, has not been recognized, only very little of the music has been explained.

Three very characteristic excerpts are now given. ►[Ex. 517, 518, 519]◄ There can hardly be any doubt that decisive progress in contrapuntal setting has been achieved. The treatment of the voice leading is purposeful, inasmuch as the single tones, intervals and chords have a clear function. In spite of all the individual expression of the single voices, a strong correlation between them is manifested, stronger than in the products of the Notre Dame School. This enables the ear to follow the individual course of each melody more readily than actual independent voice leading would ever permit. The correlation of the single voices in creating an organic whole is especially interesting in Ex. 519, where the descending line of the melodic structure is expressed by the motetus alternating with the triplum, the final tone being performed by both voices in unison (see the graphs). Observe also the motetus at the end of Ex. 518 which ushers in the "bass" tone F, structurally due at this point.

For a somewhat longer illustration, an excerpt from Motet No. 54 is given.[4] ►[Ex. 520]◄ The section as a whole is subdivided into several prolongations. The first two are dovetailed, since the tenor melody continues beyond the first prolongation, meas. 3. In meas. 6, however, the tenor concludes its first part so that meas. 7 forms a clear end of the preceding and, simultaneously, the beginning of a new prolongation.

---

[4] The motets cited by number are from Aubry's edition.

The melody around the structural F moves first to the lower neighbor note E, then a third down to D and finally a fourth down to C, the inner voice of the governing ⅚ chord, before returning once more to F. Again we find the melodic outline to be expressed by the motetus and triplum voices mutually; in spite of the individuality of each voice part, they join in bringing out the essential outline and content of the melody. The motetus and triplum represent two melodic components creating a resultant third melodic line which governs this section and molds it into an organic whole.

Within the rich repertoire of motets which have come down to us, there are also those which show direction of voice leading or the structural factor of chord prolongation although the inner organization of the prolongations appears problematic. Let us turn to Motet No. 9. Careful listening conveys a feeling of direction, even if somewhat vague, from C to F. ►[Ex. 521]◄ Another example is meas. 1 to 12 of Motet No. 40. Although the reading of meas. 9-12 appears to be clear, meas. 1-8 seem to allow for the two possible explanations given in the graphs. ►[Ex. 522]◄

All these subtle differences must be weighed carefully before one can begin to understand thirteenth-century music. Structural hearing divulges the large and the small differences in musical conception, the difference between structural and non-structural polyphony, and the difference between clear, directed or ambiguous writing. All of this is so important that the fact of stylistic identity may be occasionally misleading.

Turning to the problem of form, it appears that such sections and passages as have been discussed are at the same time the form sections of a motet. Very similar to the organum of the Notre Dame School, the thirteenth-century motet presents in many cases a row of chord prolongations or progressions from one chord to another which are more or less interrelated on the basis of the principle of repetition. Often motets use one single chord as basis for all prolongations; sometimes different chords serve as the foundation. The motet as a whole thus represents a row of units, but does not constitute an organic whole within the framework of a single structural progression.

Concerning the principle of repetition, it appears insufficient to discuss the problem of form on the basis of the tenor repetitions alone, for one finds that a tenor melody often, but by no means always, coincides with the length of a chord prolongation. The simultaneous effect of all the voices must be considered, otherwise the form of the piece as a whole can never be clarified.

The next three examples, two of them by Adam de la Halle, are very remarkable in the assurance of their formal construction. They present a rudimentary use of interruption and seem to constitute the earliest examples of this forming principle. ►[Ex. 523, 524, 525]◄ The first example illustrates what one might call the contrapuntal version of interruption inasmuch as the bass moves to the supertonic as the dividing chord. Ex. 524 is from a monophonic *Ballade* and characteristic for the technique under discussion. The third example is of special interest. The line of the top voice is clearly indicative of interruption. The bass, however, goes in octaves with the top voice at the points of structure. Therefore, we are not confronted with a composition presenting tonal unity, but with a work expressing a unified progression from A to F. Ex. 521 and 525 would then present works to which the term "modulatory" could accurately be applied.

*

*   *

One cannot conclude even a cursory discussion of the thirteenth century without mentioning a deeply significant trait appearing for the first time in the motets of this period: the earliest groping attempts towards a harmonic conception of music.

The beginning of Motet No. 24 will serve as illustration. ►[Ex. 526]◄ It is impossible to assert with any amount of certainty that the composers instinctively felt that they were moving to the chord built on the fifth degree of the scale and that this chord stands in any relation to the preceding and following tonic chords. It is rather more convincing to believe that these earliest stages of a harmonic concept were neither felt nor consciously planned. Nevertheless, the fact of a tonic-dominant-tonic progression is obvious. Within the Codex Bamberg there even occur passages showing such progressions in a prolonged form. ►[Ex. 527]◄

These early attempts in harmonic writing, of course, do not change the general picture of a completely contrapuntal (and predominantly structural) style of polyphony. Architectonic principles of tonal organization which appear in the Notre Dame School are further developed and consolidated in the motet of the thirteenth century. They are the techniques of chord prolongation and the well-directed motion between two chords.

*

*   *

In the music of the fourteenth century, counterpoint remains the governing factor, but a strengthening of the harmonic principle is to be found in quite a number of works. For instance in Machaut's compositions there are many sections which show the increased influence of harmonic thinking. Two excerpts from *Virelai* No. 38 and *Virelai* No. 32 are offered. ►[Ex. 528, 529]◄

Turning to three-part compositions, we find again that prolonged motions to the V occur. The last measures of *Ballade* No. 3 serve as an example. ►[Ex. 530]◄ This excerpt shows a clearly defined motion to the dominant and therefore gives further evidence of the awakening of the harmonic concept. At the same time it is typical of Machaut's contrapuntal technique, the understanding of which presents the foremost problem of fourteenth-century music. While passages such as this can readily be explained, there are three- and four-part compositions which often show a heretofore unparalleled degree of complexity. The increased use of small note-values, with the consequent enrichment of the rhythmic treatment of the single voice parts, so characteristic of the period of the *Ars Nova*, frequently gives the impression of contrapuntal overactivity, making the recognition of musical direction very difficult. These problems are intensified by the complexities of fourteenth-century notation and by *musica ficta*, which thus far has by no means been clarified.

Thus the musical understanding of many works by Machaut presents a baffling problem.[5] The visual characteristics of the single voices and the voice leading in general have been described and much has been written about the highly individual character of his art in comparison with that of the anonymous composers of the thirteenth century. Much has been said regarding Machaut as the true representative of a new art and about his great impact on the development of music. The musical contents of his works, however, remain on the whole an uninvestigated field. Although this is equally true of thirteenth-century music, the importance attached to Machaut is so much greater, that the lack of a musical approach of analysis to his works must be felt all the more. Especially in our time, the style of Machaut has attracted the attention of young composers. In their reaction to the nineteenth century and their struggle for a new style his works have become in a way a new symbol. How strange then that one should idolize a composer to whom one has all approaches—aesthetic, historical and sociological—save the all-important one to the music itself. Let us therefore

[5] A very interesting analysis of a *Ballade* by Machaut may be found in Hindemith's book, *Craft of Musical Composition*.

discard all wishful thinking and admit that, as far as understanding Machaut's music is concerned, we are only at the very beginning.

However, in spite of all the difficulties that his works present, structural hearing is able to penetrate and clarify a great number of them, which at first hearing seem to elude any explanation beyond the description of single characteristics. But more than in previous examples, large dimensional hearing is essential since the strong activity of melody and counterpoint add so much vertical weight to the voice leading, thus hampering the element of musical direction. There is much contrapuntal detail work within single measures and this makes new demands on our capacity to grasp the continuity of a phrase, section or the composition as a whole.

Contrapuntal and rhythmic activity characterize the next example which is taken from the *Rondeau* No. 13. ►[Ex. 531]◄ On a greater scale than previously observed, there seems to occur a veritable battle between the individual impulse of the single part and the structural direction of the phrase as a whole. The reader should observe the density of the counterpoint of meas. 3 to 7. The D chord prevails in meas. 4 and 5, notwithstanding the G in the tenor in meas. 4, and acts as a neighbor-note chord of E which, in spite of the strong melodic impulse and the lack of clarifying motivic profile, nevertheless constitutes the chord of higher structural order. The last E chord in meas. 7 is structurally relatively weak, because the voice leading has a tendency to continue. In relation to the meaning of the whole excerpt, the E chord is a prolonged structural chord between I and V. This progression, combined with the structural motion of the top voice, shines through the maze of highly individual voice leading, and gives direction to the whole passage.

To call this type of voice leading "linear" counterpoint is extremely misleading. The single voices in a contrapuntal setting may be treated individually to a varying degree and they may seem at first hearing, as in fourteenth-century music, to exist for their own horizontal development only. In structural music, however, even the most individual sounding voice in a polyphonic composition will in its last analysis be found to cooperate with the structural meaning of the whole. The single voices, "free" as they may seem to be, will always be subordinate to the structural direction which they mutually help to express.

A number of works by Machaut fail, however, to divulge any structural direction and coherence in their voice leading. Some of the four-part *ballades* especially, seem to be enigmatic except for occasional vague circlings around certain chords. In regard to such works, the term "linear" is of no help either. For, if the voice parts should really go their own ways, disregarding a mutual structural purpose, then the composition could hardly be deemed of artistic quality. It is, of course, entirely possible that much of this music demands more patience and more research before it will unfold its meaning. Many more works by this fascinating composer will have to be analyzed before definite answers to these problems can be found.

The fact that we are only at the beginning of musical recognition of fourteenth-century music also precludes a completely satisfactory writing of the voice-leading graphs. Often these graphs will have to be taken as first attempts only, but I am convinced that the shortcomings will be overcome as soon as the musical motion of the works in question has been grasped. So far, however, the exact status of the voice leading in many cases is anything but clear. In addition the "pure" counterpoint of this period, comparable to the abstraction of counterpoint in regard to seventeenth-, eighteenth- and nineteenth-century music (see Chapter III), only begins to be recognizable. In contrast to the contrapuntal principles of later centuries, it definitely presents a different conception of dissonance and of progressions in fifths, octaves and fourths.

Much therefore remains to be done until a clearer picture can be drawn. Nevertheless, at this stage some definite insight can be gained, provided we are willing to concentrate on the actual musical motion and the problems of its coherence.

To substantiate this statement two of Machaut's works shall be quoted in their entirety, the *Virelai* No. 31 and the *Ballade* No. 26. First we present the *Virelai*. ►[Ex. 532]◄ This piece shows a remarkable assurance in the treatment of form combined with much greater melodic subtlety than was encountered in the thirteenth-century motet. As a whole it presents a three-part form (the A¹ part constituting a repetition of meas. 1-22) in which the technique of interruption on a contrapuntal basis (see the examples from Adam de la Halle's works) plays a major structural role. In fact this *Virelai* and the following *Ballade* belong, according to our present knowledge, to the first compositions showing structural and thus tonal unity (see Graph b). Quite apart from the obvious parallelisms created through the use of interruption in structure and main prolongations, the whole piece abounds with subtle, variation-like repetitions (see Graph a). It should be noticed in addition that the composition, clearly in D, starts with four meas. which act in a capacity somewhat similar to an incomplete harmonic progression constituting the beginning of a number of compositions of later centuries. Here we encounter not a harmonic but a contrapuntal drive to the tonic. Ascertaining the first structural tone of the top voice may at first seem difficult. The tone F, however, appears without any doubt as the structural starting point of the top voice, the tone A being a tone of the middle voice (see meas. 2), shifted an octave higher in meas. 5.

In the *Ballade* the architectonic assurance is likewise remarkable. Comparable to the beginning of the *Virelai* it starts with the subdominant, and in this instance one can not fail to have a premonition of later introductory IV-V-I progressions. ▶[Ex. 533]◀ The parallelisms with their power to foster the impression of an organic whole are startling and it seems to us that in such compositions we are hearing contrapuntal entities on a remarkably developed level. Together with similar works they presage future techniques by keenly anticipating the large organisms of later times.

In concluding this section it may be said that among Machaut's works (as in the thirteenth-century motets) the musical differences—as far as musical direction, continuity and coherence are concerned—are very great. Stylistic descriptions and terms are insufficient because they are unable to take these differences into account, the style being the same whether a work is complex, straightforward, clear or obscure. As long as we are unable to penetrate his problematic compositions, it appears that Machaut presents two contrasting characteristics: Machaut as pioneer in structural polyphony and its expressive possibilities, and Machaut absorbed in rhythmic and contrapuntal speculations and experiments. The latter, however, have materially enhanced the contrapuntal setting in general and have contributed much to the development of melodic writing.

*

*   *

In whatever way the results of future analytical research will affect present-day conclusions, it appears certain that the first half of the fifteenth century (the English and Burgundian Schools) shows a strong reaction to the rhythmic and contrapuntal exuberance found in many compositions of the fourteenth century. However, like all reactions in truly creative periods, they do not revert to any epoch prior to the one in opposition to which their principles are aimed. Structural polyphony emanates from the contrapuntal turmoil of the fourteenth century on an advanced level of often truly classical clarity. In musical terms, a main characteristic of the English and Burgundian Schools is the fact that counterpoint is less active for its own sake and serves more the mutual constructive aim of all the voice parts.

The beginning of Dunstable's *Sub tuam protectionem* is typical of fifteenth-century structural polyphony. ►[Ex. 534]◄

Harmony plays a distinct, but subordinate part in comparison to the contrapuntal progression which is the main feature of this example. It cannot be emphasized too strongly that the increased use of the triad as a vertical chord or in a chord-outlining form in the melody, and above all the frequently occurring progressions of sixth chords, do *not* in themselves mean a further development of harmonic thinking. The reader knows by now that such chords may be used within a completely contrapuntal setting. On the other hand, a harmonic framework may appear in works in which the triad plays only a very subordinate role, as occasionally in works by Machaut. Here is one more instance where in analysis the lack of a clear distinction between harmonic and contrapuntal factors has done much to obscure the true meaning of composition.

Although triads and sixths are no criteria for harmonic writing, a further development of the harmonic concept may be observed in works of this period. We point to the increased use of I-IV-V-I progressions. This progression may be heard in meas. 1 to 12 (Ex. 534) and is used here as a harmonic prolongation within a contrapuntally conceived whole. Observe once again the cooperation of the voice parts, when the middle voice becomes the bass of the dominant in meas. 10.

In another example by the same composer, meas. 1-19 from the Chanson *Puisque m'amour*, the contrapuntal and the harmonic conceptions are for the first time more in equilibrium. ►[Ex. 535]◄ The tonic as referred to in the graph applies only to the section discussed. While in former examples we had found single harmonic progressions either as frameworks for relatively short passages or, as in the preceding excerpt, acting in a prolonging capacity of a contrapuntal progression of higher structural order, we now encounter harmonic prolongations of a framework at least partly harmonic.

It would be wrong, however, to believe that structural polyphony from this time on proceeds to develop without interference from a non-structural and non-directed way of writing. Once more, in a number of works of the second half of the fifteenth century, counterpoint for the sake of counterpoint creates a density of texture which obscures and hinders musical direction. This is not dissimilar to events of the fourteenth century, although the style and the counterpoint itself have changed considerably. On the whole, however, the fifteenth century and the beginning of the sixteenth show a constantly growing development of directed music and this author can not conceal his personal conviction that the fifteenth century is a musical period exceeding the fourteenth century in creative achievement. The expressiveness of the music is certainly no less strong, and the power for creating tonal direction and coherence is much greater. It can be said very definitely that a larger percentage of compositions of the fifteenth century, in fact larger than of any previous period, can be explained. As a matter of fact the number is so great that it is impossible within the framework of these cursory discussions to give even a limited cross section of structural music and its achievements in this period. We shall therefore confine ourselves to highlighting a few problems and to quoting a few selected examples in order to round out this introduction to a new analytical approach to the music of the Middle Ages and the early Renaissance.

We turn first to the *Rondeau, Adieu m'amour* by Dufay. ►[Ex. 536]◄ The greater correlation of the voices within the course of voice leading, so strongly initiated by Dunstable, is further and subtly developed in works of this kind. They point convincingly to the great strides structural music has made since the period of Machaut. This applies also to the appearance of clear outer-form organizations. This *Rondeau*, for instance, is composed in a two-part prolongation-form. The second part shows the structural progression, in itself subdivided through interruption. Observe that the post-interruption section offers an interesting parallelism with section A, with the melody in contracted form moving upward in thirds to the structural tone C. Expressiveness and lucidity of style appear in a balance heretofore hardly to be found.

The same can be said about the following movement from a Mass by Obrecht which shows that the harmonic conception has been decisively elaborated. We refer to the Osanna from the *Missa "Je ne demande"* by Obrecht, a composition in through-composed form. ►[Ex. 537]◄

That in spite of all the startling innovations of the fifteenth century, old techniques still are being used because they are fundamental techniques of structural music, may be gathered, for instance, from the Kyrie of Isaac's *Missa Carminum*. The principle of repetition and variation dating back to the twelfth century can be found here on a higher architectural level. ►[Ex. 538]◄

Finally, as an example which appears as a crowning summary of all previous achievements and which at the same time links up with the developments discussed throughout Part II, the complete first section from a Motet by Josquin des Prés is given. ► [Ex. 539] ◄ Once more we should like to remind the reader that only a careful study of the graphs will reveal to him the detailed analysis and consequently the contents of a work. Our often brief comments are only intended to point out some items of specific interest.

With Ex. 539 we have come to our last illustration and to the end of our investigations. Although it would be premature to draw detailed and final conclusions from this preparatory study of music from the eleventh to the sixteenth century, we believe we have presented sufficient reasons and material for our previous statement that research in the field of musicology should concentrate more on the problems of continuity and structure. Even this short survey indicates that structural hearing opens up new aspects of this fascinating early music.

The inception of the principle of tonality and certain of its techniques expressing themselves in the construction of tonal units of various length and complexity goes as far back as the Organa of St. Martial and Santiago de Compostela. A continuous development of structural polyphony from the twelfth to the twentieth century may with justification be assumed. Whether we encounter the use of modes or the major-minor system, whether the contrapuntal voice leadings are different from those of later periods or whether harmonic thinking expresses itself in a different manner than later on in the eighteenth century, the music of the Middle Ages and the Renaissance demonstrates the same basic principles of direction, continuity and coherence as music from the Baroque period to the twentieth century.

Tonal coherence or tonality, as defined in Chapter VIII, has its roots and its first great development in the music of the Middle Ages. Its range and possibilities, therefore, appear even greater than outlined in Part II. The time will arrive when the full scope of tonality can be surveyed and then it should become possible to add to the existing histories of music a much-needed history of tonal continuity and coherence.

Conclusion

The Language of Western Music

All music conceived on the fundamental principles presented throughout this book shows direction and definite functions of tones and chords in relation to the structure of the whole. Such music may be called structural or tonal music. The terms tonal or structural are therefore interchangeable; they symbolize the same fundamental characteristics.

Tonality, in the new and broader sense as conceived in this book, represents a musical language. Within its orbit there occur works as contrasting as a motet of the thirteenth century and compositions by Machaut, Dufay, Frescobaldi, Mozart, Wagner, Debussy or Bartók. This language far transcends the style of specific periods and of certain composers because it is able to find expression in the most divergent styles and settings. In whatever style this musical language happens to express itself, whether in instrumental music, in song or opera, whether the style is gothic, baroque, classic or impressionistic, the basic characteristics of musical direction, continuity and coherence are the same and constitute a common denominator. This convincingly demonstrates that all these composers speak the same language, but in the form of the most contrasting styles.

Although we are only at the beginning of a new period of musical insight, theory and musicology, it is possible to state that structural or tonal music allows for the greatest possible variety, elasticity and individuality within the fundamental principles of structural direction and organization as represented in any period from the twelfth to the twentieth century. On the basis of these principles, musical expression, modern in every sense, appears entirely possible. This type of modern music brings about a continuation of the age-old elements of structural unity, nevertheless exhibiting beyond any doubt the stylistic characteristics of our time.

However, if compositions are definitely not within the wide tonal realm as outlined in these chapters, if they clearly are not representative of structural music, then we may ask: What is this music's constructive principle and what are the principles of its musical continuity? If it is representative of a new and different type of music not based on tonal direction, what possibilities for the achievement of artistic unity and variety does it offer instead?

We think here of Schönberg and his development of the twelve-tone system. The principles of this approach deal with possibilities of musical coherence and continuity very different from those discussed throughout these pages. It can not be denied, however, that his is a truly new and in itself convincing musical language. And so the question remains: Will music continue to express itself in the structural language of tonality revitalized by the new aspects of tonal expression which have been developed by composers as different as Hindemith, Bartók and Stravinsky, or will the twelve-tone system become the musical art's language of the future?

Whichever of these two languages will be developed further in the future, and whatever form of musical expression may conceivably grow out of some eventual contact between certain principles of tonality and of twelve-tone music—it does not seem likely that we shall ever again be satisfied with a merely descriptive type of musical theory. I firmly believe that there is a need for a theory of music and composition which never loses contact in all its branches and disciplines with what seems to me to be its principal goal and justification: leading the ear and mind to understand all details as organic offshoots of the whole, which means the perception of total musical organization. This is the goal of structural hearing, which touches on a fundamental problem of composing regardless of style and period—the achievement of coherence and unity.

VOLUME TWO

Acknowledgments

Grateful acknowledgment is made to the following publishers for permission to use copyrighted material:

Associated Music Publishers, Inc. (Ex. X, 410, 411, 445, 453).

Boosey & Hawkes, Inc. (Ex. 239, 241, 377, 386, 406, 407, 412, 416, 419, 452).

Elkan-Vogel Co., Inc. for Durand et Cie. (Ex. 290).

Leeds Music Corp. (Ex. 380, 451).

E. B. Marks Music Corp. (Ex. 413).

Oxford University Press, Ltd. (Ex. 319, 331).

Salabert, Inc. (Ex. 414).

I wish, furthermore, to thank the following for permission to reprint material from their publications:

Harvard University Press, for various quotations from *Historical Anthology of Music; Oriental, Medieval and Renaissance*, Vol. I, Revised edition, 1949 (Ex. 184, 185, 510, 513, 515, 524, 525).

E. B. Marks Music Corp. for Ex. 415.

Oxford University Press, Ltd. for Ex. 209.

G. Schirmer, Inc. for Ex. 418 and for the excerpts from Ruth and Thomas Martin's translation of *The Magic Flute* (Ex. 483).

F.S.

Contents

Musical Illustrations

Notes to the Reader

Ideally, a book of this type would present every musical quotation discussed, along with its voice-leading graphs. This proved impractical for reasons of space; therefore, the following plan has been adopted. With very few exceptions the examples in Part I, Part II through Chapter Six and in Part III appear in complete form (music and graphs). In Chapter Seven the music has been omitted for most quotations from standard literature and for the quotations of large excerpts. Chapter Eight, which deals with complete compositions, offers exclusively voice-leading graphs without the music. Since all the music omitted is from available editions, it is hoped that this procedure will not be disadvantageous to the reader.

It has been found practical to print many examples and their graphs (especially the larger ones) running across facing pages, in order to make the course of voice leading clearer for the eye, and to avoid awkward turning of pages as much as possible. The first such example is Ex. X. If there is doubt about the continuity, the reader is advised to orient himself by means of the measure numbers.

In the quotations from music of earlier times, treble and bass clefs have been consistently used, even if the transcriptions in the indicated sources do not follow this procedure. Furthermore, in some compositions, transpositions and change of note-values have been carried out, thus reverting to the readings of earlier sources.

List of Musical Illustrations

Notes and Glossary for the Voice-Leading Graphs

1. The note-values indicate the structural value and significance of tones and chords; they do not indicate rhythmic values.

2. The difference in structural significance is given in four different note-values: half-notes, quarter-notes, notes without stem and occasionally eighth-notes. The latter are used to indicate embellishments and appoggiaturas. The highest note-values in a graph represent tones or chords of the highest structural order. Among notes of equal value, those whose stems reach the same level are of the same structural order.

3. The relation between identical and different tones or chords, and specifically their structural connection, is indicated by dotted or solid slurs and lines, curved or horizontal arrows or by beams.

4. Horizontal, solid arrows (used mostly in regard to bass motions) indicate the direction or driving tendency of the music in general, or passing motions in particular.

5. A note in parenthesis with or without a dotted stem means a note expected on the basis of direct voice leading, but omitted or substituted for in the composition.

6. Brackets of various kinds indicate either chord prolongations ⌣⌣ or melodic parallelisms ⌐⌐ .

7. Roman numerals are assigned to harmonic chords only; the relative size of these numerals corresponds to their structural value.

8. A small Roman numeral in parenthesis indicates the chord of harmonic emphasis.

Glossary of Symbols

P	Passing tone or passing chord
N	Neighbor note or neighbor-note chord
UN and LN	Upper and lower neighbor note
IN	Incomplete neighbor note
$\frac{N}{P}$	Neighbor-passing chord
Em	Embellishing chord
CS	Contrapuntal-structural chord
DF	Double function chord
M	Mixture
‖	Interruption
D	Dividing dominant
A B or A B A[1]	Indication of form

List of Sources (*Abbreviations*)

AM   *Altniederländische Motetten*, ed. by W. Braunfels. Oratoriumsverlag, Köln.

AMI   *L'Arte musicale in Italia*, ed. by L. Torchi. G. Ricordi e C., Milano.

AUDM   *Aufführungspraxis der Musik*, by R. Haas. Akademische Verlagsgesellschaft Athenaion, Potsdam.

CM   *Cent Motets du XIIIe Siècle*, transcribed by P. Aubry. Rouart, Lerolle & Cie., Paris.

DAS CHORWERK   *Das Chorwerk*, ed. by F. Blume. G. Kallmeyer Verlag, Wolfenbüttel.

DTOE   *Denkmäler der Tonkunst in Oesterreich*. Artaria & Co., Wien.

HAM   *Historical Anthology of Music; Oriental, Medieval and Renaissance Music*, ed. by A. T. Davison and W. Apel, Vol. I. Rev. ed. Harvard University Press, Cambridge, Mass.

HDM   *Handbuch der Musikgeschichte*, ed. by G. Adler, 2nd ed. Heinrich Keller, Berlin.

EPM   *The Evolution of Piano Music (1350–1700)*, ed. by C. Sachs. E. B. Marks Music Corp., N. Y.

MET   *Music of Earlier Times (13th Century to Bach)*, ed. by J. Wolf. Broude Bros., N. Y.

MMA   *Music in the Middle Ages*, by G. Reese. W. W. Norton & Co., N. Y.

MW   Guillaume de Machaut, *Musikalische Werke*, ed. by F. Ludwig. Breitkopf & Härtel, Leipzig.

OHM   *The Oxford History of Music*. Oxford University Press, Ltd., London.

OL   Orlando di Lasso, *Sämtliche Werke*. Breitkopf & Härtel, Leipzig.

SHM   *A Short History of Music*, by A. Einstein. 2nd ed. Alfred A. Knopf, N. Y.

TC   *Sechs Trienter Codices*, ed. by G. Adler. In DTOE.
VDO   *Studien zur Vorgeschichte der Orchestersuite im 15. und
         16. Jahrhundert*, by F. Blume. Kistner & Siegel, Leipzig.
WJO   Jacob Obrecht, *Werken*, ed. by J. Wolf. Johannes Müller,
         Amsterdam.
WJP   Josquin des Prés, *Werken*, ed. by A. Smijers. G. Alsbach &
         Co., Amsterdam.

         Note: Sources for the quotations from English virginal compositions, which
         have been repeatedly reprinted, are omitted.

Musical Illustrations

I BACH Prelude No. 21 (Well-Tempered Clavier, Bk I)

II BACH Chorale (No. 294)

2

III BACH Chorale (No. 23)

IV

e

graph III a

f

chorale

V SCHUBERT Waltz, Op 18, No. 10

VI

 horizontalization of

4

VII

VIII MOZART Piano Sonata, A minor, K. 310

IX

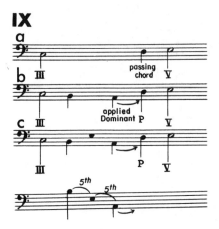

X   # HINDEMITH Piano Sonata No. 3

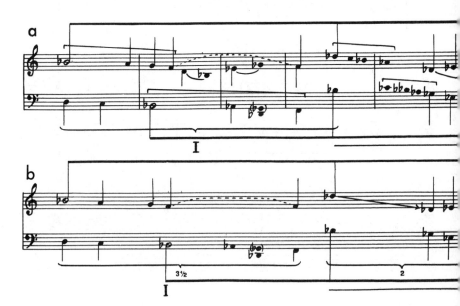

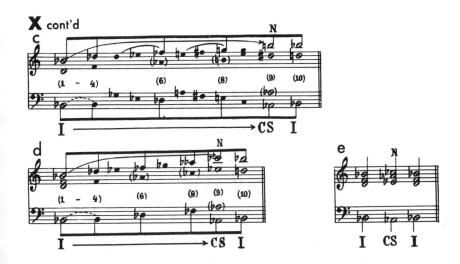

7

1 BACH Chorale (No. 6)

I ———→ V I

2 D. SCARLATTI Sonata, D minor, L. 413

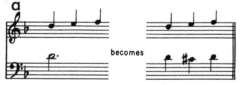

becomes

I ——————————————————→ V

3 BEETHOVEN Bagatelle, Op 119, No. 11

Andante, ma non troppo

4

5   SCHUMANN Little Piece (Album for the Young)

6   SCHUBERT Waltz, Op 9, No. 8

7   HAYDN Minuet

8   FOLK TUNE

9   SCHUMANN Album-Leaves, Op 124 No. 16

10   BEETHOVEN Piano Sonata, A Major, Op 2, No. 2

10 cont'd

a

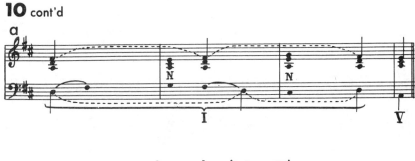

11　　　BACH Chorale (No. 7)

a

horizontalization of

b

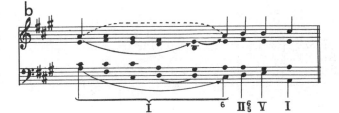

c

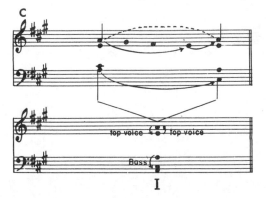

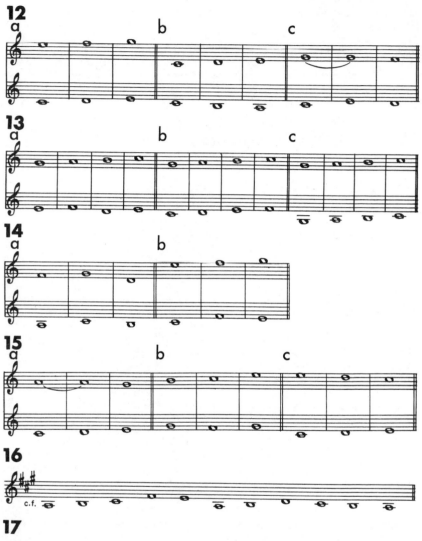

18

19

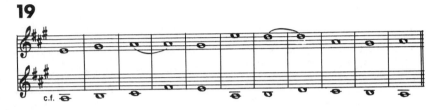

20

21

22

23

24

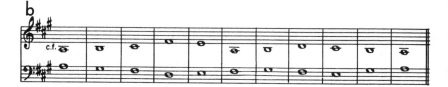

25

26

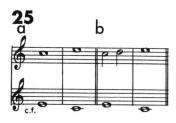

27

28

29

30

31

14

18

19

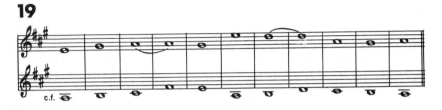

20

21

22

23

24

25

26

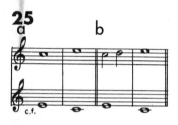

27

28

29

30

31

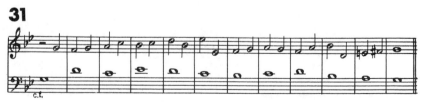

14

32

33

34

35

36

37

38

39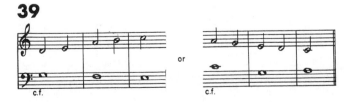

40

41

42

43

avoids

stands for

16

44

45

46

a   b   c   d

47

a   b

48

a   b

49

a   progression   b embellishment

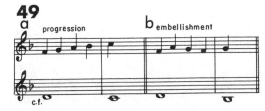

50

17

51

52

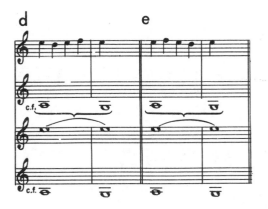

53 **54**

55

56

57

a

b

58

59

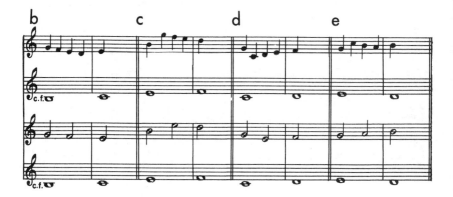

60

61

62

b

c

63

a

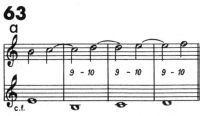

b

64

a

b

65

a

65 cont'd

66

a good   b   c   d

a not good   b   c   d

67

a   b   c   d

e   f   g   h

68   **69**

a   b   c

70

a   b   c

71   **72**

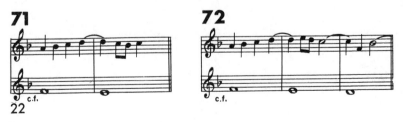

22

73

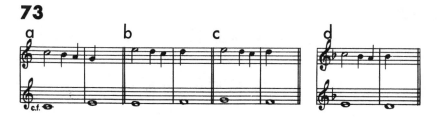

74

75

76

77

78

79

80

81

82

83

84

85

86

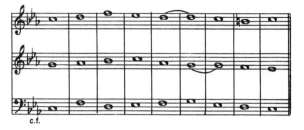

87

88

89

25

90

91

92

93

94

95

Part II Chapter Four

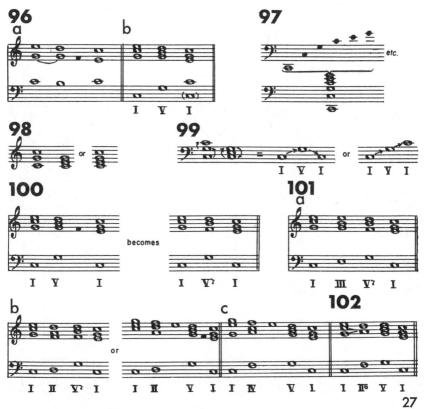

27

103

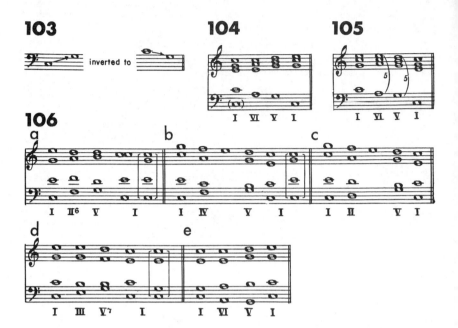

104

105

inverted to

I VI V I

I VI V I

106

a

b

c

I II⁶ V I

I IV V I

I II V I

d

e

I III V⁷ I

I VI V I

107

108

109

I V⁷ I

I III V⁷ I

I III V⁷ I

110

a

b

or

I II V I

I II⁶ V I

I IV V⁷ I

c

111

a

b

I VI V I

I IV♭ V I

I III♯ V I

112

I   IV $^6_4$ $^5_3$ V   I

113

I   II$^6_5$ V   I

114

I   IV^7 V^7 I

115

I   II^6 V^7 I

instead of

I   II^6 V   I

116

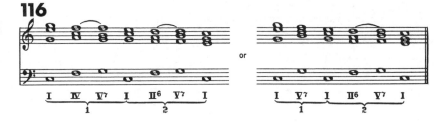

I   IV   V^7 I   II^6 V^7 I
      1   2

or

I   V^7 I   II^6 V^7 I
      1   2

117

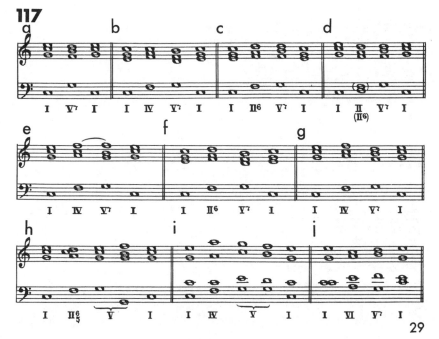

a   b   c   d

I   V^7 I   I   IV   V^7 I   I   II^6 V^7 I   I   II   V^7 I
                                                                                (II^6)

e   f   g

I   IV   V^7 I   I   II^6 V^7 I   I   IV   V^7 I

h   i   j

I   II$^6_4$ V   I   I   IV   V   I   I   VI   V^7 I

118

119 BACH Chorale (No. 337)

120 BACH Chorale (No. 88)

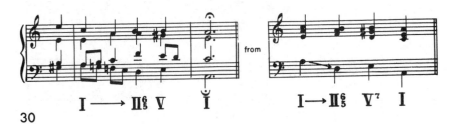

121

or

I ⟶ II V⁷ I   I ⟶ II V⁷ I

122 BACH Chorale (No. 348)

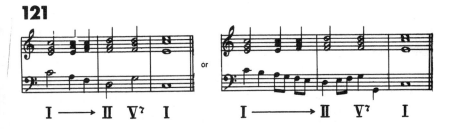

I ⟶ II V I

123 BACH Chorale (No. 246)

I ⟶ II⁶₅ V I

a

I ⟶ II⁶₅ V I

124

I ⟶ V⁷ I

125

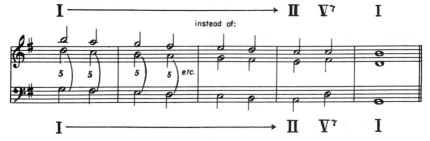

instead of:

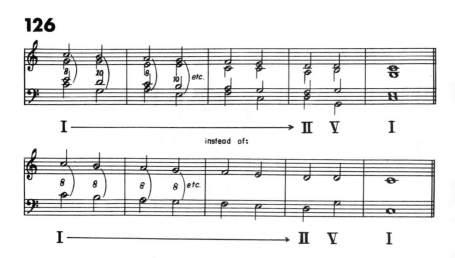

126

instead of:

127
a

127 cont'd

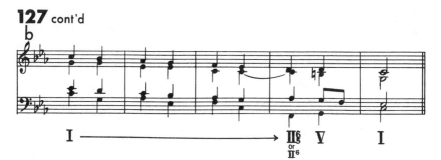

I ——————————————————————→ II⁶₆ V   I
                                      or
                                      II⁶

128

   from

I → II V I   I II V⁷ I

129

a

I   II V⁷   I

b

I   II   V   I

c

   5 6   5 6   5 6

I ——————————————————→ V   I
                      ⁶₄ ⁷

d

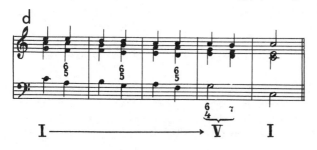

      ⁶₅   ⁶₅   ⁶₅

I ——————————————————→ V   I
                      ⁶₄ ⁷

130

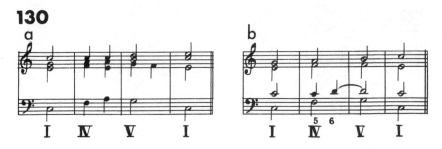

I   IV   V   I   I   IV   V   I
                                 5 6

131   CHOPIN Waltz, Op 34, No. 2

I ⟶ IV   6   V

132   BACH Gavotte (French Suite No. 5)

I ⟶ IV   V   I

133   BRAHMS Piano Sonata, F minor, Op 5

Allegro maestoso

a

$$I \longrightarrow V \left(\begin{smallmatrix} 6 & 5 \\ 4 & 3 \end{smallmatrix}\right)$$

134

I   *   II   V   I

135

a   b

6                    $\frac{5}{3}$

136

a   b   c   d   e

$\frac{6}{4}$ 7 $\frac{6}{5}$ $\frac{4}{3}$ 2

136 cont'd

137

138

139

140 BACH Chorale (No. 330)

141 SCHUBERT Waltz, Op 50, No. 1

36

142   CHOPIN Waltz, E Major (Posth.)

143   MOZART Piano Sonata, C Major, K. 545

144   SCHUBERT Ländler Op 67 No. 5

145   BACH Chorale (No. 346)

146

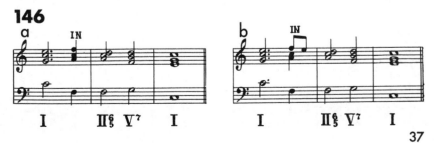

147 BACH Little Prelude, C minor

148

149

150

becomes

151

152 BACH Prelude No. 1 (Well-
Tempered Clavier, Bk I)

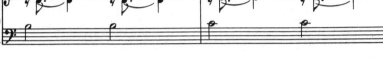

153

154   C. P. E. BACH Minuetto

155   CHOPIN Waltz, Op 69, No. 2

156   JOSQUIN Missa: Pange lingua

[From DAS CHORWERK, Vol. I]

157

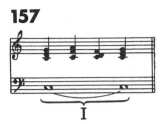

158 BACH Prelude No. 6 (Well-Tempered Clavier, Bk I)

159

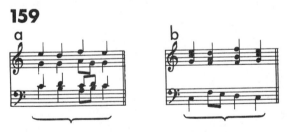

160 BACH Chorale (No. 11)

160 cont'd

161

162 BACH Chorale (No. 366)

163 BACH Chorale (No. 367)

164

a   b

I   II   V⁷   I
     (II⁶)   I

165

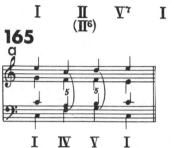

a   b

I   IV   V   I

166

    becomes   

167

a   b   c

d   e   f

   or      

g   h

168 BACH Chorale (No. 24)

169 BACH Prelude No. 2 (Well-Tempered Clavier, Bk II)

170 BACH Little Prelude, F Major

171

or

171 cont'd

172

a   b   c

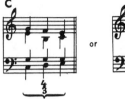 or

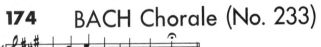

173

174 BACH Chorale (No. 233)

a

b

I   V   I

175 BACH Chorale (No. 367)

a

b

I   II⁶₅ V I

176 BACH Chorale (No. 362)

a

6

b

I   II⁶₅ V I

6

177 BACH Chorale (Peters No. 118)

a

$$I \qquad IV^7 \; V \quad I$$

b

$$I \qquad IV^7 \; V \quad I$$

178

a

$$I \qquad II^6$$

b

$$I \qquad II$$

c

$$I \qquad II^6$$

179   BACH Chorale (No. 110)

a

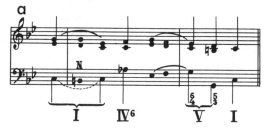

$$I \qquad IV^6 \qquad \overset{6}{\underset{4}{}}\ \overset{5}{\underset{3}{}} \qquad I$$
$$\hphantom{I \qquad IV^6 \qquad} V \hphantom{\qquad I}$$

b

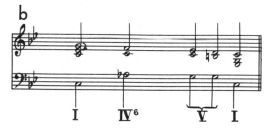

$$I \qquad IV^6 \qquad V \qquad I$$

180

a

b

181

a

$$I \qquad IV^7\ V \qquad I$$
$$\hphantom{I \qquad} 6 \hphantom{\qquad}$$

b

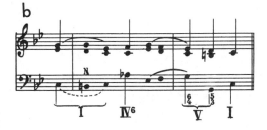

182 BACH Chorale (No. 42)

a

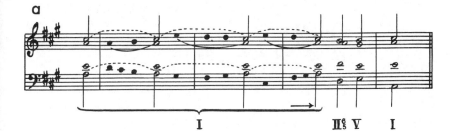

b

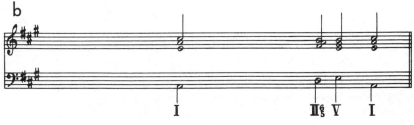

183 MOZART Piano Sonata, D Major, K. 311.

184 JOSQUIN Motet: Tu pauperum refugium

Tu pau - pe - rum re - fu - gi - um,

[From HAM, Vol. I, No. 90]

185 GIACOMO FOGLIANO Ave Maria

San - cta Ma - ri - a, Ma - ter De - i, o - ra pro no - bis

[From HAM, Vol. I, No. 94]

186 BARTÓK Piano Pieces for Children, No. 32

Allegro ironico

186 cont'd

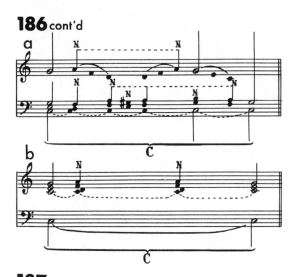

187

188

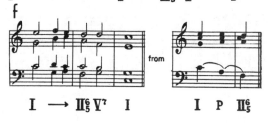

189

a

$$\text{I} \qquad \text{IV}^6 \qquad \text{V} \qquad \text{I}$$

b

$$\text{I} \qquad \text{IV} \qquad \text{V} \qquad \text{I}$$

190

a

or   etc.

$$\text{I} \;\longrightarrow\; \text{II}^6 \; \text{V}^7 \; \text{I} \qquad\qquad\qquad \text{I}$$

b

from   etc.

$$\text{I} \;\longrightarrow\; \text{II}^6_5 \; \text{V}^7 \; \text{I} \qquad\qquad\qquad \text{I} \quad \text{P} \quad \text{II}$$

191

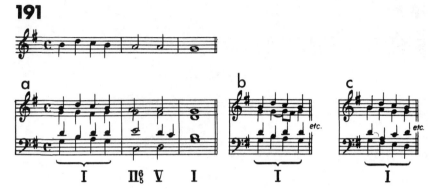

192

54

193

a

$$\text{I} \qquad \text{II}^6_5 \qquad \text{V} \qquad \text{I}$$

b

$$\text{I} \qquad \text{II}^6 \qquad \text{V} \qquad \text{I}$$

194

a

$$\text{I} \qquad \text{II}^6_5 \qquad \overset{5}{4}\quad\overset{5}{3} \qquad \text{V} \qquad \text{I}$$

b

etc.

$$6$$

$$\text{I}$$

c

etc.

$$\overset{5}{3}$$

$$\text{I}$$

55

194 cont'd

d

I ⟶ II⁶₅ V I

from

I → II⁶₅ V I

195

a

b

c

d

196

a Interval-filling

b Interval-outlining

c ornamental

197

a

b

198 MOZART Piano Sonata, F Major, K. 280

199   MOZART Piano Sonata, C Major, K. 279

200   BACH Courante (Partita No. 5)

201   MOZART Piano Sonata, C Major, K. 279

202 HANDEL Double

203 MOZART Rondo, A minor, K. 511

204

or

205 MENDELSSOHN Song Without Words, Op 62, No. 1

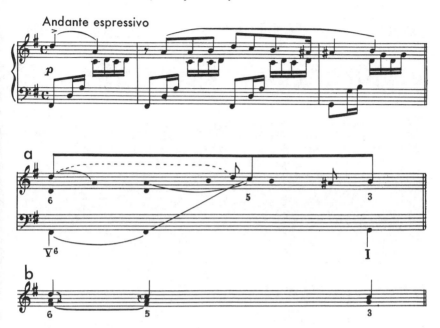

206 BEETHOVEN Piano Sonata, F minor, Op 2, No. 1

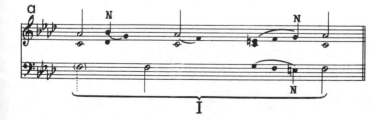

207 MOZART Fantasia, D minor, K. 397

Adagio

a

b

208 MOZART Piano Sonata, C minor, K. 457

Molto allegro

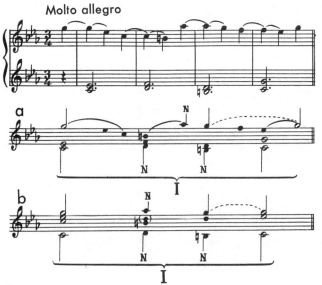

209 CARISSIMI Cantata: Mary Stuart

Ah mo - ri - re, ah mo - ri - re, ah mo - ri - - - - re

[From OHM, Vol. III]

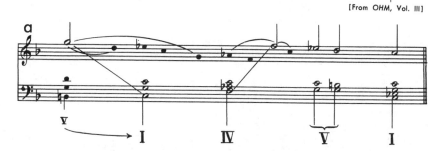

210 HAYDN Piano Sonata, C Major, No. 35

Allegro con brio

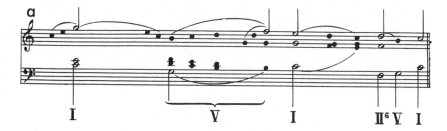

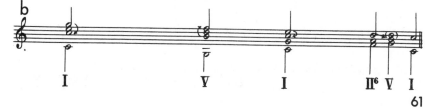

210 cont'd

211   HAYDN Piano Sonata, D Major, No. 19

212   FROBERGER Suite: "Auf die Mayerin"

[From *DTOe*, Vol. VI]

213 MOZART Courante (Suite, K. 399)

I   II V   I II⁶ → V I   I II⁶→V I

214 HAYDN Piano Sonata, G Major, No. 27

I   II⁶   V   I

215 FOLK TUNE

I   II⁶   V   I

216 CHOPIN Nocturne, Op 32, No. 1

217 MOZART Piano Sonata, F Major, K. 280

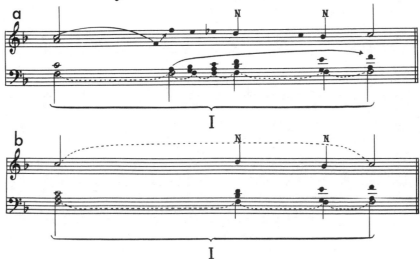

218 MENDELSSOHN Song Without Words, Op 102, No. 2

219 MOZART Aria ("Don Giovanni")

219 cont'd

quel - che a lei pia - ce, ___ vi - ta mi _ ren - de, etc.

220 CLEMENTI Sonatina, G Major, Op 36, No. 2

221 BEETHOVEN Piano Sonata,
E Major, Op 109

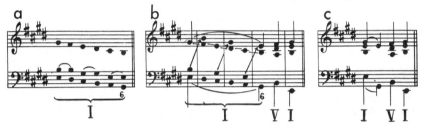

222 BEETHOVEN Symphony No. 9

223 SCHUBERT Ländler, Op 18, No. 2

 becomes

I V I

224 C. P. E. BACH Fantasia

N

225 BACH Praeludium (Partita No. 1)

a

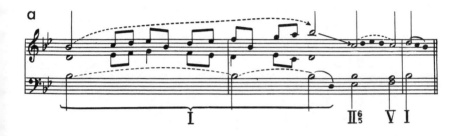

226 BEETHOVEN Piano Sonata,
G Major, Op 79

226 cont'd

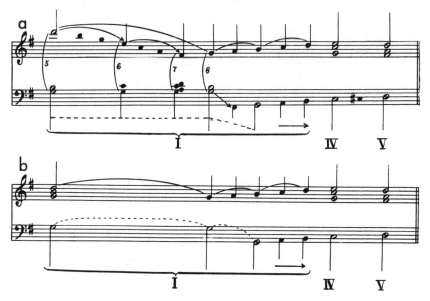

a

b

227   HANDEL Variation 1 (Air from Suite No. 3)

a

b

228 BACH Courante (Suite pour le clavecin, E♭ Major)

a

b

229 BEETHOVEN Piano Sonata, E Major, Op 14, No. 1

229 cont'd

a

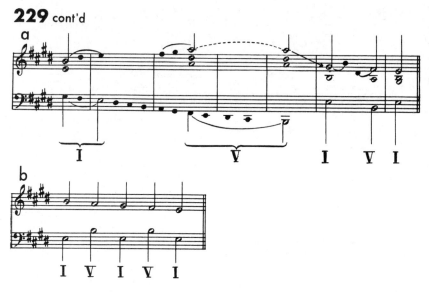

I   V   I V I

b

I V I V I

230   MOZART Trio, E♭ Major, K. 498

Andante

p

a   b   c

231   BACH Praeambulum (Partita No. 5)

a4 9 7 °5

C⁶

a

C⁶

232   BACH Aria variata

233   MOZART Piano Sonata, C Major, K 545

234   SCHUMANN Melody (Album for the Young)

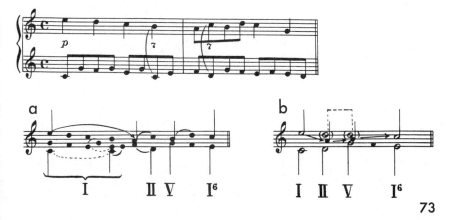

235 MOZART Fugue, C Major
(Fantasia, K. 394)

which avoids

236 BACH Chorale (No. 64)

10   8   6

237 BACH Chorale (Peters No. 43)

238 **HANDEL Minuet**

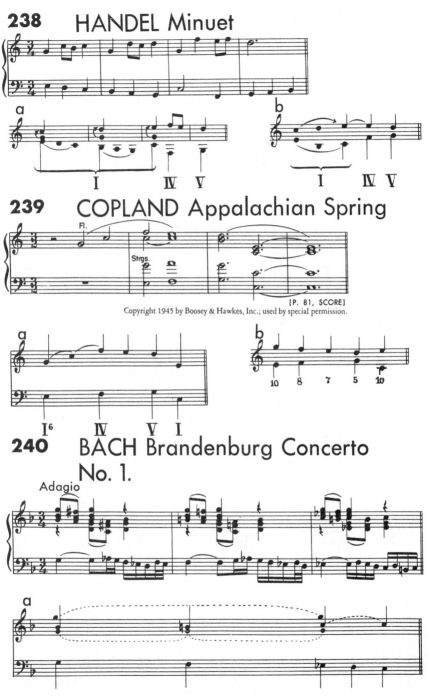

a

I   IV V

b

I   IV V

239 **COPLAND Appalachian Spring**

Fl.

Strgs.

[P. 81, SCORE]

a

b

10 8   7   5 10

I⁶   IV   V I

240 **BACH Brandenburg Concerto No. 1.**

Adagio

a

241 # BARTOK Ukrainian Song (Petite Suite)

242

243 # BYRD Pavane: The Earle of Salisbury

244 MOZART Piano Sonata, G Major, K. 283

245 GOTTLIEB MUFFAT Air (Suite, B♭ Major)

246 BACH Prelude No. 10 (Well-Tempered Clavier, Bk I)

a

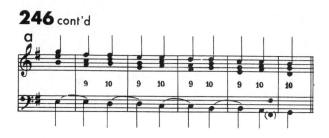

247 HAYDN Piano Sonata, C Major, No. 21

Allegro

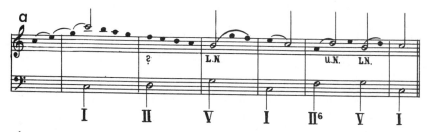

a

b

c

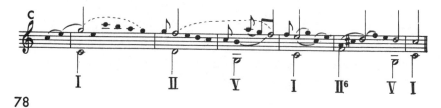

248 MOZART Piano Sonata, G Major, K. 283

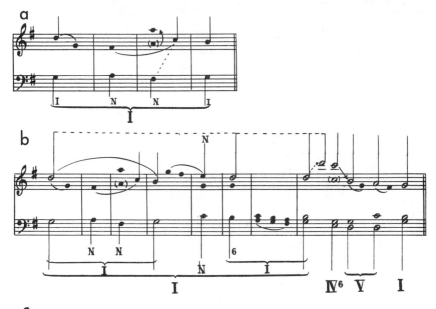

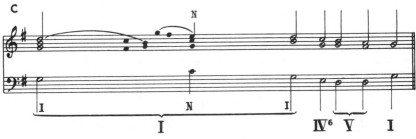

249 BACH Little Prelude, C minor

80

250 CHOPIN Mazurka, Op 41, No. 4

251 CHOPIN Etude, Op 25, No. 5

252 SCHUMANN Kreisleriana, Op 16, No. 8

a

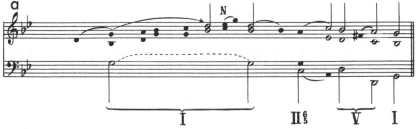

253

a   **b**

254 BEETHOVEN Piano Sonata, G Major, Op 14, No. 2

254 cont'd

a

etc.

I

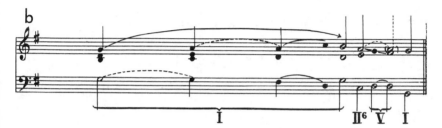

b

I   II⁶ V I

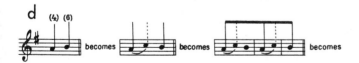

c

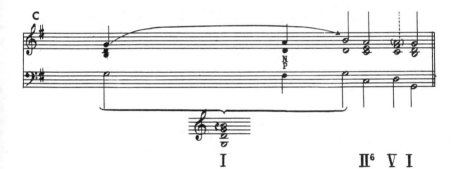

N
P

I   II⁶ V I

d (4) (6)

becomes   becomes   becomes

255

256

257

258

259

I II⁶ V I

260

I V I II⁶ V I

261

I II⁶ V I

262

a

b

I IV V I

c

263

I II⁶ V I

86

263 cont'd

264

a

divided through
interruption (‖)

I V I

b

I V I V I
(D)

265   BEETHOVEN Piano Sonata,
E Major, Op 14, No. 1

Allegretto

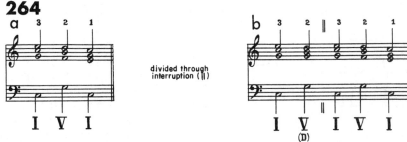

p

p   cresc.   sf

a

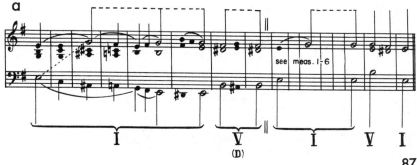

see meas. 1–6

I   V   I   V   I
(D)

266 ## HAYDN Symphony, G Major, No. 100

267 ## MOZART Quartet ("Don Giovanni")

Non ___ ti fi-dar, o mi-se-ra, di quel ri-bal-do cor!

Me già tra-dì quel bar-ba-ro, te vuol tra-dir an-cor!

267 cont'd

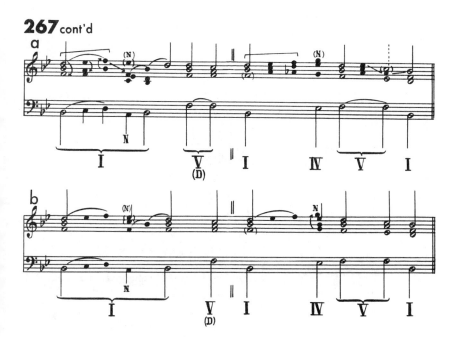

268 BASSE DANSE

[From VDO, App. P. 35]

89

269 BACH Chorale (No. 192)

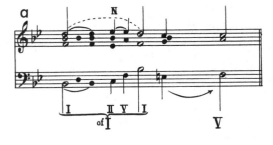

270

271 GIBBONS The Queene's Command

JOSQUIN Motet: Ave Maria

Ma - ri - a ple - na gra - ti - a, coe - le - sti - a, ter -

Ma - ri - a ple - na gra - ti - a, coe - le - sti - a, ter -

Ma - ri - a ple - na gra - ti - a, coe - le - - sti - a, __ ter - re -

Ma - ri - a ple - na gra - ti - a, coe - le - sti - a, ter -

re - stri - a, mun - - - dum re - plens lae - - - ti - - - - - - ti - a.

re - stri - a, mun - - - dum re - plens __ lae - ti - ti - - - - - - - - - - a.

- stri - a, __ mun - - - dum re - - - - plens lae - - ti - ti - a.

re - stri - a, mun - dum __ re - plens lae - ti - - - - - - - - ti - - a.

[From AM, P. 9]

273 cont'd

a

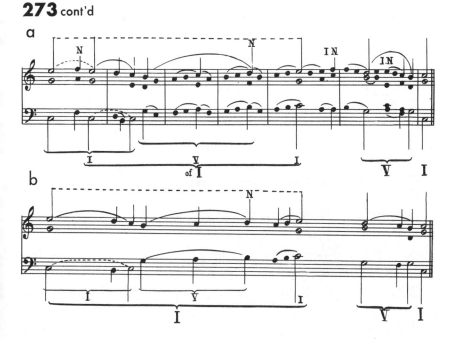

b

274   CLÉREAU Missa: In me transierunt

Ky - ri - e - e - ley - - - - - son, e - ley - - - - - - - - - - - - - son

[From *HDM*, Vol. I, P. 330]

a

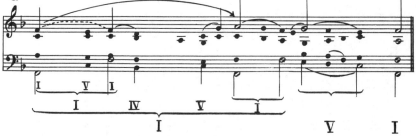

275

a

I   II V I

I   II⁶   V   I

b

I   V   I
of I   N   I

of I   IV⁶ V   I

276   BACH Chorale (No. 5)

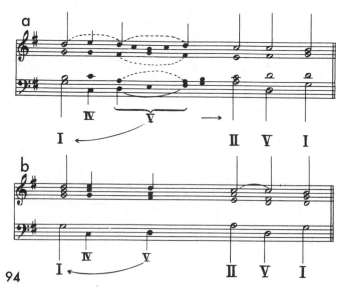

a

IV

I   V   →   II   V   I

b

I   IV   V   II   V   I

277 MOZART Piano Sonata, D Major, K. 576

278

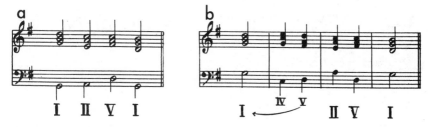

279 SCHUMANN Bunte Blätter, Op 99

280 BACH Prelude No. 7 (Well-Tempered Clavier, Bk II)

a

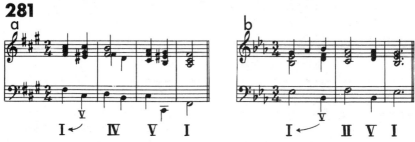

I ← V   II V I

281

a

I ← IV V I

b

I ← V II V I

282 SCHUBERT Ländler, Op 18, No. 10

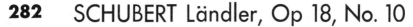

V → I

283 CHOPIN Etude, Op 10, No. 4

Presto

f

V → I

284 CHOPIN Mazurka, Op 63, No. 2

285 CHOPIN Mazurka, Op 24, No. 3

286 SCHUMANN Der Nussbaum

287 SCHUMANN Dichterliebe, No. 5

Ich will mei-ne See - - - - le tau - - - - - - chen

288 BEETHOVEN Piano Sonata,
Eᵇ Major, Op 31, No. 3

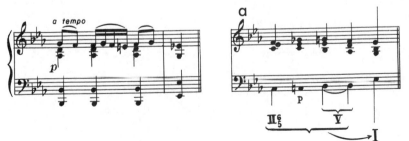

289 BEETHOVEN Piano Sonata,
Eᵇ Major, Op 81a

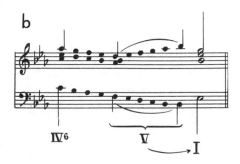

290 RAVEL Rigaudon (Tombeau de
Couperin)

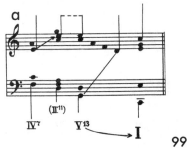

291

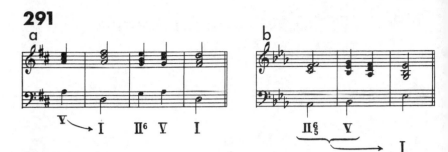

292

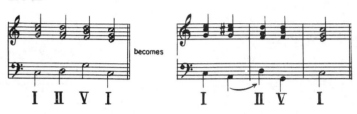

becomes

293 SCHUBERT Waltz Op 127, No. 3

294 SCHUBERT Piano Sonata,
D Major,

295 SCHUBERT Waltz, Op 10, No. 6

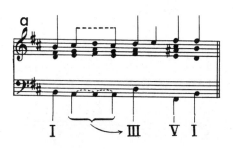

296 SCHUMANN Humoreske, Op 20

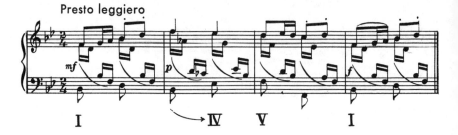

Presto leggiero

I   IV V   I

297 CHOPIN Waltz, Op 64, No. 2

Tempo giusto

a

I V I

298 BEETHOVEN Piano Sonata,
C Major, Op 2, No. 3

Allegro assai

298 cont'd

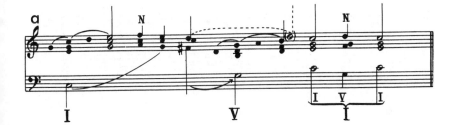

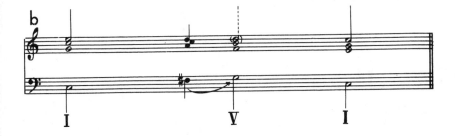

299 SCHUMANN Fantasiestücke, Op 12, No. 3

300 LISZT Liebestraum (Nocturne No. 3)

Poco allegro, con affetto

dolce cantando

a

I   V   I

301

a

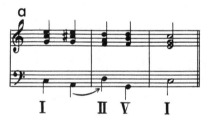

I   II V   I

b

I   VI V   I

c

I   III V   I

d

I   IV   V   I

302

contrapuntal   harmonic

303   SCHUMANN Scenes from
          Childhood, Op 15, No. 1

I   o⁷ → V   I

304   CHOPIN Mazurka, Op 17, No. 2

Lento, ma non troppo

a

I   II   V   I   V   I
        of III

305 SCHUMANN Album-Leaves,
Op 124, No. 10

Mit Lebhaftigkeit

a

I   of V   I⁶   VI   V   I

306

a

I   of III   V   I

b

I   of V   I

c

I   of II   V   I

d

I   of VI   V   I

307 SCHUMANN Album-Leaves,
Op 124, No. 5

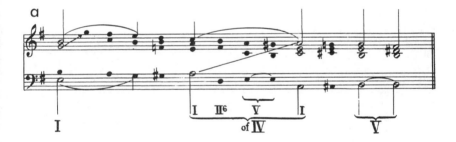

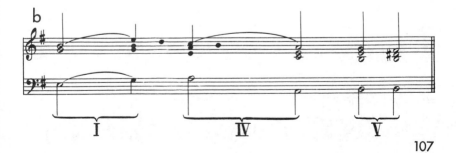

BRAHMS Intermezzo, Op 118, No. 2

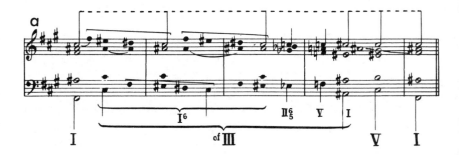

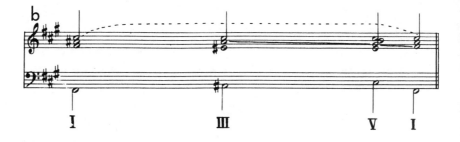

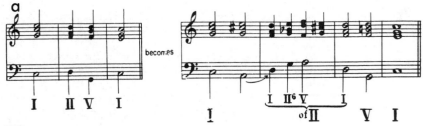

309 cont'd

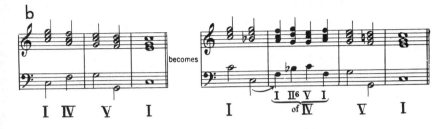

b

I IV V I   I I II⁶ V I   V I
                         of IV

310   SCHUMANN Auf dem Rhein

Ziemlich langsam

Auf dei-nem Grun-de ha-ben sie an-ver-borg'-nem__ Ort

a

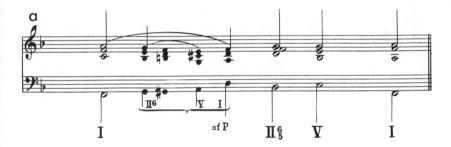

I   II⁶   V I   II⁶₅ V   I
        of P

b

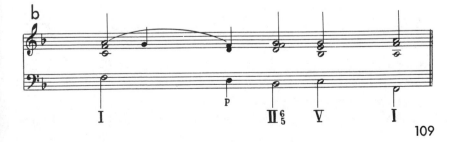

I   II⁶₅ V   I

311 CHOPIN Mazurka, Op 59, No. 2

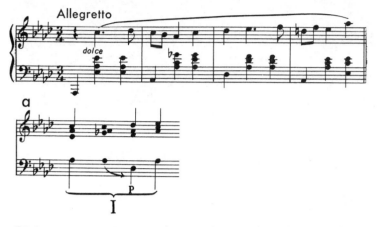

312 BACH Chorale (No. 55)

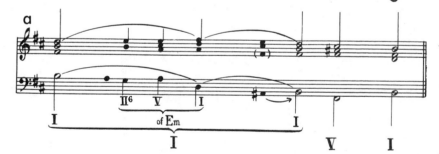

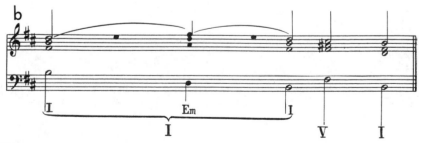

313 BACH Chorale (No. 177)

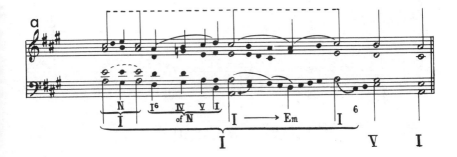

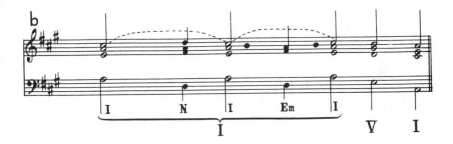

314

315 ## CHOPIN Mazurka, Op 68, No. 2 (Posth.)

316 ## SCHUBERT German Dance, No. 7

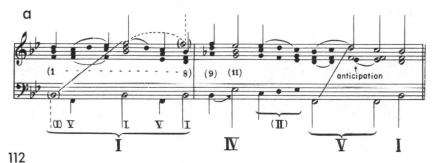

316 cont'd

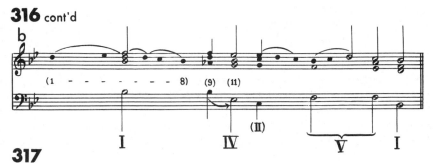

317

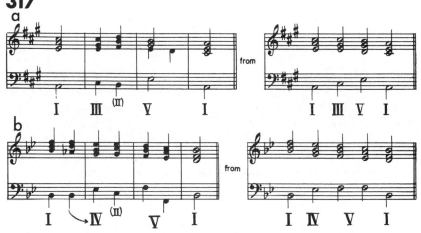

318 HAYDN Piano Sonata, G minor, No. 44

113

319 # PURCELL Overture, "Dido and Aeneas"

a

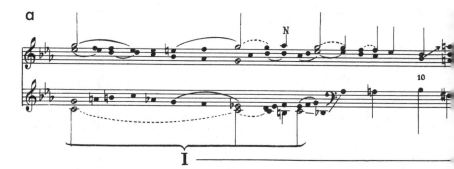

b

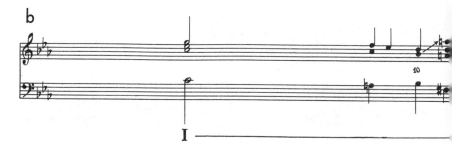

320 # PEERSON The Primerose

319 cont'd

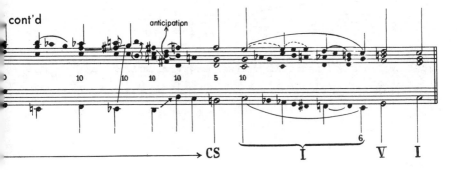

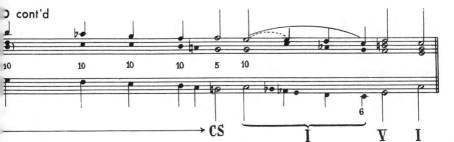

320 cont'd

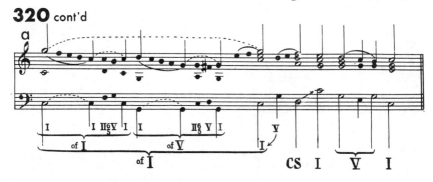

321 BACH Chorale (No. 229)

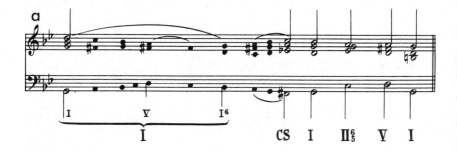

I   V   I⁶

I

CS   I   II$_5^6$ V   I

322

a

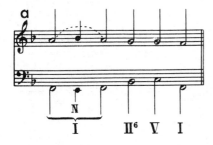

N

I   II⁶   V   I

b

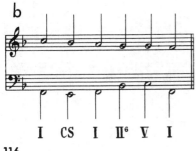

I   CS   I   II⁶   V   I

323 COUPERIN La Bandoline

I CS I⁶
(CS) II⁶ V I

324 CHOPIN Nocturne, Op 9, No. 2

324 cont'd

a

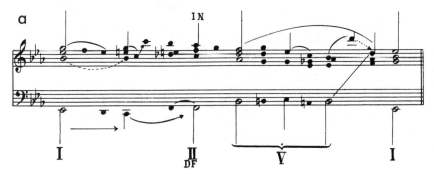

I   II DF   V   I

b

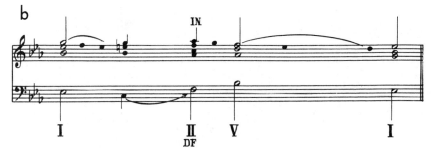

I   II DF   V   I

325 SCHUMANN Piano Concerto

325 cont'd

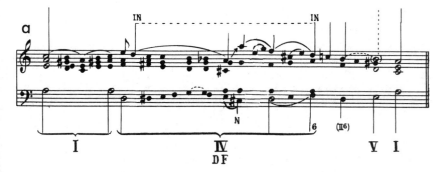

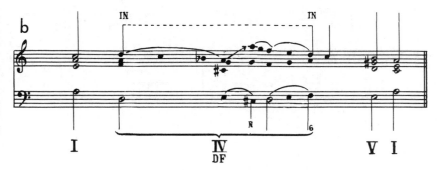

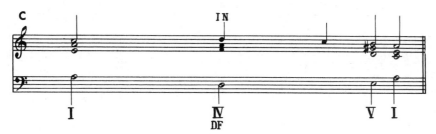

326

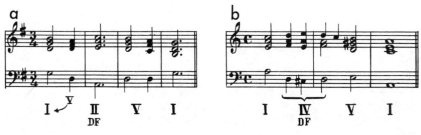

327   BACH Chorale (No. 320)

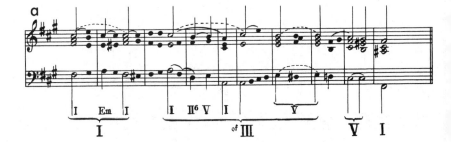

a

I   Em   I   I   II⁶ V   I   V   V   I
    I   of III

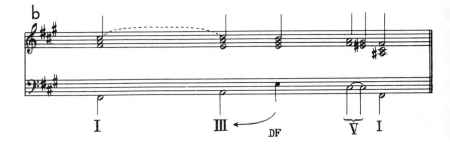

b

I   III ←── DF   V   I

328   BACH Chorale (No. 280)

I   IV   (II)   V   I
              DF

329 HANDEL Courante (Suite No. 14)

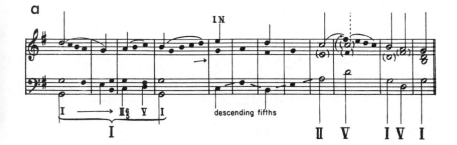

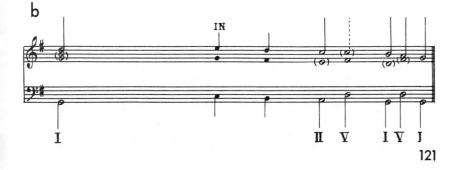

330 SCHUBERT Impromptu, Op 90, No. 2

a

331 VAUGHAN-WILLIAMS
Symphony No. 5

332 MOZART Rondo, K. 494

332 cont'd

333 SCHUBERT Waltz Op 77, No. 10

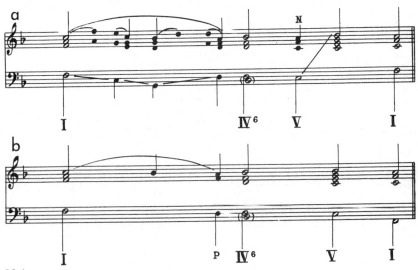

334   SCHUBERT Täuschung

$I \longrightarrow VI \ V \ I$

335   WEBER Overture, "Der Freischütz"

I

I I

336 HAYDN String Quartet, Op 76, No. 4

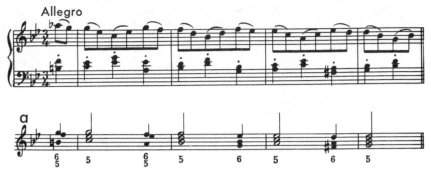

337 SCHUBERT Piano Sonata, B♭ Major

338

a
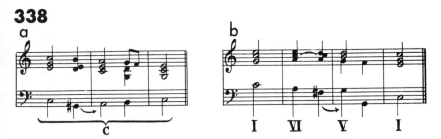
c

b

I   VI   V   I

c

I ——————————————→ II   V   I

d

I ——————————————→ II   V   I

339   BACH Chorale (No. 361)

a

I ———→ IV ———→ V̲   I

340

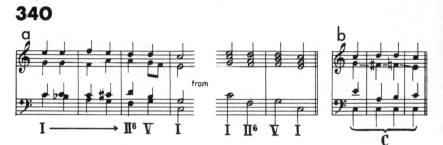

from

c

341

342

343

344

or
(meas.2)

345

346

347 BACH Chorale (No. 166)

I II⁶₅ ——→ V I

348 BACH Chorale (No. 167)

I ——————→ IV ——→ V I

349 HAYDN String Quartet, Op 76, No. 1

Adagio sostenuto

a

I N ——→ N V

b

I N N V

350 CHOPIN Mazurka, Op 24, No. 3

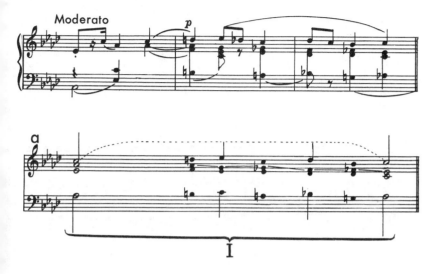

351 WOLF Schlafendes Jesuskind

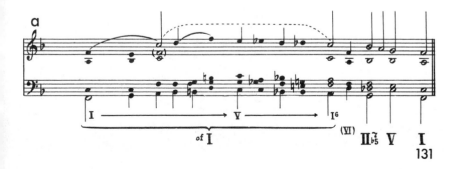

352

a

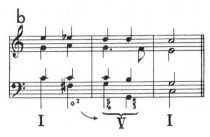

b

c

d

353

a

b

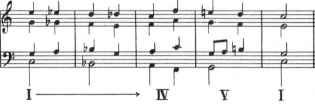

c

354

a

I   II⁶   V   I

b

I   P   II⁶   V   I

c

I ⟶   P   II⁶   V   I

355

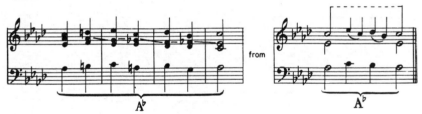

from

A♭   A♭

356

C

133

357 CHOPIN Mazurka, Op 30, No. 4

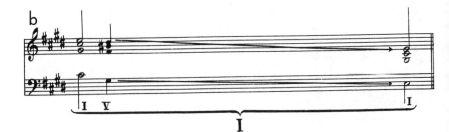

SCHUMANN Novelette, Op 21, No. 2

Ausserst rasch und mit Bravour

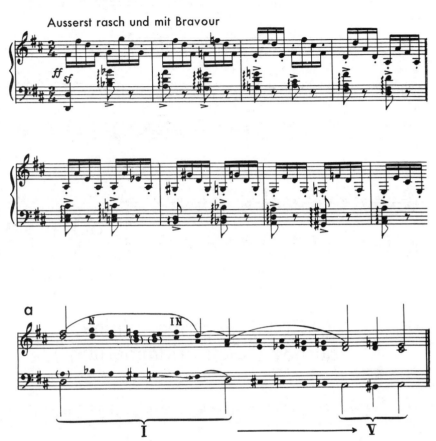

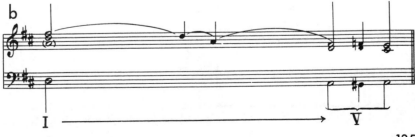

359 ## CHOPIN Mazurka, Op 17, No. 4

Lento, ma non troppo

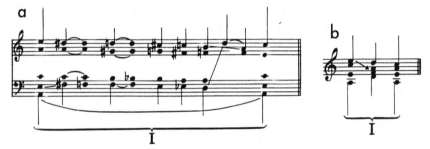

a

b

I

I

360 ## WAGNER Siegfried's Rhine Journey ("Götterdämmerung")

Rasch

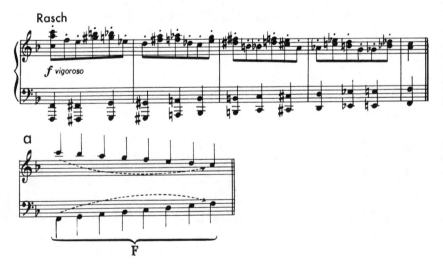

f vigoroso

a

F

CHOPIN Mazurka, Op 7, No. 2

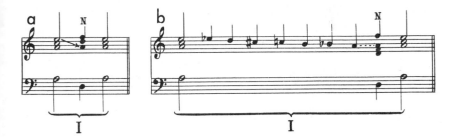

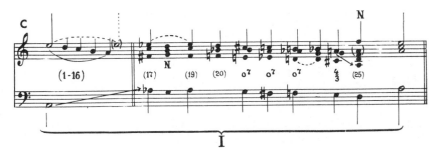

362 CHOPIN Mazurka, Op 6, No. 1

a

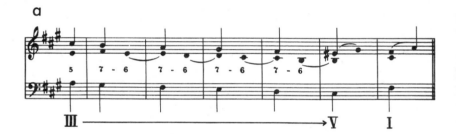

b

c

362 cont'd

d

e

363 SCHUMANN Novelette, Op 21, No. 8

Munter, nicht zu rasch

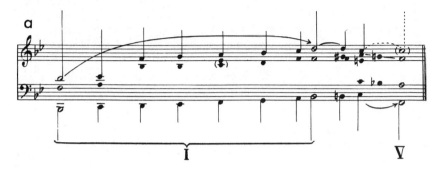

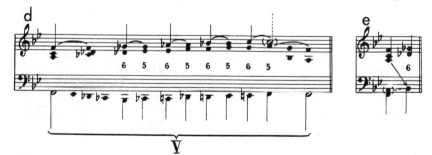

363 cont'd

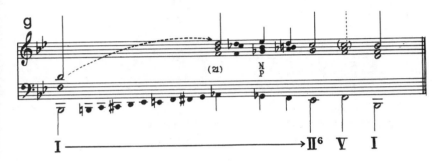

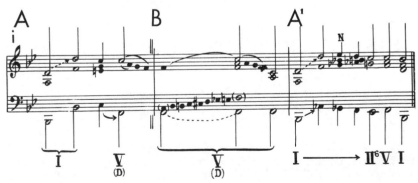

364

a

I   V   I

b

I ⟶ V I

c

I ⟶ V I

365

becomes

366   SCHUBERT Tränenregen

Ziemlich langsam

I   II   V

367 WAGNER "Götterdämmerung," (Act I)

368

becomes

369

a

b

370

I   *   V   I   I   *   V   I

I   VI   *   V   I

371   WAGNER Prelude, "Tristan und Isolde"

372   **373**

374

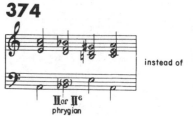

375 BEETHOVEN Piano Sonata, C# minor, Op 27, No. 2

376 WEBER "Der Freischütz" (Act II, No. 6)

R. STRAUSS "Ariadne auf Naxos"

Mezzo movimento

[P. 216, PIANO-VOCAL SCORE]

a

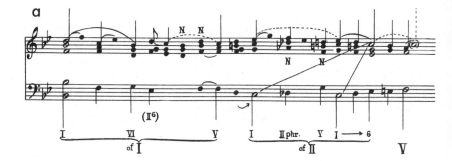

b

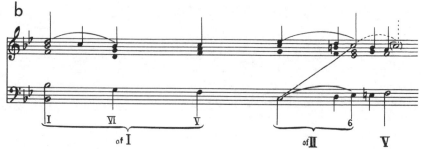

CHOPIN Nocturne, Op 27, No. 1

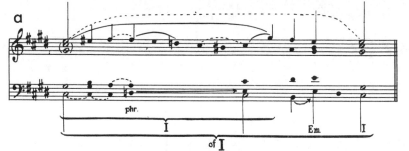

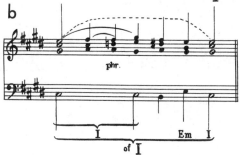

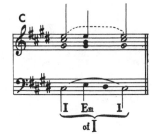

379

380 PROKOFIEFF Gavotte, Op 77, No. 4

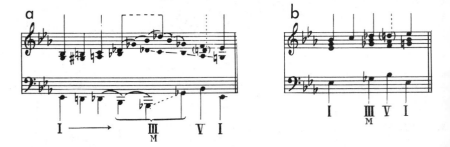

381 R. STRAUSS Don Juan

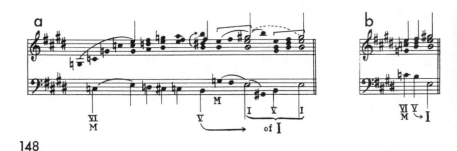

382   # WOLF In dem Schatten meiner Locken

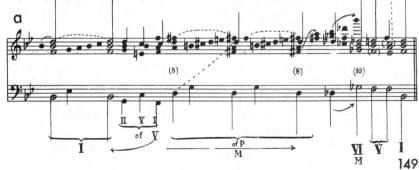

382 cont'd

383 BEETHOVEN Piano Sonata,
C minor, Op 13

Adagio cantabile

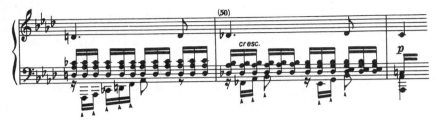

384 SCHUBERT Piano Sonata, C minor

a

b

c

385 SCHUBERT Pause

Ziemlich geschwind

Nun lie-be Lau-te, ruh' an dem Na-gel hier, und weht ein

385 cont'd

meiner Lie - bes - pein? Soll es das Vor - spiel - neu - er Lie - der sein?

a

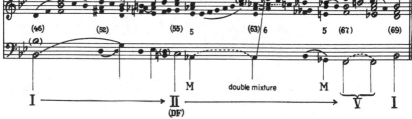

double mixture

b

386 MAHLER Das Lied von der Erde, No. 6

Langsam

Ich — su - che Ru - he, Ru - he für — mein — ein - - - - - sam Herz!

386 cont'd

a

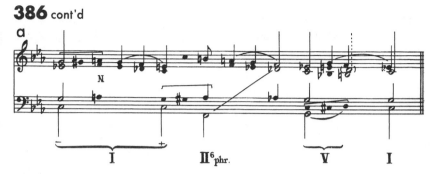

I   II⁶phr.   V   I

387   CHOPIN Mazurka, Op 68, No. 4 (Posth.)

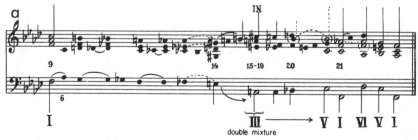

387 cont'd

b

double mixture

c

double mixture

388 MOZART Piano Sonata, F Major, K. 280

Adagio

a

I   II⁶₅   V   VI (for I)   V   I
    (DF)

389 SCHUBERT Trio, B♭ Major, Op 99

HAYDN Piano Sonata, F Major, No. 29

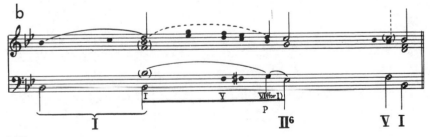

391   SCHUMANN Forest Scenes, No. 6

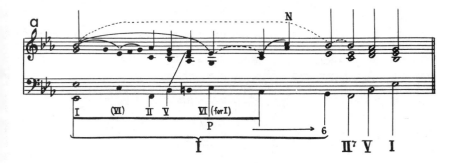

392   BACH Chorale (No. 5)

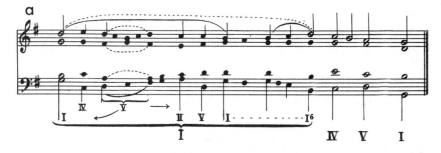

CHOPIN Waltz, Op 64, No. 2

394 SCHUBERT Piano Sonata, Bb Major

394 cont'd

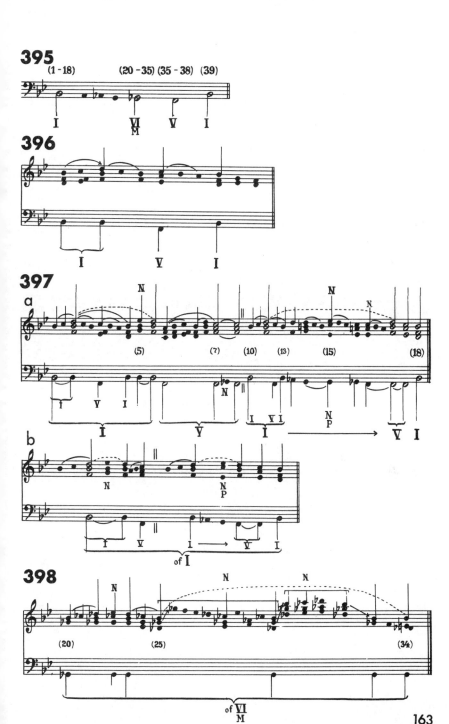

399

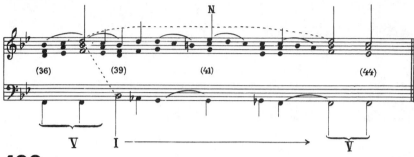

400

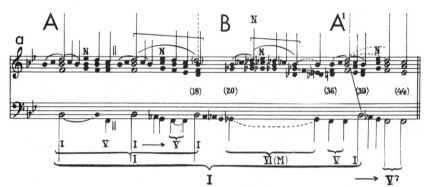

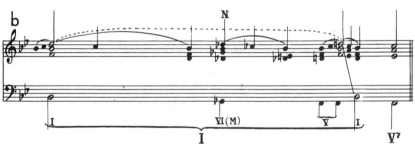

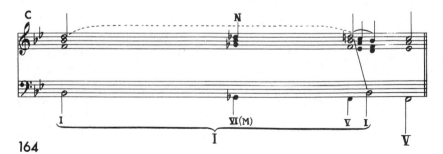

401 HAYDN String Quartet, Op 20, No. 5

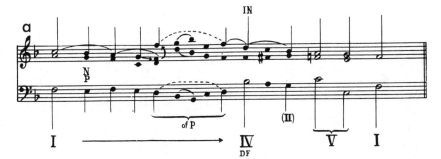

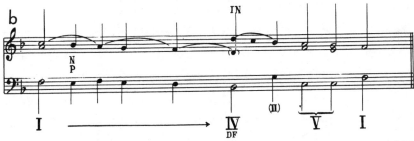

165

402   LASSO Motet: Recordare Jesu pie

[From *OL*, Vol. 15]

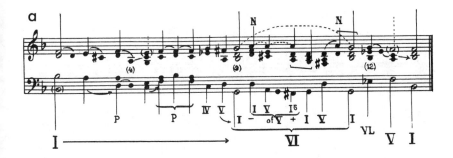

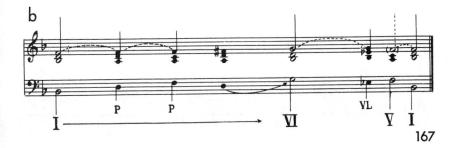

403 GASTOLDI Balletto: Speme amorosa

[From SHM, No. 20]

a

I IV V I   IV   V   I
                 DF

b

(1-4)   (5-8)

WAGNER "Tristan und Isolde"
(Act II)

Nun führst du in dein Ei - - gen,dein Er - - be mir zu

zei - - gen; wie flöh' ich wohl das Land, das al - le Welt um-spannt?

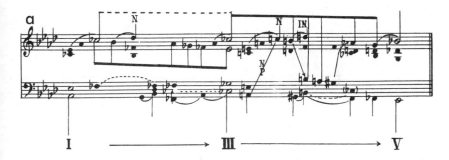

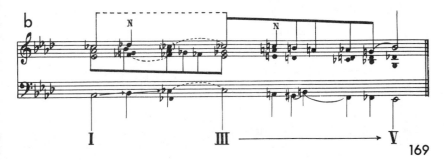

FRANCK Prelude, Aria and Finale

a

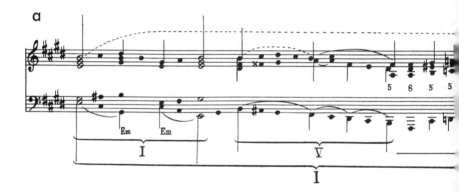

b

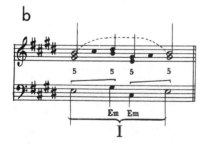

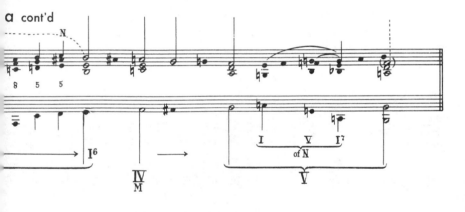

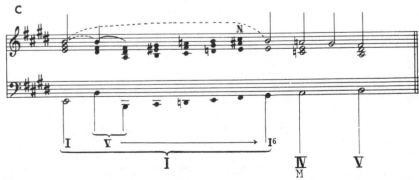

406 R. STRAUSS Quintet ("Ariadne auf Naxos")

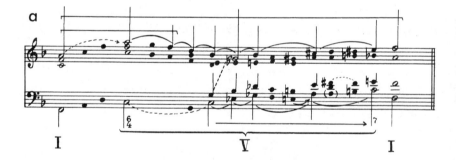

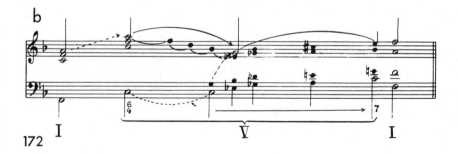

407 R. STRAUSS Quintet ("Ariadne auf Naxos")

Poco tranquillo

a

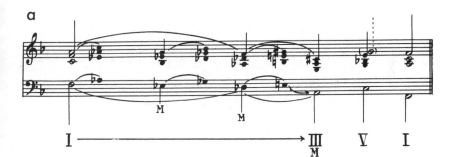

b

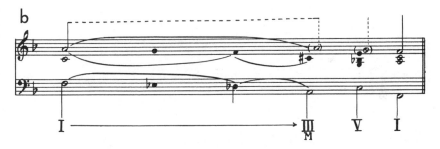

408 BIZET Seguidilla ("Carmen," Act I)

Allegretto

Près des rem - parts de Sé - vil - - - - le,

173

408 cont'd

Chez ___ mon a - mi ___ Lil - las Pas - tia _____ J'i -

rai dan - ser la Sé - gue - dille Et boi - re du Man - za - nil - la ____

_____ J'i - rai chez mon a - mi Lil - las Pas - tia. ____

409 CHOPIN Polonaise-Fantasy

a

a

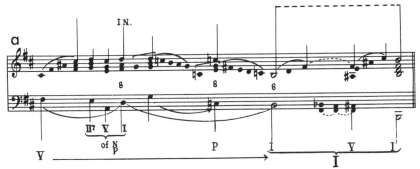

a cont'd

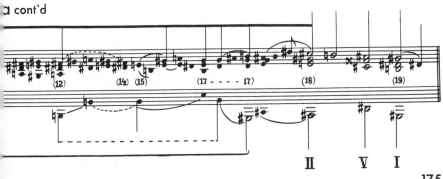

b

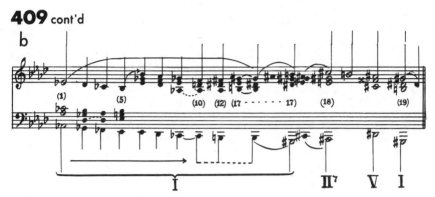

c

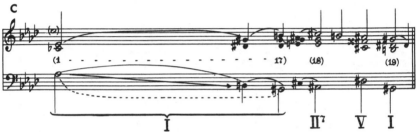

d

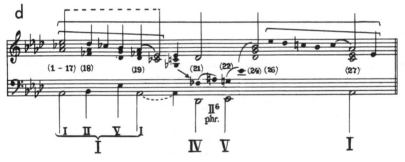

e

f

410   # HINDEMITH Piano Sonata No. 2.

a

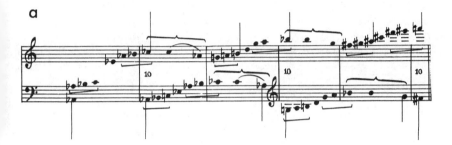

b

c

411 MARTINŮ Sonata for Cello and Piano No. 2.

Largo

412 COPLAND 3 Excerpts from "Our Town," No. 1

Moderate, with calm

a

411 cont'd

a

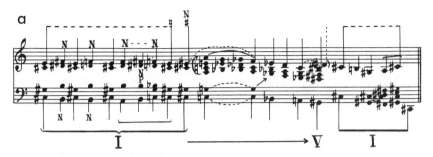

b

412 cont'd

a cont'd

413 **WAGENAAR** Ciacona

a

b

c

from

D

D

414 **MARTINŮ** Sonata for Violin and Piano No. 2

Larghetto

a

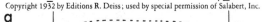

$B\flat$ $\frac{6}{4}$

415 RAVEL Jeux d'eau

Allegretto

415 cont'd

a

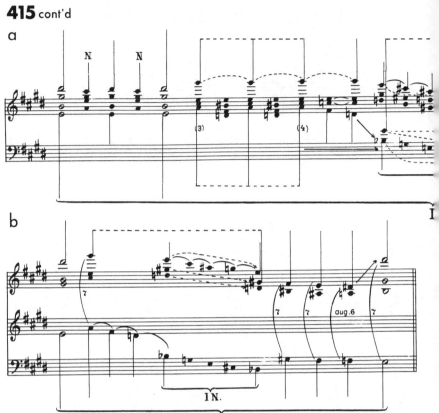

416 COPLAND Piano Sonata

cont'd

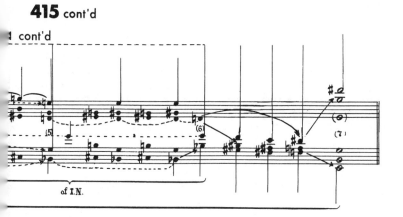

c

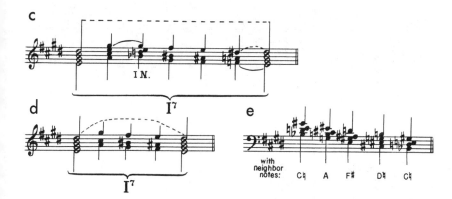

d

e

416 cont'd

a

186

cont'd

F ($\underline{V}$)

cont'd

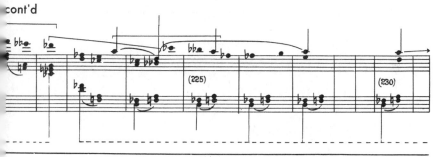

F ($\underline{V}$)

b

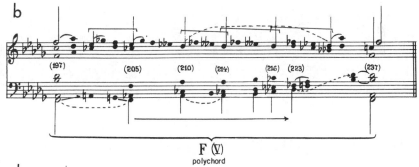

F ($\underline{V}$)
polychord

d

(197-237)

417 STRAVINSKY Symphony in Three Movements

a

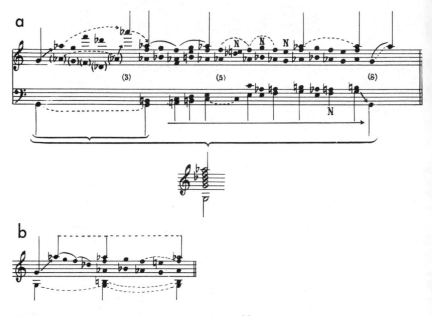

b

418 BARTOK Bagatelle Op 6, No. 4

419 R. STRAUSS "Elektra"

420 BEETHOVEN Piano Concerto No. 4, G Major

421

422

423

contracted with

424   BACH Cantata: Du wahrer Gott und Davids Sohn

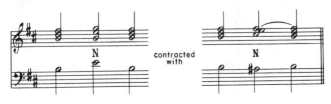

425   SCHUMANN Romance, Op 28, No. 1

Allegro marcato

a

anticipation

b   instead of:

426 ## COUPERIN La Favorite

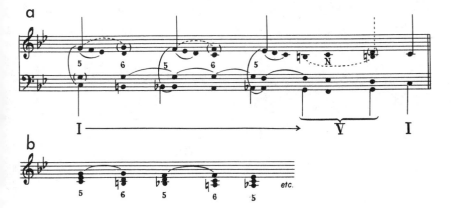

427 ## BYRD Sacerdotes Domini

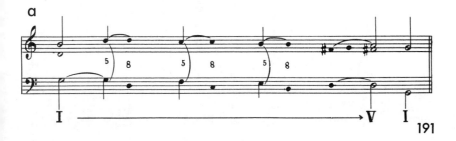

428 MOUSSORGSKY Ballet of the Unhatched Chickens (Pictures from an Exhibition)

Scherzino

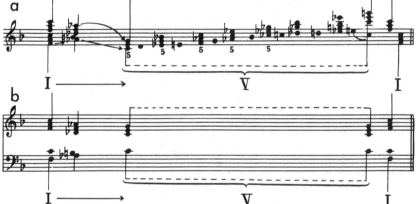

a

b

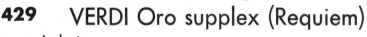

I ⟶   V   I

429 VERDI Oro supplex (Requiem)

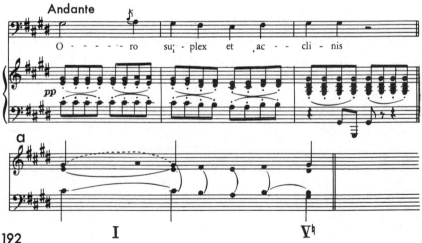

Andante

O - - - - ro su,-plex et ,ac - - cli - nis

a

I   V♮

430 BEETHOVEN Piano Sonata,
C Major, Op 53. Introduzione

431 CHOPIN Polonaise, Op 26

431 cont'd

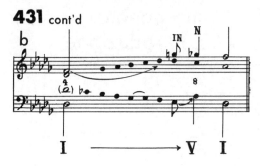

CHOPIN Mazurka, Op 59, No. 2

432
a

b

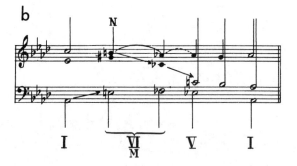

431 cont'd

c

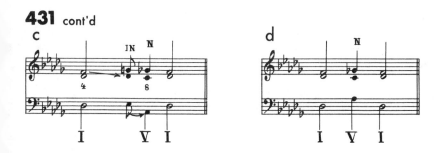

d

432 cont'd

cont'd

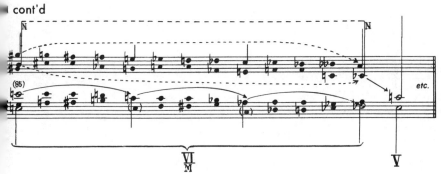

433   CHOPIN Polonaise, Op 40

a

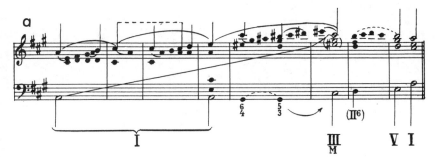

434

Instead of

we hear

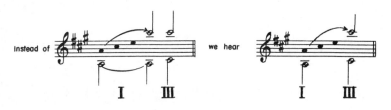

435   FARNABY A Toye

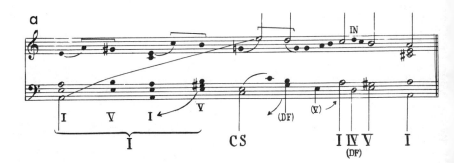

436   MENDELSSOHN Overture,
        "A Midsummer Night's Dream"

Allegro di molto

437 SCHUBERT Piano Sonata, C minor

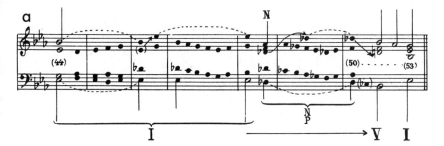

a

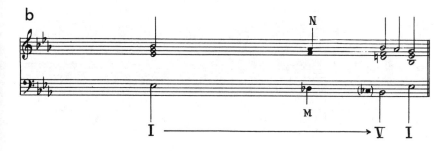

b

438 SCHUBERT Fantasia-Sonata

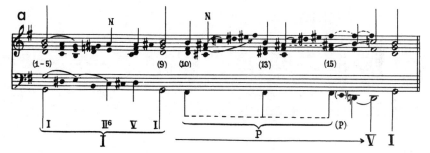

a

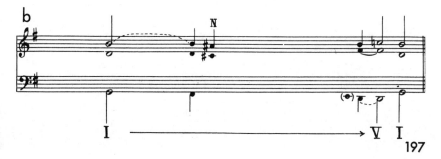

b

439   SCHUMANN Piano Quintet

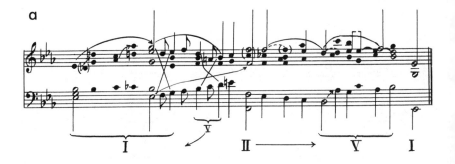

441   BARTÓK From 10 Easy Pieces for Piano

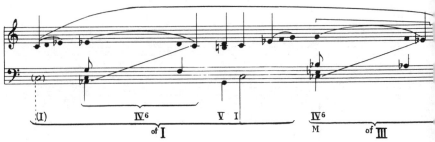

439 cont'd

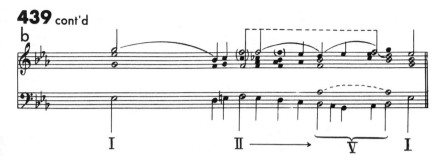

440 BEETHOVEN Piano Sonata, G Major, Op 31, No. 1

441 cont'd

a cont'd

442 **BEETHOVEN** Piano Sonata,
F minor, Op 2, No. 1

a

443 **BEETHOVEN** Piano Sonata,
C minor, Op 10, No. 1.

a

444 **MOZART** Piano Sonata, C Major,
K. 279

a

442 cont'd

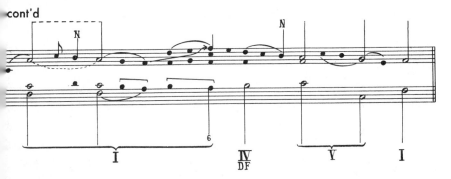

443 cont'd

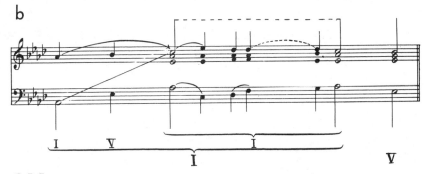

444 cont'd

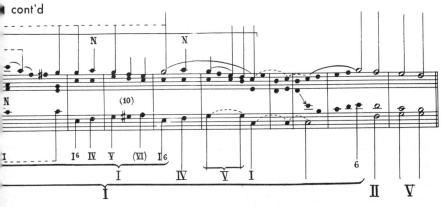

445   MAHLER Kindertotenlieder, No. 1

Nun will die

Sonn'   so   hell   auf - geh'n,   als sei _____ kein

a

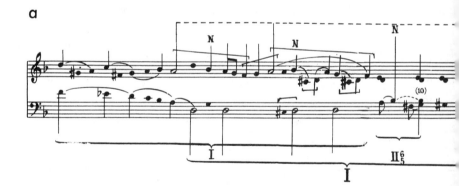

446

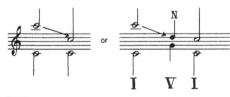

445 cont'd

Un - glück, kein _ Un - glück _ die _ Nacht _____ ge - scheh'n! __

cont'd

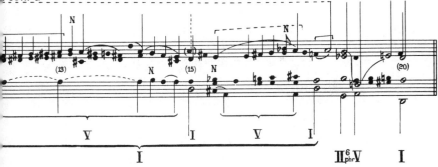

447 ALLEMANDE

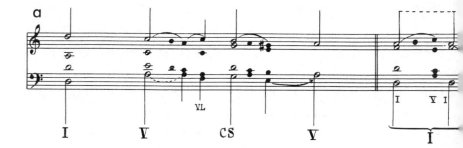

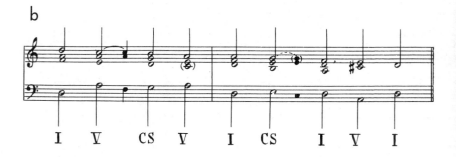

447 cont'd

[From MET, No. 39]

:ont'd

I   V   I

I   CS   I   V   I

448   SCHUBERT Die Krähe

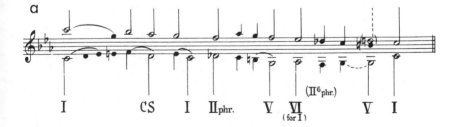

a

I   CS   I   II$_{phr.}$ V   VI   V   I
                                 (II$^{6}_{phr.}$)
                              (for I)

449 RAMEAU Choeur des Spartiates
("Castor et Pollux," Act I)

450 BEETHOVEN Piano Sonata,
E minor, Op 90

449 cont'd

450 cont'd

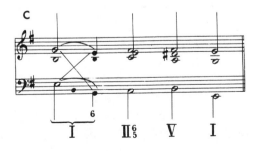

451　PROKOFIEFF Piano Sonata No. 8, Op 84

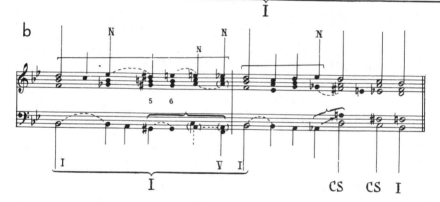

451 cont'd

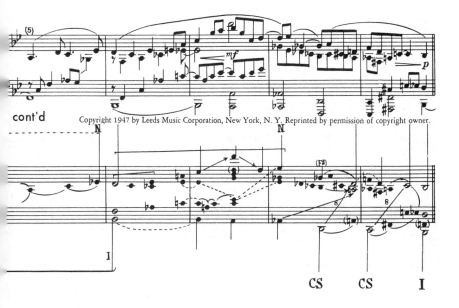

cont'd

452 BARTÓK String Quartet No. 5

Adagio molto

452 cont'd

Un poco più Andante

a

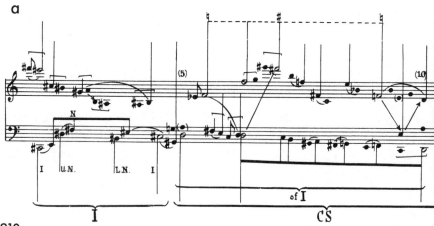

cont'd

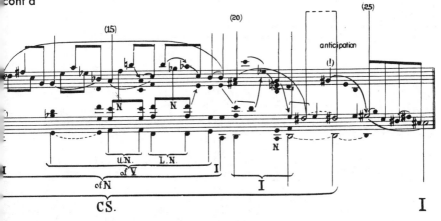

452 cont'd

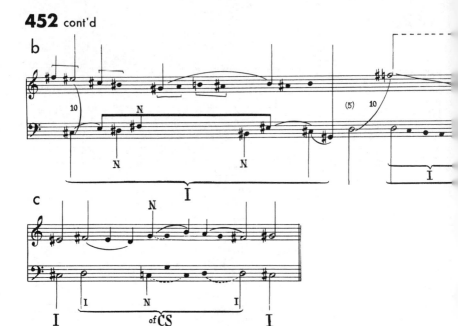

453 HINDEMITH Piano Sonata No. 1

With quiet motion, in quarters

452 cont'd

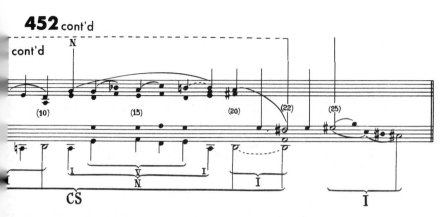

453 cont'd

a

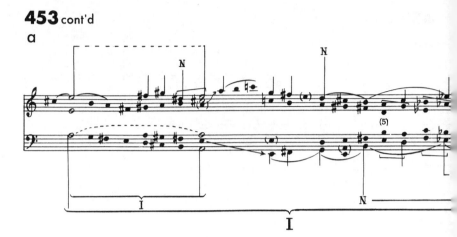

a cont'd

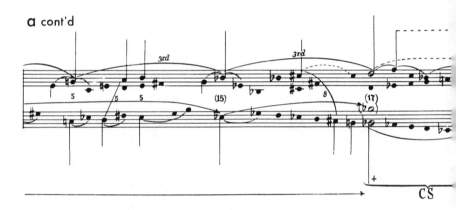

b

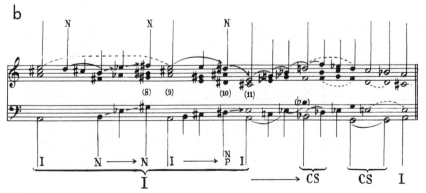

cont'd

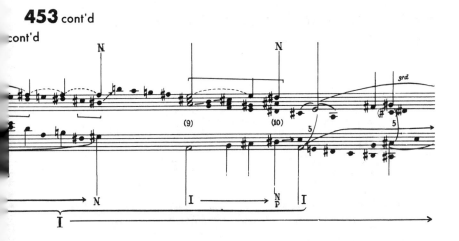

cont'd

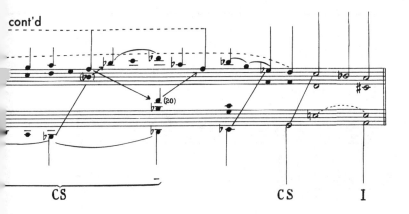

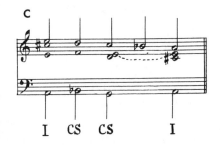

a

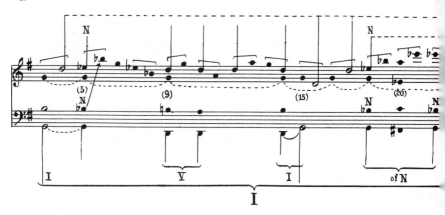

a cont'd

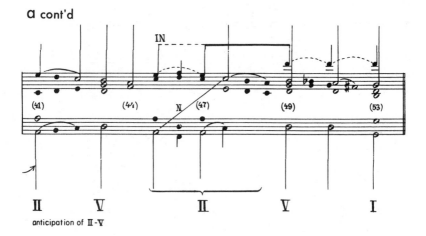

cont'd

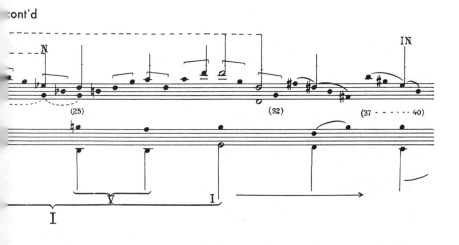

b

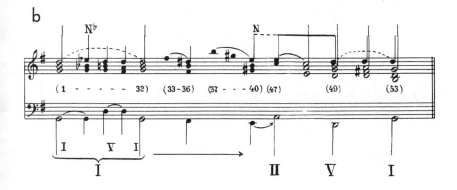

455 DEBUSSY Prélude à l'après-midi d'un faune

cont'd

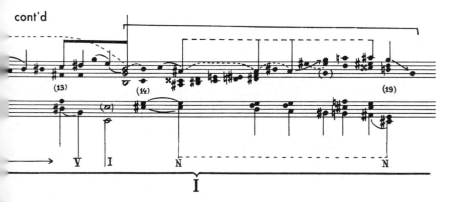

cont'd

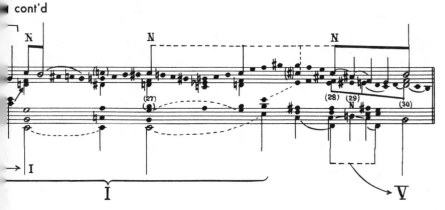

cont'd

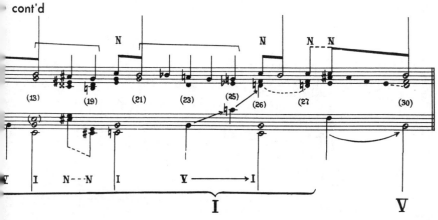

456 CHOPIN Nocturne, Op 48, No. 2

a

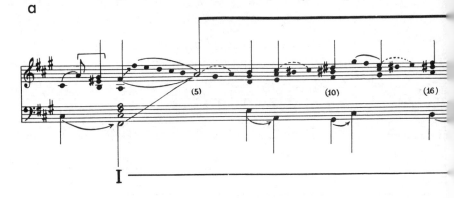

b

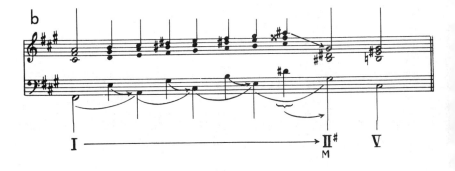

457 PROKOFIEFF Piano Sonata No. 3

a

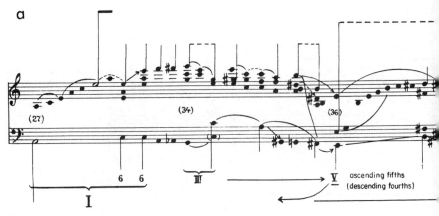

cont'd

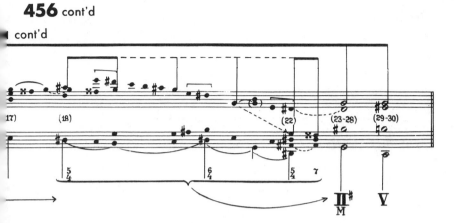

C

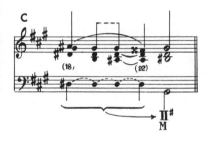

cont'd

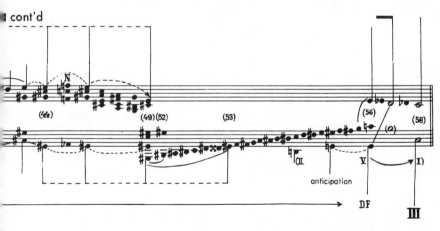

anticipation

b

d

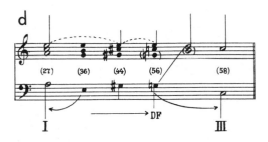

458   BEETHOVEN Piano Sonata,
D Major, Op 10, No. 3

a

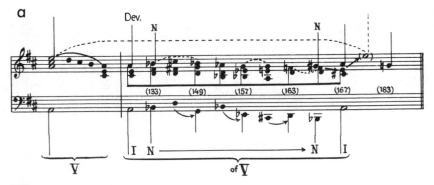

457 cont'd

c

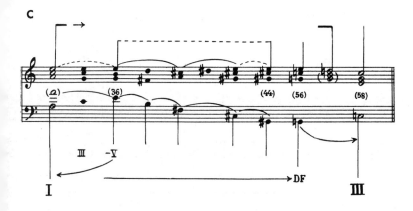

458 cont'd

b

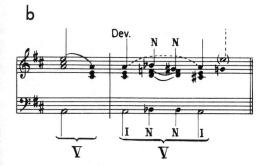

459 HAYDN Symphony D Major, No. 104

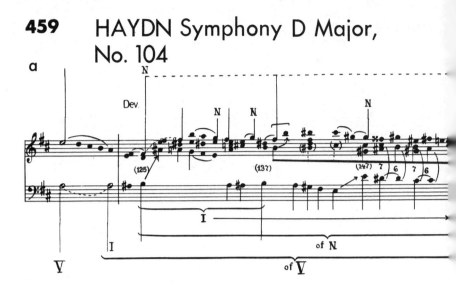

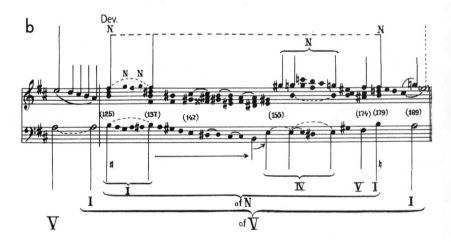

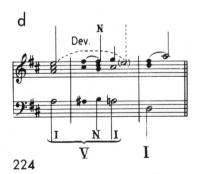

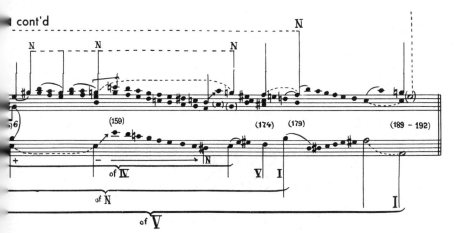

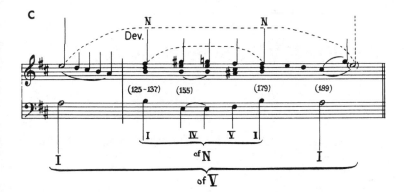

460

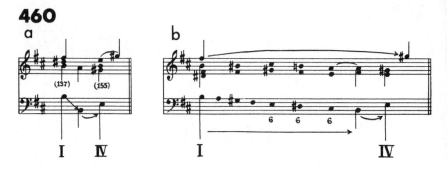

461 BEETHOVEN Piano Sonata,
Bᵇ Major, Op 22

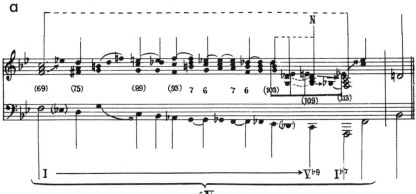

462 BEETHOVEN Symphony No. 7

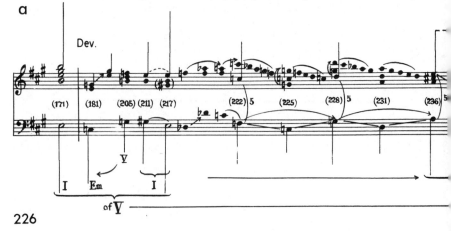

460 cont'd

c

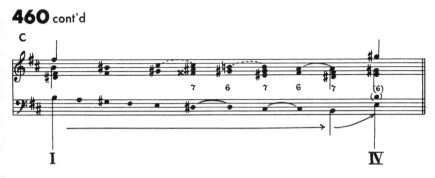

461 cont'd

b   c

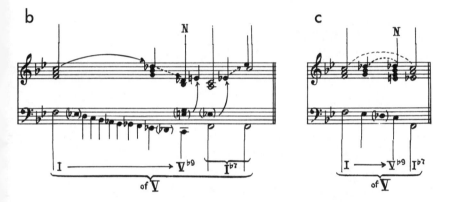

462 cont'd

cont'd

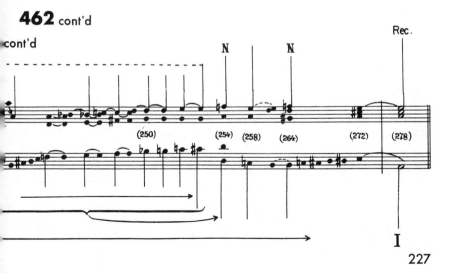

227

462 cont'd

b

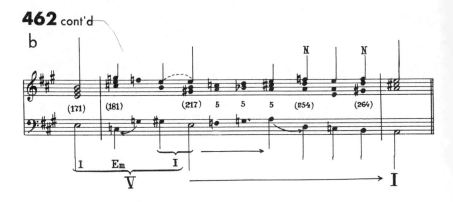

(171) (181) (217) 5 5 5 (254) (264)

I Em I

V I

463 BEETHOVEN Piano Sonata, C minor, Op 10, No. 1

a

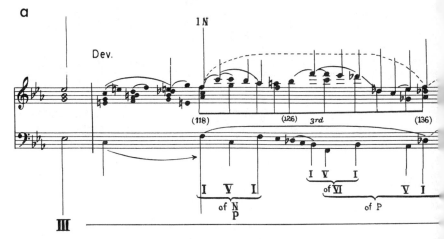

Dev.

1N

(118) (126) 3rd (136)

I V I

of N/P

I V I

of VI

V I

of P

III

b

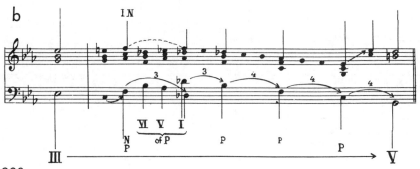

1N

3 3 4 4 4

VI V I

N/P of P

P P P

III V

462 cont'd

c

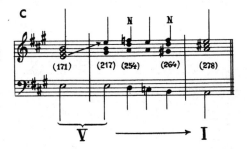

463 cont'd

cont'd

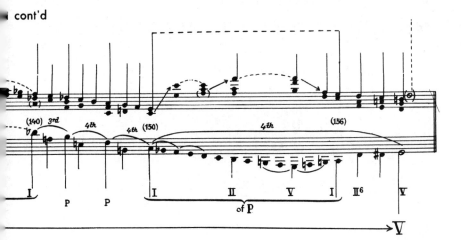

c

d

464 BEETHOVEN Piano Sonata, F minor, Op 57

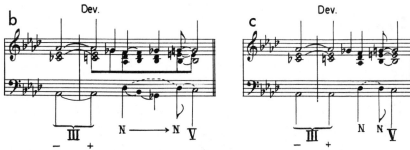

465

466

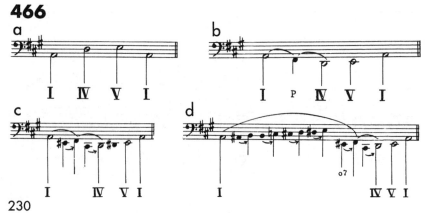

467

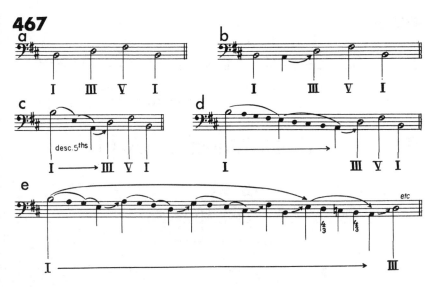

468

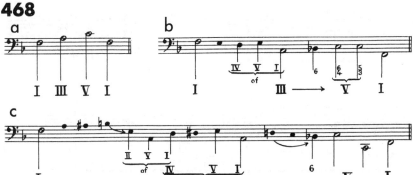

469

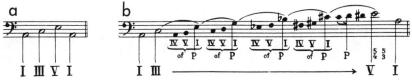

470

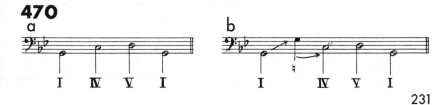

c

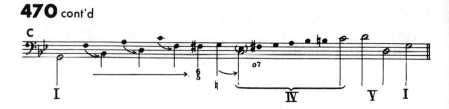

471 WAGNER "Parsifal," (Act I)

a

b

c

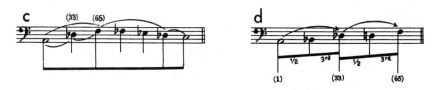

d

e

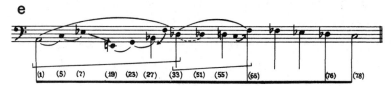

g cont'd

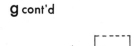

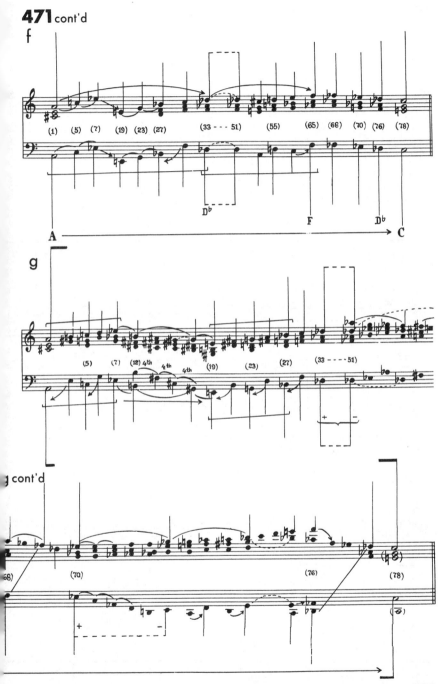

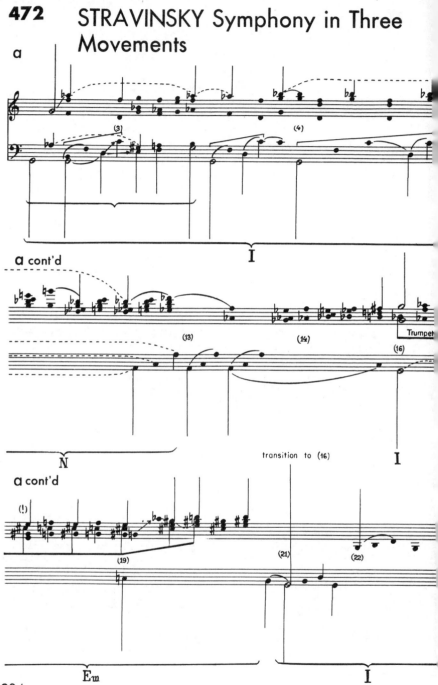

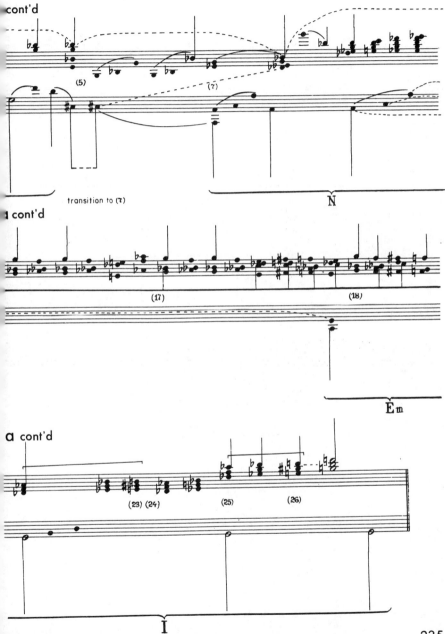

cont'd

(5)

(7)

transition to (7)

N

cont'd

(17)   (18)

Em

a cont'd

(23) (24)   (25)   (26)

I

472 cont'd

b

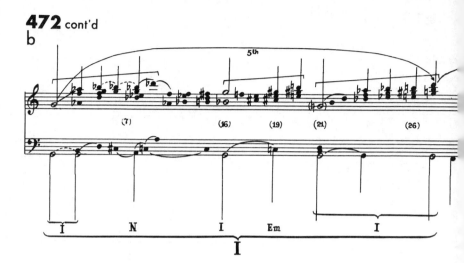

c

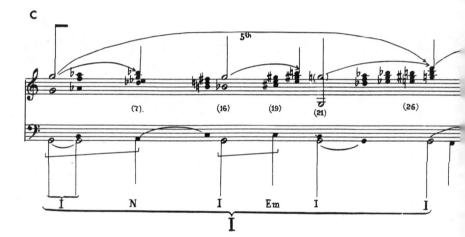

d

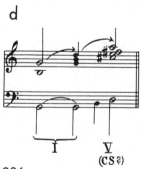

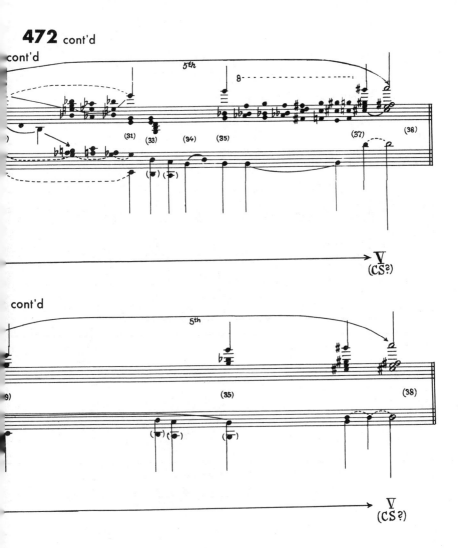

473   DOWLAND Ayre: What if I
never speed

[From *HAM*, Vol. I, No. 163]

a

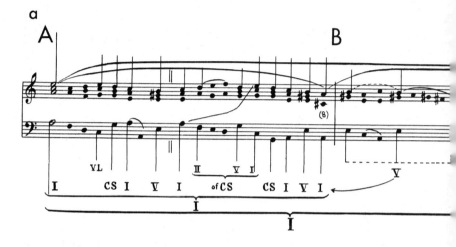

b

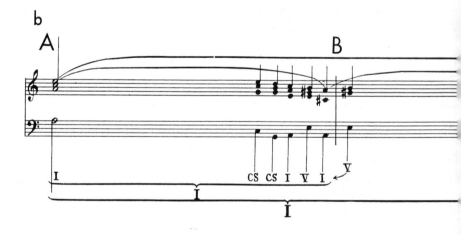

cont'd

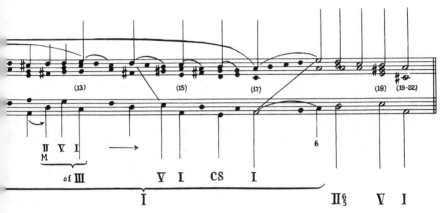

) cont'd

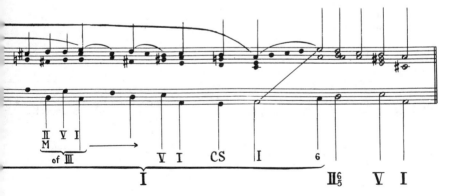

BACH Fugue No. 5 (Well-Tempered Clavier, Bk I)

a

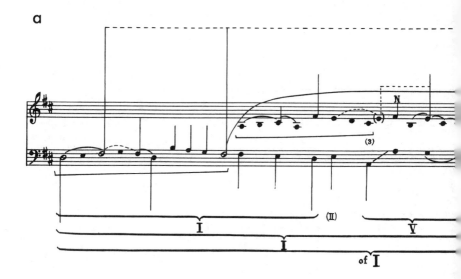

a cont'd

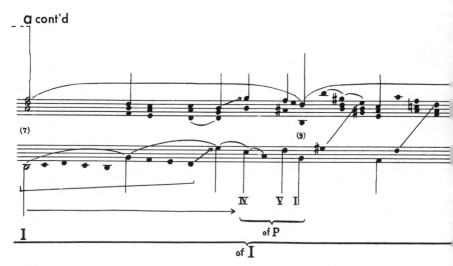

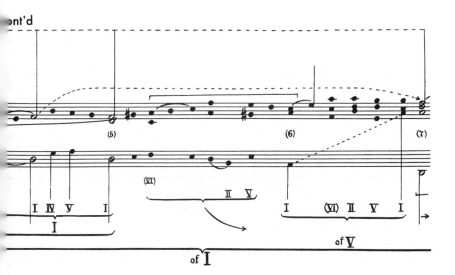

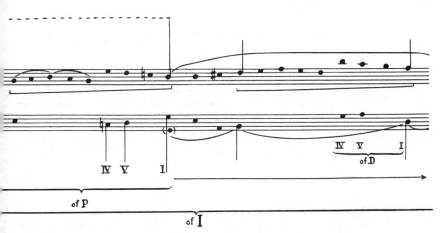

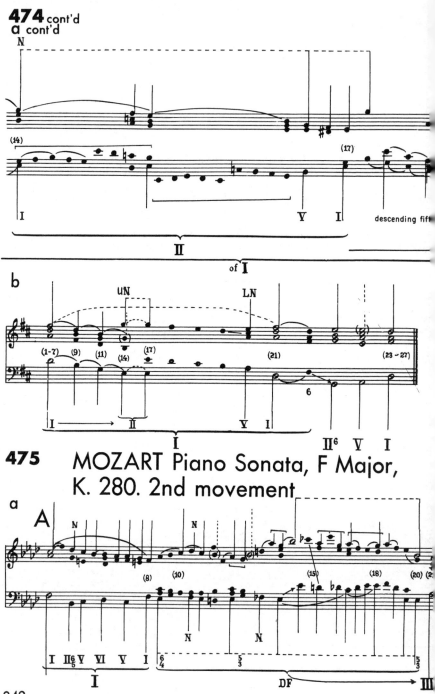

475 MOZART Piano Sonata, F Major, K. 280. 2nd movement

◀ cont'd

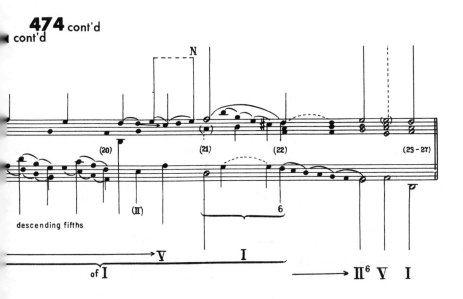

a cont'd

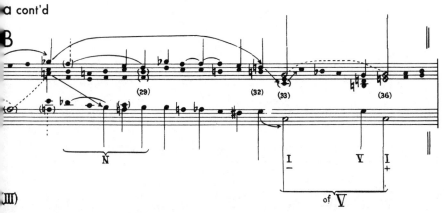

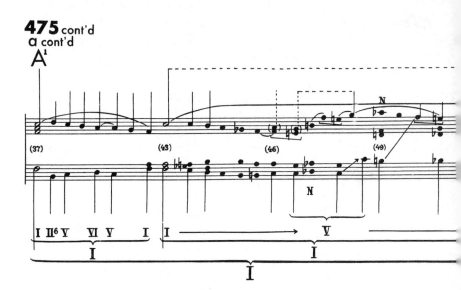

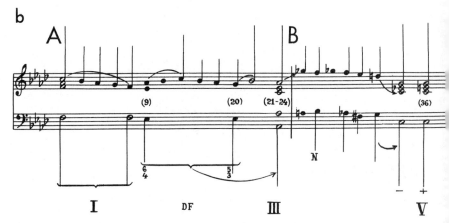

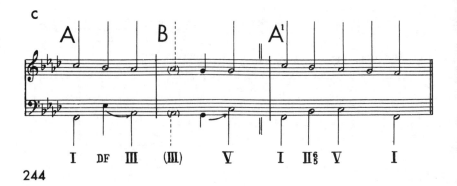

SCHUBERT Liebesbotschaft

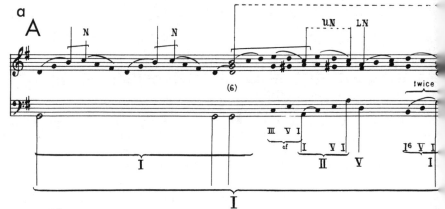

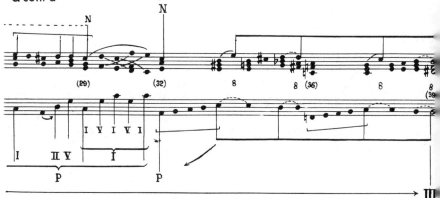

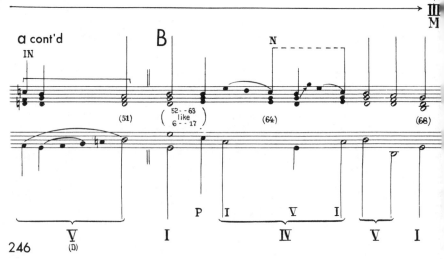

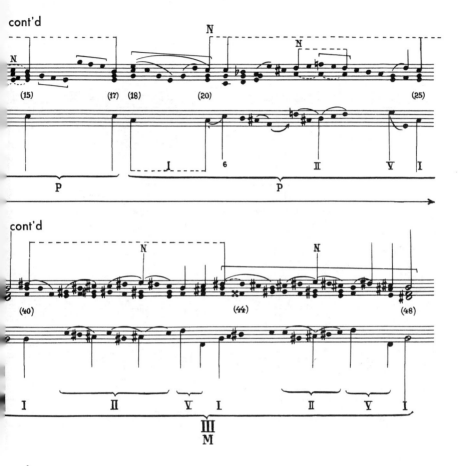

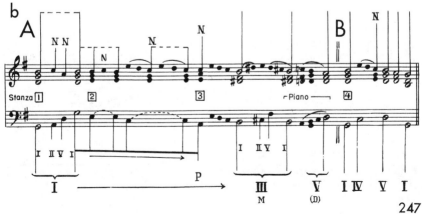

BRAHMS Intermezzo, Op. 119, No. 1

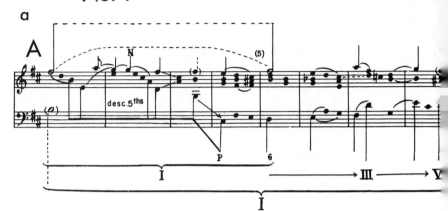

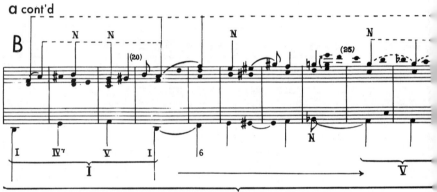

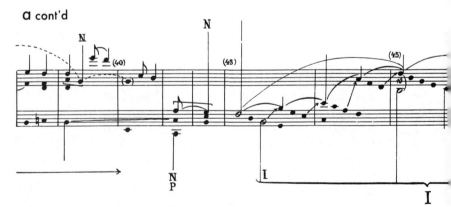

a cont'd

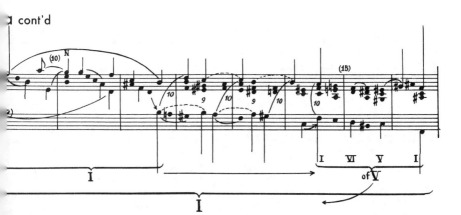

a cont'd

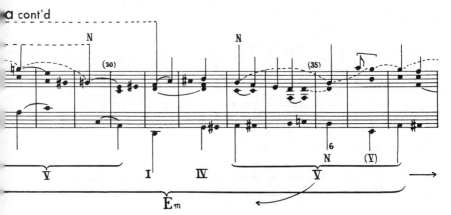

a cont'd

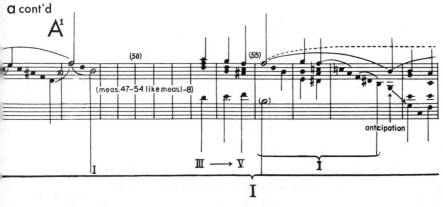

477 cont'd

a cont'd

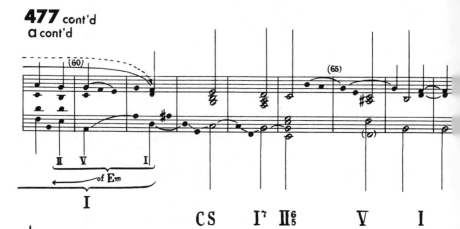

b cont'd

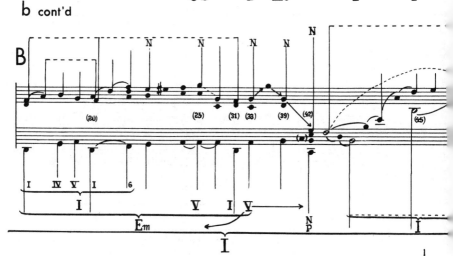

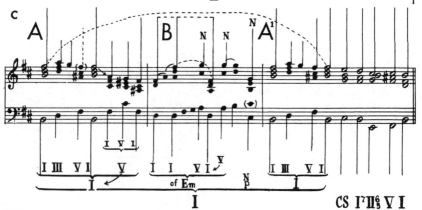

250

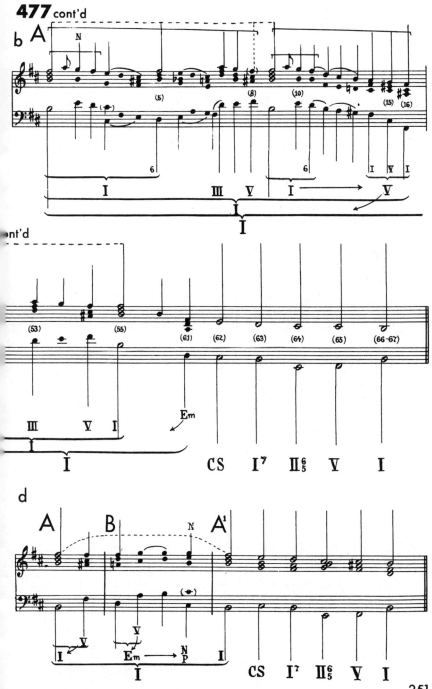

a

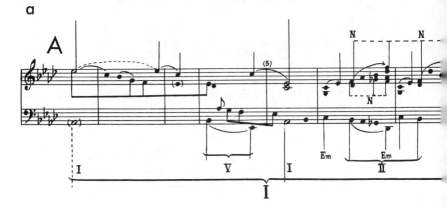

a cont'd

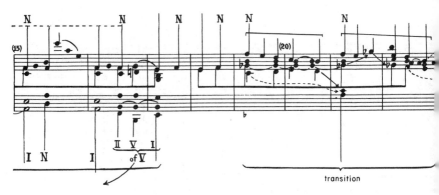

a cont'd

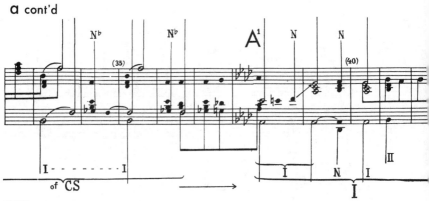

cont'd

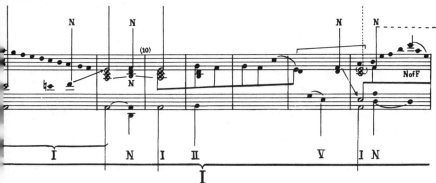

cont'd

B

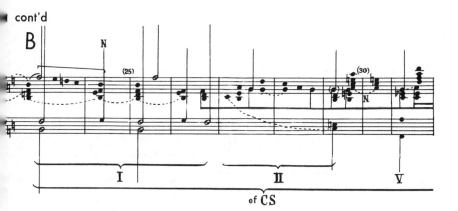

of CS

cont'd

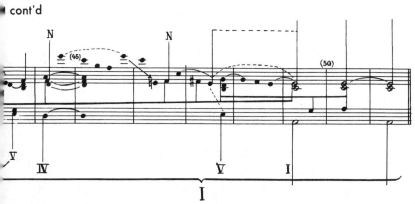

478 cont'd

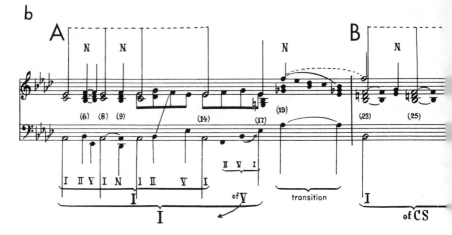

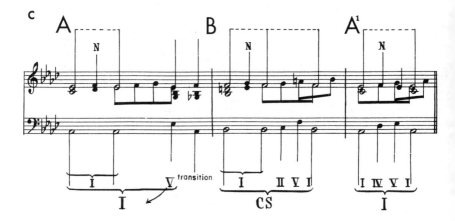

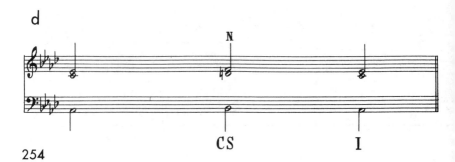

b cont'd

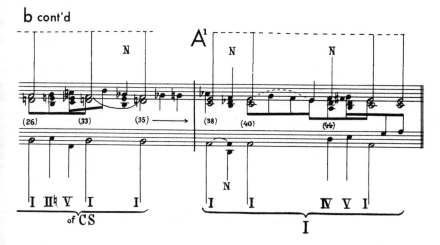

e

Melodic prolongations:

GESUALDO Madrigal: Io pur respiro

[From *HAM*, Vol. I, No. 161]

a

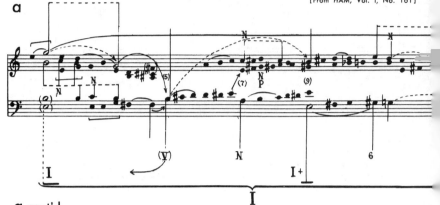

a cont'd

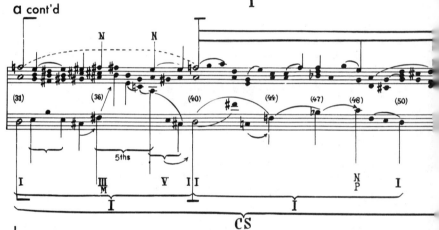

b

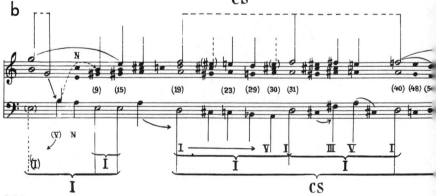

cont'd

BARTÓK Piano Concerto No. 3.
1st movement

a

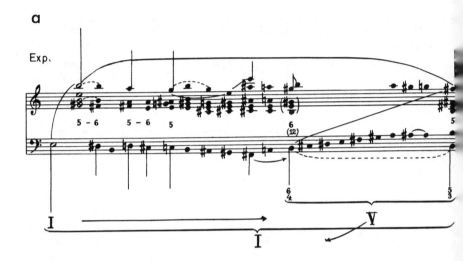

a cont'd

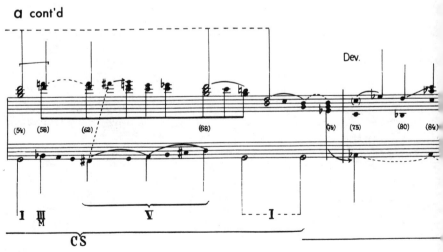

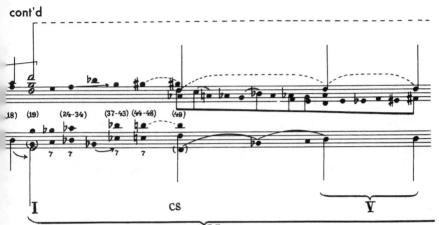

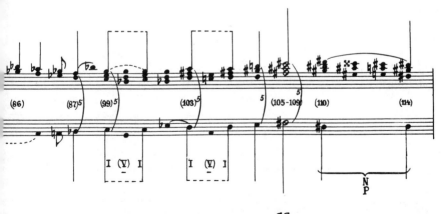

a cont'd

a cont'd

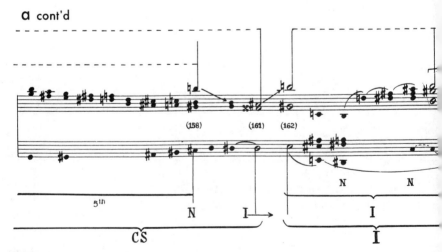

cont'd

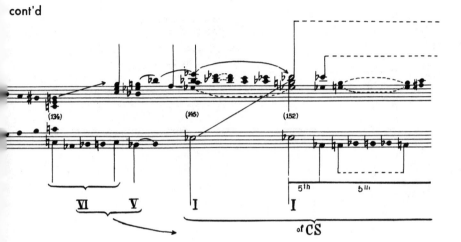

cont'd

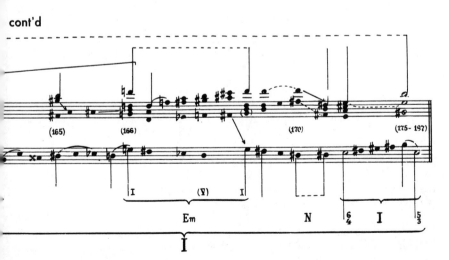

b

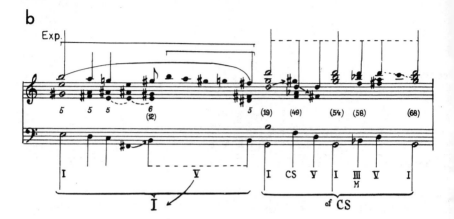

b cont'd

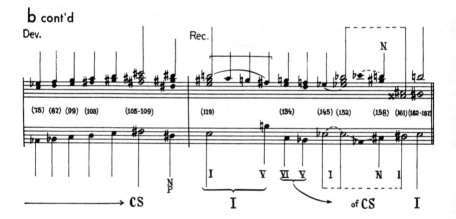

c

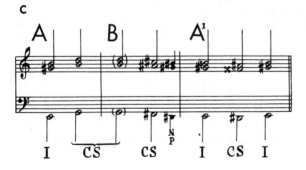

481

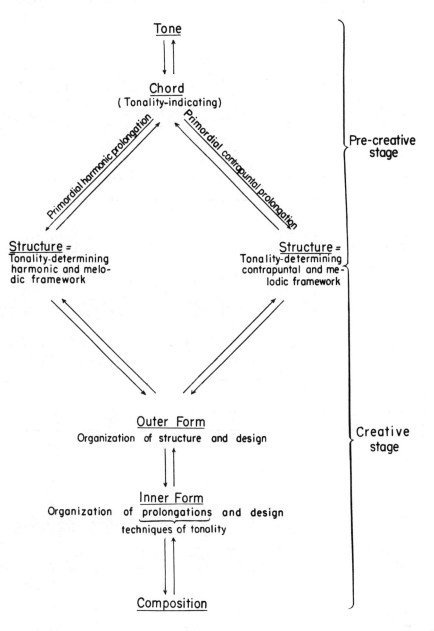

263

482 ## MARENZIO Madrigal: Io piango

[From *SHM*, No. 18]

a

a cont'd

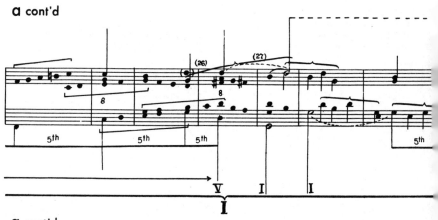

a cont'd

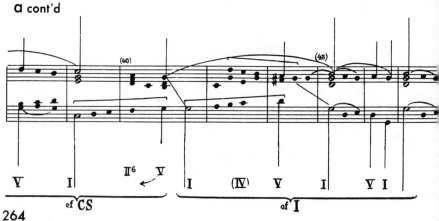

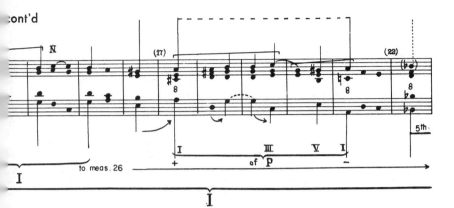

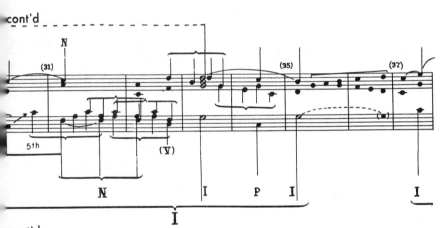

b

c

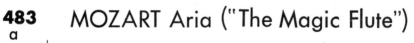

483 MOZART Aria ("The Magic Flute")

a

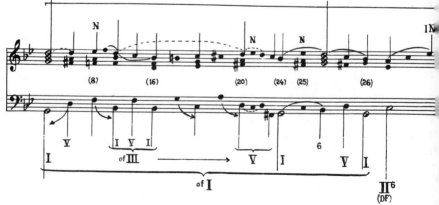

484 FRESCOBALDI Corrente

[From AMI, Vol. III, P. 207]

a

485 cont'd

a cont'd

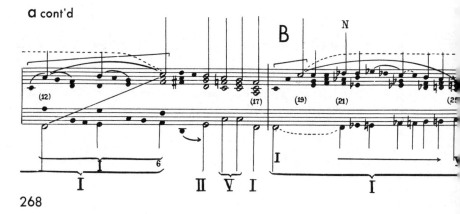

cont'd

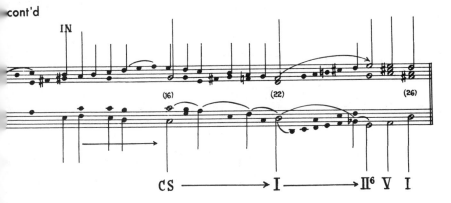

485   BRAHMS Feldeinsamkeit

a

486 FRESCOBALDI La Frescobalda

[From *EPM*, P. 33]

a

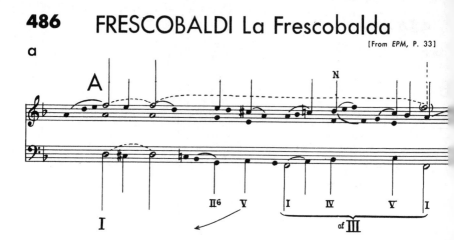

b

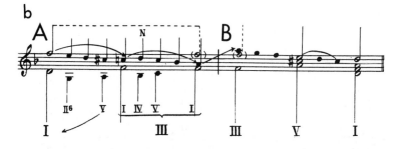

487 D. SCARLATTI Sonata, G Major, L. 490

a

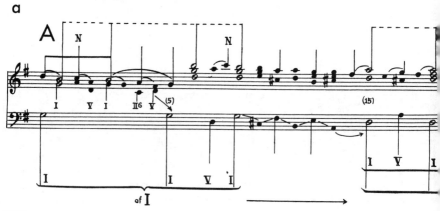

486 cont'd

cont'd

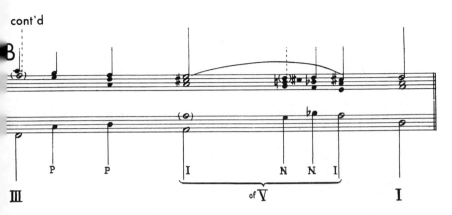

III   P   P   I   N   N   I   I

of V

c

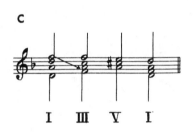

I   III   V   I

487 cont'd

cont'd

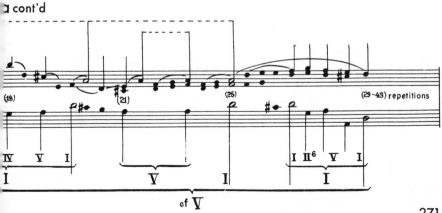

(29-43) repetitions

IV   V   I   I II⁶ V   I

I   V   I   I

of V

487 cont'd

a cont'd

488

WOLF In der Frühe

272

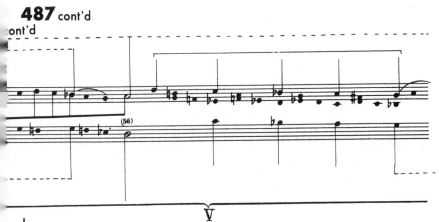

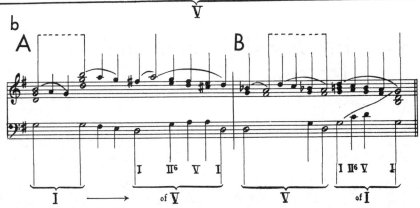

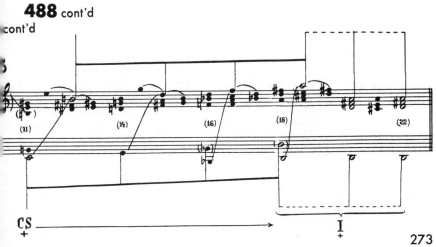

488 cont'd

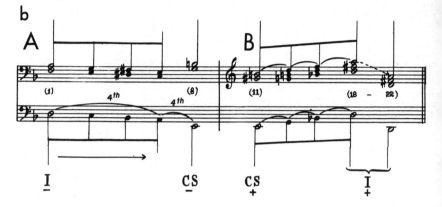

489 HINDEMITH Interludium (Ludus Tonalis)

488 cont'd

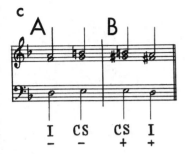

c

A   B

I   CS   CS   I
–   –   +   +

489 cont'd

ont'd

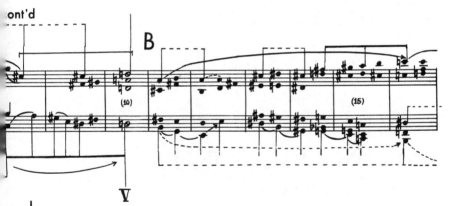

B

(10)   (15)

V

b

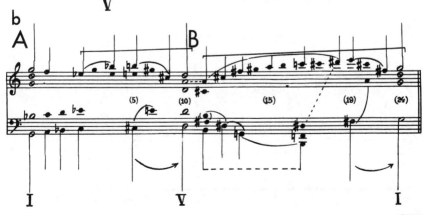

A   B

(5)   (10)   (15)   (19)   (24)

I   V   I

c

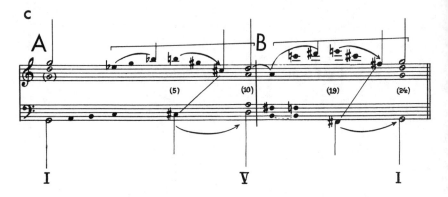

e

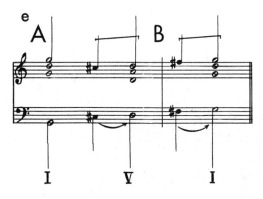

490 BYRD Pavane: The Earle of Salisbury

a

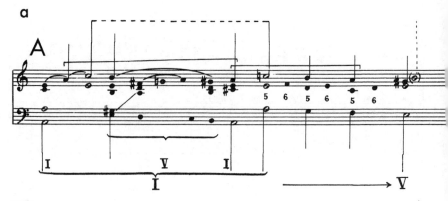

489 cont'd

d

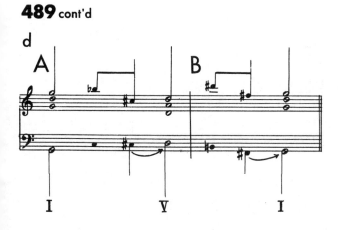

I   V   I

490 cont'd

a cont'd

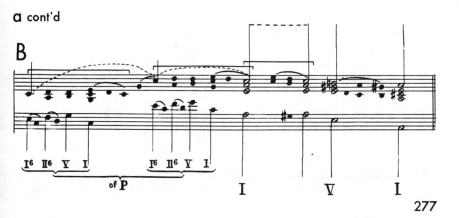

I⁶ II⁶ V I   I⁶ II⁶ V I

of P

I   V   I

277

b

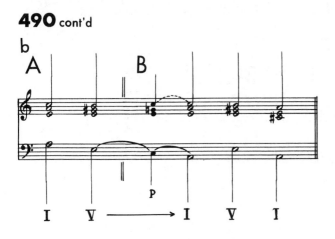

491   BEETHOVEN String Quartet,
Op 18, No. 5. 3rd movement

a

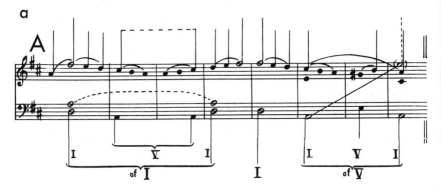

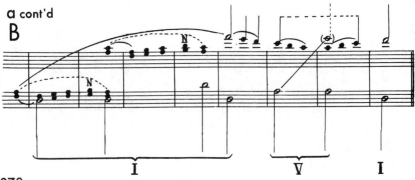

b

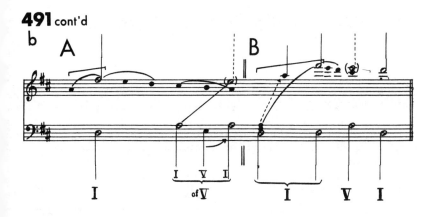

492 CHOPIN Prelude, Op 28, No. 1

a

b

493 BACH Little Prelude, G minor

494 BRAHMS Waltz, Op 39, No. 8

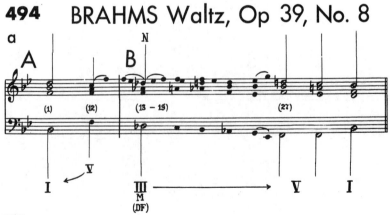

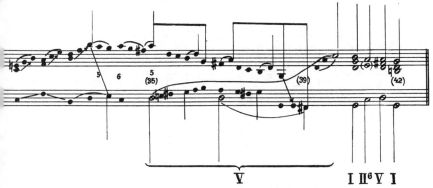

495 BACH Minuet 2 (Partita No. 1)

496

a

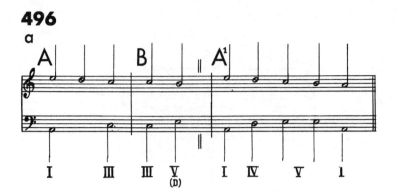

497 SCHUBERT Symphony, B minor.
1st movement

a

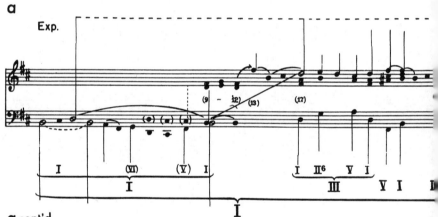

a cont'd

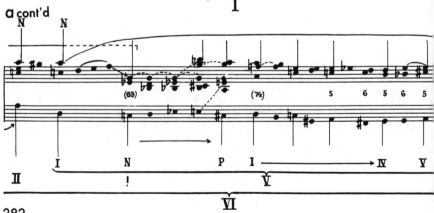

b

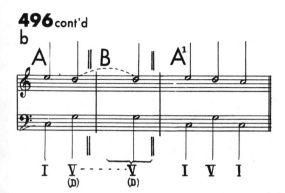

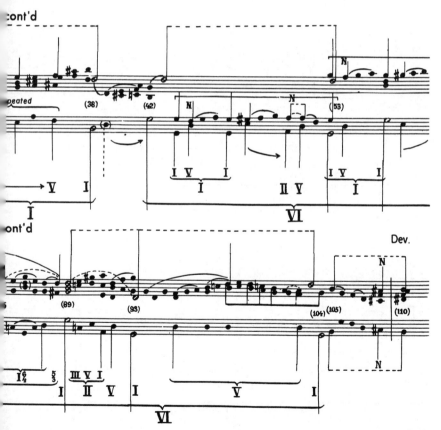

a cont'd

Dev.

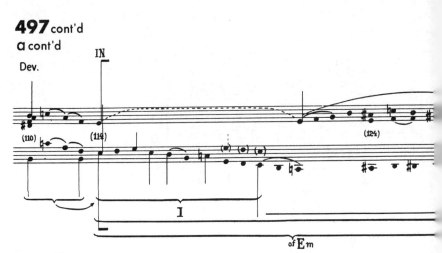

a cont'd

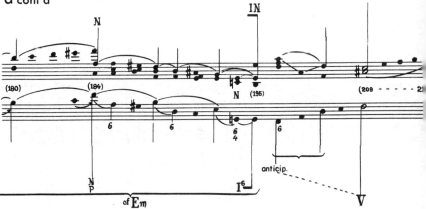

a cont'd

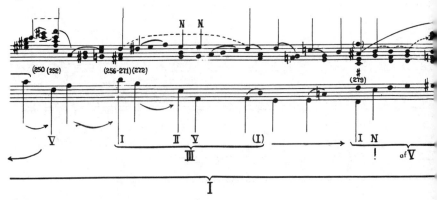

497 cont'd

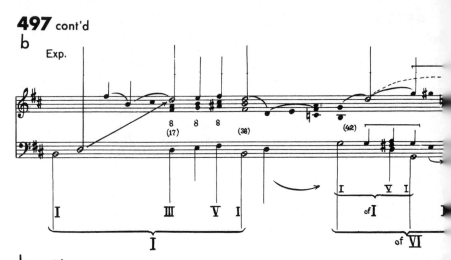

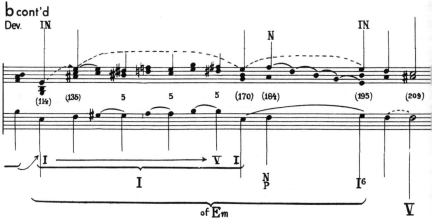

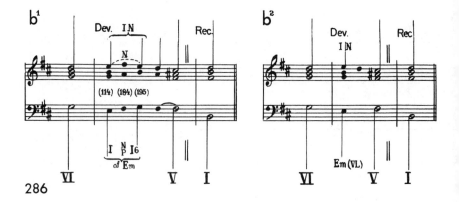

cont'd

cont'd

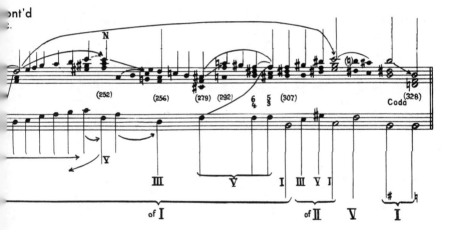

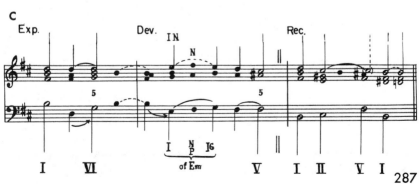

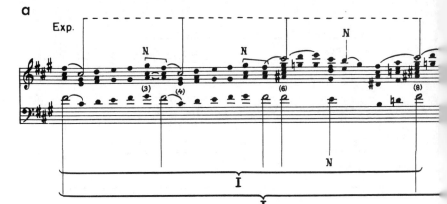

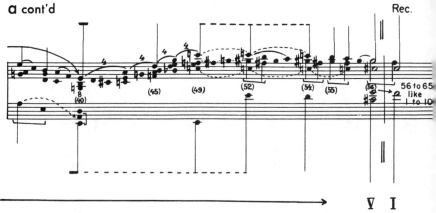

ont'd

cont'd
ev.

to E meas. 40

to E meas 40

cont'd

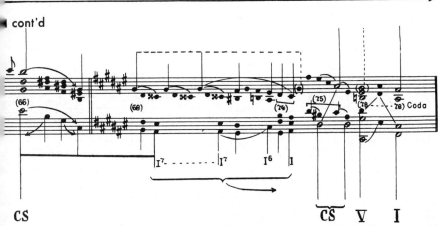

CS

CS   V   I

498 cont'd

b

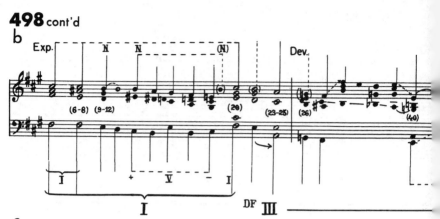

c

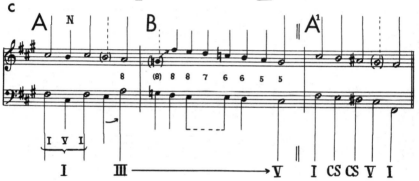

500 CHOPIN Nocturne, Op 9, No. 2

a

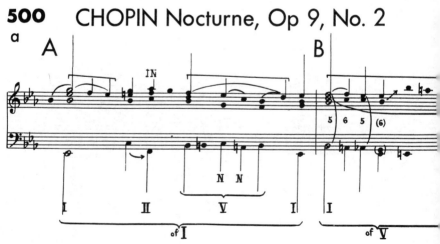

498 cont'd

ont'd

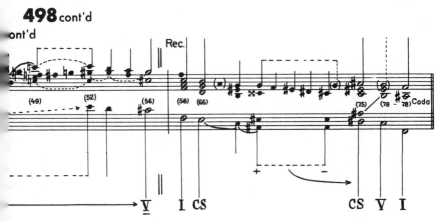

499 CHOPIN Mazurka, Op 17, No. 2

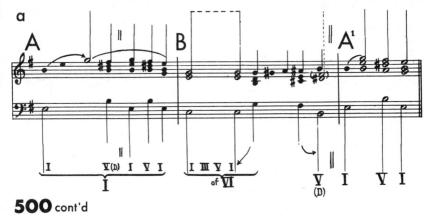

500 cont'd

cont'd

500 cont'd

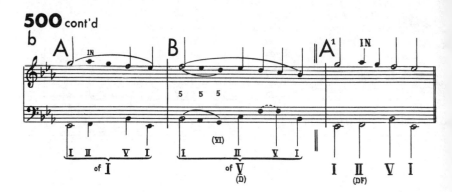

501 cont'd

a cont'd

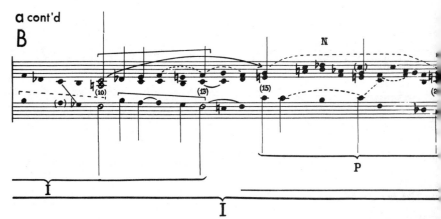

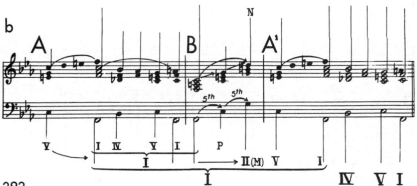

MONTEVERDI Madrigal:
Lasciatemi morire

a

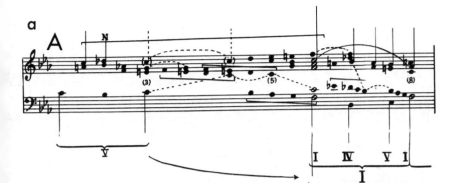

cont'd

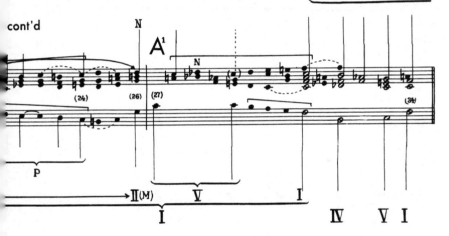

c

a

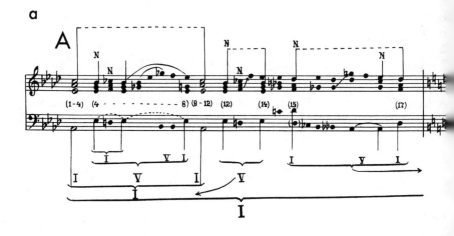

a cont'd

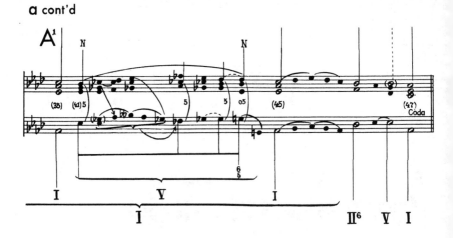

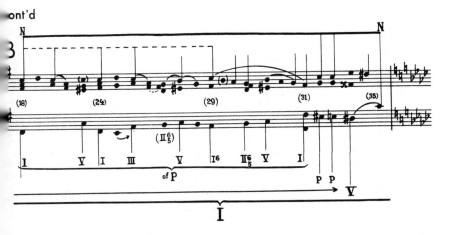

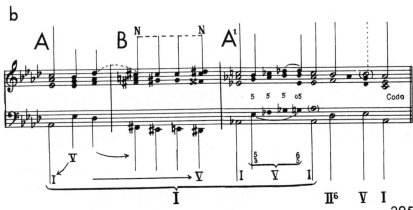

503 BRAHMS Symphony No. 3.
1st movement

a

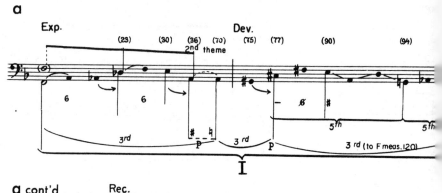

a cont'd

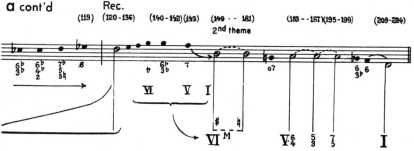

504 BARTÓK Bourrée (Mikrokosmos, Bk IV)

a

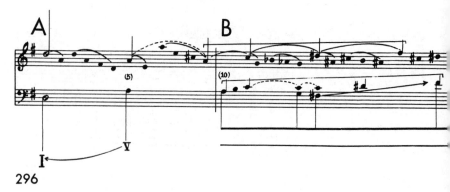

cont'd

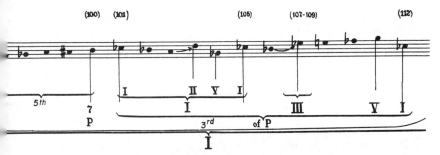

b

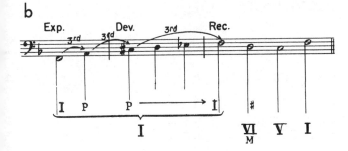

cont'd

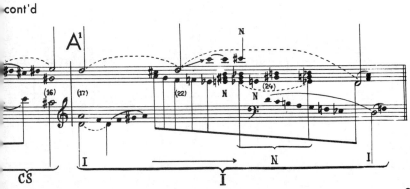

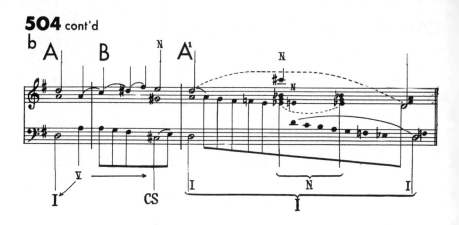

504 cont'd

505 HINDEMITH Piano Sonata No. 2
1st movement

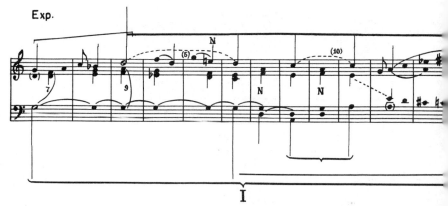

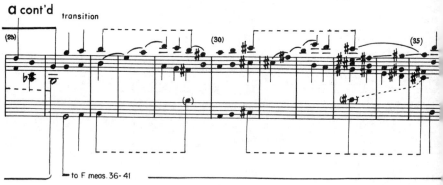

504 cont'd

C

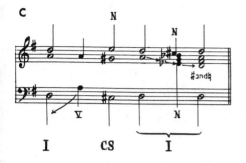

I   CS   I

505 cont'd

:ont'd

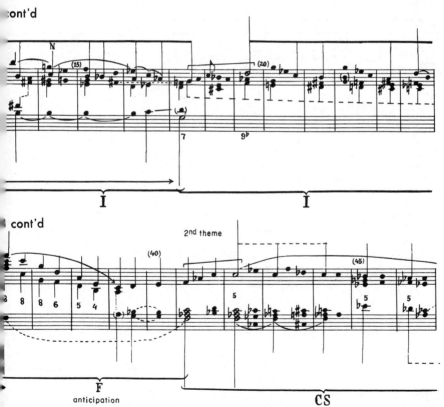

cont'd

2nd theme

F
anticipation

CS

505 cont'd

a cont'd

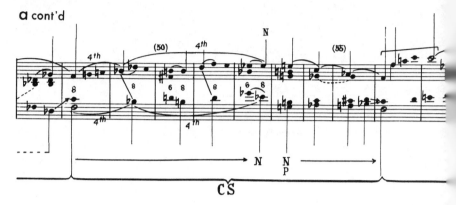

a cont'd

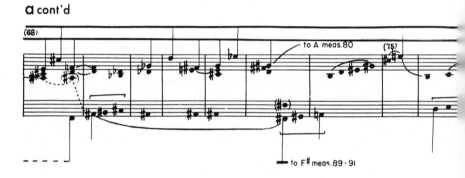

a cont'd

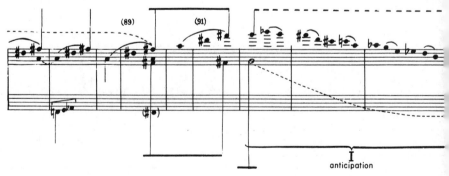

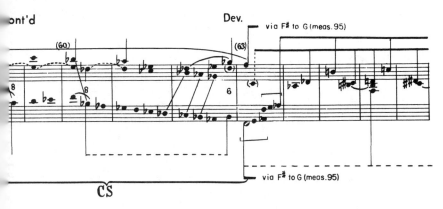

cont'd

Dev.

via F# to G (meas. 95)

(60) (63)

via F# to G (meas. 95)

CS

cont'd

(80) N N (85)

N N

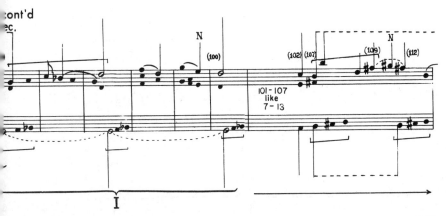

cont'd
ec.

N

(100) (102) (107) (109) N (112)

101-107
like
7-13

I

a cont'd

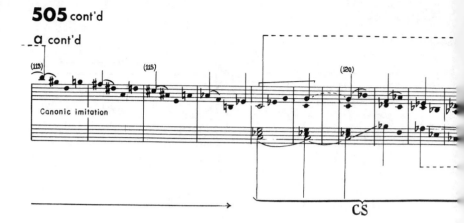

Canonic imitation

CS

a cont'd

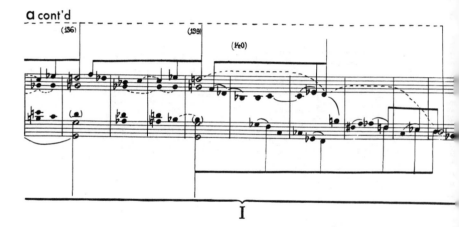

I

b

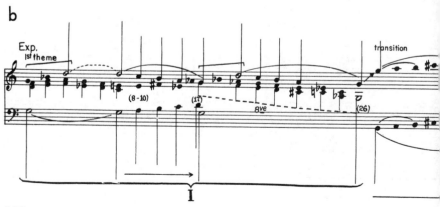

Exp.
1st theme

transition

I

cont'd

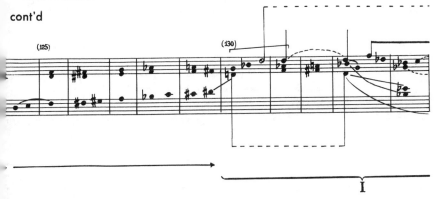

cont'd

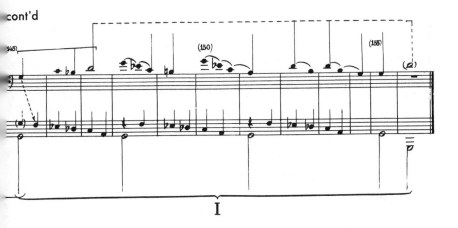

cont'd

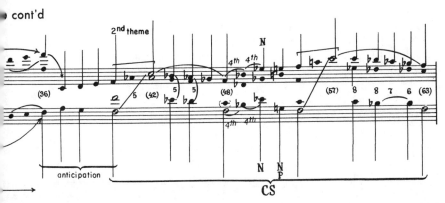

b cont'd

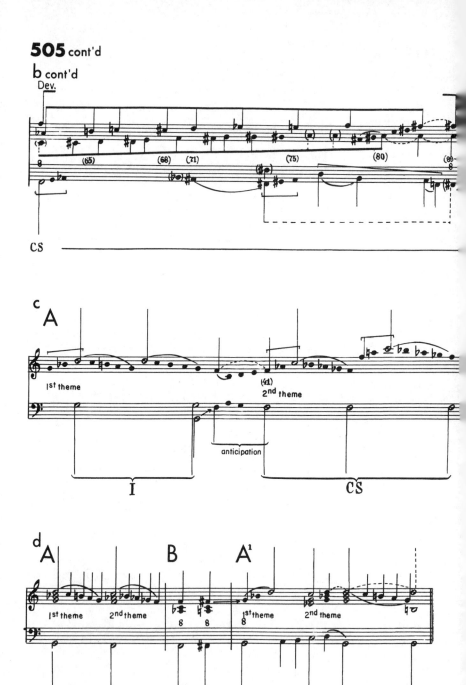

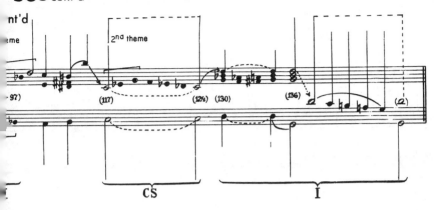

nt'd

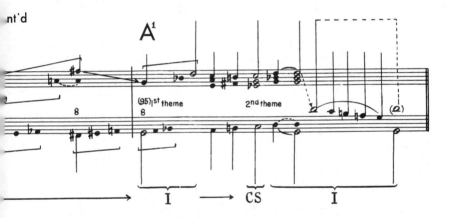

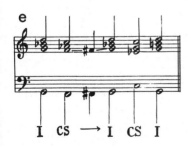

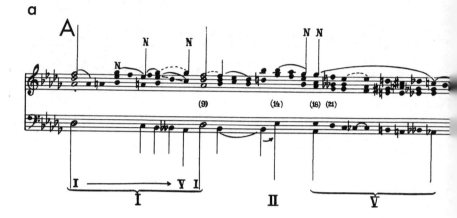

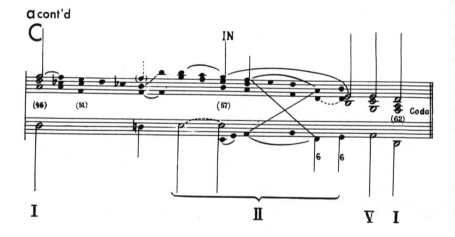

cont'd

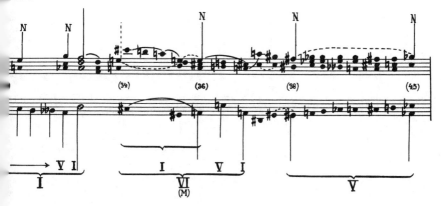

b

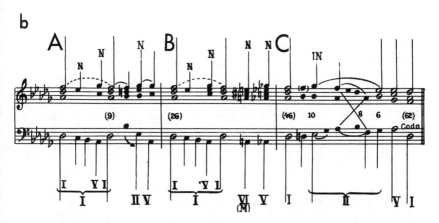

507 MOZART Fantasia, C minor, K. 475

a
Adagio

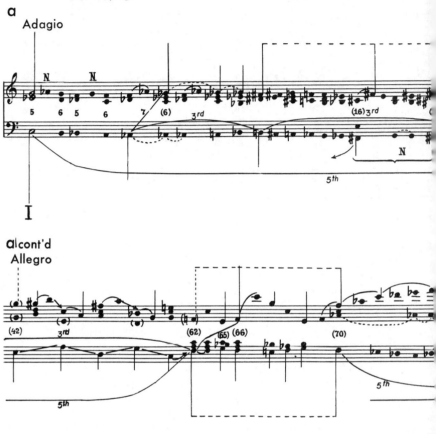

a cont'd
Allegro

a cont'd
Andantino

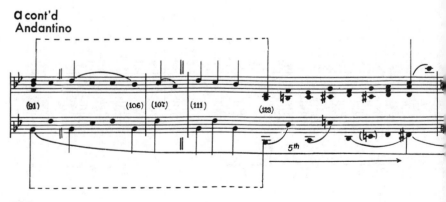

cont'd

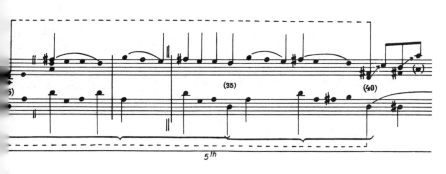

cont'd

cont'd
più Allegro
to A♭ meas. 143

a cont'd

b

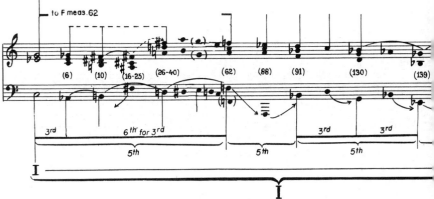

c

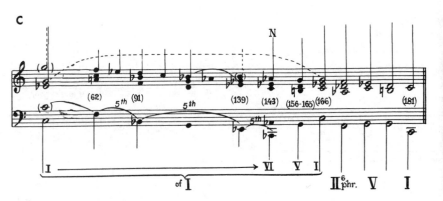

507 cont'd

ont'd

cont'd

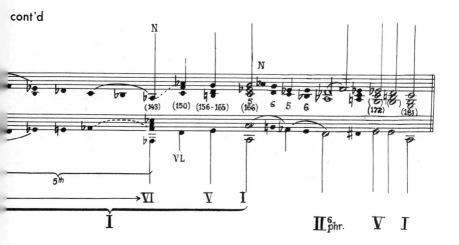

508 CHOPIN Nocturne, Op 37, No. 2

a

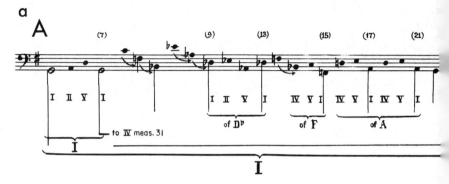

a cont'd

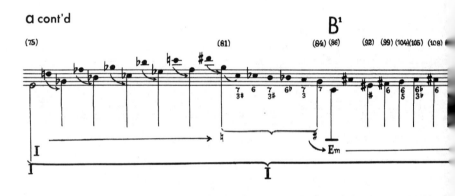

b

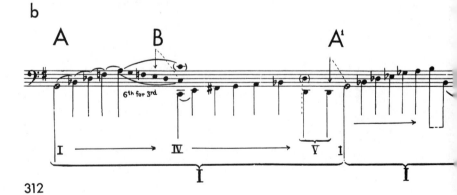

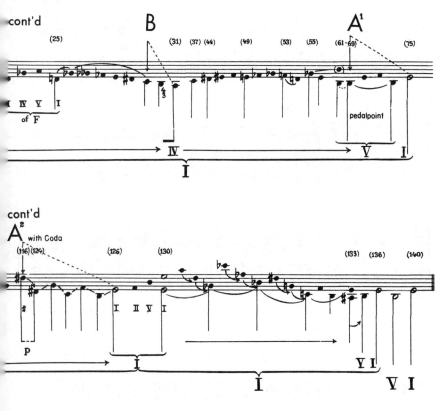

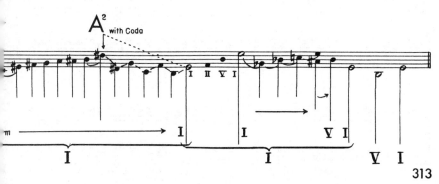

313

509 ## LASSO Christe Dei soboles

[From *HDM*, Vol. I, P. 333]

Part III Chapter Two

510 ## ALLELUIA ANGELUS DOMINI

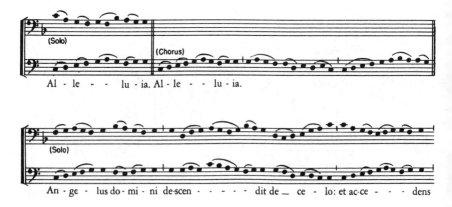

re-vol - - - - vit la - - - pi-dem et __ se-de-bat su-per e-um. ____

[From *HAM*, Vol. I, No. 26c]

511   BENEDICAMUS DOMINO
(School of St. Martial)

Be - - - - - - - - - - - ne - - - - - - - - - - -

etc.

di - - - - - - - - - - - - - - ca - - - mus ____

[From *HDM*, Vol. I, P. 179]

a

N

b   Be - ne - di - ca - mus

c

512 BENEDICAT ERGO (School of Compostela)

Be - ne - di - cat er - go plebs fi - de - - - lis

do - - - - - - - - - - - - - - - - - - mi - - no

[From *HDM*, Vol. I, P. 182]

a

a cont'd

513 VIDERUNT HEMANUEL (School of St. Martial)

Vi - de - - runt ____ He - - ma - nu - - - - - - - - el

[From *HAM*, Vol. I, No. 27a]

a

C?

G

514 LEONINUS Alleluia Pascha

Alleluia, etc.

[From AUDM, PP. 94-95]

a

317

515   # ORGANUM (Style of Perotinus)

[From *HAM*, Vol. I, No. 31]

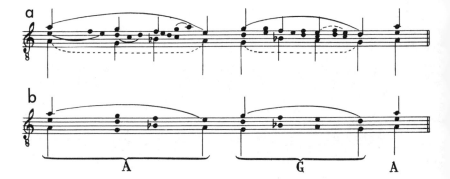

516   # PEROTINUS Organum Triplum

[From HDM, Vol. I, P. 226]

a

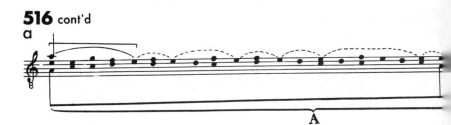

A

a cont'd

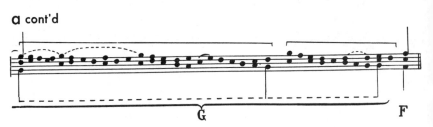

G   F

517   MOTET

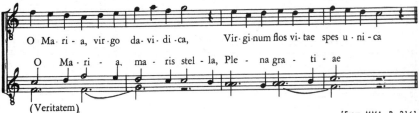

O Ma·ri·a, vir·go da·vi·di·ca,   Vir·gi·num flos vi·tae spes u·ni·ca

O   Ma·ri·a,   ma·ris stel·la, Ple·na gra·ti·ae

(Veritatem)

[From MMA, P. 316]

a

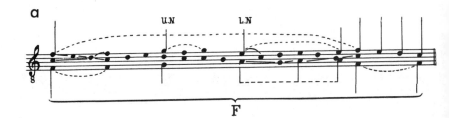

U.N   L.N

F

b

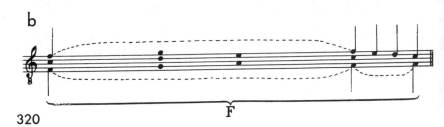

F

nt'd

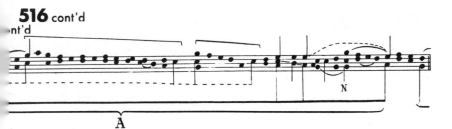

A

b

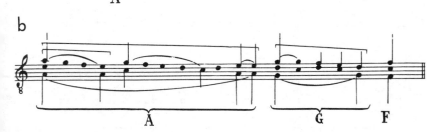

A   G   F

518   MOTET

Quant flou - rist la vi - o - le - te, La rose et la flour de glay,

Non _____ or - pha - num te de - se - ram. Sed ef - fe - ram

Et gaudebit.

[From CM, No. 67]

a

F   Motetus

b   c

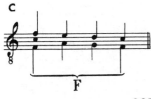

F   F

519 **MOTET**

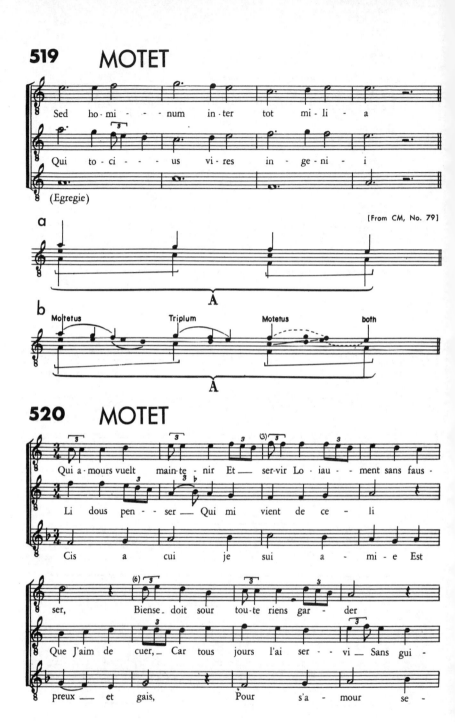

Sed ho-mi-num in-ter tot mi-li-a

Qui to-ci-us vi-res in-ge-ni-i

(Egregie)

[From CM, No. 79]

a

A

b

Motetus   Triplum   Motetus   both

A

520 **MOTET**

Qui a-mours vuelt main-te-nir Et ser-vir Lo-iau-ment sans faus-

Li dous pen-ser Qui mi vient de ce-li

Cis a cui je sui a-mi-e Est

ser, Bien se doit sour tou-te riens gar-der

Que J'aim de cuer, Car tous jours l'ai ser-vi Sans gui-

preux et gais, Pour s'a-mour se-

322

520 cont'd

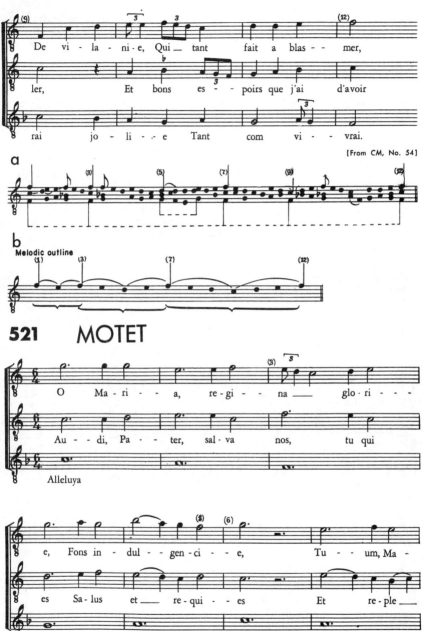

[From CM, No. 54]

a

b

Melodic outline

521 MOTET

O Ma - ri - - a, re - gi - - na — glo ri - - -

Au - - di, Pa - - ter, sal - va nos, tu qui

Alleluya

e, Fons in - dul - - gen - ci - - e, Tu - - um, Ma -

es Sa - lus et — re - qui - - es Et re - ple —

323

521 cont'd

ter, ex- o- - ra — Fi - li - - um, Ut pro no - -

nos spi - ri - tu di - vi - - no, Ut — gra - ci -

a

C

b

522 MOTET

L'au · tre jour par un ma - - - ti - net M'en — a - -

Hier — ma - ti - net Trou - vai sans son

Omnes,

lai - es be - ni - ant Et trou·vai sans son ber - ge - ret

ber - ge - ret Pas - toure es - ga - re - - - e;

[From CM, No. 40]

521 cont'd

bis ex - o - - - ret _____ Do - mi - - - - - num.

as a - ga - - - mus _____ Do - mi - - - - - no.

cont'd

[From CM, No. 9]

A   G   F

522 cont'd

a

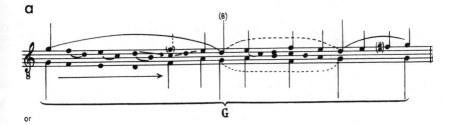

G

or

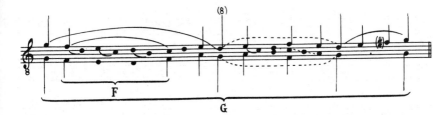

F

G

523 RONDEAU: Amours et ma dame aussi

A-mours et ma dame aus - - si jointes mains vous proi mer - chi!
etc.

[From MMA, P. 322]

a

524 ADAM DE LA HALLE Li maus d'amer (1st part)

Li maus d'a - - - mer me plaist miex a sen - - - - - tir

K'a main-ta- mant ne fait li dons de joi - e, etc.

[From HAM, Vol. I, No. 36a]

525 ADAM DE LA HALLE Rondeau: Tant con je vivrai

Tant con je vi - - - vrai N'a - me - - -

rai   au - - - - - - - trui   que _____ vous. etc.

[From HAM, Vol. I, No. 36b]

a

526   MOTET

Entre, etc.

Chief, etc.

Aptatur

[From CM, No. 24]

a

I   V   I

527 MOTET

Au dous, etc.

Biaus, etc.

Manere

[From CM, No. 18]

528 MACHAUT Virelai (No. 38)

De _ tout . sui si con - for - - - te - e

[From MW, Vol. I]

529 MACHAUT Virelai (No. 32)

Da - me mon _ cuer em - por - tes

[From MW, Vol. I]

530 MACHAUT Ballade (No. 3)

(flour etc.)

[From MW, Vol. I]

a

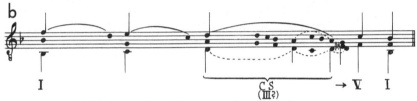

b

I   C S (III?)   → V   I

531 MACHAUT Rondeau (No. 13)

Da - me, — se —— vous n'a - vez a - per - ce - u

que ———————— je vous aim de ———— cuer, etc.

a

b

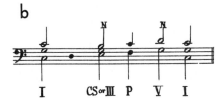

532   MACHAUT Virelai (No. 31)

1.5 Plus du - - re_ que un dy - a - - mant   ne que_ pier-re_ d'a - - y -
4. par un_ ac - cueil _ at -trai - - ant,   m'ont au _ cuer en _ re - -sgar-

mant est _ vo dur - -té,   da - me qui_ n'a -ves pi - - té, de_
dant si _ fort na - -vré   que_ ja - mais_ joi - e n'a - - vré, ju - -

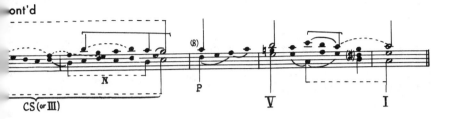

vostre a - - mant qu'o ci - - es en _ de - - si - rant vostre _ a - mi - tié.

sques a - - tant que vo _ gra -ce _ quil _ a - tant m'au - - res don - - né.

2. Da - me, _ vo pu - - re _ biau - té qui _ tou - tes _ passe,

3. simple et _ plein d'u - - mi - li - té, de _ dou - ceur _ fi - -

a _ mon - gré, et _ vo _ sam - blant

ne _ pa - ré, en _ sous - ri - - - ant,

[From MW, Vol. I]

331

532 cont'd

a
A

I

a cont'd

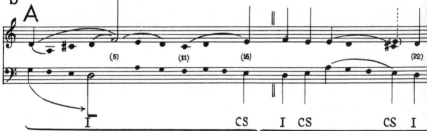

B

I   CS   I   CS I

b
A

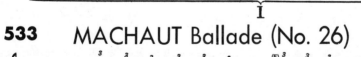

CS I CS   CS I

I

I

533 MACHAUT Ballade (No. 26)

Don - nez —————— signeurs, donnez a toutes mains, ne re te
S'on - neur a vez et de richesses meins, pour vous se

332

ront li _ grant et   li

533 cont'd

l'on · neur.   me · neur   cha — — scuns ___ di —

ra: ___ ci a vaillant si·gneur. Et terre aus·siqu'est despen . . . . . du — — — — — e

a

A

(3)   (6)   N   (9)

a cont'd

B

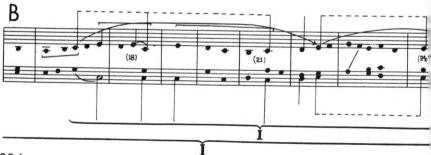

(18)   (21)   (24)

533 cont'd

vaut trop mieus que ter - - re per - - du - - - - - - - - - - - e

[From MW, Vol. I]

cont'd

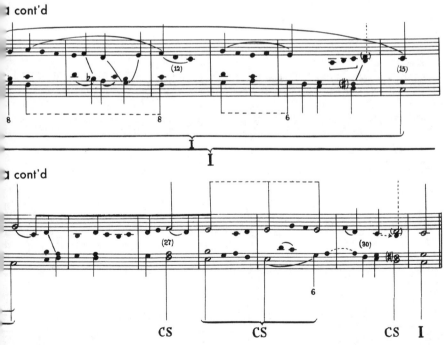

CS   CS   CS I

533 cont'd

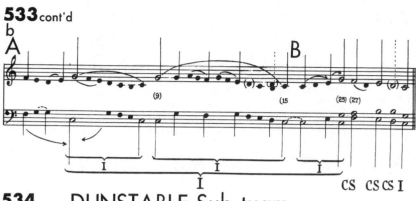

534 DUNSTABLE Sub tuam
protectionem

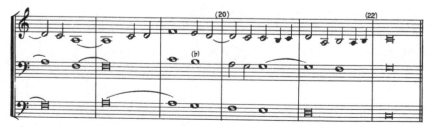

[From *TC*, Vol. I, P. 198]

534 cont'd

535 DUNSTABLE Puisque m'amour

Puis-que m'a mour— m'a pris en ——— des ———— plai-

sir

535 cont'd

a

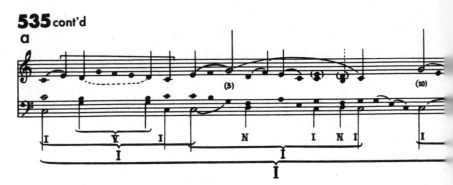

536 DUFAY Adieu m'amour

535 cont'd

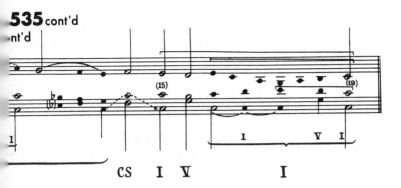

536 cont'd

Le di - re_a dieu ___ tant ___ fort ___ me bles - - - - - - se

Le di - re_a-dieu tant ___ fort me bles - - - - - - - - se ___

Qu'il me sam - ble que mo - rir ___ doy - - - - - - - -

Qu'il me sam - ble que mo - rir doy - - - - - - - - - -

e

e.

a

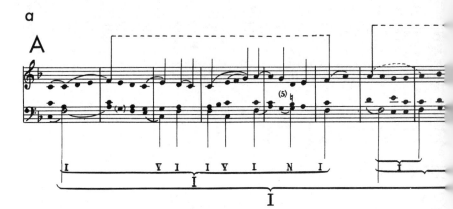

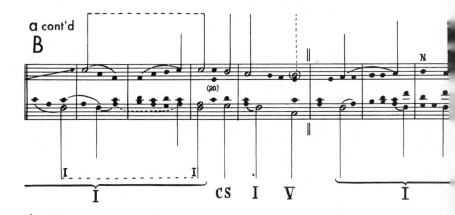

b

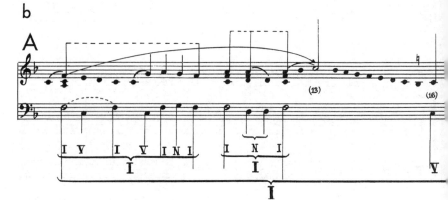

536cont'd

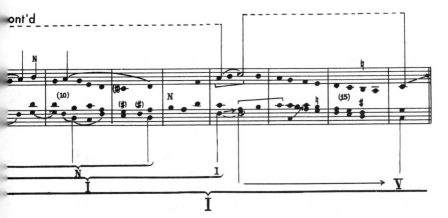

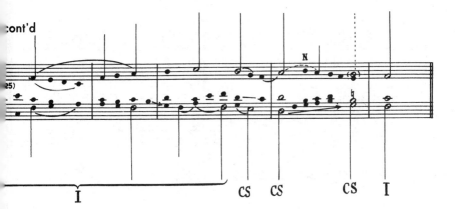

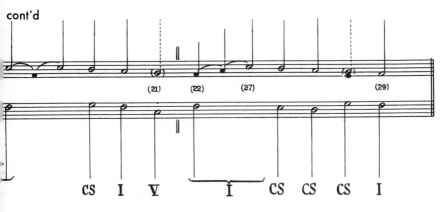

537   OBRECHT Osanna (Missa: Je ne demande)

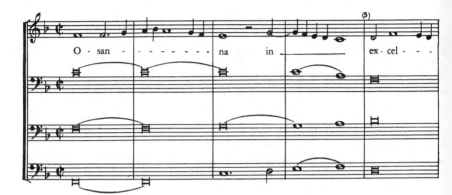

O - san - - - - - - - - na   in _____ ex - cel - - -

- - - - - - - - sis,   etc.

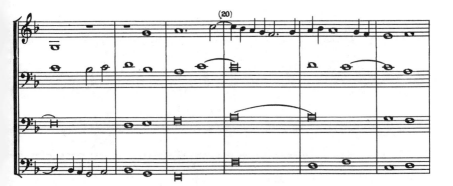

[From *WJO, Missen,* Vol. 1, No. 1]

a

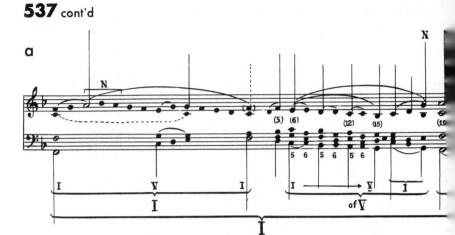

b

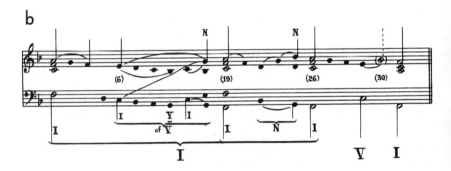

538 ISAAC Kyrie (Missa Carminum)

Ky - - ri - - - - e ——— e - - lei - - son, etc.

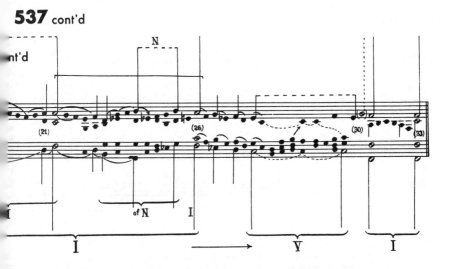

[From DAS CHORWERK, Vol. VII]

a

539   JOSQUIN Motet: O Domine Jesu
Christe (1st part)

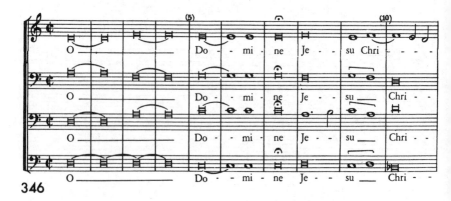

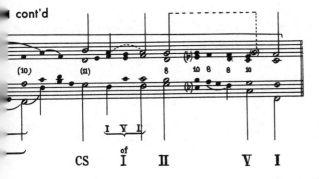

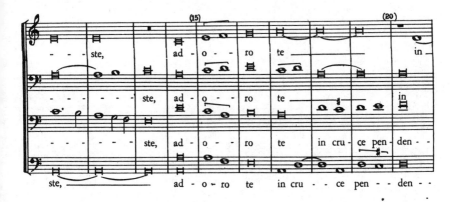

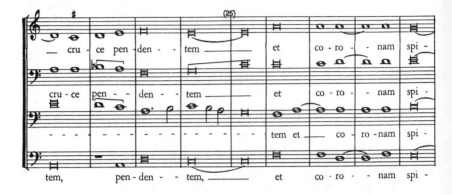

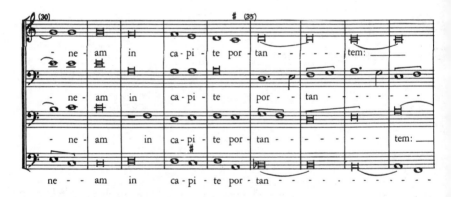

a

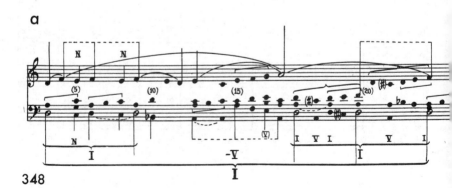

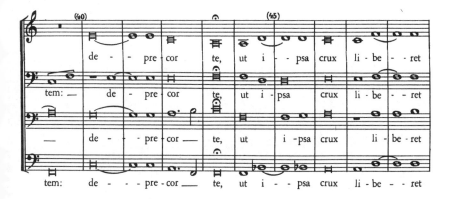

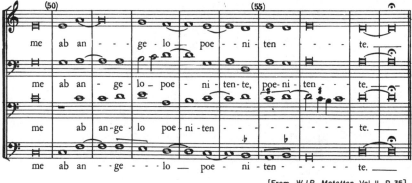

[From *WJP, Motetten,* Vol. II, P. 35]

cont'd

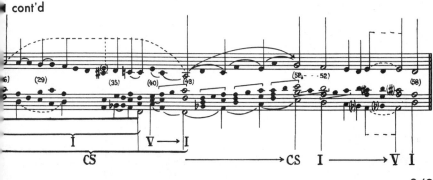

A CATALOG OF SELECTED
DOVER BOOKS
IN ALL FIELDS OF INTEREST

A CATALOG OF SELECTED DOVER
BOOKS IN ALL FIELDS OF INTEREST

CONCERNING THE SPIRITUAL IN ART, Wassily Kandinsky. Pioneering work by father of abstract art. Thoughts on color theory, nature of art. Analysis of earlier masters. 12 illustrations. 80pp. of text. 5⅜ x 8½.   23411-8

ANIMALS: 1,419 Copyright-Free Illustrations of Mammals, Birds, Fish, Insects, etc., Jim Harter (ed.). Clear wood engravings present, in extremely lifelike poses, over 1,000 species of animals. One of the most extensive pictorial sourcebooks of its kind. Captions. Index. 284pp. 9 x 12.   23766-4

CELTIC ART: The Methods of Construction, George Bain. Simple geometric techniques for making Celtic interlacements, spirals, Kells-type initials, animals, humans, etc. Over 500 illustrations. 160pp. 9 x 12. (Available in U.S. only.)   22923-8

AN ATLAS OF ANATOMY FOR ARTISTS, Fritz Schider. Most thorough reference work on art anatomy in the world. Hundreds of illustrations, including selections from works by Vesalius, Leonardo, Goya, Ingres, Michelangelo, others. 593 illustrations. 192pp. 7⅛ x 10¼.   20241-0

CELTIC HAND STROKE-BY-STROKE (Irish Half-Uncial from "The Book of Kells"): An Arthur Baker Calligraphy Manual, Arthur Baker. Complete guide to creating each letter of the alphabet in distinctive Celtic manner. Covers hand position, strokes, pens, inks, paper, more. Illustrated. 48pp. 8¼ x 11.   24336-2

EASY ORIGAMI, John Montroll. Charming collection of 32 projects (hat, cup, pelican, piano, swan, many more) specially designed for the novice origami hobbyist. Clearly illustrated easy-to-follow instructions insure that even beginning papercrafters will achieve successful results. 48pp. 8¼ x 11.   27298-2

THE COMPLETE BOOK OF BIRDHOUSE CONSTRUCTION FOR WOOD-WORKERS, Scott D. Campbell. Detailed instructions, illustrations, tables. Also data on bird habitat and instinct patterns. Bibliography. 3 tables. 63 illustrations in 15 figures. 48pp. 5¼ x 8½.   24407-5

BLOOMINGDALE'S ILLUSTRATED 1886 CATALOG: Fashions, Dry Goods and Housewares, Bloomingdale Brothers. Famed merchants' extremely rare catalog depicting about 1,700 products: clothing, housewares, firearms, dry goods, jewelry, more. Invaluable for dating, identifying vintage items. Also, copyright-free graphics for artists, designers. Co-published with Henry Ford Museum & Greenfield Village. 160pp. 8¼ x 11.   25780-0

HISTORIC COSTUME IN PICTURES, Braun & Schneider. Over 1,450 costumed figures in clearly detailed engravings–from dawn of civilization to end of 19th century. Captions. Many folk costumes. 256pp. 8⅜ x 11¾.   23150-X

STICKLEY CRAFTSMAN FURNITURE CATALOGS, Gustav Stickley and L. & J. G. Stickley. Beautiful, functional furniture in two authentic catalogs from 1910. 594 illustrations, including 277 photos, show settles, rockers, armchairs, reclining chairs, bookcases, desks, tables. 183pp. 6½ x 9¼. 23838-5

AMERICAN LOCOMOTIVES IN HISTORIC PHOTOGRAPHS: 1858 to 1949, Ron Ziel (ed.). A rare collection of 126 meticulously detailed official photographs, called "builder portraits," of American locomotives that majestically chronicle the rise of steam locomotive power in America. Introduction. Detailed captions. xi+ 129pp. 9 x 12. 27393-8

AMERICA'S LIGHTHOUSES: An Illustrated History, Francis Ross Holland, Jr. Delightfully written, profusely illustrated fact-filled survey of over 200 American lighthouses since 1716. History, anecdotes, technological advances, more. 240pp. 8 x 10¾. 25576-X

TOWARDS A NEW ARCHITECTURE, Le Corbusier. Pioneering manifesto by founder of "International School." Technical and aesthetic theories, views of industry, economics, relation of form to function, "mass-production split" and much more. Profusely illustrated. 320pp. 6⅛ x 9¼. (Available in U.S. only.) 25023-7

HOW THE OTHER HALF LIVES, Jacob Riis. Famous journalistic record, exposing poverty and degradation of New York slums around 1900, by major social reformer. 100 striking and influential photographs. 233pp. 10 x 7⅞. 22012-5

FRUIT KEY AND TWIG KEY TO TREES AND SHRUBS, William M. Harlow. One of the handiest and most widely used identification aids. Fruit key covers 120 deciduous and evergreen species; twig key 160 deciduous species. Easily used. Over 300 photographs. 126pp. 5⅜ x 8½. 20511-8

COMMON BIRD SONGS, Dr. Donald J. Borror. Songs of 60 most common U.S. birds: robins, sparrows, cardinals, bluejays, finches, more–arranged in order of increasing complexity. Up to 9 variations of songs of each species.
Cassette and manual 99911-4

ORCHIDS AS HOUSE PLANTS, Rebecca Tyson Northen. Grow cattleyas and many other kinds of orchids–in a window, in a case, or under artificial light. 63 illustrations. 148pp. 5⅜ x 8½. 23261-1

MONSTER MAZES, Dave Phillips. Masterful mazes at four levels of difficulty. Avoid deadly perils and evil creatures to find magical treasures. Solutions for all 32 exciting illustrated puzzles. 48pp. 8¼ x 11. 26005-4

MOZART'S DON GIOVANNI (DOVER OPERA LIBRETTO SERIES), Wolfgang Amadeus Mozart. Introduced and translated by Ellen H. Bleiler. Standard Italian libretto, with complete English translation. Convenient and thoroughly portable–an ideal companion for reading along with a recording or the performance itself. Introduction. List of characters. Plot summary. 121pp. 5¼ x 8½. 24944-1

TECHNICAL MANUAL AND DICTIONARY OF CLASSICAL BALLET, Gail Grant. Defines, explains, comments on steps, movements, poses and concepts. 15-page pictorial section. Basic book for student, viewer. 127pp. 5⅜ x 8½. 21843-0

THE CLARINET AND CLARINET PLAYING, David Pino. Lively, comprehensive work features suggestions about technique, musicianship, and musical interpretation, as well as guidelines for teaching, making your own reeds, and preparing for public performance. Includes an intriguing look at clarinet history. "A godsend," *The Clarinet,* Journal of the International Clarinet Society. Appendixes. 7 illus. 320pp. 5⅜ x 8½. 40270-3

HOLLYWOOD GLAMOR PORTRAITS, John Kobal (ed.). 145 photos from 1926-49. Harlow, Gable, Bogart, Bacall; 94 stars in all. Full background on photographers, technical aspects. 160pp. 8⅜ x 11¼. 23352-9

THE ANNOTATED CASEY AT THE BAT: A Collection of Ballads about the Mighty Casey/Third, Revised Edition, Martin Gardner (ed.). Amusing sequels and parodies of one of America's best-loved poems: Casey's Revenge, Why Casey Whiffed, Casey's Sister at the Bat, others. 256pp. 5⅜ x 8½. 28598-7

THE RAVEN AND OTHER FAVORITE POEMS, Edgar Allan Poe. Over 40 of the author's most memorable poems: "The Bells," "Ulalume," "Israfel," "To Helen," "The Conqueror Worm," "Eldorado," "Annabel Lee," many more. Alphabetic lists of titles and first lines. 64pp. 5³⁄₁₆ x 8¼. 26685-0

PERSONAL MEMOIRS OF U. S. GRANT, Ulysses Simpson Grant. Intelligent, deeply moving firsthand account of Civil War campaigns, considered by many the finest military memoirs ever written. Includes letters, historic photographs, maps and more. 528pp. 6⅛ x 9¼. 28587-1

ANCIENT EGYPTIAN MATERIALS AND INDUSTRIES, A. Lucas and J. Harris. Fascinating, comprehensive, thoroughly documented text describes this ancient civilization's vast resources and the processes that incorporated them in daily life, including the use of animal products, building materials, cosmetics, perfumes and incense, fibers, glazed ware, glass and its manufacture, materials used in the mummification process, and much more. 544pp. 6⅛ x 9¼. (Available in U.S. only.) 40446-3

RUSSIAN STORIES/RUSSKIE RASSKAZY: A Dual-Language Book, edited by Gleb Struve. Twelve tales by such masters as Chekhov, Tolstoy, Dostoevsky, Pushkin, others. Excellent word-for-word English translations on facing pages, plus teaching and study aids, Russian/English vocabulary, biographical/critical introductions, more. 416pp. 5⅜ x 8½. 26244-8

PHILADELPHIA THEN AND NOW: 60 Sites Photographed in the Past and Present, Kenneth Finkel and Susan Oyama. Rare photographs of City Hall, Logan Square, Independence Hall, Betsy Ross House, other landmarks juxtaposed with contemporary views. Captures changing face of historic city. Introduction. Captions. 128pp. 8¼ x 11. 25790-8

AIA ARCHITECTURAL GUIDE TO NASSAU AND SUFFOLK COUNTIES, LONG ISLAND, The American Institute of Architects, Long Island Chapter, and the Society for the Preservation of Long Island Antiquities. Comprehensive, well-researched and generously illustrated volume brings to life over three centuries of Long Island's great architectural heritage. More than 240 photographs with authoritative, extensively detailed captions. 176pp. 8¼ x 11. 26946-9

NORTH AMERICAN INDIAN LIFE: Customs and Traditions of 23 Tribes, Elsie Clews Parsons (ed.). 27 fictionalized essays by noted anthropologists examine religion, customs, government, additional facets of life among the Winnebago, Crow, Zuni, Eskimo, other tribes. 480pp. 6⅛ x 9¼. 27377-6

FRANK LLOYD WRIGHT'S DANA HOUSE, Donald Hoffmann. Pictorial essay of residential masterpiece with over 160 interior and exterior photos, plans, elevations, sketches and studies. 128pp. 9¼ x 10¾. 29120-0

THE MALE AND FEMALE FIGURE IN MOTION: 60 Classic Photographic Sequences, Eadweard Muybridge. 60 true-action photographs of men and women walking, running, climbing, bending, turning, etc., reproduced from rare 19th-century masterpiece. vi + 121pp. 9 x 12. 24745-7

1001 QUESTIONS ANSWERED ABOUT THE SEASHORE, N. J. Berrill and Jacquelyn Berrill. Queries answered about dolphins, sea snails, sponges, starfish, fishes, shore birds, many others. Covers appearance, breeding, growth, feeding, much more. 305pp. 5¼ x 8¼. 23366-9

ATTRACTING BIRDS TO YOUR YARD, William J. Weber. Easy-to-follow guide offers advice on how to attract the greatest diversity of birds: birdhouses, feeders, water and waterers, much more. 96pp. 5³⁄₁₆ x 8¼. 28927-3

MEDICINAL AND OTHER USES OF NORTH AMERICAN PLANTS: A Historical Survey with Special Reference to the Eastern Indian Tribes, Charlotte Erichsen-Brown. Chronological historical citations document 500 years of usage of plants, trees, shrubs native to eastern Canada, northeastern U.S. Also complete identifying information. 343 illustrations. 544pp. 6½ x 9¼. 25951-X

STORYBOOK MAZES, Dave Phillips. 23 stories and mazes on two-page spreads: Wizard of Oz, Treasure Island, Robin Hood, etc. Solutions. 64pp. 8¼ x 11. 23628-5

AMERICAN NEGRO SONGS: 230 Folk Songs and Spirituals, Religious and Secular, John W. Work. This authoritative study traces the African influences of songs sung and played by black Americans at work, in church, and as entertainment. The author discusses the lyric significance of such songs as "Swing Low, Sweet Chariot," "John Henry," and others and offers the words and music for 230 songs. Bibliography. Index of Song Titles. 272pp. 6½ x 9¼. 40271-1

MOVIE-STAR PORTRAITS OF THE FORTIES, John Kobal (ed.). 163 glamor, studio photos of 106 stars of the 1940s: Rita Hayworth, Ava Gardner, Marlon Brando, Clark Gable, many more. 176pp. 8⅜ x 11¼. 23546-7

BENCHLEY LOST AND FOUND, Robert Benchley. Finest humor from early 30s, about pet peeves, child psychologists, post office and others. Mostly unavailable elsewhere. 73 illustrations by Peter Arno and others. 183pp. 5⅜ x 8½. 22410-4

YEKL and THE IMPORTED BRIDEGROOM AND OTHER STORIES OF YIDDISH NEW YORK, Abraham Cahan. Film Hester Street based on *Yekl* (1896). Novel, other stories among first about Jewish immigrants on N.Y.'s East Side. 240pp. 5⅜ x 8½. 22427-9

SELECTED POEMS, Walt Whitman. Generous sampling from *Leaves of Grass*. Twenty-four poems include "I Hear America Singing," "Song of the Open Road," "I Sing the Body Electric," "When Lilacs Last in the Dooryard Bloom'd," "O Captain! My Captain!"–all reprinted from an authoritative edition. Lists of titles and first lines. 128pp. 5³⁄₁₆ x 8¼. 26878-0

THE BEST TALES OF HOFFMANN, E. T. A. Hoffmann. 10 of Hoffmann's most important stories: "Nutcracker and the King of Mice," "The Golden Flowerpot," etc. 458pp. 5⅜ x 8½. 21793-0

FROM FETISH TO GOD IN ANCIENT EGYPT, E. A. Wallis Budge. Rich detailed survey of Egyptian conception of "God" and gods, magic, cult of animals, Osiris, more. Also, superb English translations of hymns and legends. 240 illustrations. 545pp. 5⅜ x 8½. 25803-3

FRENCH STORIES/CONTES FRANÇAIS: A Dual-Language Book, Wallace Fowlie. Ten stories by French masters, Voltaire to Camus: "Micromegas" by Voltaire; "The Atheist's Mass" by Balzac; "Minuet" by de Maupassant; "The Guest" by Camus, six more. Excellent English translations on facing pages. Also French-English vocabulary list, exercises, more. 352pp. 5⅜ x 8½. 26443-2

CHICAGO AT THE TURN OF THE CENTURY IN PHOTOGRAPHS: 122 Historic Views from the Collections of the Chicago Historical Society, Larry A. Viskochil. Rare large-format prints offer detailed views of City Hall, State Street, the Loop, Hull House, Union Station, many other landmarks, circa 1904-1913. Introduction. Captions. Maps. 144pp. 9⅜ x 12¼. 24656-6

OLD BROOKLYN IN EARLY PHOTOGRAPHS, 1865-1929, William Lee Younger. Luna Park, Gravesend race track, construction of Grand Army Plaza, moving of Hotel Brighton, etc. 157 previously unpublished photographs. 165pp. 8⅞ x 11¾. 23587-4

THE MYTHS OF THE NORTH AMERICAN INDIANS, Lewis Spence. Rich anthology of the myths and legends of the Algonquins, Iroquois, Pawnees and Sioux, prefaced by an extensive historical and ethnological commentary. 36 illustrations. 480pp. 5⅜ x 8½. 25967-6

AN ENCYCLOPEDIA OF BATTLES: Accounts of Over 1,560 Battles from 1479 B.C. to the Present, David Eggenberger. Essential details of every major battle in recorded history from the first battle of Megiddo in 1479 B.C. to Grenada in 1984. List of Battle Maps. New Appendix covering the years 1967-1984. Index. 99 illustrations. 544pp. 6½ x 9¼. 24913-1

SAILING ALONE AROUND THE WORLD, Captain Joshua Slocum. First man to sail around the world, alone, in small boat. One of great feats of seamanship told in delightful manner. 67 illustrations. 294pp. 5⅜ x 8½. 20326-3

ANARCHISM AND OTHER ESSAYS, Emma Goldman. Powerful, penetrating, prophetic essays on direct action, role of minorities, prison reform, puritan hypocrisy, violence, etc. 271pp. 5⅜ x 8½. 22484-8

MYTHS OF THE HINDUS AND BUDDHISTS, Ananda K. Coomaraswamy and Sister Nivedita. Great stories of the epics; deeds of Krishna, Shiva, taken from puranas, Vedas, folk tales; etc. 32 illustrations. 400pp. 5⅜ x 8½. 21759-0

THE TRAUMA OF BIRTH, Otto Rank. Rank's controversial thesis that anxiety neurosis is caused by profound psychological trauma which occurs at birth. 256pp. 5⅜ x 8½. 27974-X

A THEOLOGICO-POLITICAL TREATISE, Benedict Spinoza. Also contains unfinished Political Treatise. Great classic on religious liberty, theory of government on common consent. R. Elwes translation. Total of 421pp. 5⅜ x 8½. 20249-6

MY BONDAGE AND MY FREEDOM, Frederick Douglass. Born a slave, Douglass became outspoken force in antislavery movement. The best of Douglass' autobiographies. Graphic description of slave life. 464pp. 5⅜ x 8½. 22457-0

FOLLOWING THE EQUATOR: A Journey Around the World, Mark Twain. Fascinating humorous account of 1897 voyage to Hawaii, Australia, India, New Zealand, etc. Ironic, bemused reports on peoples, customs, climate, flora and fauna, politics, much more. 197 illustrations. 720pp. 5⅜ x 8½. 26113-1

THE PEOPLE CALLED SHAKERS, Edward D. Andrews. Definitive study of Shakers: origins, beliefs, practices, dances, social organization, furniture and crafts, etc. 33 illustrations. 351pp. 5⅜ x 8½. 21081-2

THE MYTHS OF GREECE AND ROME, H. A. Guerber. A classic of mythology, generously illustrated, long prized for its simple, graphic, accurate retelling of the principal myths of Greece and Rome, and for its commentary on their origins and significance. With 64 illustrations by Michelangelo, Raphael, Titian, Rubens, Canova, Bernini and others. 480pp. 5⅜ x 8½. 27584-1

PSYCHOLOGY OF MUSIC, Carl E. Seashore. Classic work discusses music as a medium from psychological viewpoint. Clear treatment of physical acoustics, auditory apparatus, sound perception, development of musical skills, nature of musical feeling, host of other topics. 88 figures. 408pp. 5⅜ x 8½. 21851-1

THE PHILOSOPHY OF HISTORY, Georg W. Hegel. Great classic of Western thought develops concept that history is not chance but rational process, the evolution of freedom. 457pp. 5⅜ x 8½. 20112-0

THE BOOK OF TEA, Kakuzo Okakura. Minor classic of the Orient: entertaining, charming explanation, interpretation of traditional Japanese culture in terms of tea ceremony. 94pp. 5⅜ x 8½. 20070-1

LIFE IN ANCIENT EGYPT, Adolf Erman. Fullest, most thorough, detailed older account with much not in more recent books, domestic life, religion, magic, medicine, commerce, much more. Many illustrations reproduce tomb paintings, carvings, hieroglyphs, etc. 597pp. 5⅜ x 8½. 22632-8

SUNDIALS, Their Theory and Construction, Albert Waugh. Far and away the best, most thorough coverage of ideas, mathematics concerned, types, construction, adjusting anywhere. Simple, nontechnical treatment allows even children to build several of these dials. Over 100 illustrations. 230pp. 5⅜ x 8½. 22947-5

THEORETICAL HYDRODYNAMICS, L. M. Milne-Thomson. Classic exposition of the mathematical theory of fluid motion, applicable to both hydrodynamics and aerodynamics. Over 600 exercises. 768pp. 6⅛ x 9¼. 68970-0

SONGS OF EXPERIENCE: Facsimile Reproduction with 26 Plates in Full Color, William Blake. 26 full-color plates from a rare 1826 edition. Includes "The Tyger," "London," "Holy Thursday," and other poems. Printed text of poems. 48pp. 5¼ x 7. 24636-1

OLD-TIME VIGNETTES IN FULL COLOR, Carol Belanger Grafton (ed.). Over 390 charming, often sentimental illustrations, selected from archives of Victorian graphics–pretty women posing, children playing, food, flowers, kittens and puppies, smiling cherubs, birds and butterflies, much more. All copyright-free. 48pp. 9¼ x 12¼. 27269-9

PERSPECTIVE FOR ARTISTS, Rex Vicat Cole. Depth, perspective of sky and sea, shadows, much more, not usually covered. 391 diagrams, 81 reproductions of drawings and paintings. 279pp. 5⅜ x 8½. 22487-2

DRAWING THE LIVING FIGURE, Joseph Sheppard. Innovative approach to artistic anatomy focuses on specifics of surface anatomy, rather than muscles and bones. Over 170 drawings of live models in front, back and side views, and in widely varying poses. Accompanying diagrams. 177 illustrations. Introduction. Index. 144pp. 8⅜ x11¼. 26723-7

GOTHIC AND OLD ENGLISH ALPHABETS: 100 Complete Fonts, Dan X. Solo. Add power, elegance to posters, signs, other graphics with 100 stunning copyright-free alphabets: Blackstone, Dolbey, Germania, 97 more—including many lower-case, numerals, punctuation marks. 104pp. 8⅛ x 11. 24695-7

HOW TO DO BEADWORK, Mary White. Fundamental book on craft from simple projects to five-bead chains and woven works. 106 illustrations. 142pp. 5⅜ x 8.
20697-1

THE BOOK OF WOOD CARVING, Charles Marshall Sayers. Finest book for beginners discusses fundamentals and offers 34 designs. "Absolutely first rate . . . well thought out and well executed."–E. J. Tangerman. 118pp. 7¾ x 10⅝. 23654-4

ILLUSTRATED CATALOG OF CIVIL WAR MILITARY GOODS: Union Army Weapons, Insignia, Uniform Accessories, and Other Equipment, Schuyler, Hartley, and Graham. Rare, profusely illustrated 1846 catalog includes Union Army uniform and dress regulations, arms and ammunition, coats, insignia, flags, swords, rifles, etc. 226 illustrations. 160pp. 9 x 12. 24939-5

WOMEN'S FASHIONS OF THE EARLY 1900s: An Unabridged Republication of "New York Fashions, 1909," National Cloak & Suit Co. Rare catalog of mail-order fashions documents women's and children's clothing styles shortly after the turn of the century. Captions offer full descriptions, prices. Invaluable resource for fashion, costume historians. Approximately 725 illustrations. 128pp. 8⅜ x 11¼. 27276-1

THE 1912 AND 1915 GUSTAV STICKLEY FURNITURE CATALOGS, Gustav Stickley. With over 200 detailed illustrations and descriptions, these two catalogs are essential reading and reference materials and identification guides for Stickley furniture. Captions cite materials, dimensions and prices. 112pp. 6½ x 9¼. 26676-1

EARLY AMERICAN LOCOMOTIVES, John H. White, Jr. Finest locomotive engravings from early 19th century: historical (1804–74), main-line (after 1870), special, foreign, etc. 147 plates. 142pp. 11⅜ x 8¼. 22772-3

THE TALL SHIPS OF TODAY IN PHOTOGRAPHS, Frank O. Braynard. Lavishly illustrated tribute to nearly 100 majestic contemporary sailing vessels: Amerigo Vespucci, Clearwater, Constitution, Eagle, Mayflower, Sea Cloud, Victory, many more. Authoritative captions provide statistics, background on each ship. 190 black-and-white photographs and illustrations. Introduction. 128pp. 8⅞ x 11¾.
27163-3

LITTLE BOOK OF EARLY AMERICAN CRAFTS AND TRADES, Peter Stockham (ed.). 1807 children's book explains crafts and trades: baker, hatter, cooper, potter, and many others. 23 copperplate illustrations. 140pp. 4⅝ x 6.   23336-7

VICTORIAN FASHIONS AND COSTUMES FROM HARPER'S BAZAR, 1867–1898, Stella Blum (ed.). Day costumes, evening wear, sports clothes, shoes, hats, other accessories in over 1,000 detailed engravings. 320pp. 9⅜ x 12¼. 22990-4

GUSTAV STICKLEY, THE CRAFTSMAN, Mary Ann Smith. Superb study surveys broad scope of Stickley's achievement, especially in architecture. Design philosophy, rise and fall of the Craftsman empire, descriptions and floor plans for many Craftsman houses, more. 86 black-and-white halftones. 31 line illustrations. Introduction 208pp. 6½ x 9¼.   27210-9

THE LONG ISLAND RAIL ROAD IN EARLY PHOTOGRAPHS, Ron Ziel. Over 220 rare photos, informative text document origin (1844) and development of rail service on Long Island. Vintage views of early trains, locomotives, stations, passengers, crews, much more. Captions. 8⅞ x 11¾.   26301-0

VOYAGE OF THE LIBERDADE, Joshua Slocum. Great 19th-century mariner's thrilling, first-hand account of the wreck of his ship off South America, the 35-foot boat he built from the wreckage, and its remarkable voyage home. 128pp. 5⅜ x 8½.
40022-0

TEN BOOKS ON ARCHITECTURE, Vitruvius. The most important book ever written on architecture. Early Roman aesthetics, technology, classical orders, site selection, all other aspects. Morgan translation. 331pp. 5⅜ x 8½.   20645-9

THE HUMAN FIGURE IN MOTION, Eadweard Muybridge. More than 4,500 stopped-action photos, in action series, showing undraped men, women, children jumping, lying down, throwing, sitting, wrestling, carrying, etc. 390pp. 7⅞ x 10⅝.
20204-6 Clothbd.

TREES OF THE EASTERN AND CENTRAL UNITED STATES AND CANADA, William M. Harlow. Best one-volume guide to 140 trees. Full descriptions, woodlore, range, etc. Over 600 illustrations. Handy size. 288pp. 4½ x 6⅜.   20395-6

SONGS OF WESTERN BIRDS, Dr. Donald J. Borror. Complete song and call repertoire of 60 western species, including flycatchers, juncoes, cactus wrens, many more–includes fully illustrated booklet.   Cassette and manual 99913-0

GROWING AND USING HERBS AND SPICES, Milo Miloradovich. Versatile handbook provides all the information needed for cultivation and use of all the herbs and spices available in North America. 4 illustrations. Index. Glossary. 236pp. 5⅜ x 8½.
25058-X

BIG BOOK OF MAZES AND LABYRINTHS, Walter Shepherd. 50 mazes and labyrinths in all–classical, solid, ripple, and more–in one great volume. Perfect inexpensive puzzler for clever youngsters. Full solutions. 112pp. 8⅛ x 11.   22951-3

PIANO TUNING, J. Cree Fischer. Clearest, best book for beginner, amateur. Simple repairs, raising dropped notes, tuning by easy method of flattened fifths. No previous skills needed. 4 illustrations. 201pp. 5⅜ x 8½. 23267-0

HINTS TO SINGERS, Lillian Nordica. Selecting the right teacher, developing confidence, overcoming stage fright, and many other important skills receive thoughtful discussion in this indispensible guide, written by a world-famous diva of four decades' experience. 96pp. 5⅜ x 8½. 40094-8

THE COMPLETE NONSENSE OF EDWARD LEAR, Edward Lear. All nonsense limericks, zany alphabets, Owl and Pussycat, songs, nonsense botany, etc., illustrated by Lear. Total of 320pp. 5⅜ x 8½. (Available in U.S. only.) 20167-8

VICTORIAN PARLOUR POETRY: An Annotated Anthology, Michael R. Turner. 117 gems by Longfellow, Tennyson, Browning, many lesser-known poets. "The Village Blacksmith," "Curfew Must Not Ring Tonight," "Only a Baby Small," dozens more, often difficult to find elsewhere. Index of poets, titles, first lines. xxiii + 325pp. 5⅝ x 8¼. 27044-0

DUBLINERS, James Joyce. Fifteen stories offer vivid, tightly focused observations of the lives of Dublin's poorer classes. At least one, "The Dead," is considered a masterpiece. Reprinted complete and unabridged from standard edition. 160pp. 5$\frac{3}{16}$ x 8¼. 26870-5

GREAT WEIRD TALES: 14 Stories by Lovecraft, Blackwood, Machen and Others, S. T. Joshi (ed.). 14 spellbinding tales, including "The Sin Eater," by Fiona McLeod, "The Eye Above the Mantel," by Frank Belknap Long, as well as renowned works by R. H. Barlow, Lord Dunsany, Arthur Machen, W. C. Morrow and eight other masters of the genre. 256pp. 5⅜ x 8½. (Available in U.S. only.) 40436-6

THE BOOK OF THE SACRED MAGIC OF ABRAMELIN THE MAGE, translated by S. MacGregor Mathers. Medieval manuscript of ceremonial magic. Basic document in Aleister Crowley, Golden Dawn groups. 268pp. 5⅜ x 8½. 23211-5

NEW RUSSIAN-ENGLISH AND ENGLISH-RUSSIAN DICTIONARY, M. A. O'Brien. This is a remarkably handy Russian dictionary, containing a surprising amount of information, including over 70,000 entries. 366pp. 4½ x 6⅛. 20208-9

HISTORIC HOMES OF THE AMERICAN PRESIDENTS, Second, Revised Edition, Irvin Haas. A traveler's guide to American Presidential homes, most open to the public, depicting and describing homes occupied by every American President from George Washington to George Bush. With visiting hours, admission charges, travel routes. 175 photographs. Index. 160pp. 8¼ x 11. 26751-2

NEW YORK IN THE FORTIES, Andreas Feininger. 162 brilliant photographs by the well-known photographer, formerly with *Life* magazine. Commuters, shoppers, Times Square at night, much else from city at its peak. Captions by John von Hartz. 181pp. 9¼ x 10¾. 23585-8

INDIAN SIGN LANGUAGE, William Tomkins. Over 525 signs developed by Sioux and other tribes. Written instructions and diagrams. Also 290 pictographs. 111pp. 6⅛ x 9¼. 22029-X

ANATOMY: A Complete Guide for Artists, Joseph Sheppard. A master of figure drawing shows artists how to render human anatomy convincingly. Over 460 illustrations. 224pp. 8⅜ x 11¼. 27279-6

MEDIEVAL CALLIGRAPHY: Its History and Technique, Marc Drogin. Spirited history, comprehensive instruction manual covers 13 styles (ca. 4th century through 15th). Excellent photographs; directions for duplicating medieval techniques with modern tools. 224pp. 8⅜ x 11¼. 26142-5

DRIED FLOWERS: How to Prepare Them, Sarah Whitlock and Martha Rankin. Complete instructions on how to use silica gel, meal and borax, perlite aggregate, sand and borax, glycerine and water to create attractive permanent flower arrangements. 12 illustrations. 32pp. 5⅜ x 8½. 21802-3

EASY-TO-MAKE BIRD FEEDERS FOR WOODWORKERS, Scott D. Campbell. Detailed, simple-to-use guide for designing, constructing, caring for and using feeders. Text, illustrations for 12 classic and contemporary designs. 96pp. 5⅜ x 8½.
25847-5

SCOTTISH WONDER TALES FROM MYTH AND LEGEND, Donald A. Mackenzie. 16 lively tales tell of giants rumbling down mountainsides, of a magic wand that turns stone pillars into warriors, of gods and goddesses, evil hags, powerful forces and more. 240pp. 5⅜ x 8½. 29677-6

THE HISTORY OF UNDERCLOTHES, C. Willett Cunnington and Phyllis Cunnington. Fascinating, well-documented survey covering six centuries of English undergarments, enhanced with over 100 illustrations: 12th-century laced-up bodice, footed long drawers (1795), 19th-century bustles, 19th-century corsets for men, Victorian "bust improvers," much more. 272pp. 5⅜ x 8¼. 27124-2

ARTS AND CRAFTS FURNITURE: The Complete Brooks Catalog of 1912, Brooks Manufacturing Co. Photos and detailed descriptions of more than 150 now very collectible furniture designs from the Arts and Crafts movement depict davenports, settees, buffets, desks, tables, chairs, bedsteads, dressers and more, all built of solid, quarter-sawed oak. Invaluable for students and enthusiasts of antiques, Americana and the decorative arts. 80pp. 6½ x 9¼. 27471-3

WILBUR AND ORVILLE: A Biography of the Wright Brothers, Fred Howard. Definitive, crisply written study tells the full story of the brothers' lives and work. A vividly written biography, unparalleled in scope and color, that also captures the spirit of an extraordinary era. 560pp. 6⅛ x 9¼. 40297-5

THE ARTS OF THE SAILOR: Knotting, Splicing and Ropework, Hervey Garrett Smith. Indispensable shipboard reference covers tools, basic knots and useful hitches; handsewing and canvas work, more. Over 100 illustrations. Delightful reading for sea lovers. 256pp. 5⅜ x 8½. 26440-8

FRANK LLOYD WRIGHT'S FALLINGWATER: The House and Its History, Second, Revised Edition, Donald Hoffmann. A total revision–both in text and illustrations–of the standard document on Fallingwater, the boldest, most personal architectural statement of Wright's mature years, updated with valuable new material from the recently opened Frank Lloyd Wright Archives. "Fascinating"–*The New York Times*. 116 illustrations. 128pp. 9¼ x 10¾. 27430-6

CATALOG OF DOVER BOOKS

PHOTOGRAPHIC SKETCHBOOK OF THE CIVIL WAR, Alexander Gardner. 100 photos taken on field during the Civil War. Famous shots of Manassas Harper's Ferry, Lincoln, Richmond, slave pens, etc. 244pp. 10⅝ x 8¼.   22731-6

FIVE ACRES AND INDEPENDENCE, Maurice G. Kains. Great back-to-the-land classic explains basics of self-sufficient farming. The one book to get. 95 illustrations. 397pp. 5⅜ x 8½.   20974-1

SONGS OF EASTERN BIRDS, Dr. Donald J. Borror. Songs and calls of 60 species most common to eastern U.S.: warblers, woodpeckers, flycatchers, thrushes, larks, many more in high-quality recording.   Cassette and manual 99912-2

A MODERN HERBAL, Margaret Grieve. Much the fullest, most exact, most useful compilation of herbal material. Gigantic alphabetical encyclopedia, from aconite to zedoary, gives botanical information, medical properties, folklore, economic uses, much else. Indispensable to serious reader. 161 illustrations. 888pp. 6½ x 9¼. 2-vol. set. (Available in U.S. only.)   Vol. I: 22798-7
Vol. II: 22799-5

HIDDEN TREASURE MAZE BOOK, Dave Phillips. Solve 34 challenging mazes accompanied by heroic tales of adventure. Evil dragons, people-eating plants, blood-thirsty giants, many more dangerous adversaries lurk at every twist and turn. 34 mazes, stories, solutions. 48pp. 8¼ x 11.   24566-7

LETTERS OF W. A. MOZART, Wolfgang A. Mozart. Remarkable letters show bawdy wit, humor, imagination, musical insights, contemporary musical world; includes some letters from Leopold Mozart. 276pp. 5⅜ x 8½.   22859-2

BASIC PRINCIPLES OF CLASSICAL BALLET, Agrippina Vaganova. Great Russian theoretician, teacher explains methods for teaching classical ballet. 118 illustrations. 175pp. 5⅜ x 8½.   22036-2

THE JUMPING FROG, Mark Twain. Revenge edition. The original story of The Celebrated Jumping Frog of Calaveras County, a hapless French translation, and Twain's hilarious "retranslation" from the French. 12 illustrations. 66pp. 5⅜ x 8½.
22686-7

BEST REMEMBERED POEMS, Martin Gardner (ed.). The 126 poems in this superb collection of 19th- and 20th-century British and American verse range from Shelley's "To a Skylark" to the impassioned "Renascence" of Edna St. Vincent Millay and to Edward Lear's whimsical "The Owl and the Pussycat." 224pp. 5⅜ x 8½.
27165-X

COMPLETE SONNETS, William Shakespeare. Over 150 exquisite poems deal with love, friendship, the tyranny of time, beauty's evanescence, death and other themes in language of remarkable power, precision and beauty. Glossary of archaic terms. 80pp. 5³⁄₁₆ x 8¼.   26686-9

THE BATTLES THAT CHANGED HISTORY, Fletcher Pratt. Eminent historian profiles 16 crucial conflicts, ancient to modern, that changed the course of civilization. 352pp. 5⅜ x 8½.   41129-X

CATALOG OF DOVER BOOKS

THE WIT AND HUMOR OF OSCAR WILDE, Alvin Redman (ed.). More than 1,000 ripostes, paradoxes, wisecracks: Work is the curse of the drinking classes; I can resist everything except temptation; etc. 258pp. 5⅜ x 8½. 20602-5

SHAKESPEARE LEXICON AND QUOTATION DICTIONARY, Alexander Schmidt. Full definitions, locations, shades of meaning in every word in plays and poems. More than 50,000 exact quotations. 1,485pp. 6½ x 9¼. 2-vol. set.
Vol. 1: 22726-X
Vol. 2: 22727-8

SELECTED POEMS, Emily Dickinson. Over 100 best-known, best-loved poems by one of America's foremost poets, reprinted from authoritative early editions. No comparable edition at this price. Index of first lines. 64pp. 5³⁄₁₆ x 8¼. 26466-1

THE INSIDIOUS DR. FU-MANCHU, Sax Rohmer. The first of the popular mystery series introduces a pair of English detectives to their archnemesis, the diabolical Dr. Fu-Manchu. Flavorful atmosphere, fast-paced action, and colorful characters enliven this classic of the genre. 208pp. 5³⁄₁₆ x 8¼. 29898-1

THE MALLEUS MALEFICARUM OF KRAMER AND SPRENGER, translated by Montague Summers. Full text of most important witchhunter's "bible," used by both Catholics and Protestants. 278pp. 6⅝ x 10. 22802-9

SPANISH STORIES/CUENTOS ESPAÑOLES: A Dual-Language Book, Angel Flores (ed.). Unique format offers 13 great stories in Spanish by Cervantes, Borges, others. Faithful English translations on facing pages. 352pp. 5⅜ x 8½. 25399-6

GARDEN CITY, LONG ISLAND, IN EARLY PHOTOGRAPHS, 1869–1919, Mildred H. Smith. Handsome treasury of 118 vintage pictures, accompanied by carefully researched captions, document the Garden City Hotel fire (1899), the Vanderbilt Cup Race (1908), the first airmail flight departing from the Nassau Boulevard Aerodrome (1911), and much more. 96pp. 8⅞ x 11¾. 40669-5

OLD QUEENS, N.Y., IN EARLY PHOTOGRAPHS, Vincent F. Seyfried and William Asadorian. Over 160 rare photographs of Maspeth, Jamaica, Jackson Heights, and other areas. Vintage views of DeWitt Clinton mansion, 1939 World's Fair and more. Captions. 192pp. 8⅞ x 11. 26358-4

CAPTURED BY THE INDIANS: 15 Firsthand Accounts, 1750-1870, Frederick Drimmer. Astounding true historical accounts of grisly torture, bloody conflicts, relentless pursuits, miraculous escapes and more, by people who lived to tell the tale. 384pp. 5⅜ x 8½. 24901-8

THE WORLD'S GREAT SPEECHES (Fourth Enlarged Edition), Lewis Copeland, Lawrence W. Lamm, and Stephen J. McKenna. Nearly 300 speeches provide public speakers with a wealth of updated quotes and inspiration–from Pericles' funeral oration and William Jennings Bryan's "Cross of Gold Speech" to Malcolm X's powerful words on the Black Revolution and Earl of Spenser's tribute to his sister, Diana, Princess of Wales. 944pp. 5⅜ x 8⅜. 40903-1

THE BOOK OF THE SWORD, Sir Richard F. Burton. Great Victorian scholar/adventurer's eloquent, erudite history of the "queen of weapons"–from prehistory to early Roman Empire. Evolution and development of early swords, variations (sabre, broadsword, cutlass, scimitar, etc.), much more. 336pp. 6⅛ x 9¼. 25434-8

AUTOBIOGRAPHY: The Story of My Experiments with Truth, Mohandas K. Gandhi. Boyhood, legal studies, purification, the growth of the Satyagraha (nonviolent protest) movement. Critical, inspiring work of the man responsible for the freedom of India. 480pp. 5⅜ x 8½. (Available in U.S. only.)   24593-4

CELTIC MYTHS AND LEGENDS, T. W. Rolleston. Masterful retelling of Irish and Welsh stories and tales. Cuchulain, King Arthur, Deirdre, the Grail, many more. First paperback edition. 58 full-page illustrations. 512pp. 5⅜ x 8½.   26507-2

THE PRINCIPLES OF PSYCHOLOGY, William James. Famous long course complete, unabridged. Stream of thought, time perception, memory, experimental methods; great work decades ahead of its time. 94 figures. 1,391pp. 5⅜ x 8½. 2-vol. set.
Vol. I: 20381-6   Vol. II: 20382-4

THE WORLD AS WILL AND REPRESENTATION, Arthur Schopenhauer. Definitive English translation of Schopenhauer's life work, correcting more than 1,000 errors, omissions in earlier translations. Translated by E. F. J. Payne. Total of 1,269pp. 5⅜ x 8½. 2-vol. set.   Vol. 1: 21761-2   Vol. 2: 21762-0

MAGIC AND MYSTERY IN TIBET, Madame Alexandra David-Neel. Experiences among lamas, magicians, sages, sorcerers, Bonpa wizards. A true psychic discovery. 32 illustrations. 321pp. 5⅜ x 8½. (Available in U.S. only.)   22682-4

THE EGYPTIAN BOOK OF THE DEAD, E. A. Wallis Budge. Complete reproduction of Ani's papyrus, finest ever found. Full hieroglyphic text, interlinear transliteration, word-for-word translation, smooth translation. 533pp. 6½ x 9¼.   21866-X

MATHEMATICS FOR THE NONMATHEMATICIAN, Morris Kline. Detailed, college-level treatment of mathematics in cultural and historical context, with numerous exercises. Recommended Reading Lists. Tables. Numerous figures. 641pp. 5⅜ x 8½.
24823-2

PROBABILISTIC METHODS IN THE THEORY OF STRUCTURES, Isaac Elishakoff. Well-written introduction covers the elements of the theory of probability from two or more random variables, the reliability of such multivariable structures, the theory of random function, Monte Carlo methods of treating problems incapable of exact solution, and more. Examples. 502pp. 5⅜ x 8½.   40691-1

THE RIME OF THE ANCIENT MARINER, Gustave Doré, S. T. Coleridge. Doré's finest work; 34 plates capture moods, subtleties of poem. Flawless full-size reproductions printed on facing pages with authoritative text of poem. "Beautiful. Simply beautiful."—*Publisher's Weekly.* 77pp. 9¼ x 12.   22305-1

NORTH AMERICAN INDIAN DESIGNS FOR ARTISTS AND CRAFTSPEOPLE, Eva Wilson. Over 360 authentic copyright-free designs adapted from Navajo blankets, Hopi pottery, Sioux buffalo hides, more. Geometrics, symbolic figures, plant and animal motifs, etc. 128pp. 8⅜ x 11. (Not for sale in the United Kingdom.)   25341-4

SCULPTURE: Principles and Practice, Louis Slobodkin. Step-by-step approach to clay, plaster, metals, stone; classical and modern. 253 drawings, photos. 255pp. 8⅛ x 11.
22960-2

THE INFLUENCE OF SEA POWER UPON HISTORY, 1660–1783, A. T. Mahan. Influential classic of naval history and tactics still used as text in war colleges. First paperback edition. 4 maps. 24 battle plans. 640pp. 5⅜ x 8½.   25509-3

THE STORY OF THE TITANIC AS TOLD BY ITS SURVIVORS, Jack Winocour (ed.). What it was really like. Panic, despair, shocking inefficiency, and a little heroism. More thrilling than any fictional account. 26 illustrations. 320pp. 5⅜ x 8½.
20610-6

FAIRY AND FOLK TALES OF THE IRISH PEASANTRY, William Butler Yeats (ed.). Treasury of 64 tales from the twilight world of Celtic myth and legend: "The Soul Cages," "The Kildare Pooka," "King O'Toole and his Goose," many more. Introduction and Notes by W. B. Yeats. 352pp. 5⅜ x 8½.
26941-8

BUDDHIST MAHAYANA TEXTS, E. B. Cowell and others (eds.). Superb, accurate translations of basic documents in Mahayana Buddhism, highly important in history of religions. The Buddha-karita of Asvaghosha, Larger Sukhavativyuha, more. 448pp. 5⅜ x 8½.
25552-2

ONE TWO THREE . . . INFINITY: Facts and Speculations of Science, George Gamow. Great physicist's fascinating, readable overview of contemporary science: number theory, relativity, fourth dimension, entropy, genes, atomic structure, much more. 128 illustrations. Index. 352pp. 5⅜ x 8½.
25664-2

EXPERIMENTATION AND MEASUREMENT, W. J. Youden. Introductory manual explains laws of measurement in simple terms and offers tips for achieving accuracy and minimizing errors. Mathematics of measurement, use of instruments, experimenting with machines. 1994 edition. Foreword. Preface. Introduction. Epilogue. Selected Readings. Glossary. Index. Tables and figures. 128pp. 5⅜ x 8½.   40451-X

DALÍ ON MODERN ART: The Cuckolds of Antiquated Modern Art, Salvador Dalí. Influential painter skewers modern art and its practitioners. Outrageous evaluations of Picasso, Cézanne, Turner, more. 15 renderings of paintings discussed. 44 calligraphic decorations by Dalí. 96pp. 5⅜ x 8½. (Available in U.S. only.)   29220-7

ANTIQUE PLAYING CARDS: A Pictorial History, Henry René D'Allemagne. Over 900 elaborate, decorative images from rare playing cards (14th–20th centuries): Bacchus, death, dancing dogs, hunting scenes, royal coats of arms, players cheating, much more. 96pp. 9¼ x 12¼.
29265-7

MAKING FURNITURE MASTERPIECES: 30 Projects with Measured Drawings, Franklin H. Gottshall. Step-by-step instructions, illustrations for constructing handsome, useful pieces, among them a Sheraton desk, Chippendale chair, Spanish desk, Queen Anne table and a William and Mary dressing mirror. 224pp. 8⅛ x 11¼.
29338-6

THE FOSSIL BOOK: A Record of Prehistoric Life, Patricia V. Rich et al. Profusely illustrated definitive guide covers everything from single-celled organisms and dinosaurs to birds and mammals and the interplay between climate and man. Over 1,500 illustrations. 760pp. 7½ x 10⅛.
29371-8